LEARNING TO LEARN

THE SKILL AND WILL OF COLLEGE SUCCESS

SECOND EDITION

Scott W. VanderStoep

HOPE COLLEGE

Paul R. Pintrich

LATE, UNIVERSITY OF MICHIGAN

PEARSON

Prentice Hall

Upper Saddle River, New Jersey
Columbus, Ohio

Library of Congress Cataloging-in-Publication Data

VanderStoep, Scott W.
  Learning to learn: the skill and will of college success / Scott W. VanderStoep,
Paul R. Pintrich.
     p. cm.
  Includes bibliographical references and index.
  ISBN 978-0-13-158606-2 (pbk.)
  1. Study skills.   2. Learning, Psychology of.   I. Pintrich, Paul R.   II. Title.
  LB2395.V395 2008
  378'.1702812—dc22

                                                                    2007003544

Vice President and Executive Publisher: Jeffery W. Johnston
Executive Editor: Sande Johnson
Editorial Assistant: Lynda Cramer
Production Editor: Alexandrina Benedicto Wolf
Production Coordination: Thistle Hill Publishing Services, LLC
Design Coordinator: Diane C. Lorenzo
Cover Designer: Jeff Vanik
Cover Image: SuperStock
Production Manager: Susan Hannahs
Director of Marketing: David Gesell
Marketing Manager: Amy Judd
Marketing Coordinator: Brian Mounts

This book was set in Sabon by Integra Software Services. It was printed and bound by
Edwards Brothers. The cover was printed by Phoenix Color Corp.

Pearson Education Ltd.   Pearson Education Australia Pty. Limited
Pearson Education Singapore Pte. Ltd.   Pearson Education North Asia Ltd.
Pearson Education Canada, Ltd.   Pearson Educación de Mexico, S.A. de C.V.
Pearson Education—Japan   Pearson Education Malaysia Pte. Ltd.

10 9 8 7 6 5 4 3 2 1
ISBN-13: 978-0-13-158606-2
ISBN-10:   0-13-158606-8

To Jill

In memory of Paul

CONTENTS

Chapter 3

MOTIVATION: PREPARING TO USE YOUR WILL COMPONENTS   37

Chapter 4

MANAGING YOUR RESOURCES I: EXTERNAL TOOLS   57

Chapter 5

MANAGING YOUR RESOURCES II: INTERNAL TOOLS   77

Chapter 6

IMPROVING YOUR ATTENTION AND MEMORY   93

Chapter 7

IMPROVING YOUR COGNITION AND METACOGNITION   117

Chapter 11

TAKING TESTS   199

Chapter 12

CRITICAL THINKING   223

Chapter 13

PROBLEM SOLVING   239

Chapter 14

CONCLUSION: ASSESSING YOUR PROGRESS, PLANNING YOUR FUTURE   271

Appendix

PREFACE

It takes two things to be successful in life: skill and will. This is true not just in academic pursuits but also in athletics, music, employment, and relationships. Successful people in all walks of life are both skillful and willful. Skill is the competency to do things well. Will is the motivation to do things well. In college, the skill component is the cognitive aspect of learning. It involves setting goals and plans and trying to enact them. It also involves working to become proficient at reading, writing, studying, note taking, and test taking. The will component involves motivating yourself with different goals, trying hard, persisting, and finding what things motivate you to excel.

This book is about skill and will, and improving both. Some students have high skill and low will: "He is so smart, but he's lazy." Some students have low skill and high will: "She's not very smart, but she works really hard." And some students are low or high on both. Whatever the case, this book will help you improve both your skill and your will.

The philosophy of this book is simple: to get smarter and learn more, you need to improve your skill and your will. Being skillful (smart, intelligent) alone won't be sufficient. Being willful (motivated, driven) alone won't be sufficient. Having just one component will always leave you performing below your potential. So this book encourages you to reflect on both your skill and your will, and offers many suggestions for improving both.

ACKNOWLEDGMENTS

This part is hard for me to write. I'm doing it alone. Many of you know that Paul Pintrich died unexpectedly on July 12, 2003, less than a year after the first edition of this book was published. His name remains on the cover and his fingerprints indelibly cover each page. He was taken from us too soon, and he is missed by all who knew him. The first acknowledgment goes to him.

Both Paul and I had the unique pleasure of learning under the tutelage of Wilbert (Bill) J. McKeachie. If you studied college student learning at the University of Michigan anytime in the last 60 years, Bill had an impact on your professional life. Bill served as Scott's mentor when he was in graduate school and as Paul's mentor during his postdoctoral studies. Most important, he created the Learning to Learn course at Michigan. He trained both of us as his teaching assistants for this course, which sparked our interest in developing this book. As Paul said in the first edition of the book, he would probably not even be a college professor if it were not for Bill's support, encouragement, and mentoring in those early years. He is a wonderful mentor, superb educator, and a living testimony to the fact that nice guys can indeed finish first.

Paul mentored many graduate students who meant so much to him. The close-knit group that wandered through Ann Arbor during the last 20 years made up the fabric of Paul's professional community: David Smith, Julie Turner, Teresa Garcia, Rob Roeser, Tim Urdan, Eric and Lynley Anderman, Chris Wolters, Shirley Yu, Barbara Hofer, Allison Ryan, Elizabeth Linnenbrink, Akane Zusho, AnneMarie Conley, Toni Kempler, Brian Sims, Christina Rhee, and Peter Simmonds. All of these great people helped in direct and indirect ways in the development of this book and now serve as Paul's ambassadors, teaching and advising a new generation of students.

Paul loved the Combined Program in Education and Psychology at the University of Michigan. He would want to recognize his colleagues in CPEP: Phyllis Blumenfeld, Jacque Eccles, Stuart Karabenick, Martin Maehr, Ron Marx, the late Carol Midgley, and Janie Knieper. He would probably save his final acknowledgments for his best friend, Alan Wigfield, and his fantastic spouse and friend (and fine educator in her own right), Elisabeth De Groot. Paul's legacy lives in all these folks.

At Hope College, student Anne Hoekstra provided assistance in conducting data analyses on the Learning Inventory. Colleagues in the Psychology Department and Hope administrators are always supportive of my professional life. Hope College is a great place to work, and my coworkers are truly people of Hope. My children, Amy, Allison, and Mark, endured another writing project, and they even want me to produce a *Learning to Learn Junior*. Jill VanderStoep balanced her own professional and family responsibilities and provided manifold witness to what it means to be a great spouse. "I'll love you with all the madness in my soul."

We thank our editor Sande Johnson, editorial assistant Lynda Cramer, production editor Alex Wolf, and project editor Amanda Dugan.

A special note of appreciation to Brian Sims of North Carolina A & T State University for preparing the Instructor's Manual. We know many people who teach from this book are trained in something other than education or psychology. For those of you with different academic training, I believe you will find the Instructor's Manual to have some great teaching ideas.

We wish to thank the following reviewers for their insights: Peg Adams, Northern Kentucky University; Andrea Berta, University of Texas at El Paso; Patricia A. Haught, West Virginia University; Howard Hayward, Lewis University; Kathleen McGough, Broward Community College; Dana McMurray, University of Montana; Joel V. McGee, Texas A & M University; and Patricia Parma, Palo Alto College.

Students or faculty who wish to comment, correct, or suggest ideas for future editions should send an e-mail to vanderstoep@hope.edu.

Scott VanderStoep

Becoming a Self-Regulated Learner

Chapter Goals

This chapter will help you:

- Develop an initial assessment of areas of strength in your learning
- Develop an initial assessment of areas in need of growth in your learning
- Identify growth areas in your learning and think about ways to make improvements
- Have an overview of the book so that if a particular need becomes urgent, you know where to look to find suggestions

Key Terms

advanced organizer	motivation
critical thinking	problem solving
goal setting	resource management
ill-defined problems	self-regulated learner
learning strategy	skill
learning style	test anxiety
metacognition	will

CHAPTER 1

This book has one goal—to help college students become better learners. Each of the authors has spent several years teaching a course in learning and study skills. Each of the authors has also spent many years researching student learning and motivation in college, high school, and middle school. We believe the best way to become a better learner is to listen to practical advice based on educational and psychological research. This book is designed to teach readers about human learning and motivation, and in so doing identify specific and practical ways that readers can improve their own learning and motivation.

WHO SHOULD READ THIS BOOK?

This book is designed for college students who want to excel in college. We suspect that most readers will be first- or second-year students. The book contains helpful advice for students of all ages, and we also believe it describes strategies that will assist you in life after college. (In fact, both of us found that writing the book provided us with helpful reminders about how to improve our own work and personal life.) In short, this book is for all college students who are trying to improve their learning and achievement.

WHY SHOULD YOU USE THIS BOOK?

Many individuals are successful in school and in other settings, such as at work, at home, and in social situations. These individuals are not just "very smart" or "highly intelligent." There are a number of reasons these individuals do well in many different situations, but two general reasons are what we will call **skill** and **will**. *Skill* refers to the various types of knowledge and strategies that individuals learn and that all individuals can acquire throughout their lives. Skill is not an innate, genetic capacity for learning. It is changeable and it is learnable by all. Some people may have more innate intellectual ability, but this book focuses on the fact that each student can improve in knowledge and strategies. Thus, everyone can get smarter by reading this book. *Will* refers to the various ways individuals attempt to motivate and regulate themselves in their daily lives. Will involves taking charge of your life and being in control of your motivation, learning, and overall behavior.

A recurring theme in this book is that successful individuals are always using both skill and will as they engage in different activities. Students need to have both knowledge and strategies for learning and the motivation to use them. Perhaps you know students who are high in knowledge and strategies but can't seem to get motivated to use their expertise. These are the students who may do well in high school when their time and work are more structured by others (e.g., teachers, parents), but then can't seem to motivate themselves in more unstructured situations such as college. This book can help. On the other hand, some students who are motivated may work very hard and study all the time, but without the appropriate knowledge and strategies, they don't study as effectively as they could and therefore don't do as well as they should in school. For as hard as these students work, they could do better with strategy instruction. This book can help. The purpose of this book is to help you learn how to be both skillful and willful in your learning.

In other words, to help you become what we call a **self-regulated learner**. A self-regulated learner is one who actively plans, monitors, and controls her own learning and behavior. The lessons you learn about self-regulation in this book are also crucial in other areas of your life (Baumeister, 2005).

THE PERSPECTIVE OF THIS BOOK

Dozens of "study skills" books are currently available. What is different about this one? That is, why should you use this one instead of another one you see on the college bookshelf? The first difference between this book and other study-skills books is that we consistently base our suggested study skills on psychological research that we and others have done with college students. In this book we translate our own research findings into real-life suggestions for ways you can become a better learner. Many other researchers have studied effective learning extensively, and we will draw on their findings as well. So, these suggestions are not based on our intuitions, or what might have worked for *us* in school, or "folklore" that has been passed down from previous generations of college students. Instead, these suggestions come from our efforts to digest many research studies from the fields of cognitive, motivational, and educational psychology and to create real-life applications for you. This approach ensures that the suggestions in this book have been shown to be valid for many other college students.

A second difference is that our goal is to create self-regulated learners. A self-regulated learner is both skillful and willful in learning, actively planing, monitoring, and controling her or his own behavior. The self-regulated learner is able to recognize when and why you need to study in certain ways. Instead of wandering blindly through your courses, trying learning strategies randomly, you should be able to recognize which learning strategies are needed for different types of school tasks. This will make you more efficient because you won't be spending too much time on schoolwork that doesn't require it, and you won't be using a learning strategy that is inappropriate for a certain task. For example, the best way to study for some types of tests is to do lots of memorization, whereas for other tests, the best preparation is to make lists, draw charts, and expand your notes. Using an inappropriate study approach can be a disaster. The key to being a self-regulated learner is to spend the right amount of time and use the appropriate learning strategies.

SKILL AND WILL: THE KEYS TO COLLEGE SUCCESS

Let's talk more about skill and will, the two things you need to succeed in college. Skill refers to the collection of learning and thinking strategies that you have at your disposal for tackling various academic tasks. Psychologists call the skill component "cognition." Cognition is an often-used term in psychology and education, and it is used in many different contexts. When we use the word *cognition*, we mean the mental operations involved in accomplishing school tasks—basically, it's the learning part of doing well in school. Sometimes cognition refers to the learning activities you engage in (these are the main focus of this book), and sometimes it refers to the knowledge you have acquired. Some of the cognitive (skill) activities that you are likely to need in college include reading comprehension, memorization of facts or definitions, writing essay exams and term papers, and solving mathematics problems.

Right now you may be thinking, "My memory is not very good" or "I am a slow reader" or "I am unorganized." If you have these thoughts, you may be apprehensive about your chances for success in college. We have good news for you: These skill components can be improved with practice. This book covers the different skill (cognitive) components that students need to do well in college. We will explain the psychological rationale behind each of these cognitive components, and then go over ways you can improve your cognitive performance. Without the proper skills, you won't do well in college.

Success in college takes skill—sophisticated cognitive strategies—but it also takes will. In general, will refers to your motivation: Are you dedicated to success? Specifically, will refers to the extent to which you set goals for yourself and how well you follow through on pursuing your goals and monitoring your progress. Will also refers to how well you handle the anxiety and stress associated with being in college, how you handle change, and how eagerly you search for meaning and relevance in what you study. When you get good grades, does your confidence increase? When you get bad grades, do you learn from your mistakes and persevere in the face of disappointment? All of these components make up what we refer to as will.

So, it is important to remember that to do your best in college, you need both of these components—cognition and motivation, or skill and will. You may already have a lot of cognitive ability (skill). That is, you are a good reader, a good writer, and you have a good memory. But you may lack will. Maybe you don't spend enough time studying for your courses. Or maybe you don't have any academic or professional goals. Or maybe you work hard but get very anxious during tests or when writing papers. Or maybe you lack self-confidence that you can succeed. All of us have heard this said about people we know: "She's really bright, she just doesn't apply herself." This may be someone with high skill and low will. If you are this type of person, then you will want to concentrate more on the will components of this book, such as motivation, anxiety, and self-confidence.

On the other hand, you may work very hard and be highly motivated to succeed. That is, you may have set goals for yourself, you may spend a lot of time studying for your classes, and you may have a strong desire to be successful. But you may lack skill. Maybe you are not very good at writing answers to essay questions, or maybe you have a hard time remembering what you read in your textbooks. If you are this type of person, then you will want to concentrate on the skill components of this book, such as improving your memory, effective learning strategies, effective reading and writing, problem solving, and critical thinking.

A story of one college student (in a class called Learning to Learn, incidentally) illustrates the importance of cognition and motivation for school success. During class one day, the teacher was talking about goal setting and the importance of recognizing how much a student could accomplish in a given period of time. One of the points the teacher made was that if students set manageable goals, this would increase their motivation for subsequent tasks. To illustrate this, the teacher passed out two photocopied pages from an introductory psychology textbook. He asked the students to estimate how long they thought it would take them to read these pages. (Of course, most study sessions will involve reading more than two pages, but the teacher did this simply to illustrate the concept of goal setting.) Almost all of the 20 students in that class estimated it would take them between 10 and 15 minutes to read the pages. One student, however, estimated it would take him 40 minutes to read two textbook pages!

Why is this story relevant to a discussion of skill and will? It didn't matter how motivated this person was, this student was not going to succeed in college if he read this slowly. That is, he may have had will, but he clearly lacked skill. He could study 18 hours a day, 7 days a week, but he would still struggle with such a low skill level. So, the teacher encouraged him to seek extra academic support to improve his reading speed. What is interesting is that the student kept insisting, up to this point, that his problem was that he was "lazy." He thought he could do the work if he applied himself. He thought he had a "will" problem, when he really had a "skill" problem. We hope that this book will help you identify your own weaknesses in learning so that you can begin to work on them right away.

Whatever type of student you are, you need both sophisticated cognitive strategies and motivation to succeed. Maybe you already have a high degree of motivation and you also use good study skills (i.e., you have high skill and high will). If such is the case, this book will allow you to refine your skills even more, so that you can reach a higher level of academic success.

LEARNING STYLE VERSUS LEARNING STRATEGY: IS THERE A DIFFERENCE?

We use the phrase **learning strategy** to refer to an approach to completing cognitive tasks. Many people refer to **learning style**, which is a preferred method of completing cognitive tasks (Sternberg, 1997). We will use *strategy* more than *style*, although it is a matter of preference. The main reason we prefer *strategy* is because strategies are easily changeable based on the task. Your strategy for algebra class will be different than that for your English composition class. Conversely, style can imply a stable way of doing something. (For example, "I have a visual learning style.") If you pigeonhole yourself into only one type of learning, you will face difficulty when you encounter professors or courses that don't match that style. So we say *strategy*; it's flexible across many subject areas.

THE LEARNING INVENTORY

To identify your strengths and weaknesses as a learner, you need a diagnostic tool. We have developed such a tool to measure your academic motivation and your learning strategies. The instrument contains 63 items, with approximately four to six items corresponding to each chapter in the book. For each section your responses will receive a score, which you (and perhaps your professor) can use to help determine your strengths and weaknesses as a learner. The chapters in this book are designed around the sections of this instrument. As we go through each chapter, we will ask you to refer back to your score on that particular set of items. Your score on those items will serve as an assessment of your particular learning characteristics and help you see where your opportunities for improvement lie.

We have designed a Learning Inventory specifically designed to correspond with the chapters of this book. We present the entire Learning Inventory in this chapter. Then in each chapter we present the specific items corresponding to each chapter at the beginning of that particular chapter. Before you read any more, we would like you to complete the entire Learning Inventory at this time (Activity 1.1). For the self-assessment to be helpful, it is important that you answer all of the questions honestly. These are your opinions about yourself; there are no right or wrong answers. We will then revisit the set of items relating to each chapter at the beginning of that chapter. Then, at the end of the book you will retake this instrument as part of the final chapter. This will allow you to compare your scores at the beginning and the end of reading this book. In the next section of this chapter, we describe the different sections of the Learning Inventory.

ACTIVITY 1.1 *The Learning Inventory*

Mark the responses that best describe your approach to college.

GOAL SETTING

	Never or almost never	Rarely	Frequently	Always or almost always
1. When choosing between a hard class and an easy class, I consider my potential grade more than the interest or challenge the class would bring.	④	③	②	①
2. When thinking about the future, I think about the potential positive impact of doing well in college, and the potential negative impact doing poorly might have on my future.	①	②	③	④
3. When I am given a large assignment, I try to do it all in one night.	④	③	②	①
4. When faced with a large task, I make lists of things I need to do to reach the final goal.	①	②	③	④
5. I take mistakes personally and see them as a sign of failure.	④	③	②	①

Mark the responses that best describe your motivation for college.

MOTIVATION

	Never or almost never	Rarely	Frequently	Always or almost always
6. I feel trapped into taking the classes that I take. I don't feel I can take classes that interest me.	④	③	②	①
7. When faced with a difficult homework problem, I am likely to wander down the hall and ask someone in my hall rather than work on my own.	④	③	②	①
8. I doubt whether I can succeed in college.	④	③	②	①
9. I get discouraged when courses are difficult or boring.	④	③	②	①
10. Being successful in college is more a function of ability and luck than effort and persistence.	④	③	②	①
11. Even when a class is boring, I try to find something interesting to get out of it.	①	②	③	④

Indicate the extent to which you engage in these behaviors.

RESOURCE MANAGEMENT: EXTERNAL	None of the time	Some of the time	Most of the time	All of the time
12. I set up a weekly schedule each term.	①	②	③	④
13. I make a to-do list and set priorities from list.	①	②	③	④
14. I set aside weekly times for studying.	①	②	③	④
15. I maintain a study area free of distractions.	①	②	③	④
16. I form peer study groups in my classes.	①	②	③	④
17. I take initiative in getting help from faculty.	①	②	③	④
18. I listen to music or watch TV when studying.	④	③	②	①
19. I fall asleep when studying.	④	③	②	①

Mark the responses that best describe your approach to college.

RESOURCE MANAGEMENT: INTERNAL	None of the time	Some of the time	Most of the time	All of the time
20. I sleep eight hours or more each day.	①	②	③	④
21. I eat nutritionally sound meals each day.	①	②	③	④
22. I exercise three or more times per week.	①	②	③	④
23. I feel stressed about school on a regular basis.	④	③	②	①
24. I get along with people most of the time.	①	②	③	④

Mark the responses that best describe your approach to college.

ATTENTION AND MEMORY	Never or almost never	Rarely	Frequently	Always or almost always
25. Rote memorization is my most preferred way of learning material.	④	③	②	①
26. When I have trouble remembering something, I think of things that are related to what I'm asked to remember.	①	②	③	④
27. I listen to lyrical music when I study.	④	③	②	①
28. I am easily distracted.	④	③	②	①
29. I usually study in a noisy place.	④	③	②	①

Mark the responses that best describe your approach to learning.

METACOGNITION				
	Never or almost never	Rarely	Frequently	Always or almost always
30. I generate questions to help me understand class material.	①	②	③	④
31. I notice or look for examples of what I'm learning in one class in other classes or in my life outside of school.	①	②	③	④
32. I try to make comparisons and find similarities between what I read in textbooks and what I hear in lectures.	①	②	③	④
33. I monitor my progress to assess whether I am learning what I set out to learn.	①	②	③	④
34. I vary my approach to learning depending on the class and type of assignment.	①	②	③	④

Mark the responses that best describe your note-taking habits.

NOTE TAKING

35. I miss class
  - ④ never
  - ③ once or twice a semester
  - ② once or twice a month (4–8 times a semester)
  - ① once or twice a week (over 15 times a semester)

36. I find it hard to concentrate
  - ① at least once per class period
  - ② at least once per week
  - ③ only one or two times a month
  - ④ I almost never have trouble concentrating in class (my mind wanders only once or twice a semester during class)

37. I ask questions or provide a comment in class
  - ④ once a week or more
  - ③ once a month or more
  - ② only one or two times a semester
  - ① I do not participate in class unless called on by the professor

38. Positive features of my note taking (mark all that apply):
  - (+1) I look over my notes after class.
  - (+1) I go back and expand and/or clarify my notes after class.
  - (+1) I review my notes with the professor or with a classmate.
  - (+1) People who have borrowed my notes have commented on how organized and easy to understand they are.

39. Negative features of my note taking (mark all that apply):
  - (−1) I try to write down what the professor says verbatim.
  - (−1) I lose track of what the professor is saying because I am trying to write down as much as possible.

-1 The only time I look at my notes is a day or two before the test to review.

-1 I have a hard time understanding my notes when I go back to them because I can't read the writing or understand the abbreviations, or there are parts missing.

Mark the responses that best describe your approach to taking tests.

TEST TAKING

	Never or almost never	Rarely	Frequently	Always or almost always
40. After I get a multiple-choice test back, I look at the ones I got wrong and realize I made a "stupid mistake".	4	3	2	1
41. I study the same way for essay and multiple-choice tests.	4	3	2	1
42. I try to make comparisons and note similarities between what I read in textbooks and what I hear in lectures.	1	2	3	4
43. My nervousness distracts me from clear thinking during tests.	4	3	2	1
44. I jot down an outline for an essay answer before I begin writing.	1	2	3	4

Indicate the extent to which you do the activities listed while reading.

READING

	None of the time	Some of the time	Most of the time	All of the time
45. I set a goal before I begin.	1	2	3	4
46. I ask myself questions about the text.	1	2	3	4
47. I change my strategy based on the difficulty of the text.	1	2	3	4
48. I take notes during the reading.	1	2	3	4
49. I reread when I don't understand.	1	2	3	4
50. I listen to music.	4	3	2	1
51. I fall asleep.	4	3	2	1

Indicate the extent to which you engage in the following behaviors when you are writing.

WRITING

	None of the time	Some of the time	Most of the time	All of the time
52. I make an outline.	1	2	3	4
53. I feel rushed.	4	3	2	1

54. I proofread.	①	②	③	④
55. I allow a friend to read my writing.	①	②	③	④
56. I turn in the first version I print out.	④	③	②	①
57. I have multiple pieces of information available when sitting at the computer, such as a textbook, Web sites, and note cards.	①	②	③	④

Mark how true each of the following statements is of you.

CRITICAL THINKING

	None of the time	Some of the time	Most of the time	All of the time
58. I often find myself questioning things I hear or read in this course to decide if I find them convincing.	①	②	③	④
59. When a theory, interpretation, or conclusion is presented in class or in readings, I try to decide if there is good supporting evidence.	①	②	③	④
60. I treat the course material as a starting point and try to develop my own ideas about it.	①	②	③	④
61. I try to play around with ideas of my own related to what I am learning in this course.	①	②	③	④
62. Whenever I read or hear an assertion or conclusion in this class, I think about possible alternatives.	①	②	③	④

Note. The preceding five items are from the Motivated Strategies for Learning Questionnaire (Pintrich, Smith, Garcia, & McKeachie, 1991.)

Mark the responses that best describe your approach to problem solving.

PROBLEM SOLVING

	Never or almost never	Rarely	Frequently	Always or almost always
63. I enjoy puzzles, problems, and brainteasers.	①	②	③	④
64. When faced with difficult problems, I have a hard time deciding how to begin.	④	③	②	①
65. When I hear someone state a position or argument, I skeptically try to think of alternative explanations.	①	②	③	④
66. I am good at thinking "outside the box."	①	②	③	④
67. I find personal testimonials on TV commercials convincing.	④	③	②	①

IDENTIFYING WHO YOU ARE AS A LEARNER

What Did You Find Out?

Now that you have completed the Learning Inventory, it's time to examine your scores. Add all of your scores for each section, and divide by the number of questions in that particular section. (For the note-taking section, the numbers will be slightly different because of the different types of questions.) This will be your average score for each section. Activity 1.2 provides a scoring guide.

Learning Inventory

ACTIVITY 1.2

Scale	Number of items	Total score	Scale score (Total score divided by number of items)
Goal Setting	5		
Motivation	6		
Resource Management: External	8		
Resource Management: Internal	5		
Attention and Memory	5		
Metacognition	5		
Note Taking	11		
Test Taking	5		
Reading	7		
Writing	6		
Critical Thinking	5		
Problem Solving	5		

Later, a brief description of each of the scales is provided. We also provide a mean score for each of the scales based on a sample of students who have completed the Learning Inventory previously.[*]

As we give you these averages (what social scientists call norms), we must offer a strong word of caution. Although we believe the scores of other students are informative for you, we also want to make it absolutely clear that you should not view this as a contest. The point is not to try to have higher scores than the averages we present here, or to have higher scores than others

[*] These means are based on scores of 80 college students from a 4-year college or university (with the exception of Resource Management: Internal, which is based on 40).

in your class. The point is to provide you with descriptive information about what might be your strengths and weaknesses as a learner. To do this, you can compare your scores on one scale to scores on another scale, or, even more important, compare your score at the beginning of the book to your score on that same scale at the end of the book. This will be a good measure of change. You should focus on two things. First, you should analyze which aspects of the learning process you are doing well with, and which aspects of the learning process you may need additional help with. Second, at the end of this book, you should notice on which sections of the instrument your scores have changed. This will give you an idea of the ways this book has changed your learning behavior. We go through the scales in the order that we cover them in the book.

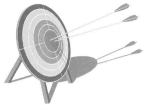

© Anna Stodolskaya – FOTOLIA

Goal Setting. (Scale Mean = 2.76) All successful people set goals. Without goals, you will not achieve as much. Chapter 2 will teach you about **goal setting** to focus and direct your work. It is important to have short-term and long-term goals, and these goals should be difficult yet realistic. Fear of making mistakes can hurt people's performance; it is important to remember that making mistakes is a normal part of the learning process, and in fact, mistakes are a sign of appropriate risk taking. Taking risks is how we learn.

Motivation. (Scale Mean = 2.86) **Motivation** is how we direct and energize our behavior. Staying motivated involves coping well with failure and disappointment when they occur (and they occur for everyone). Chapter 3 covers strategies for building self-confidence, developing healthy self-explanations for your success and failure, and identifying effective reinforcers to reward your effort.

Resource Management: External. (Scale Mean = 2.46) **Resource management** involves properly organizing and utilizing the tools at your disposal. One resource management strategy is organization. Organization is easy to say and hard to do. Walking into certain professors' offices will tell you that even getting a PhD doesn't guarantee organization. The truth is, regardless of ability or educational level, we would all do better if we were more organized. Chapter 4 will teach you about valuable resource-management tools such as the importance of a flexible weekly schedule, finding the right places to study, effective group studying, and the importance of faculty mentoring.

Resource Management: Internal. (Scale Mean = 2.67) These five questions address how well you manage your internal resources. Chapter 5 will cover important topics related to healthy living. Young adults are at their peak in terms of physical health and strength. Unfortunately, the stress of college and poor decision making create risks for students. This chapter stresses the importance of nutrition, sleep, avoiding dangerous excesses, and healthy interpersonal communication.

Attention and Memory. (Scale Mean = 2.73) The most important inner component of learning is effective mental activity; that is, attending to and learning course material. Chapter 6 covers ways to improve your attention, strategies for storing information effectively into long-term memory, and tips for pulling out the right information at the right time.

Metacognition. (Scale Mean = 2.72) **Metacognition** is an awareness and control of your own learning. School learning is enhanced when you have an awareness of your own learning. Chapter 7 covers ways to improve your metacognition, such as previewing material, asking questions of yourself and others, and building pictures (mental and actual) of the material you are learning.

Note Taking. (Scale Mean = 1.82) Note taking is essential to college success. Chapter 8 describes note taking as both a product and a process. Having good notes is important for storage of material, but how you actually take notes will also improve your learning. Like most activities, there are good ways and bad ways to do it, and this chapter describes healthy note taking.

Reading. (Scale Mean = 2.56) Being a good reader involves many of the same strategies that are involved in other school tasks. However, too often people don't set reading goals, they don't ask questions or engage the text, they simply want to finish and are not aware of how much they are actually understanding, and they pick poor environments in which to read. In Chapter 9 we develop a profile of a good reader and encourage you to adapt your behavior to fit that profile.

Writing. (Scale Mean = 2.75) Good writing begins before you ever put pen to paper (or fingers to keyboard). In Chapter 10 we develop a plan for effective writing that involves prewriting strategies and describe ways to build good sources for your text, strategies for translating your ideas to text, and effective revision techniques.

Test Taking. (Scale Mean = 2.57) Not all tests are created equal. Therefore, different tests require different strategies for success. In Chapter 11 we explore how to study for multiple-choice tests and for essay tests. **Test anxiety** will likely arise sometime in your life if it hasn't already. We examine the root of the anxiety and suggest ways to handle it.

Critical Thinking. (Scale Mean = 2.58) **Critical thinking** is the ability to use acquired knowledge in flexible and meaningful ways. If you always accept what you read or hear as true, if reading material doesn't prompt you to ask questions or read other material, and if you don't think in terms of "what's the evidence" for a particular claim, you're probably not a great critical thinker—yet. But Chapter 12 will teach you ways to become a better critical thinker.

Problem Solving. (Scale Mean = 2.93) Similar to critical thinking, **problem solving** is the act of moving from a state of not knowing how to complete a task to being able to complete the task. Different types of problems involve different solution strategies. In Chapter 13 we explore how to solve concrete problems like those found on SAT exams as well as **ill-defined problems**—problems for which not everyone will agree on the correct answer.

This concludes our journey through the book's learning-assessment inventory. Are you disappointed with some of your scores? That's OK. That's what this book is for. Now that you have made a preliminary diagnosis, you can begin to think about ways to improve your learning. As you read this book, we will ask you to think back to your scores on these scales. We will reference this instrument during the appropriate chapters of the book.

UNIVERSITY RESOURCES

Colleges and universities of all sizes have more resources than most students realize. Your university is bigger than you think and has a lot to offer you. Use these facilities and people.

Health Clinic

Sleep deprivation, stress, and living in close proximity to others all contribute to putting you at high risk for infection. Many of these illnesses will be viral, so you can only treat the symptoms. But even for viral infections your health clinic will be able to recommend over-the-counter treatments. For bacterial infections like strep throat (common among college students), the health clinic can diagnose and treat with antibiotics. Best of all, these services are almost always free or available at a small cost. In addition, the health clinic can assist with advice about health topics ranging from immunization for international travel to repercussions of unprotected sex.

Counseling Center

We believe an important yet underused resource on many college campuses is the counseling center. As an example, the first author brings the director of the college's counseling center to speak to one of his classes each semester. It is amazing how few of those students even know where the counseling center is before that day. Whereas health clinics address issues of physical health, counseling centers address issues of mental and emotional health. Counseling centers provide both *intervention*, treating the causes of and symptoms resulting from mental illness, and *prevention*, working to reduce the risk of mental-health problems before they occur. The most common form of intervention on college campuses is one-on-one therapy with a licensed counselor, social worker, or clinical psychologist. Prevention could include yoga, relaxation sessions, or workshops for fraternities and sororities. On the first author's campus, more than 1 in 5 graduating seniors use the counseling center at least once during their college career. This statistic should reduce any anxiety you have about using this service, and we encourage you to take advantage of it.

Library

Too many students underuse the library. The resources available are far richer than most people understand. Too often students (and, dare we say, professors?) simply "Google" a topic when they want to learn something or when a paper is due. Googling is a good first start, but there are more sophisticated databases available at a university library. We encourage you to schedule a tour with a reference librarian—a university staff person trained in using library research resources—*very* early in your first semester to make maximum use of the learning goldmine that awaits you at the library.

BEFORE YOU MOVE ON: A FEW SURVIVAL TIPS

In this section we offer some strategies to help you in a crisis. Consider this your emergency tool kit that you can use before you finish reading this book. These survival skills come from a convocation address offered by one of our colleagues, Dr. James Herrick. Here are his seven survival skills:

© EuToch – FOTOLIA

1. *Never sit in the back row.* Although there may be no harm, and we don't cite specific research on this, in general people in the back row develop a bad rep. It might be unjustified, but we believe it's there. Along with the reputation of being a "back bencher" comes a host of other dilemmas: it's harder to hear; it's harder to see; you feel anonymous, so that maybe you talk when you don't think you can be heard; and you sit with other back benchers who also feel anonymous. So, move up and see your engagement increase.

2. *Never ask for an extension.* Professors often grant extensions, but this is a bad habit to get into. Asking for an extension is a slippery slope—it becomes easier the next time you do it. There are at least two problems. First, we don't believe that extra time produces better quality. Rarely does an extension improve paper quality or even give you more study time (because the extra time gets filled with other activities). Second, the extra time you take to finish the extended assignment pushes back all of the other assignments, gives you less time for them, and makes it more likely that you'll need to ask for an extension for the *next* assignment.

3. *Set your own schedule.* Don't let friends tell you what to do and when to do it. You will ultimately take the credit or blame for everything that happens in your life, so don't let others determine how you spend your time. If you have a test the next day, don't go out. If you've got a Monday midterm, and you know that you'll be with your family on Sunday, skip the football game on Saturday. College needs to be fun, but you are here to learn. Make that your first priority. You'll be happy you did.

4. *Attend every class.* It's too expensive to miss class. It's expensive because you are paying for your education, and if you divided your total tuition bill by the number of classes per year, you might be less inclined to miss. It's also expensive because there are valuable things that go on in each class and you can't afford to miss them. It's also expensive because when you miss class, you hurt your credibility with the professor. Obviously, there are times when you can't attend because of illness or family emergency. But beyond that you should be there every time. Attendance is a bigger problem with early classes. On mornings with early classes, we strongly suggest that you get enough sleep the night before. Finally, missing class puts you behind, and falling behind is always counterproductive.

5. *Read every assignment.* Just like asking for extensions and skipping class, failing to read assignments makes it harder to keep up. It is especially important to read before class. This gives you an **advanced organizer**—a framework for understanding and interpreting knowledge.

6. *Do every problem.* Professors don't give throwaway assignments. We give assignments because we think they are important and because we believe they will help you learn the material. Whether it's a math problem, journal entry, or online quiz, doing assignments helps you learn.

7. *Visit every professor at least once.* It's probably self-serving to say this, but we believe professors are interesting people. They also (and this sounds less self-serving) like to talk about their subject area. We recommend having at least one conversation with each of your professors each semester. You will learn something about them and about the field they teach.

CHAPTER SUMMARY

There are two keys to successful learning: skill and will. You need good learning strategies (skill) as well as an effective motivational orientation (will). Intelligent students who are not motivated, and hardworking students with poor learning strategies will both fail to live up to their academic potential.

This chapter has given you an initial assessment of your motivation and learning strategies. The rest of the book will focus on the different components of learning and motivation. The following chapters will present some of the underlying educational and psychological principles of successful learning, but the main focus will be to offer concrete suggestions to improve your skill and will.

Goal Setting

PREPARING TO USE YOUR SKILL COMPONENTS

Chapter Goals

This chapter will help you:

- Begin to set goals so you can direct and focus your work on things you value

- Identify both long-term and short-term goals you have, as both are important for college success

- Challenge yourself with difficult, yet realistic, goals

- Realize that having a competitive (performance) goal may not be good all the time, and why under most circumstances, focusing on your own learning is better than trying to outdo others

- Realize that making mistakes is how humans learn, and trying simply to avoid mistakes won't make you smarter

Key Terms

goals

long-term goals

mastery goal

outcome goals

performance goal

process goals

short-term goals

CHAPTER 2

This chapter introduces you to goal setting: an important aspect of the skill component of learning. The chapter provides a general overview of how to prepare to use your skills by setting goals and getting ready for learning. Many of the other chapters in this book will address the specific cognitive skills measured in the Learning Inventory. Goals are also measured separately on the Learning Inventory, and some aspects of goal setting and planning are also part of the items in the metacognition scale. To assess your current views of learning and setting goals, do Activity 2.1, which comprises the five goal-setting items from the Learning Inventory.

ACTIVITY 2.1 *Learning Inventory: Goal-Setting Items*

Circle the statements that best describe your approach to college. When you are finished, add the corresponding points for all items.

1. When choosing between a hard class and an easy class, I consider my potential grade more than the interest or challenge the class would bring:
   - (4) never or almost never
   - (3) rarely
   - (2) frequently
   - (1) always or almost always

2. When thinking about the future, I think about the potential positive impact of doing well in college, and the potential negative impact doing poorly might have on my future:
   - (1) never or almost never
   - (2) rarely
   - (3) frequently
   - (4) always or almost always

3. When I am given a large assignment, I try to do it all in one night:
   - (4) never or almost never
   - (3) rarely
   - (2) frequently
   - (1) always or almost always

4. When faced with a large task, I make lists of the things I need to do to reach the final goal:
   - (1) never or almost never
   - (2) rarely
   - (3) frequently
   - (4) always or almost always

5. I take mistakes personally and see them as a sign of failure:
   - (4) never or almost never
   - (3) rarely
   - (2) frequently
   - (1) always or almost always

SCORING:

The following categorization can be used as a rough indicator of your views about goal setting.

16 and above: You probably have a healthy perspective on school learning, with the right amount of focus on goal setting, planning, and mastery. This chapter can serve as a helpful review of important aspects of learning.

11–15: You probably have a moderately good perspective on school learning. However, you may have to rethink some of your ideas. This chapter will help you identify some ways you can change your thinking toward school learning.

10 and below: This chapter is definitely for you. It will help you focus on some of the important aspects of effective school learning. We encourage you to read this chapter carefully and to use the suggestions we offer to change your orientation to learning in college.

Everyone has goals for life in general, goals to accomplish at work, goals to accomplish in school, and even goals for smaller tasks, such as a goal for what to accomplish when reading a chapter in a textbook or writing a paper for a class. The problem for most people is not that they don't have goals, it is more that they aren't aware of all of their goals, and their goals may be too vague and general to be of best use for them as a guide in decision making. Moreover, if you aren't aware of your goals or your goals are too vague, then it is difficult to monitor your progress toward them to become a self-regulated learner. This chapter involves you in thinking about your goals for life as well as your goals for school and for the specific academic tasks you will encounter in different courses.

WHY SET GOALS?

Goals are important because they influence our thinking, our emotions, and our actions. You can think of goals as the things that energize and guide our action. Goals will help you make decisions about which paths you will follow as you go about your daily life. Depending on your goals, you will choose different activities, and these different paths will lead you to pursue some goals and not to pursue others.

There are other aspects of goals that are important as well. Goals differ in many ways: some are long-term goals, like having a successful career or happy family life. Others are short-term goals, such as getting an A on a midterm chemistry exam or finding a date for Saturday night. Goals also differ in how specific they are. All students want to "do well," but that is a vague, general goal. In contrast, a goal of being a nurse is a specific goal. Devising a plan for a specific goal is easier than for a general goal. The specific goal of becoming a nurse will lead to the general goal of being happy.

Goals can also be arranged in a hierarchy, with some goals serving as subgoals for other, larger goals. So, a student might want to get an A on her midterm chemistry exam because that is a subgoal for doing well in her chemistry course, which is a subgoal for having a high overall GPA. And, of course, having a high GPA is a subgoal for gaining admission to medical school, which allows her to reach a larger goal of becoming a medical doctor and having a successful career. We now will discuss these different aspects of goals and how you, as a self-regulated learner, can best think about them.

LONG-TERM AND SHORT-TERM GOALS

Long-term goals are goals you may have for your life in general, your goals for your career and employment, your goals for family life, and even your goals for college. These goals will not be reached in a few days or even weeks or months. In addition, your ideas about these goals may be rather vague and general, such as "have a happy and successful life and career," or "get married and have a nice family," or "get my college degree in 4 years." As you go through life, your ideas about these general life goals may become more specific as you gain more self-knowledge and experience. For example, you may decide that a successful career means becoming a medical doctor or that you will become a teacher for an urban school district or that you will become an entrepreneur and design fuel-efficient machines.

© andresr – FOTOLIA

These definitions of your long-term goals will evolve over the course of your college career. You don't need to worry now if you don't have very specific long-term goals. However, you do need to have specific **short-term goals**. Psychological research has shown that individuals who set short-term goals are better able to monitor their progress toward these goals and regulate their behavior to come closer to achieving their long-term goals (Pintrich & Schunk, 2002; Watson & Tharp, 1997). For example, if you have a long-term goal of being successful in life, how would you monitor your progress toward this goal? How would you know if you are getting closer to it or what strategies you could use to bring it closer? In contrast, research has shown that short-term goals can be monitored more readily than long-term goals can, and individuals can usually think of ways to accomplish these short-term goals. For example, imagine you have a short-term goal of doing an excellent final paper for a history class. This is much closer in time than "having a successful career," and you can probably think of some strategies for writing a good final paper (chapter 10 also discusses strategies for writing papers), whereas if you try to think of specific strategies to "have a successful career," you may get lost or overwhelmed.

The main idea about this dimension of goals is that long-term goals are fine, but individuals also need to set short-term goals for themselves. In terms of college, short-term goals should include specific goals for your courses as well as for the different academic tasks you will do in these courses.

STRATEGY SUGGESTION

Short-term course goals should be set at least weekly so you can monitor them regularly.

Of course, for specific academic tasks, short-term goals should be relevant to the task at hand. For example, if you have three chapters to read in a textbook, you might set short-term goals of reading and studying each chapter in three separate studying sessions to make the task more manageable. Another example of a specific academic task that can benefit from short-term goal setting is writing a 20-page final paper for a course. For most students, generating 20 pages of text is quite a large goal, and it can seem insurmountable. However, if the task is broken up into short-term goals such as generating an outline of sections, doing research for each section, and then writing each section separately, followed by editing of the whole paper, these smaller goals are much more easily accomplished than trying to accomplish a larger goal of writing a 20-page paper.

In fact, both of the authors of this book set short-term goals for writing chapters of this book, and within chapters, writing sections of each chapter. For example, the goal for writing this chapter was to write it within a 2-week period, and within that 2-week period, each section was set for one or two sessions of writing time (a 3-hour session set aside for writing). This short-term goal setting not only made the task manageable, but it improved our confidence and motivation. If both of us thought only about writing a whole book all the time, this goal was too intimidating and distant and would make it hard for us to continue on the task. Breaking the task into smaller short-term goals such as chapters and then sections within chapters allowed us to complete these tasks and feel successful. And, after a while, these sections and chapters built up so that the book was finally completed.

In a wonderful essay entitled "The Considerable Satisfaction of Two Pages a Day," published in the *Chronicle of Higher Education*, writer Jay Parini says that he achieves success by writing only two pages a day. Imagine: two pages a day, 5 days a week for 2 weeks, and your 20-page paper is done. Two pages a day, 5 days a week for a whole year, and you've completed a 500-page "paper"—a 200-page book! All big dreams are best accomplished by breaking them into little pieces.

Activity 2.2 suggests some ways to think about both long-term and short-term goals. You should list some long-term goals you have for your life in general as well as for college. Then, try to think of some more short-term goals that will help you accomplish these long-term goals. Use the strategy suggestion below to help you in this activity.

STRATEGY SUGGESTION

Make some of your goals into short-term goals that can be accomplished within a few days or a week.

Setting Long-Term and Short-Term Goals

List some of your long-term goals in the areas below. For each long-term goal on the left, think of several more short-term goals.

LONG-TERM GOALS
Academic/School

_____

_____

_____

_____

Career

_____

_____

_____

Personal Life/Social Relations

_____

_____

_____

Recreation

_____

_____

_____

SHORT-TERM GOALS
Academic/School

_____

_____

_____

_____

Career

_____

_____

_____

Personal Life/Social Relations

_____

_____

_____

Recreation

_____

_____

_____

SPECIFIC AND MEASURABLE GOALS

Another important dimension of goals is that they should be specific and measurable. It is difficult to monitor goals that are vague. If you have a goal of "doing well" in college, what does that mean? How will you know when you have reached that goal? Even a more short-term goal such as "doing well in an English course" is still vague, and progress toward that goal is difficult to monitor.

In contrast, more specific goals that include measurable or actual overt behaviors are more easily monitored. For example, doing well in college can be defined more specifically, such as, "I will try to maintain a 3.3 (B +) overall GPA." This is easily measurable and specific, albeit a little long term. When you think about goals for courses or academic tasks, remember that specific and measurable short-term goals can help you monitor and regulate your academic behavior. So, for doing well in an English class, your goal might become, "I will get an A − in my English Literature class this semester." At the more specific task level, "do all the assigned reading before the next class" and "make two or three contributions to the next class discussion" would be specific and measurable goals that you could easily assess in this English class.

In addition, an important aspect of setting specific goals is to think about how your goals can be linked to different situations (Watson & Tharp, 1997). That is, some goals may be situation specific and more easily accomplished in some situations than in other situations. For example, suppose you have a goal of "being less shy." That is fairly general and vague, but suppose you revise that goal to mean two different kinds of goals. One subgoal for becoming less shy might be, "talk in a class discussion and offer my ideas to the class." This subgoal is often hard for many students. However, when you think about your different classes, you decide that it is easier to do this in your English course, where there are only 25 students and the professor encourages and structures class time to facilitate discussion, rather than in a large lecture class in psychology.

In this case, the English class affords you a better opportunity to achieve your goal, and you would be better off trying to talk (and become less shy about your ideas) in this class than in other classes or situations that are not structured as well for you to achieve your goal. So, you might revise your general goal about being less shy to "talk and share my ideas in English class this semester," which is more specific and tied to a particular situation.

A second subgoal of becoming less shy might be, "talk to other students socially." Again, this is a somewhat vague goal, but you may think about different situations in which this is easier to do than others. For example, it may be easier to talk to students you meet in your classes than trying to go up and start talking to other students at a party where you don't know anyone. In the class situation, at least you can begin a social conversation by talking about the class, the work, and the professor because you have these things in common and you may at least recognize one another. In the party situation, you may not know anyone and don't necessarily have anything in common with others except for attending the same college (perhaps this is the reason that many conversations at college parties start off with a discussion of classes and professors, to establish some common ground). Accordingly, the class situation may offer you a better chance to reach your goal of talking to other students socially, so you may revise your goal of "being less shy" to "talk with other students in my classes socially before and after class time." This is easier and more specific than a goal of "talking to other students" or "becoming less shy." The main idea is that an important aspect of making your goals more specific is that you think about which situations will allow you to accomplish them more easily.

Activity 2.3 asks you to take some of your short-term goals from Activity 2.2 and make them into more specific and measurable goals. Use the strategy suggestions below to help you in this activity.

STRATEGY SUGGESTIONS

Make your goals specific and measurable. Avoid vague and general statements, and try to make your goals reflect actual behavior that you could observe.

Think of specific situations where you could more easily accomplish your goals.

Making Short-Term Goals More Specific and Measurable

Short-Term Goal	Specific/Measurable	Situation
Choose some of your short-term goals from Activity 2.2 and list them here.	For each goal in the first column, how could you make it more specific? How could you measure it?	For each goal, list situations where you could and could not accomplish it.

CHALLENGING BUT REALISTIC GOALS

A third dimension of goals that is important to keep in mind when goal setting is to make them challenging but realistic. It is good to have high goals and high standards, but an important aspect of becoming a self-regulated learner is also to know your relative strengths and weaknesses. It may be motivating at one level to have a goal of becoming the next LeBron James in basketball or Jenny Finch in softball, but the overwhelming majority of us are not going to be able to reach those heights. And, for some individuals, if they set those unrealistic goals and then can't meet them, they get discouraged and may give up the activity completely. It is much more motivating to set challenging but realistic goals, reach them, and feel good about accomplishing them, and then go on to set somewhat higher goals for the next round of the activity.

In terms of academic activities, if you have been an average student in high school, with a C or lower GPA (2.0), it may be unrealistic for you to set a goal of getting a 4.0 GPA for your first semester in college. This is not as unrealistic as becoming the next LeBron James, but it may be more realistic to strive first for a 3.3 (B+) or 3.7 (A−) average in your first semester. This is a challenging goal if you are normally a 2.0 student. Setting a goal of getting the same C average you had in high school is neither motivating nor challenging, so you should set your goal so that it is challenging but realistic, such as a 3.3 GPA. If you achieve this level, then the following semester you can set your goal even higher. In contrast, if you did set a very challenging goal of a 4.0 GPA and did not attain it, you would feel less successful and good about yourself than if you did attain a more realistic goal.

Activity 2.4 asks you to think about your short-term goals from the previous two activities and set three different levels of these goals: easy, challenging but realistic, and too difficult. Use the strategy suggestion below for this activity.

STRATEGY SUGGESTION

Make your goals challenging but realistic. Make them something you have to try hard to attain—not too easy, but also not too difficult.

ACTIVITY 2.4   *Making Your Goals Challenging but Realistic*

List some of your goals from Activity 2.2 here. For each goal, try to think of three levels of challenge: an easy level, a challenging but realistic level, and a too-difficult level.

GOAL 1

Easy Level _____

Challenging Level _____

Too-Difficult Level _____

GOAL 2

Easy Level _____

Challenging Level _____

Too-Difficult Level _____

GOAL 3

Easy Level _____

Challenging Level _____

Too-Difficult Level _____

PROCESS GOALS AND OUTCOME GOALS

Another important dimension of goals concerns the setting of process goals versus outcome goals. **Outcome goals** concern the final product of the activity. For example, in our discussion in the previous paragraph, GPA would be an outcome goal. It reflects a general product of your 4 years in college or your first semester in college. In sports activities, winning a contest or game would be an outcome goal. In contrast, **process goals** refer to how you might achieve your final outcome goal. In an academic task, these might include learning how to write a research paper, learning how to solve calculus problems, or learning how to take essay exams. In the sports domain, process goals might include mastering the various skills needed to play well; for example, learning the different strokes in tennis well enough that one could win a tennis match (an outcome goal). Achieving process goals should lead to better outcome goals.

Research (see Zimmerman, 2000) has suggested that when students are first learning a skill or strategy, process goals are more helpful than outcome goals. Then, after students have acquired the skill at a high level of expertise and are trying to use it in new situations, outcome goals are more useful for achieving high levels of performance. For example, when you are learning how to play tennis, it is much better to focus on process goals: learning how to serve and to hit different strokes such as the forehand and backhand. In addition, even more specific process subgoals can be helpful. For example, when learning to serve, you might focus on the different "subprocesses" of serving, including tossing the ball up, drawing the racket back, and then following through on the actual serve stroke.

By focusing on these process goals as you learn to play tennis, you can improve the different strokes without worrying about whether you won or lost the tennis match. In fact, this is why coaches in many sports often stress practice time and breaking down the skills into different process goals: it lets individuals acquire the appropriate skills in a nonthreatening situation. In contrast, during a competition, the subprocess skills should already be learned and fairly automatic so that the individual can concentrate on playing well enough to win.

In learning situations, this same general idea holds. When you are first acquiring a skill or strategy, it is probably better to focus on the processes involved and not worry about your overall outcome goal (of a score, a grade, or your GPA). In fact, a great deal of research on students' general goal orientation (see Pintrich, 2000; Pintrich & Schunk, 2002) has found that a general focus on skill mastery and learning has many benefits to students. In contrast, a performance focus that emphasizes competition or avoiding "looking dumb" in front of others has negative consequences for students. This research has been done with elementary students, high school students, and college students. It seems to be applicable to all ages and levels in school. The next section of this chapter summarizes this research and what it means for you as a learner.

MASTERY AND PERFORMANCE GOAL ORIENTATION

Figure 2.1 displays a general summary of these two different goal orientations and how they can influence your cognition, motivation, and behavior. As you can see in Figure 2.1, students who are operating under a **mastery goal** define their success in terms of improvement, mastery, progress, and learning. In an academic situation, if you were operating with a mastery goal, you would focus on learning and improvement and not worry about grades or trying to beat out other students.

FIGURE 2.1   Mastery and performance goal orientations.

DIMENSIONS	MASTERY GOALS	PERFORMANCE GOALS
Success defined as	Improvement, progress, mastery, learning	Higher grades, besting others, winning at all costs
Value placed on	Effort, attempting challenging tasks	Avoiding failure
Reasons for effort	Intrinsic meaning and interest	Demonstrating one's worth in activity
How work is evaluated	Absolute criteria, progress from previous performance	Norms, social comparisons with others
Errors viewed as	Informational, part of learning	Failure, lack of ability
OUTCOMES		
Cognition	Use of deeper processing strategies. More self-regulation, metacognition	Use of more surface or rote learning strategies
Motivation/affect	Adaptive self-efficacy beliefs. More intrinsic interest, value	More anxiety, stress. Less intrinsic interest, more extrinsic motivation
Behavior	More adaptive help seeking. More risk taking. More effort at challenging tasks	Less likely to seek help. Less likely to take risks. Less likely to try difficult tasks

Source: From *Motivation in Education: Theory, Research, and Applications,* 2nd ed., by P. R. Pintrich and D. Schunk, 2002, Upper Saddle River, NJ: Merrill/Prentice Hall. Adapted with permission of the author.

In contrast, if you adopted a **performance goal,** you would define your success in terms of getting better grades than others. You could do very well in some cases if you have the high knowledge and skills necessary, but in many cases, especially when you are learning something new, it is not reasonable to expect that you will be the top scorer. When you just start learning to play golf, you are not going to be able to beat many other more experienced golfers. In the same way, in a very competitive situation such as a classroom where a grading curve limits the number of A's, not all students can get the highest grades. In this case, it is inevitable that some students will not succeed if their goal is to have the highest grades in the course. Some students with high performance will do well, but not all will get the top scores.

Another aspect of the mastery–performance goal distinction concerns what is valued. As shown in Figure 2.1, with a mastery goal orientation, students generally value effort and attempt challenging tasks. That is, if you had a mastery goal orientation, you would see effort and trying hard at challenging tasks as important. In contrast, with a performance goal orientation, students try to avoid failure, and they value demonstrating how smart they are relative to other students. In some cases, people who have a performance goal believe that if you try hard, it means you are not smart. Generally, most of us believe that a person who is smart or skilled at something doesn't have to try as hard. This makes "failure" difficult to deal with. Furthermore, this belief can be self-defeating when you confront a challenging task that requires effort.

When the first author's son was eight years old, he was a math whiz. He had lots of confidence in math, but he convinced himself that to be good at math meant to be fast at math. This has had the negative consequence of him giving up if he can't solve a problem right away. His parents have tried very hard to show him that being smart is not the same as being fast. What matters is effort. Time will tell if the lesson was successful.

With a performance goal orientation, if faced with the possibility of failure, you might be less likely to try hard because you want to appear smart (or avoid looking dumb). In addition, as Covington (1998) pointed out, you can protect yourself (psychologically speaking) by not trying hard. If you do well without much effort, you can assume you are "smart" and feel good about yourself. On the other hand, if you do poorly, you can rationalize your failure by saying that you were not really trying, thereby protecting your self-worth. Of course, in the long run, not trying hard at challenging goals and tasks will *not* be beneficial for your overall success.

Two other dimensions of the mastery–performance goal distinction (as shown in Figure 2.1) are how work is evaluated and how errors are viewed. Students with mastery goals tend to use absolute criteria that reflect task success and progress. For example, if you had a mastery goal, you would tend to evaluate your success in terms of doing well on the task, such as understanding the reading material or writing a good essay. In the same manner, you would see errors as potentially helpful to you in giving you feedback about areas you need to improve in. In contrast, performance-oriented students would tend to use evaluation criteria based on social comparison with others. For example, if you were performance oriented, you would check to see how well you did compared to others. If you got better scores or grades than other students or friends, you would be satisfied, regardless of your actual learning. You also would not view errors as learning opportunities, but instead as evidence of your failure, and would usually try to avoid them (say, by picking easy tasks).

Outcomes

All these aspects of mastery and performance goals can lead to different outcomes in terms of your thinking, motivation, emotions, and behavior. Again, a great deal of research has studied how these different goal orientations can lead to different outcomes. The main finding from this research is that adopting a mastery goal is quite beneficial, both in and out of school. Performance goals can lead to higher achievement, but sometimes there are costs associated with these goals.

Cognition. Figure 2.1 summarizes the outcomes that are associated with the two different goal orientations. First, in terms of thinking (cognition), students who adopt a mastery goal are more likely to engage in various self-regulatory learning strategies. If you are focused on learning and mastery, then you are more likely to use strategies that help you learn. In contrast, if you are focused on getting better grades than others, you may just use the easiest strategy available to you, which may or may not be helpful to your learning. In addition, mastery-oriented students are much more likely to plan and think about their learning. If you are concentrating on learning, you are more likely to think about what you are reading or studying. For example, if you read something and don't understand it at first, you are more likely to go back and read it again and try to understand it if your main goal is learning and mastery. In contrast, if you only care about grades and doing better than others, you may not spend as much time thinking about the material, and you may just keep on reading, even when you are not sure you understand what you just read.

Motivation. In terms of motivation, adopting a mastery goal seems to be related to many positive beliefs. First, if you focus on learning and mastery, then generally your confidence about your capabilities (what we will call self-efficacy; see Chapter 3) is high. In contrast, if you are oriented to trying always to be better than others, your self-efficacy may not be so high. In some cases, you may feel confident that you can do better than most other students; in other situations, you may feel much less confident about your potential for being successful in competing with others. Mastery-oriented students also seem to be much more intrinsically interested in the course material than performance-oriented students are. This makes sense: If your goal is only to do better than others, you may not appreciate the importance of what you are learning. Finally, in terms of emotions, students who adopt mastery goals are much less anxious and worried than are students who adopt performance goals. Again, if your main goal is besting others or not failing and looking stupid, you will probably be anxious about your grades and worried about how you look to others. In contrast, if you are focused on improving and mastery, there is no reason to be anxious as long as you make some progress over your own previous performance.

Behavior. In terms of behavior, mastery goals are also more beneficial than performance goals. Students who adopt a mastery goal are more likely to try hard, persist at the task, and ask for help in useful and adaptive ways in comparison to performance-oriented students. For example, if you are performance oriented, you may not want to try as hard as you can because you don't want other people to think you are unable. Or you may actually increase your effort level by focusing on beating out others in a competitive manner. Nevertheless, you still may be more anxious about how others are doing and your chances of beating them in terms of grades. Also, you are less likely to seek help from others because you don't want them to think you are stupid. In contrast, if you have a mastery goal, you are more likely to ask for help from others such as friends, peers, teachers, and parents in a way that will help you learn.

Are performance goals ever helpful? After all, don't we live in a competitive world where those who win move on? Perhaps. And yes, competition does help some of the people some of the time. And if it works for you, go for it. But we offer this caution: No matter what you do, you will always find someone who is better than you are. If only being the best will satisfy you, you will never be satisfied. If this causes you to give up, you need to change your approach. We recommend switching your focus from *being* the best to *doing* your best (from performance to mastery).

Activity 2.5 asks you to think about your own goals in terms of the process–outcome distinction as well as the mastery–performance distinction. The strategy suggestions below should help you think about how to make some of your goals more process oriented and mastery oriented.

STRATEGY SUGGESTIONS

When you are learning something for the first time, it helps to focus on the process of learning, not the outcome.

Try to keep a focus on mastery, self-improvement, and progress over your own previous performance; this will be helpful to you over time.

Try to see errors as information that you can use for improvement, not as evidence of failure.

Evaluate yourself in terms of how you did on the task, regardless of how others did on the task.

Process and Outcome Goals and Mastery and Performance Orientations

List the challenging goals from Activity 2.4 here. For each of these goals, try to determine if it is a process or outcome goal and if you have a mastery or performance orientation to the goal.

Goal	Process or outcome?	Mastery or performance?	Criteria you will use to evaluate yourself

MULTIPLE GOALS AND A HIERARCHY OF GOALS

All of this discussion of the different aspects of goals makes it clear that students can have multiple goals for college. When you enter college, you have some general goals for your career and your life, and you probably have somewhat more specific goals for college. In addition, as the preceding sections have suggested, you should try to have some specific and short-term goals for the different courses you will take and, within those courses, the different academic tasks you will encounter.

Sometimes with all these different goals, you may encounter conflict between goals. For example, you may want to make a lot of friends and socialize, and this may conflict with your goal of doing well and studying in college. The important issue is that you become aware of these potential conflicts and think about strategies for lessening the problem. One way to do this is to think about a hierarchy of your multiple goals and how they may fit together.

FIGURE 2.2   Carlos's and Jane's goals hierarchies.

GOALS	CARLOS	JANE
Life Goal	Be happy and successful	Become a doctor
College Goals	Do well in college Have a girlfriend	Earn a high GPA in science courses Make friends
Course Goals	Do well in courses Learn in courses	Do well in science courses Do better than others on exams and labs

Figure 2.2 displays the hierarchy of goals for two hypothetical students: Carlos and Jane. The first step in creating a hierarchy of goals is to think about your general life goals. In Carlos's case, his main life goal is to be happy and successful, whereas Jane's is more specific: to become a doctor. The next level down in the hierarchy in Figure 2.2 concerns their goals for college. Carlos wants to do well in college and has a more specific goal of having a girlfriend. Jane has a more specific goal of being a premed major with a high GPA, and a more general goal of making friends. Underneath these general college goals, Carlos and Jane both have more specific goals for their courses. Carlos wants to do well in all his classes, but he also has some goals for learning in his courses. Jane is mainly focused on her grades and one of a few of her subgoals for the courses seems to adopt a performance orientation toward grades and competing with others.

When you examine these hierarchies of goals, do you see any potential for conflicts? For example, do you think the social goals of both of these students might interfere with achieving their academic goals? In many cases, the academic and social goals of college students can easily conflict. That is, as students try to make friends, go to parties to meet people, try to have a boyfriend or a girlfriend, or spend a lot of free time socializing, they devote less time and attention to studying and academic tasks.

This does not have to be the case. One solution is to think of ways you can meet multiple goals through the same strategies. For example, you may form study groups for your classes. In a study group, you can make friends as you work on the course material and possibly learn better (see Chapter 4 for suggestions on how to work with peers). Of course, in Jane's case, given that she has a performance goal of doing better than other students in her chemistry class, she may not want to use a study group if she thinks that she will be helping the other students in her group do well. If she is competitive in all her classes, she may have a harder time making friends, and this would be a conflict in her goals that would be hard to overcome. On the other hand, if she is aware of this potential conflict and does not want to change her competitive goals, she may want to seek out friends among people who are not in her classes.

Another important aspect of making a hierarchy of your goals is that it may help you decide which of your many goals are more important than the others. In Jane's case, she might decide that making friends is more important than beating out everyone in her chemistry class. She will still want to get an A in chemistry, but she may decide that doing better than her classmates is not as important as having some friends in chemistry she can study with for exams. This type of awareness of your goals and how important each goal is to you is important for self-regulation. If you are trying to achieve two conflicting goals, you may experience stress, anxiety, and general dissatisfaction as you find that by approaching one goal, you move farther away from accomplishing another goal. By making some decisions about which goals are more important to you, you may be able to avoid these conflicts. This does not mean that you have to give up one or the other goal; it means that if you are in a situation that does not allow you to accomplish both goals at once, you can make an informed choice about which goal to pursue. This kind of informed decision making is another important aspect of becoming a self-regulated learner.

Activity 2.6 asks you to draw your own hierarchy of goals and to see which goals you think are most important to you. In addition, you should think about the possibility of your goals conflicting with one another. What are your strategies for dealing with potential conflicts? The following strategy suggestions may help you with this activity.

STRATEGY SUGGESTION

Examine your goal hierarchy and goals and try to see how you can avoid conflicts. Try to think of ways you can accomplish more than one goal with the same strategy (e.g., studying with peers can facilitate both academic and social goals).

Developing a Hierarchy of Your Goals

Given your goals from Activities 2.2–2.5, arrange them in a hierarchy as in Figure 2.2. Place more general and important goals at the top, and more specific goals closer to the bottom. You might want to use the four general levels shown in Figure 2.2.

Level 1: General Life and Career Goals

_____

_____

Level 2: Goals for College Years

_____

_____

Level 3: Goals for Specific College Classes

_____

_____

Level 4: Goals Within College Classes

_____

_____

© pryzmat – FOTOLIA

PATHWAYS AND ROADBLOCKS TO REACHING YOUR GOALS

In our discussion so far, we have talked about how to set different types of goals and how to make your goals more attainable. Still, there will always be obstacles to your goals. You can deal with some of them by thinking ahead about potential obstacles and finding ways to avoid them. In addition, positive factors or pathways are always available to help you reach your goals. Again, thinking of these pathways can help you maintain your focus on your goals and achieve them. Some of these facilitators are attitudes: different ways to frame the obstacles. Therefore, as you think of the roadblocks to your goals, you also may think of potential pathways.

There are some general roadblocks that many of us face in trying to attain our goals. Watson and Tharp (1997) pointed out several common ones you may face in your attempts to reach your goals. They include:

1. *Not expecting mistakes.* One obstacle that may hinder you is if you expect to be able to reach your goals easily and without mistakes. If you have this expectation and then make mistakes and things don't go smoothly, you may lose motivation for persisting at your goal. A mastery orientation that frames mistakes as an opportunity to learn can be helpful in overcoming this roadblock. If mistakes give you important feedback about how to improve, then mistakes can be helpful, not harmful. The main issue is how you use these mistakes to improve yourself. So, a potential pathway to your goals is to view mistakes as an opportunity to learn.

2. *Blaming mistakes or poor performance on a lack of general intelligence.* In an academic domain, many students give up simply because they think their intelligence is insufficient. These students believe that they do poorly or fail because they don't have what it takes intellectually. Moreover, they think they can't change this general ability. As we pointed out before, almost all the knowledge, skills, and strategies needed in academic settings are learnable. This learnable view of intelligence will be more helpful to you than the view that intelligence cannot change. Believing you can become smarter can be a pathway to your goals.

3. *Blaming poor performance on your personality.* This roadblock parallels the previous one. It just blames your mistakes on your personality traits, rather than your intellectual traits. For example, people may blame their poor study habits on a general personal trait, such as "I'm just not the studying type of person" or "I'm just not cut out to sit down and study. I'm too much of a free spirit, and I always wait until the last minute because I don't want to destroy my creativity." Students also may blame their personality traits for poor performance in different subject areas by suggesting that they are "just not the math or science type of person" or "just not the creative type" for English.

This does not just apply to academic situations. As Watson and Tharp (1997) pointed out, people can create this type of obstacle in other areas as well, such as trying to control eating, smoking, drinking, or exercising. For example, when trying to quit overeating, some people may say, "I just lack self-control; I'm just one of those people who are too impulsive and I can't control myself." Again, believing that your choices or mistakes come from some unchangeable part of yourself makes it difficult to believe in the possibility of improvement. This type of belief is an obstacle to change. If you think you can't change yourself or that you lack self-control or the ability to control your own behavior, you will be less likely to try to change.

As noted before, a more changeable view of personality that suggests that you can improve and gradually have some control and regulation over your own behavior will be more helpful in your attempts to become a self-regulated learner. As you read about the last two obstacles, remember that this changeable view of personality can be a pathway to better progress.

4. *Staying in situations that evoke unwanted behavior.* Watson and Tharp (1997) pointed out that many of us have difficulty in making changes in our behavior because we continue to put ourselves in situations that bring out the behavior we are trying to change. For example, if you are trying to quit smoking or stop drinking, then going to bars with friends will not help you meet these goals. You may swear that you will not smoke or drink and that you are just going to be sociable. But once in that situation, there are all kinds of reminders of the behaviors you are trying to avoid. One way to avoid this problem is to avoid situations that you know will generate the unwanted behavior. So, in this example, try to think of other places to socialize with your friends, such as a no-smoking coffeehouse. Controlling the situation or context can help you reach your goals.

In the academic domain, the places where you choose to study may have too many distractions, especially other students to talk with, even though you need to study alone. For example, at one of our universities, the first floor of the library has a big open area with large tables for studying. In the evenings this space is crowded with students who are ostensibly studying, but upon closer observation, you can see that many of them are just talking and gossiping, checking out the other students, and so on. Very little academic work is getting done here. Students who go to this space in the library every night for three hours but still do poorly may wonder why they are not doing better. It is likely that they are spending too much time socializing, talking, and people watching and not enough time concentrating. These students should try to change where they study. They should avoid this space as it is too tempting to socialize there, and it contains far too many distractions. A better strategy would be to go to the private study carrels on the upper floors of the library, to study without distractions. Then, when it is time for a break, they may come down to the first floor and socialize.

5. *Having friends or peers continually tempt you.* As Watson and Tharp (1997) explain, one of the biggest roadblocks to reaching your goals may be your friends and peers. That is, they may encourage you to smoke or drink, even if you are trying to quit. They may tempt you not to study in favor of hanging out with them. One of the important tasks for most college students involves finding a balance between individual goals and a general goal of having a good set of friends. Of course, we are not suggesting in any way that you change your friends if they are not supporting your efforts to change and reach your goals. Rather, we hope to make you aware of the possibility that sometimes your friends or peers may present you with obstacles. You need to think about how your friends support or do not support you in making progress toward your goals.

In terms of academics, if all your friends also study regularly, then it is easier for you to have a regular study schedule. They will support your going to the library in the evening, and you may all go together and then take breaks together or go out after studying. The difficulty is more likely to arise when you try to develop some regular study habits and your friends are urging you to come and hang out with them. At this point, you have to make some choices about how to handle the situation. It may help to explain to your friends why you have to study now and make plans to meet them later. Or you can ask them to support you in your attempts to study as you explain to them why you may need to study now, even if they do not. It is not always easy, and sometimes you may have to avoid your friends for a short time as you try to implement your plans. Once you get your plans for studying going and feel comfortable with them, then you may be able to make plans to socialize with your friends at other times.

In summary, roadblocks are sure to face you as you attempt to reach your goals. First, you need to become aware of the different kinds of roadblocks and then decide how you will attempt to overcome them. In many cases, the roadblocks are your own beliefs about your general ability and personality. The idea that your knowledge, skills, and aspects of your personality and behavior can change can be a powerful pathway as you try to reach your goals. In addition, you may need to examine certain situations, including your friendships, in terms of how they help or hurt your attempts to reach your goals. If you become aware of these situations and their pros and cons, you will be better equipped to think of strategies for reaching your goals.

Activity 2.7 asks you to examine the goals you have been working on in the previous activities. You will list some of the potential roadblocks to these goals, then strategies for overcoming the roadblocks. As much as we try to avoid it, things go wrong. Plans go awry. Dreams don't always come true. We can both attest to the fact that the major difference between students who are successful and those who are not is that the successful students persevere in the face of failure and blocked goals. It's not a question of whether bad things will happen to you in college, because they will. Bad test grades, failed friendships, deaths of friends. They will happen to you. Those who are able to overcome those roadblocks and continue to move forward toward their short- and long-term goals will be successful in college and beyond.

ACTIVITY 2.7 *Overcoming Roadblocks and Reaching Your Goals*

List some of your goals from Activities 2.2–2.6 here. For each goal, list possible roadblocks and possible strategies you might use to reach the goal.

Goal	Roadblocks to Goal	Potential Strategies to Reach Goal

CHAPTER SUMMARY

This chapter has discussed the psychology of goal setting and has suggested a number of strategies you might use for setting goals. The most important thing to remember is that we all have goals, but we need to become aware of them to make them most useful to us. By becoming aware of our goals, we can plan and monitor our actions to come closer to reaching our goals. In addition, you can benefit the most from goal-setting strategies that help you do the following in terms of your academic work:

- Make sure you set some short-term goals for your courses.
- Try to make these goals specific and measurable.
- Think of specific situations where you can accomplish these goals.
- Make your goals challenging but realistic.
- Try to keep a process and mastery orientation to your goals, especially when you are learning things for the first time.
- Think about your multiple goals and which ones are more important to you than others.
- Think ahead about what roadblocks you might face in reaching your goals.
- Given these roadblocks, try to think of strategies that might help you overcome them.

Following these strategies will help you become more effective in reaching your goals. They will not guarantee success all the time, but they will help you get started on the right path to better performance and achievement. We now turn to another important aspect of meeting your goals: your motivation for learning.

Motivation

PREPARING TO USE YOUR WILL COMPONENTS

Chapter Goals

This chapter will help you:

- Understand how to motivate yourself
- Assess your motivation—identify how you view yourself and your motivation and confidence for learning
- Be better able to cope with failure and disappointment so that you don't get discouraged and stop trying
- Assess what you value, what is important to you in college, and what topics interest you

Key Terms

attributions

choice behavior

expectancy

extrinsic rewards

motivation

reinforcers

self-concept

self-efficacy

self-esteem

situational interest

value

CHAPTER 3

T his hapter is about the will component of learning. It is about what motivates you to do well and to learn in academic settings. It is about the energy you bring to college learning, what you value in college, and your beliefs about your own success and failure. The specific items from the Learning Inventory attempt to determine what motivates you. Activity 3.1 shows these six items. We encourage you to complete them before you read any further.

ACTIVITY 3.1 *Assessing Your Will*

Circle the statements that best describe your motivation for college. When you are finished, add the corresponding points for all items.

1. I feel trapped into taking the classes that I take. I don't feel I can take classes that interest me.
   - (4) never or almost never
   - (3) rarely
   - (2) frequently
   - (1) always or almost always

2. When faced with a difficult homework problem, I am likely to wander down the hall and ask someone in my hall rather than working on my own.
   - (4) never or almost never
   - (3) rarely
   - (2) frequently
   - (1) always or almost always

3. I doubt whether I can succeed in college.
   - (4) never or almost never
   - (3) rarely
   - (2) frequently
   - (1) always or almost always

4. I get discouraged when courses are difficult or boring.
   - (4) never or almost never
   - (3) rarely
   - (2) frequently
   - (1) always or almost always

5. Being successful in college is more a function of ability and luck than effort and persistence.
   - (4) never or almost never
   - (3) rarely
   - (2) frequently
   - (1) always or almost always

6. Even when a class is boring, I try to find something interesting to get out of it.
   - (4) never or almost never
   - (3) rarely
   - (2) frequently
   - (1) always or almost always

SCORING: The following categorization can be used as a rough indicator of your views about motivation.

21 and above: You probably have a healthy perspective on motivation, with adaptive beliefs about yourself, school, and rewards. This chapter can serve as a helpful review of important components of will.

15–20: You probably have a moderately good perspective on motivation. However, you may have to rethink some of your ideas. This chapter will help you identify some ways you can change your thinking about motivation.

14 and below: This chapter is definitely for you. It will help you focus on some of the important aspects of effective motivation. We encourage you to read this chapter carefully and to use the suggestions we offer to change your orientation to learning in college.

Everyone is motivated by different things. In this chapter we want you to ask yourself about what motivates you. What motivates you to study? What motivates you to try hard? What motivates you to try different things? The word *motivation* is derived from the Latin verb *movere*, which means "to move." This fits our commonsense ideas about motivation as something that gets us going, that helps to get us off the couch to do something and then keeps us moving. We define **motivation** as something that energizes and directs our behavior. Motivation is affected by our beliefs—beliefs about ourselves and beliefs about schoolwork. We hope that after reading this chapter, you will discover that motivation has multiple components. It is not just one "thing," and individuals are not just "motivated" or "unmotivated." There are many ways to be motivated, and these different qualities of motivation lead to different behaviors. We now explore those different aspects.

THE PROFILE OF A MOTIVATED PERSON

What do motivated people look like? A generation ago, psychologists thought someone was either motivated or unmotivated for different activities—sort of an on–off switch of energized behavior. Students who had the motivation switch "on" for school were expected to do well, and those low in achievement motivation would not do well. These older theories also viewed motivation as a personality trait—something about you rather than something about the task (Pintrich & Schunk, 2002). Currently, psychologists see motivation as changeable based on a variety of external factors. For example, you're probably not motivated for every class; your motivation depends on the topic, type of classroom environment, type of professor, and other things. Psychologists have proposed a number of different motivational components that are relevant to increasing your motivation. In this section (and chapter as a whole) we will discuss those components and suggest strategies that you might use to increase your own motivation.

In the previous chapter, we discussed goals and goal orientation, which are an important aspect of both your cognition and your motivation. In this chapter, we will discuss some other important components of motivation and how they can influence your behavior. Figure 3.1 shows two general aspects of motivation, expectancy and value. Expectancy is a belief about yourself—what you believe will happen when you study for a test, come up to bat with the bases loaded, or

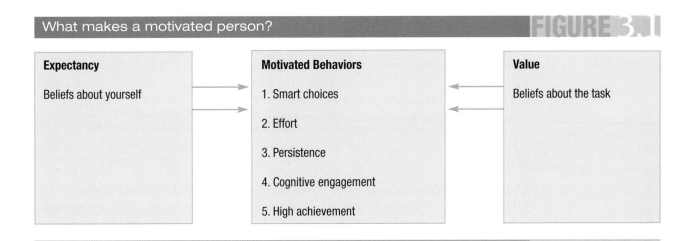

What makes a motivated person?   **FIGURE 3.1**

Expectancy		Motivated Behaviors		Value
Beliefs about yourself	→	1. Smart choices	←	Beliefs about the task
		2. Effort		
		3. Persistence		
		4. Cognitive engagement		
		5. High achievement		

ACTIVITY 3.2   *Evidence for Motivation*

Ask five people on campus or at your job the following question:

"What are the five things that a motivated person does that makes him or her motivated?"

Aspect	Person 1	Person 2	Person 3	Person 4	Person 5
	_____	_____	_____	_____	_____
	_____	_____	_____	_____	_____
	_____	_____	_____	_____	_____
	_____	_____	_____	_____	_____
	_____	_____	_____	_____	_____

Aspects that were mentioned more than once:

_____   _____

_____   _____

try out for a theater performance. Value is the importance you place on the activity, such as your interest in the topic or your desire to get a good grade. Both expectancy and value feed our motivation in five different ways. These five factors make up the profile of a motivated person. Before we discuss what psychologists have identified as important aspects of a motivated person, do Activity 3.2 to get an "on the street" feel for what others think motivation looks like.

Smart Choices

First, as Figure 3.1 shows, a motivated person shows five different behaviors. The first thing a motivated person does is to make smart choices. Motivation is related to the decisions and choices we make as we go about our lives. For example, if you are motivated for academic work, then you will probably choose to study and work on your course work rather than to hang out and watch TV or play sports or go partying. If you are working full-time and also going to school, this shows that you are still motivated for academic activities, as you could always spend your free time in other ways. College students make choices about what classes to take, what majors to go into, and what careers to follow. If you are motivated for a particular subject area, then you may choose to go on to major in this subject. These choices are related to your motivation and goals, as we discussed in Chapter 2.

Effort

The second aspect of motivated behavior is trying hard, putting forth effort. When you asked people in Activity 3.2 what aspects comprise a motivated person, did anyone mention effort, or trying hard? Many people do. Teachers use this term to describe their motivated students, parents use it to describe their motivated children, and both teachers and parents bemoan the lack of effort in their unmotivated students or children. In college you will have to try harder and put forth more effort than you ever had to in high school, junior high, or elementary school. Your effort or lack of effort will have a great deal to do with your ultimate success in college.

Persistence

The third aspect of motivated behavior is persistence. This is closely related to effort, but it involves sticking with something until you complete it. The task may be challenging or it may be boring or uninteresting, but motivated students persist until the task is completed. In addition, self-regulated students know when to stop persisting at a task and ask for help. It is not a good strategy to keep trying if you are not able to complete it after a sustained effort. Getting help with the task is a useful strategy, and it does not imply that you are not able.

Cognitive Engagement

The fourth aspect of motivated behavior is harder to see in terms of actual behavior. It goes on mentally, sort of behind the scenes. We call it cognitive engagement. It refers to how you think about a task. Do you think deeply, really studying it, mulling it over in your head, thinking about different ways to accomplish your goal? Or are you just going through the motions, reading your textbook but not really thinking about the material? Motivated students are more likely to be cognitively engaged and to use a variety of helpful strategies.

High Achievement

The fifth and final aspect of motivated behavior refers to your actual achievement and performance. Students who do well in their classes, get high grades, get good scores, learn the material, and master the skills taught are generally motivated. Students who are not motivated may not spend the needed time or effort, they may not use appropriate strategies, and they may not do as well as they are capable of doing. High motivation and high achievement go hand in hand. They feed off of one another. So finding ways you can experience success will fuel your motivation for the thing on which you just succeeded. Recently, the first author's oldest child experienced a fairly poor performance pitching in a middle-school softball game. Despair and lack of enthusiasm followed, until 3 days later when, given another chance, she did very well. It was amazing, but not surprising, to watch her motivation for playing, practicing, and talking about softball increase greatly because of this success. Motivation leads to success, and success leads to motivation.

Now you know the five important aspects of a motivated person. Recall that at the beginning of the chapter we said that these aspects are created by two general dimensions: expectancy and value. We now move on to discuss these two general dimensions. This will complete the picture of a motivated student.

EXPECTANCY

Expectancy concerns what you believe about yourself. It asks the question, "Am I able to do this task?" Basically, expectancy involves judgments of how capable you believe yourself to be and how much control you have over yourself and the situation.

Self-Concept

At a basic level, expectancy refers to **self-concept**—general beliefs about yourself. These beliefs could be about anything, such as whether you think you are smart, sociable, athletic, good-looking, friendly, nice, honest, caring, or ethical. **Self-esteem** is then defined in terms of how you feel about yourself, based on these beliefs. For example, do you feel good about yourself based on how you think you look or how athletic you are? That is, you may think you weigh too much (low self-concept), and then feel bad (low self-esteem) about your weight and looks. On the other hand, you may think you are somewhat overweight (low self-concept), but not have low self-esteem about that because your physical looks are not that important to you.

Your self-concept and self-esteem are important, but they are not as important for school learning as are two other, more specific beliefs: self-efficacy and attributions. Lots of pop psychology talks about the dangers of low self-esteem. And low self-esteem can sometimes be a problem. But in fact, most research shows that self-esteem has very little relation to actual learning in the classroom. Instead, the research shows that other, more specific beliefs like self-efficacy and attributions have a stronger relation to learning. We discuss these two aspects next.

Self-Efficacy

© Andrey Khrolenok – FOTOLIA

We stated that self-concept refers to general beliefs. In contrast, **self-efficacy** refers to *specific* judgments of your capabilities to perform in a *specific* situation. In more colloquial terms, self-efficacy may be called self-confidence. So, you may have a fairly good self-concept of your athletic ability and think you are a good tennis player. However, today you are playing a much better player and thus you are not feeling that confident about your capability to beat her. In this case, your self-efficacy is a little lower than it might be when you are playing someone you beat regularly in tennis. In many athletic settings, you hear the athletes discussing their self-confidence. For example, when a baseball player has to bat against a really good pitcher, his self-confidence or self-efficacy may be lower than usual.

In the same fashion, for academic tasks, you may have a fairly good overall self-concept of your math ability, but in a very difficult calculus course where grading is on a curve, your self-efficacy for doing well may be a little lower. Even within a course your self-efficacy may vary. For example, at the beginning of a biology course, much of the material seems to be a review of what you had in high school, so your self-efficacy is fairly high for the first exam. However, as the course progresses, the material gets more difficult. Moreover, as the term goes on, you may fall further and further behind in your reading, so your self-efficacy for the second or third exam might be lower.

The important aspect to remember about self-efficacy is that it is changeable and under your control. Your self-efficacy changes as your skill level increases. (Competence breeds confidence.) For example, you may have low self-efficacy for doing well in a math class at the beginning of the semester, but as you progress through the material and learn how to solve different types of math problems, you become more confident. Moreover, these judgments about yourself are linked to your performance—having high self-efficacy for math is related to high performance in math. Your general self-concept is less important.

Identify a behavior or performance in four areas of your life: academic, performance (art, sports, music), social, and service (volunteering, church). For each life domain, identify: (a) a general self-concept you have about the life domain, (b) a specific behavior in which you engage from that life domain, and (c) a specific self-efficacy belief you have about that behavior.

Life Domain	General Self-Concept	Specific Behavior	Specific Self-Efficacy Belief
Academic	_____	_____	_____
Performance	_____	_____	_____
Social	_____	_____	_____
Service	_____	_____	_____

How are your general self-concept beliefs different from your specific self-efficacy beliefs?_____

_____

Is this consistent with the definitional differences between self-concept and self-efficacy described in this chapter? _____

Therefore, it is more important to think about your specific self-efficacy than your general self-concept. Before you continue reading, please do Activity 3.3.

Where does self-efficacy come from? How can one develop accurate and positive self-efficacy beliefs? Many factors influence self-efficacy beliefs, but one of the most important concerns the attributions you make after you complete a task. We turn now to a discussion of attributions.

"How'd I Do That?"   Attributions in Learning

Consider two students who do poorly on an exam. As most of us do when we encounter failure, they ask themselves, "Why did I do so poorly on this exam?" Their answers are called **attributions**, or the reasons that students give to explain their performance. One of the students, Sonja, says to herself, "It must be because I did not study enough. Next time I will have to study harder and maybe try to study differently as well." The other student, Sam, says to himself, "I must be stupid. I just can't get this college stuff no matter what I do. I must not be smart enough for college." Of these two students, which one do you think will have more confidence (self-efficacy) for the next exam? Which one do you think will be more likely to stay in the course or stay in college (positive choice behavior)?

A great deal of research has studied the role of attributions in motivation and learning, and the results are probably just what you would predict. In all the research, students who make attributions like Sonja are much more likely to feel confident and expect to do better on the next exam, in contrast to students like Sam. In fact, students who make attributions like Sonja also are more likely to persist at future tasks, such as to stay in college, than those who are like Sam. Why is this? Why are these attributions so powerful?

Students can make an infinite number of attributions for why they do well or poorly on an achievement task. Sonja and Sam have illustrated two of them. Students could attribute their success to smartness, effort, good luck, or an easy test. Students could also say that they had help from friends, they studied the right way, they know a lot about the topic, they had a good teacher, and so on. Students also can generate a great many reasons for why they did poorly, such as they are dumb, they didn't try hard, they had bad luck, the test was too hard, they were sick, they had to work late the night before, they were hung over, they studied the wrong things, the teacher was bad, and so on.

Research has shown that the two most common attributions students give for their performance are (a) general skill and (b) effort. General skill refers to how smart you think you are, and whether you know something about the topic. In other words, the "skill" part of this book. Effort is how hard you tried in general or how much you studied for a particular test. In other words, the "will" part of this book. For the students described above, Sam makes an attribution to lack of ability—being stupid. Sonja, in contrast, makes an attribution to trying harder and studying better. These different attributions clearly lead to different behaviors.

Each attribution can have three different possible variations. Your future learning and motivation will depend on what variation your attributions have (Pintrich & Schunk, 2002). The three dimensions are:

1. Location of the attribution: Is my success or failure due to something about me ("I tried hard") or not about me ("I have a good teacher")?
2. Stability of the attribution: Will the reason for my success or failure be around for a long time ("I'm stupid") or will it fade with time ("I had a hangover")?
3. Controllability of the attribution: Is the reason for my success or failure something I can control ("I worked hard") or not ("My grandma died and I didn't have time to study")?

Location. The first dimension, location, refers to whether the cause is internal or external to the individual. Attributions to ability, knowledge, skill, and effort are located inside the person, while attributions to luck, the test, teachers, or peers are located outside the person. Generally speaking, when a person succeeds at a task or on a test, attributions that are internal to the person are the most helpful. So, if you succeed at a test and attribute it to your high ability, appropriate skills, or trying hard, that will have positive consequences for your future learning. In contrast, when you fail at a task, try to see the cause as being external, such as a very difficult test or other factors outside yourself (e.g., other people not helping).

If a person fails and attributes it to lack of an internal characteristic such as intelligence and believes that intelligence can't change, this will have negative consequences for future learning. However, if the person fails and attributes it to a lack of an internal characteristic such as effort or skill (which can change), this can be helpful. This book is based on such an idea. Remember one of the main points of Chapter 1: You can become smarter. This is an internal attribution that can change. This is healthy. Believing you can't get smarter is an internal attribution that cannot change. This is not healthy.

Stability. This brings us to the most important of the three areas, stability. The research on attributions is very clear on this point: When people make attributions to stable causes, they are likely to believe that the same result will occur in the future. For example, if you succeed and attribute it to something you think is stable, like high intelligence, then you will expect to succeed in the future. In the same way, if you fail and attribute it to something you think is stable, like low intelligence, then you will expect to fail on similar tasks in the future.

The same logic works for unstable causes, such as effort or luck. If you succeed and attribute it to good luck or effort on the specific task, then you may not expect to do as well in the future because these things are unstable and may not be in effect the next time. However, if you do poorly, then attributing it to unstable causes suggests that you can have hope, as these causes may change in the future.

Perhaps you are thinking that our advice about attributions is either arrogant (bragging about success) or excuse making (not taking responsibility for failure). It is not our suggestion that you publicly make such claims, lest you be perceived as such. Rather, we encourage you to think this way in terms of your inner dialogue with yourself (how you talk to yourself), to take pride in your achievements and to rebound quickly from failure.

Controllability. Controllability refers to how much control you think you have over the reason for your success or failure. Believing that you can control the reasons for your success and failure works better than assuming you have no control. Many individuals think of general ability as not being under their control. People often think of intelligence, for example, as something that is a stable factor, perhaps determined by genetics. When they experience failure, attributing it to a lack of general ability will generally lead to a lowering of self-efficacy, because the cause of failure is perceived as not being controllable. Believing you're not smart is not helpful. In contrast, attributing a failure to lack of effort is more useful, because you can control effort. You can work harder next time and expect to do better. In the same way, attributing failure to a lack of knowledge or skills is useful, as these are inherently changeable and under your control. So, failing a test in an upper-level class when you haven't had all the prerequisites should not lower your confidence.

Strategies for Making Attributions and Self-Efficacy Judgments

Given this brief overview of attribution and self-efficacy research, we suggest the following strategies to improve the expectancy components of your motivation.

1. *Try to be accurate in your self-judgments.* There are many ways to try to change your motivation. Many self-help and popular psychology books emphasize always perceiving yourself as having no problems, as being "great" in all things, as having high self-esteem no matter what, and so forth. We believe it is more important to be realistic and accurate when you are thinking about specific academic work. If you have difficulty decoding words so that you really can't read very well, then it may be more important to recognize this problem and attempt to learn how to decode words, than just to continue to think you are a great reader. An overly optimistic but inaccurate self-concept is not helpful to you. You need to be accurate and realistic in your self-appraisals but realize that many strategies are available to you to help you improve your learning and achievement.

2. *Break a big task into smaller parts.* Self-efficacy increases when you experience mastery and success. In many cases, if you attempt a task that is too difficult, you will fail or not do well. When this happens, your self-efficacy will probably suffer, which can lead you to avoid the task in the future. In Chapter 2 we discussed

the example of writing a 20-page paper. Let's see how that example relates to self-efficacy. If you are like many college students, your self-efficacy related to writing a 20-page paper is not very high. It may be longer than any previous paper you have written, and the thought of trying to generate 20 pages of text may be daunting. You may not feel confident about your ability to generate that much text, and you may avoid the task by procrastinating, thinking that one day your creative muse will strike you and you will just pour forth the 20 pages. Unfortunately, it does not work this way, and trying to generate 20 pages the night before the deadline will not result in a very successful paper. Moreover, you will probably come away from this experience thinking to yourself, "I'm just not very good at writing papers." Putting yourself in this situation will lower your self-efficacy. In contrast, if you break a task into parts that you can manage separately (by setting short-term goals, as suggested in Chapter 2), you may experience mastery as you complete these smaller parts successfully. Self-efficacy grows from having mastery experiences, so you should try to design tasks in such a way that you can complete them successfully. For the 20-page paper, breaking the task into smaller parts, such as developing an outline, working on different sections at different times, and editing the sections, can be very helpful. In fact, when you are actually trying to generate text, it may be helpful to you to set very small short-term goals for a writing session. For example, if you go to the library for several hours of work on the paper, you may set a goal of just trying to work on one section of the paper. Moreover, you set a goal of generating three pages of text in this 3-hour session at the library. That may not seem like much, but in fact, three good pages of text is quite productive. In this case, you would feel good about having reached your goal of three pages and would probably feel confident about being able to write more pages at the next session. This is in contrast to the general goal of "working" on the paper or setting a goal of writing half the paper in one session and then feeling bad when you generate only 3 pages instead of 10.

3. *Attribute failure to unstable, internal, and controllable causes such as lack of knowledge, lack of strategies, or lack of effort.* If you can't decode words, don't attribute it to the fact that you were "born" this way and that you will always be a poor reader. This is a stable, internal, and uncontrollable attribution. In contrast, a more useful attribution is that you have not yet learned the knowledge and strategies that are important for decoding words. That is, the need to learn new knowledge and strategies is an attribution that is unstable, internal to you, and inherently under your control. You can always learn new knowledge and strategies, and in fact, that is what a big part of this book is about—teaching you new knowledge and strategies for learning.

Another useful (we know that sounds strange for what we are about to say!) attribution in a failure situation is that you just did not try hard enough—a lack of effort. It's useful because it is an unstable, internal, and controllable attribution. You can change your effort, and it is under your own control. Of course, if you really did try hard for the test or exam or paper, then it is not appropriate to say that you didn't try hard. In this case, it may be that you lack some important knowledge or strategies for learning. Many college students say they spend hours studying for exams and believe that this means they tried hard. This is probably true, but one message of this book is that in college it may not be enough just to try hard. You may have to try "smarter" or work "smarter" by using better strategies to study and learn. This book can help you learn strategies that will help you study smarter, not just harder.

4. *Take responsibility for your own academic behavior.* Students make any of a multitude of excuses as to why they don't study or why they do poorly. Some of these excuses may be valid, but in the long run, what really makes a difference in terms of your own learning is your own behavior. You need to take responsibility for your own learning and realize that it is under your control. The following attributions can limit your motivation for future tasks. To become a self-regulated learner, you should avoid them.

a. *"The teacher is no good."* In some cases, this may be true. College teachers are trained in their discipline, not in how to teach, so occasionally they may not be the best teachers. On the other hand, this is not something that you as a student have any control over. It is very unlikely that you can make teachers change the way they teach. And, in many cases, it is very difficult for you to change to another section of the course to find a better teacher. In other words, you have to find a way to adapt to the situation. Similar problems often happen in work settings. It may be difficult for you to change the nature of your work environment, your boss, or your coworkers, so rather than always complaining, you need to figure out strategies for how to work well in that situation. The same is true in classroom settings.

This book offers many strategies for becoming a better learner that can help you learn more, even when your courses may be difficult in many ways. For example, in Chapter 8, we discuss strategies for taking notes. These strategies should help you in all classes, but they may be even more useful when the professor is not the most organized or best lecturer. Thinking about active adaptive strategies that you can use to cope with the difficulties of a course will be much more productive for you in the long run than just making attributions to a bad teacher.

Other variations on external attributions to something about the course include, "The course is too big—with that many people, I can't learn"; "The class time is too early, so I'm sleepy then (or too late in the afternoon, or right after lunch)"; "The materials (readings) are too hard, disorganized, too expensive to buy, etc."; "The room the course is in has too many distractions"; "The other students in the class are all into high grades and work hard on the course, so the average person doesn't have a chance." We are sure you can even think of more external attributions to various features of the course that make it difficult for you.

The important insight from attribution theory and research is that all of these attributions to external features of the course shift the locus of responsibility away from you to external factors that you most likely have little control over. These factors are probably not going to change in the near future. Accordingly, you have to develop strategies to deal with these problems (if they are real problems, and not just excuses for you not to try hard in the course). The message is that you need to take responsibility for those aspects of the course you can do something about, especially yourself, and not to worry about those features of the course that you can't change.

b. *"I never have enough time or energy to study."* Again, this attribution shifts the responsibility for taking charge of your own studying away from you. However, in contrast to the attributions about features of the course, this one refers to something about you. It is much easier to control something about yourself than it is to change factors that are external to you. College offers many tempting activities and many demands on your time—meeting new people; going to parties, concerts, or sporting events; working part-time; taking responsibility for family duties, and so forth. We are not suggesting that you become a monk or a nun and not enjoy college life, but rather that you have an important responsibility to attend to your academic work. This means that you need to make the time to study. It should be a regular part of your daily life, not just something that you do before an exam or when a paper is due. You need to take responsibility for your academic work and make sure you schedule for it. The next chapter discusses a number of strategies for organizing your time.

c. *"I don't like any of my courses."* Here is another attribution to something about you. You may be tempted to use it when you have to take required courses for your major or for distribution requirements. It also may happen that the courses you thought you would love at first don't seem so interesting as the term goes on and the workload increases. However, don't fall prey to this attribution. You will have to do many things in life that you do not find interesting, but successful individuals find a way to do them anyway. In the same way, self-regulated learners realize that not every class or course will be the most exciting and interesting activity they ever do, but they do not shirk their responsibility for doing the work. Later in this chapter, we discuss some strategies that may help you make your courses more interesting, but the point here is that believing the course work is still your responsibility, regardless of how interesting it is, is adaptive.

d. *"I don't feel well right now"* or *"I'm not in the mood to study now."* Again, here is a more personal attribution that shifts responsibility for taking control of your own learning away from you. It is true that at times you may not feel well physically. It is easy to get overtired and fatigued in college, to get sick, or just to get so stressed out that your physical health starts to deteriorate. In these cases, you should listen to your body and take appropriate steps to take care of your physical health. For example, you do need to get plenty of rest and sleep, you should try to exercise regularly to help manage your stress, and if you do get sick, then you should see an appropriate medical professional. On the other hand, all of us have days when we feel a little tired or not quite "great," but we still have to take responsibility for getting our work done. In the same way, you should not neglect your schoolwork when you are not quite feeling wonderful. It is not adaptive to make constant excuses for not studying because you don't feel well right now.

Attributing poor performance to a "bad mood" is also not adaptive. In this case, you need to learn to manage your mental health. As with physical health, at times you might not be in the proper frame of mind to study. Your mood may be bad because you just had a fight with your roommate, you just broke up with your boyfriend or girlfriend, you just had a fight with your parents, or you are worried about money. These are occasions when it may be difficult to study because you are upset emotionally and you may not be able to concentrate. When this happens, it may make sense to take a break from working and do something else. When continuing problems cause you undue long-term emotional stress, then you may need to consult a mental-health professional. Most colleges have offices that can help you with these kinds of problems.

On the other hand, if you are just not "in the mood" to study because you would rather do something else, such as watch *Monday Night Football* or *Grey's Anatomy* on TV, this is not the most adaptive strategy. Like other examples in this section, this situation also arises in the real world. That is, in many work settings, you may not feel in the mood to get up and go to work on Monday morning after a nice long weekend. Or you may not feel like working late to finish an important project. Yet, you may have to in your job, and successful individuals are able to overcome their "mood" and get the job done. College is just like real life in this way. There will definitely be times when you are not in the mood to study or write a paper, but you will need to discipline yourself to get the job done. No matter who you are or what you are doing in college, you will need to take responsibility for your own behavior to be successful.

VALUE

The expectancy component of motivation concerns questions of your ability to do a task. In contrast, the **value** components of motivation have to do with your reasons for doing the task, such as how important you think the task is or how interesting it is to you. For the expectancy component there were two important factors: self-efficacy and attributions. For the value component, we believe there are four important factors: usefulness, extrinsic reasons, intrinsic reasons, situational reasons.

Usefulness

The first aspect of value concerns your beliefs about the usefulness of what you're doing. That is, how useful do you think the course will be to your future goals? Have you ever taken a course that you thought was useless? Was it hard to do well in it? A course may have utility or usefulness for various reasons. For example, you may not be really interested in chemistry, but if chemistry is required for you to be a premed major, the course has some utility for you. Or you may not be really interested in some aspects of a computer course, but some of the skills you learn in that course might be very useful in getting and keeping a job. When individuals see the usefulness of a course, they are more likely to be engaged in the course, to try hard, and to persist at the course activities.

Extrinsic Reasons

A second aspect of value pertains to the extrinsic reasons for doing the task. Extrinsic reasons for doing a task include seeking some kind of reward, such as good grades; a prize, honor, or award; or parental or peer approval. The reasons are outside (extrinsic to) the task; they are not part of actually doing the work. In contrast, intrinsic reasons include doing it for the sheer enjoyment. In some psychological research, extrinsic and intrinsic motivation are seen as opposing types of motivation, so that one can't be intrinsically motivated if one is extrinsically motivated. However, in this book, our perspective is that students can be motivated by a number of different reasons at the same time, and it is possible to be both extrinsically and intrinsically motivated for an academic task. For example, you may really like chemistry, but you also may need to do well in it to get into medical school.

Extrinsic reasons, such as trying to get good grades, can help students try harder. For some college students, trying to get good grades can help them maintain their commitment to their courses, ensuring that they actually attend class rather than sleeping in, and also motivate them to study. Of course, in some cases, if students become overly concerned about their grades and getting an A at all costs, they may face detrimental consequences such as too much anxiety (see Chapter 11 on test taking) or negative emotions, as well as a lack of concern with actually learning the material. Accordingly, while we think it is important for you to want to do well in college and get good grades, we also believe that this should not be the sole reason for doing your course work.

Intrinsic Reasons

In contrast, the third general reason for doing a task, intrinsic reasons, refers to the idea that people do things because they just "love" doing the task. They really like doing the work, or they find the content interesting. This type of interest is generally assumed to be somewhat stable over time. For example, one of us has always been interested in issues raised by social science and psychological articles and books, such as why people do the things they do or why they think the way they do. In contrast, mechanical or engineering activities or content, such as how machines work or why they are built a particular way, was of little interest. It is not surprising then that psychology was this author's career choice, not engineering. In this way, personal interests often shape the choices individuals make over the course of their lives. Moreover, individuals vary in their personal interests and so make different choices and decisions. Given these relations between personal interest and choices, it is important for you to become aware of your own interests and how they may affect you.

Situational Reasons

Besides intrinsic interest, research has discovered another type of interest, what is called *situational reasons*. This is the fourth value component that can influence motivation. In contrast to personal interest, situational interest changes over time. **Situational interest** refers to the interest a person feels at a particular time. For example, as noted above, one of us was never very interested in mechanical activities. However, after reading parts of David Macaulay's (1988) book *The Way Things Work*, which describes in fascinating detail and uses wonderful drawings to explicate the mechanisms for different inventions and common objects, he developed a situational interest. He became engaged in reading the book and thinking about how these things work. However, it did not result in any long-term personal interest in the subject. It did not change his overall behavior in terms of motivating him to work on his car, or to try to fix the plumbing in his house, or to read more books about these mechanical objects. The interest was only in that situation because of the features of that specific book.

In the same manner, the features of a class or a teacher or certain reading materials may spark situational interest. For example, a professor may be a very skilled lecturer and present exciting and interesting lectures that create a situational interest on your part, at least for that lecture or course. Or a class may be filled with a diverse array of students whose discussions are lively and informative, and this may create a situational interest for you. Finally, the reading materials may be interesting. For example, many college courses in law and environmental studies use the nonfiction book *A Civil Action*, a fascinating account of an environmental lawsuit in Massachusetts, as part of their readings. This book seems to create a great deal of situational interest, even if it does not generate any long-lasting personal interest in law or environmental issues.

Situational interest changes with time and circumstances, whereas personal interest is more stable over time. Situational interest may develop into a personal interest. An inspiring professor or course can interest you in a discipline, so that you choose to take more courses in the area, and you may eventually wind up majoring in the field. Given that situational interest tends to be unstable, you may need to find ways to keep required tasks interesting for you. The next section discusses strategies for changing the value aspects of motivation.

Changing Your Value Components

Research shows that there are things you can do to change the value components of motivation to improve your learning. For example, in a study of college students, Wolters (1998) found a number of strategies that self-regulated learners used to help them cope with academic tasks that were boring, uninteresting, irrelevant to their goals, not useful, or too difficult. The list provides some good ideas for how to cope with uninteresting, irrelevant, or difficult assignments you may confront in college. You may already be using some of these strategies.

1. *Make connections.* There may be times in your courses when you are not sure how the material relates to your overall goals, or the material just does not seem that relevant or important to you. This may be the case when you have to take courses that don't match your intended major or don't seem relevant to your career goals. In the Wolters (1998) study, college students suggested strategies such as trying to find ways to relate the material to their life, to their personal experiences, or to how they feel in certain situations. So, for example, in most social science courses like psychology, sociology, or anthropology, you can tie the material to your personal experiences with other people, other groups, or other cultures. It may not be most useful to your career goal, but you can use the material to help you understand your interactions with other people in your daily life in college.

Social science courses may be the easiest to apply to your personal experiences with others, but humanities and natural science courses also may be applicable and relevant to different aspects of your life as well. For example, in English courses, learning to write is an important skill that is useful in almost any career and certainly in your other college courses. In English literature classes, you may learn general analytic skills for interpreting and deconstructing texts that you can apply to interpreting what people say to you in different situations.

In the same way, you may not be able to apply specific mathematics or science content to daily life, but you may be able to apply some general strategies from mathematics and science. For example, you may be able to use the general problem-solving heuristics from mathematics, such as specifying the problem including the known and unknowns, working backward, and checking your work, to more general problems you encounter in other situations. You may be able to use the general scientific method to think about problems in your life by specifying the problem or question, collecting and interpreting data, and generating answers to your questions. In general, think about how the content of your courses connects in some way to other aspects of your life. This strategy should help you make the course material more relevant to you and keep you engaged in the course.

2. *Keep your eye on the grade.* In the Wolters (1998) study, many of the students used this general strategy when confronted with a task they felt was boring or irrelevant to them. They gave examples such as, "I would think about how I wanted a good grade," "I would remind myself about how important it is to get good grades in college," or even, "Relevancy to my life is really not an issue; understanding the material enough to succeed on the exam is." These examples all highlight how students can use self-talk about grades to help them stay on task and persist in the face of boring or irrelevant tasks.

It is important to note that grades are a fact of life in the vast majority of college courses, and they are probably not going to be replaced with other systems in the near future. Accordingly, although students may wish to complain about grades and

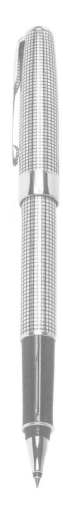

how grades may reduce their intrinsic interest, it seems more important to recognize the reality and purpose of grading. Moreover, graduate schools and many businesses rely on grades to help them select applicants. Self-regulated students recognize the importance of grades and learn to use them appropriately. All things being equal, we would want students to be intrinsically motivated. However, given that this is not always the case, we recognize (as does research) the power of grades to motivate.

3. *Use personal extrinsic rewards.* Although most college courses have external factors that can motivate you—such as grades—in some cases these grades are a little too distant to help you persist at weekly studying tasks. Recall our discussion of short-term and long-term goals from Chapter 2. In some cases, getting a good grade in a course can be a distant goal that does not seem so important to you in the 2nd or 3rd week of the semester as you try to study for the course. You can use more short-term goals and rewards to help you stay focused on your work. Wolters (1998) found that college students used **extrinsic rewards** to help them control and regulate their effort and persistence on tasks. Rewards could be watching TV, taking a nap, talking to friends, or going out with friends for ice cream or pizza.

In many cases, the rewards were just for completing the study session: after studying for, say, 3 hours, the student got the reward. It is better to make the rewards contingent on more specific goals (as we discussed in Chapter 2). For example, if you are reading for a course, it may not be enough just to give a reward for completing the assigned readings. It may be more useful to set a short-term goal of understanding the material in the readings, and then give the reward after you have demonstrated your understanding of the material by answering questions on the readings, or after you have taken detailed notes, or after you have written short summaries of the main ideas. In the same way, when writing a paper, you may break up the task into parts and reward yourself after developing a detailed outline, then after writing a certain number of pages, then after editing the whole paper. These types of specific goals, when combined with the judicious use of self-rewards, can help you maintain your motivation.

Watson and Tharp (1997) suggested several important points you should remember about rewards. First, rewards should be given after you have engaged in the behavior you want to reinforce. For example, if you want to reward yourself for studying in the library by taking breaks to chat with friends, don't start your library session by talking with friends. Go to the library with them and tell them you will meet them after a certain time in the lounge area (1 hour, 2 hours, whatever works best for you), after you have spent time studying. This makes the reward dependent on engaging in the activity you want to encourage and works better than giving yourself rewards before you have accomplished anything. Just as dessert must follow the meal, so must extrinsic rewards follow a job well done.

A second point to remember is that rewards usually work best when they follow the behavior fairly closely in time. For example, some students try to reward their studying behavior during the week by saying to themselves, "I will work hard this week and then on the weekend relax and do some other fun things." We have even heard students try to set up semester rewards such as, "I will work very hard this semester, but then really give myself a big reward at the end of the semester by taking a nice vacation." These reward strategies can be effective in some ways, but they also make you wait a fairly long time before you can obtain them. If you are studying on a Monday night, the weekend might seem rather far away. If you are studying in October, then the holiday break that comes in December and January is really a long way off. Rewards work much better when they follow the desired activity soon after you have completed it. So, if you are studying on a Monday night, breaking your studying session up with short breaks to chat with friends or getting coffee or ice cream for yourself on Monday night may be more effective. Or, if you are able to study 3 to 4 hours without a break, rewarding yourself by going out with friends for pizza at the end of the evening on Monday will be more effective than waiting until the weekend to go out with friends.

Third, remember that you can use a variety of **reinforcers,** or rewards, to help you toward your goal. Figure 3.2 lists some rewards from a list compiled by Watson and Tharp (1997). The point is that you can reinforce your behavior in many ways, and you can decide which ones will work best for you. Watson and Tharp, in their book *Self-Directed Behavior: Self-Modification for Personal Adjustment* (1997), include a list of questions to ask yourself as you try to think of rewards (see Activity 3.4). Answering them will give you some ideas for ways you can reinforce positive behavior (Watson & Tharp, 1997).

4. *Try to make the material or activity more interesting to you.* Research by Sansone, Weir, Harpster, and Morgan (1992) and also Wolters (1998) found that college students can try to make an activity more interesting by making it into a game. For example, you can make a game out of a boring math activity by seeing how many of the math problems you can get done correctly within a specified

---

Potential reinforcers.	FIGURE 3.2

Praising oneself	Taking a walk by a lake or in the forest
Going to a movie or play	Playing basketball at the rec center
Going to the beach	Going to aerobics class or the gym to work out
Going mountain climbing	Being alone
Taking a bike ride in the country	Reading a "trashy" novel
Going shopping	Playing with your cat, dog, or other pet
Listening to music	Going to a bar with friends
Watching TV	Playing video games
Doing a favorite hobby	Surfing the Web
Talking with friends on phone	Going dancing
Getting something to eat or drink	Taking a nap
Going for a pizza with friends	Taking a shower
Buying something for a friend	Visiting family
Playing with a niece/nephew	Making love
Goofing off	Playing board games with friends
Getting an ice cream	Going window shopping
Buying something that you don't need	Going bird-watching
Going to a sporting event	Going to a musical concert
Not dieting for a day	Getting a massage
Sitting in a hot tub	

Source: From *Self-Directed Behavior: Self-Modification for Personal Adjustment,* by D. Watson and R. Tharp, 1997, Pacific Grove, CA: Brooks/Cole Publishing.

Questions to Ask Yourself in Order to Develop Effective and Useful Reinforcers

Answer as many of the 20 questions in this activity as you can. Based on your answers, circle the potential rein-forces in Figure 3.2 on page 53 that you think will be the best for you.

1. What will be the rewards for you of achieving your goal?
2. What kinds of praise do you like to get from yourself and others?
3. What kinds of things do you like to do when you can freely choose to do them?
4. What kinds of things do you like to have?
5. What are your major interests?
6. What do you value most? What is most important to you?
7. What are your hobbies?
8. What kinds of people do you like to be with?
9. What do you like to do with those people?
10. What do you do for fun?
11. What do you do to get away from it all?
12. What makes you feel good?
13. What would you buy if you had an extra $25, $50, or $100?
14. What would be a nice present to receive?
15. What behaviors do you perform every day?
16. What do you do when you are not studying?
17. What would you hate to lose?
18. Of the things you do every day, which would you hate to give up?
19. What are your favorite daydreams or fantasies?
20. What are the most relaxing scenes you can imagine?

Source: From *Self-Directed Behavior: Self-Modification for Personal Adjustment,* by D. Watson and R. Tharp, 1997, Pacific Grove, CA: Brooks/Cole Publishing.

time period. You might even set it up so that you and a classmate "compete" to complete the math problems correctly. The important issue is that the game focuses on solving the math problems correctly, not just getting them done. For reading tasks, you could make understanding the text into a self-quiz game where you get points or reward yourself for answering correctly. You also could incorporate gamelike features for a reading task with a group of classmates and play the game together. Again, it is important that the game focuses on learning and understanding the material, not just memorizing parts of the text. Playing the game with classmates would probably make the reading task more interesting than just trying to struggle to read the material by yourself. These strategies might not increase your personal interest in the task, but they should at least increase situational interest and help you maintain your involvement, which we hope will get you through the end of the semester!

CHAPTER SUMMARY

This chapter has discussed the various aspects of motivation. In general, motivation has three important aspects:

1. First, there is motivated behavior. Students who are motivated are more likely to choose to do a task or continue to do it in the future. They also are more likely to try hard and exert effort. They persist at the task and are more cognitively engaged in the task. Finally, they are more likely to perform well and achieve at high levels.

2. Motivated behavior is related to two important dimensions of motivation: expectancy and value. The expectancy components concern your beliefs about whether you are capable of doing a task. One expectancy is self-efficacy—a judgment of your capabilities to do a task. Attributions reveal the reasons why you think you succeeded or failed at something. The attributions you make can have a dramatic effect on your self-confidence and your motivation.

3. The value components of motivation refer to the reasons why you do a task. Four value components are particularly relevant to school learning. First, you might do a task because it is very useful to you. Second, you can do a task for extrinsic reasons, such as wanting to get good grades or impress others. Third, maybe you are just intrinsically interested in the task. Finally, there are situational reasons—something about the class sparks your interest at that particular time.

All of these aspects of motivation are changeable and under your control. This chapter discussed the reasons you may engage in a task, as well as a number of strategies that you can use to change and control your self-efficacy and attributions. Motivation is central to doing well in any area of life, and it is important to understand that you can adapt and control your own motivation. We hope the advice we gave you in the chapter will help you do that.

Managing Your Resources I

EXTERNAL TOOLS

Chapter Goals

This chapter will help you:

- Understand the importance of a weekly schedule
- Develop a weekly schedule that is workable and flexible
- Arrange your places for studying to reduce distractions
- Understand the importance of peers to help you learn
- Develop and use a peer study group
- Understand the importance of mentoring and support from professors
- Develop at least one close relationship with a professor

Key Terms

adaptive help-seeking

dependent help-seeking

peer support

professor support

resource management

study environment management

time management

CHAPTER 4

College students don't always realize the tools they have available to them. One of the biggest challenges is to use these tools properly. Questions like "Where to study?" and "When to study?" are questions that will help you properly use these tools. Educational psychologists refer to this area of student learning as **resource management**—effective use of tools and resources. This chapter explores ways to maximize your resource management.

COLLEGE VERSUS HIGH SCHOOL

College is different from high school—that's an obvious statement. One nonobvious way it's different is that resource management in college is different from that in high school. In high school, many parts of your life are regulated by other people. Your parents may wake you up in the morning, you already have a set schedule of classes, and you have daily homework and have ways of making sure you get your work done. In addition, these teachers know you and might check on you if you miss some assignments. When you are not at school, your parents might ask you if you have done your homework. They might even have a time and place set aside for you to do your schoolwork, and they might check with you every so often to make sure you are working or even help you with some of your schoolwork. All of these supports can help you make sure you have the time and resources to get your work done.

© Stephen Coburn – FOTOLIA

In contrast, most college students do not have their parents around to wake them up in the morning, to check homework, or to provide other types of help. In college, no one is there in the morning telling you to wake up and get to class. No one is there in the evening to check to see if you are doing your schoolwork. In fact, you can stay up all night playing video games or partying and no one will tell you to go and study. If you are working full- or part-time and going to school part-time, it is even more difficult to find the time to study, and getting up in the morning might be even harder if you have worked late the night before. In addition, in college, you do not see your professors every day. Professors vary in how well they get to know their students (more contact at smaller colleges). Even if they do know you, they are not going to monitor you and your work, and in fact, in many cases, they will not even know if you come to class or not!

This is very different from high school and offers you a lot more freedom and flexibility. At the same time, it means you have much more responsibility to manage your time and other resources well. Many very good high school students go off to college and welcome their newfound freedom, but unfortunately, some of them spend a great deal of time on nonacademic pursuits. These students just do not manage their time well. The resulting poor grades should not be a surprise, but in fact, many first-year college students are surprised at how poorly they do. In fact, the time during or right after the first year of college is when students are most likely to drop out of college. This is a difficult transition year, and it is important that you learn how to manage yourself and your resources to do well. Harvard University professor Richard Light (2001) interviewed many college students and found that the most successful college students are those who manage their resources well, especially the resource of time. This chapter will help you with the transition from high school to college and give you strategies for managing your resources well.

Before you read further, complete Activity 4.1 to help you assess your skill at managing your resources. These are the items relevant to managing your resources from the Learning Inventory provided in Chapter 1. If you have high scores on Activity 4.1, you may already be doing much of what this chapter suggests. Even so, you still will likely find good ideas that you could use. By managing your resources even better, you can improve your grades and have more time left for other activities.

Assessment of Resource Management Strategies

Indicate the extent to which you engage in these behaviors.

	None of the time	Some of the time	Most of of the time	All of the time
Set up a weekly schedule each term.	①	②	③	④
Make a to-do list and make priorities from that list.	①	②	③	④
Set aside weekly times for studying.	①	②	③	④
Maintain a study area free of distractions.	①	②	③	④
Form peer study groups in your classes.	①	②	③	④
Take the initiative in getting help from professors.	①	②	③	④
Listen to music or watch TV when studying.	④	③	②	①
Fall asleep when studying.	④	③	②	①

SCORING:

26 or more: You probably have good resource-management strategies.

20–25: You are a good resource manager some of the time, but have room for improvement.

19 and below: This chapter will be very helpful for you in becoming a better manager of your resources.

MANAGING AND REGULATING YOUR TIME

One of the most important resources you have is yourself: your time, your effort, and your persistence at tasks. In Chapter 2, we discussed your goals and how you should work on developing a set of short-term and long-term goals that can help you monitor your progress. One of the most important strategies for being able to follow through on your goals is **time management:** organizing your time and schedule. In Light's (2001) study of successful college students, he found that sophomores who had a successful first year were very good at managing their time, while those who really struggled in their first year of college did not manage their time well. Poor students had a very difficult time making the transition from high school, where other people regulated their time for them, to college, where they were the ones responsible for managing their time.

Using an Appointment Book

Appointment books are not just for middle-aged professors or businesspeople who can't remember all the things they need to get done. In college, you have many different activities, such as classes, labs, sporting events, outside speakers, community service, parties, and employment. Current college students probably have a greater number of obligations than students of a previous era had (a generation ago, "going to college" was the main task). Thus, it can be very hard to keep track of all of your commitments. If you don't want to miss an important lunch or coffee date, let alone your classes, you need an appointment book to help you keep track of all your activities. If you can afford it, you might choose to use a BlackBerry or other personal digital assistant (PDA). Regardless of which method you choose, using a daily planner is critical for your success. From a psychological perspective, a daily planner will free up your cognitive resources (see Chapter 6) so that you don't have to think about your schedule and can spend more time thinking about your schoolwork.

STRATEGY SUGGESTION

Get an appointment book, calendar, or personal digital assistant (PDA) to help you keep track of your appointments, classes, to-do lists, and so forth.

These books will also help you keep from double-booking something, such as telling a person you can meet for lunch at the same time you wanted to hear an outside speaker. It will help you avoid disappointing yourself and other people. As professors, we are always impressed with students who have PDAs or daily planners because they seem organized and reliable, in contrast to a student who scribbles a time and date for a future meeting on a scrap of paper or, worse yet, his or her hand. We never know if the scrap of paper will be enough to remind the student of our meeting (it can get lost easily), whereas we know that the student with the appointment book is much more likely to show up for a meeting. The PDA or planner signals to professors and others, including your friends, that you are serious about your time and that you have made a commitment to being a responsible individual who keeps appointments.

Making a Weekly Schedule

It is also a good idea to make a weekly schedule for your classes, and to set aside times within this weekly schedule for studying. Activity 4.2 gives a schedule for 1 week, divided into 1-hour periods. On this weekly schedule, mark off all the meeting times of your classes. These are times when you should not schedule any other appointments or activities. This may seem like common sense, but you would be surprised at how many students skip classes to do other activities. You should attend every class unless there is some emergency or you are really sick. Your main job is to go to class and learn—this is why you are paying tuition. If you paid for a service such as repair work on the plumbing in your house, and the person did not come and do the work, you would not be very happy about not getting the work done and not getting your money's worth. It is the same with college, except you are the one who must go to class to receive the service. You should make sure you get your money's worth by going to every class.

Make a weekly schedule for classes and studying times.

Now look at the times you have blocked out for your class schedule. What does your week look like? Where can you fit in study time? Many students assume that they will fit in studying time in the evenings, after dinner, which is certainly a good idea. Often, however, nonacademic activities (e.g., part-time work, fraternity meetings) arise in the evenings. If you have set aside the evenings for study time, you will feel conflicted by wanting to do two important things at the same time.

A Weekly Time Schedule

ACTIVITY 4.2

	Monday	Tuesday	Wednesday	Thursday	Friday	Saturday	Sunday
7 A.M.							
8 A.M.							
9 A.M.							
10 A.M.							
11 A.M.							
Noon							
1 P.M.							
2 P.M.							
3 P.M.							
4 P.M.							
5 P.M.							
6 P.M.							
7 P.M.							
8 P.M.							
9 P.M.							
10 P.M.							
11 P.M.							

We have found that students often have large parts of the day between classes when they could study, but they don't utilize those times. For example, say you have a Spanish class on Monday, Wednesday, and Friday from 9:00 to 10:00 a.m., and your next class on those days is not until 1:00 p.m. The time between 10:00 a.m. and noon is a very good time to set aside for studying. You can have lunch from noon to 1:00 p.m. and if you schedule those hours between 10:00 and noon to study, you will be more likely to study then, and it leaves you more free time, or at least flexibility, in the evening for other activities. Many students would just go back to their dormitory or apartment and hang out, play video games, e-mail, or watch TV. We strongly encourage you to use that time productively. Since you are already on campus, why not go to the library and spend those 2 hours studying? In the long run, those 6 hours a week of set-aside study time will help keep you caught up in your classes and also give you more flexibility in the evening.

STRATEGY SUGGESTION

Use the computer only 1 hour a day for e-mailing, surfing, IM-ing, and other nonessential activities.

Besides class and study times, you should include other activities on your weekly schedule, such as eating, socializing, basic chores (laundry, food shopping, room/apartment cleaning, etc.), exercising, and working (if you work part-time or full-time). All of these activities take time, and you need to think about and plan how to include them in your schedule. To make your schedule for these activities, you will start by thinking about how long it takes to do them as well as how important they are for you.

Eating. For example, it is a basic fact of life that you need to eat and sleep, and you must make sure that you have time for both of these crucial activities. Some students seem to think they can go without eating or sleeping for days, but they are just kidding themselves. These are basic needs, and if you don't fulfill them, you will suffer in the long run, both mentally and physically. Some people need to eat at least three times a day and at fairly regular times. Others seem able to be much more flexible about their eating times. You need to figure out what patterns help you function best and then include those patterns in your schedule. If you are someone who has to eat breakfast or else you feel sluggish or headachy all day, then make sure you find the time in your schedule to eat breakfast. This is true for one of the authors: he has to have something to eat when he gets up in the morning at 7:30 a.m. or else he is cranky and useless most of the day. In contrast, his wife really doesn't feel like eating, and in fact, the idea of eating that early in the morning makes her a little nauseated. She has coffee but doesn't eat much until closer to noon on most days. The important point is that both of them understand their own eating preferences and build them into their daily and weekly schedules.

© Paul Bodea – FOTOLIA

Sleeping. The same goes for sleeping. It is a truism that most college students have somewhat unusual sleep patterns, staying up much later in the evening, and into the early morning hours, than most other people. We are always amazed when we teach early-morning classes and informally survey our students about their bedtime the night before. College students stay up very late: too late in our opinion. But this just seems to come with college life, and there are some physiological reasons (as well as social reasons) why adolescents stay up late. There is no point in telling you to try to go to sleep at a reasonable hour if your room-mates are staying up until 1:00 or 2:00 a.m. most nights. The important point is that you try to get a minimum of 7 hours of sleep each night, regardless of when you go to bed. A great deal of research has been done on sleep and its psycholog-ical effects on memory, learning, and thinking, and it clearly shows how impor-tant sleep is. You will feel much better both psychologically and physically if you get enough sleep. Also, if you are someone who wants to go to sleep early and your roommates don't, then you need to work out a way to satisfy both goals. Perhaps they can go to someone else's room or apartment so you can go to sleep. Or you might need to change roommates. When you are picking roommates for next year or housemates for an apartment, you should think about issues like this.

Exercise. Finally, it is important for you to find time for some type of physical exercise. It can be jogging, swimming, biking, playing some type of sports, going to a Pilates class, yoga, lifting weights, or even just taking good long walks—whatever you like to do and can do easily. Again, the research on the benefits of exercise is very clear. The physical benefits are obvious: controlling and regulating your weight, helping to build and maintain muscle tone, and just general physical health. More important, at least from our point of view as psychologists, physical exercise has some very good mental-health benefits. It helps to relieve stress and can make you feel better about yourself. It helps you feel more energetic and able to take on other tasks. It is good for you in many ways, both physically and men-tally, and you should make time in your busy schedule for it.

STRATEGY SUGGESTION

Include other activities in your weekly schedule, not just class and studying time.

One of the authors used to run track and cross country in high school, then jogged regularly in college and graduate school. In the last 2 years of graduate school, as he was working on his dissertation and other research, he stopped run-ning. He also had shin splints that really bothered him when he ran, so it was not much fun. He did not do much regular exercise during his last 2 years of graduate school and for several years after he completed his PhD. He played softball in the summers, but that was more of a social activity than serious exercise. As you might expect, he gained weight, and more important, he felt much more stress and had a harder time getting rid of the stressful feelings when he did not exercise. He even-tually started biking long distances, such as 25 to 50 or even 100 miles, with some good friends. This was easy on his shin splints and also a way to socialize as well as get exercise, so it served two goals at once. In addition, he found that it helped to relieve some of the stress. There is something about doing some physical exer-cise that takes your mind off all your problems while you just concentrate on your body and the good feelings that come with the physical exertion.

STRATEGY SUGGESTION

Maintain your weekly schedule but also be flexible.

Staying on Track and Being Flexible

On the face of it, this suggestion seems contradictory. What it means is that you should maintain your weekly schedule but be flexible enough to break it if a specific need arises. First, it is important that you follow your schedule. Making a weekly schedule does you little good if you never follow it. So, when you make your schedule, you should be committed to following it.

One of the authors of this book has a weekly schedule that includes at least 3 days a week, and 5 if possible, where he has "writing time" scheduled. As a professor, you must publish written materials—books and journal articles. Writing is a demanding task, as we will discuss in Chapter 10, but this author soon discovered that he was most successful if he had 3-hour blocks of time to write, especially in the morning when he is fresh. If he tried to write for 1 hour here and there, it was not good for him. He would just get started and then he would have to quit to do something else. He also found that if he scheduled a whole day of 8 hours or even 6 hours, this was too long; he would get tired of writing after about 3 hours, and then waste the rest of the time. So, with some trial and error, he found that about 3 hours worked for him.

Now he schedules "writing mornings" from 9:00 to noon on his weekly schedule. He has an appointment with his computer to write, just as you have class time blocked out on your schedule. If you were a student in his class and needed an appointment and asked for some time on a Monday morning between 9:00 and noon, on one of his writing days, he would tell you, "No, I can't do it that morning; I have another appointment then, but I could meet with you sometime between one and five that day." This writing time is nonnegotiable. Even if the dean (a professor's boss) asks for a meeting then, he tells her, "Sorry, I'm tied up that morning. Can we do it some afternoon this week? Any time after 1 p.m. on Monday, Wednesday, or Friday would work for me." The point is that the writing time is on the schedule, and he goes and writes at those times even if he is busy, and whether or not he is in the "mood" to write. There are no excuses, and he does not let other activities get scheduled during those times. He treats it just like his teaching time. He has to go teach from 1:00 to 2:30 p.m. on Tuesdays and Thursdays, and he can't schedule other things during that time. It is the same for his writing time.

Of course, there are occasions when you need to be flexible and adapt your schedule. This is common when you start to work out a schedule. Many college students make a first-time weekly schedule at the beginning of the term that is so full of activities from 9:00 a.m. to midnight that it is impossible to keep. So, be realistic with your schedule. Don't try to schedule yourself from early morning to late at night every day. You need to have some downtime to nap, watch TV, IM, or just hang out. However, there are still plenty of hours in the day that you can schedule for academic and nonacademic activities. If you have a realistic schedule that helps you accomplish your multiple goals, you will be much more likely to follow it.

Also, at the beginning of the term, you might make errors in estimating how much time various activities might take. For example, you might have scheduled a certain number of hours for studying for your biology course, thinking it would be fairly easy; a review of much of what you did in high school. However, as the term progresses, you realize it is much harder than you thought, and you need to add more study time to your weekly schedule. Or you find that you need to work more hours each week in your part-time job to pay your rent and other expenses. So you raise your hours from 12 per week to 18 per week, for example, and instead of working just 2 nights a week, you work 3. If this is the case, you need to adjust your schedule to reflect these new demands. In a situation like this, you should try to keep your academic hours similar, and perhaps give up some of your social hours to the new working hours.

Finally, there will be times when you want to break your schedule because something comes up that you really want to do that was not planned for when you made your weekly schedule. One of the authors is an avid Bruce Springsteen fan, has seen him in concert 10 times from Milwaukee to New York City, and has never missed a performance in Michigan since 1991. There is no way to plan for such an activity, but if it's important to you, then you need to make time for it. You will have to make up what you missed in studying by working more time the next night. It is fine to be flexible in your schedule. If you obsess about maintaining a rigid schedule, that will just add to your stress and partially defeat the purpose of the schedule, which is to help you organize your life and time in order not to be so stressed out.

Of course, the key concept in the previous paragraph is *important activity*. Going to hear a famous speaker who will not be on campus again in the near future is a good and important activity. Helping a friend who has an emergency such as a car breakdown or who is sick and has to be taken to the hospital or who is very upset because of a romantic breakup and wants to talk is an important activity that warrants breaking your scheduled study time. Going to have coffee with a friend just to gossip about last weekend's party is not an important activity. Going to shoot some hoops or play video games or watch TV with a roommate is not an important activity. In particular, these latter two activities could easily be done at some other time. You can gossip with a friend at another time and you can certainly play basketball or video games or watch TV at many other times. (I await your judgment as to whether a Springsteen concert falls under the category of *important* activity!) So keep your schedule but realize there will be occasions when you want to be flexible to accomplish some of your goals.

STRATEGY SUGGESTION

Make a weekly and/or daily to-do list and decide which tasks are most important and should be done first.

Making To-Do Lists

To-do lists are important for several reasons. First, they help you keep track of all the things you need to do. It is easy to forget the many little daily or weekly chores in life as you focus on studying and working. One of the authors keeps a to-do list organized by the courses he teaches as well as his various research projects and other administrative duties. Within each of these groupings, he lists what he has to do and tries to think about the order in which they need to be accomplished. He also knows that if he is teaching on Tuesday, then he needs to get things done by Tuesday for that class. Your list should be organized in some similar way, grouped by your courses and other activities you are involved in, such as social activities. Not only will this keep you from forgetting things, but there is also a great sense of satisfaction that comes with crossing things off your to-do list. It gives concrete evidence that you have accomplished something.

A to-do list with priorities is an important part of organizing your time. You have a weekly schedule, and you have times set aside for studying, but now you have to think about what to do with those hours of studying. Different courses will have different requirements and assignments throughout the term. If you have a big midterm exam coming up in chemistry, then you might use most of your study time that week to prepare for it. However, Light (2001) found that good students were ones who also tried to study or do work for all their classes each week. So, even if you are preparing for a big midterm, you should not stop doing the readings and other assignments for your other classes.

When preparing for a big midterm, many students have to drop their work for other classes because they have not been keeping up all term. So now they have to cram for the exam and let their other courses slide. Of course, as they let these courses slide, they have to try to catch up with them after the midterm. It is an endless cycle, and it can be very stressful and demoralizing. The same is true for working on a big final course paper. If you wait until the end of the term to start it, you will not be able to keep up with your other courses. At the end of the term, when all your courses have final exams and papers, you will be overwhelmed with the work and your stress level will be unbearable. If you have set up times throughout the term to study and keep up in all your classes, then it will still be a lot of work at the end of the term, but you will be much more able to cope with all the demands. One of the authors gives a cumulative final in Developmental Psychology. As students complain about the enormity of the task before them, he reminds them that if they've been keeping up with all the reading, they have actually been studying for the final *all semester.*

As time is limited and you do have to sleep, you may find yourself with too many things that you want to do in college. Academic work should have priority, but, again, you don't have to work all the time. There are many other activities you should make time for, and you need to decide on a weekly basis what your priorities are and adjust your schedule accordingly.

Try Activity 4.3 to see how to construct a to-do list and set priorities among all the things you have to do this week and this term.

ACTIVITY 4.3 *Constructing a To-Do List and Setting Priorities*

Step 1. Make a list of all the courses you are taking.

Step 2. Under each of these courses, list the assignments, papers, and exams for each one. Attach a date to these, or sort them into short-term (such as this week) and long-term (such as more than a week away) tasks.

Step 3. Also list other general categories of things you have to do, such as Work, Social Activities, Community Service, and Household Chores.

Step 4. Under each of these areas, list things you have to do this week or this semester, and where possible attach a date to them.

Step 5. Now that you have a general list of all the things you have to do, go through the list and think about your priorities. For example, if you have an exam this Friday, that will have priority over a final paper that is not due until the next week. Also, set priorities in the other categories, such as Household Chores. For example, if you need to go shopping because you have no food in your apartment, that should be a higher priority than cleaning the bathroom.

Step 6. Now that you have established some priorities, take out your weekly calendar and start to put the higher priority items in appropriate places in your weekly calendar. For example, for the exam on Friday, you can study for it during one or two of your already-scheduled study times. You can go shopping for food Monday night, because you need to get food in the house for the rest of the week.

MANAGING YOUR STUDY ENVIRONMENT

Your study environment is an important resource that, like your time, you must learn to manage. Successful people in general, including successful college students, take a much more active role in managing their environment. Sternberg (1985) suggested that intelligent people are those who not only manage and regulate themselves well, but also manage and regulate their environment. They try to make the environment more supportive for them as they try to reach their goals. If the environment is not easily changed, then they try to move themselves out of that environment to another one that is more supportive. For college students, this means **study environment management.**

Make your study environment supportive of studying.

Your Study Environment

The places you study should be supportive of your academic work, not supportive of other activities like watching TV, talking with friends, or other distractions. Some books on studying recommend that you have one single place for studying and that you study in this same place all the time. To us, this seems a little rigid and also may not be realistic. For example, if you live off campus but want to study during the day between classes (as we discussed in the previous section), you need someplace on campus where you can study, as well as a place at your apartment or house. Accordingly, it seems very reasonable that you have more than one place to study. The important point is that these places should facilitate your academic work, not other activities. One of the authors wrote most of the second edition of this book on his laptop, but the last few days he has been home with sick children, so this section is being written using a flash drive on the computer in his kitchen. Such flexibility is helpful as you wander from home to school to coffee shops.

At Home. In your dorm room, apartment, or home, it is important that you have a place carved out for studying that is "your" place, where you have control and as much privacy as possible. In the usual small dorm room, it would be your desk. In an apartment or house, you should have your own private desk or table in your room. The couch in the living room is not a good place to study. First, if you set up there to study, and then get all your books out, your laptop, your papers, and so on, at some point you will have to put them away if other people come home and want to sit where you are. This is very disruptive to your studying. In addition, you may not have all the materials you need (paper, pencils, notes, etc.), so you have to keep going back to your room to get these supplies. It is much better to have all of these things in one place at your own desk and make that your study place.

In addition, the kitchen table or living room couch has too many distractions, such as other people, food, and the TV. In future chapters, when we will discuss the important role of attention and how limited our working memory is, you will understand better the importance of avoiding distractions. The main idea to remember now is that there are limits to how much you can process at one time. If you are talking to roommates, eating, watching TV, and trying to study all at the same time, your cognitive system, especially your working memory, can't process all this information at once. Something has to give, and it usually is your attention to studying, which results in less learning. The removal of distractions is a key part of organizing your study environment and will benefit your learning.

At School. If you also have a study place on campus, such as at the library, you should be careful to follow the same general rule about avoiding distractions. Pick a place that is as free of distractions as you can. For example, at one of our libraries, there is a big open area on the first floor with large tables that seat six people. Undergraduates flock to this place to study at all hours, so it is usually quite crowded and busy. At the same time, it appears that for many students, this is a place to socialize. They meet their friends, check out the other students, flirt, talk on their cell phones, and do very little studying. Even the students who are not talking to other students are constantly looking up and watching all this social activity. In fact, when we go there to look at a journal, we find it a fascinating place to watch college students. We have talked to students who noted how they used to go to this part of the library for 3 hours a night but never felt like they got much done. It is no surprise, with all these distractions, that their attention was not on their studying.

In a situation like this, you are not going to be able to change the environment. You will not succeed in changing the other students' behavior, no matter how much you ask them to be quiet. It would be much better to remove yourself from the environment and find another place to study that has fewer distractions. This same library with the social center also has separate individual study carrels on the upper floors. These carrels offer a much quieter place to study, and with four walls and a door, they also shield you from distractions such as other people walking by. These places are much better for studying. If you want to reward yourself for studying by taking a break, you can then go to an open area and socialize with other students.

An advantage of having a place to study on campus, away from your dorm room or apartment, is that it will be reserved specifically for studying. It will not be a place where you also hang out with friends, play video games, or IM. If you do have a study place in your dorm room or at home, try to use it only for studying. This is the flipside of not studying at the kitchen table, which is designed for other things like eating, but not for studying. Don't use your study place to eat, play games, talk with others, or sleep. For example, when one of the authors was in graduate school, he used to study in those individual study carrels at the library in the afternoons between classes and sometimes in the evening. Often, after an hour or two of studying, he would get a little drowsy and want to rest and close his eyes for 20 minutes or so. Being a psychologist and knowing about reinforcement and classical conditioning, he would go to a different carrel, which he deemed his "nap" carrel. In his "nap" carrel, he could take a little nap, rest, and then go back to his "study" carrel to work. This way, he did not become conditioned to take a nap when he went to the "study" carrel. In the same manner, you will be able to focus better if you make your study environment a place for studying, not other activities.

STRATEGY SUGGESTION

Try not to watch TV, IM, or do other activities while you are studying.

Television and Music

As we have noted, your attention and memory are limited and you can't concentrate on your studying very well if you are trying to do other things at the same time. This means you need to regulate your study environment to help you concentrate and attend to your studying. Some students swear they study better if the TV is on in the background or if they listen to music while they are studying. In general, we would suggest that this may not be a real aid to your attention. TV would seem to be particularly distracting as it is both visual and auditory—it has two ways to grab your attention. We recommend that you not watch TV or have it on while you are trying to study. It is just too much of a distraction and will interfere with your attention and learning.

On the other hand, we realize that many, many college students like to listen to music as they study. In some cases, they will put on their headphones from their MP3 or iPod and study this way. They often suggest to us that putting on these headphones in their dorm room or in the library helps to block out other distractions or noise that interferes with their studying. This may be the case, and if so, it may be effective for them. Of course, we would ask them why they are studying in a place with so many distractions in the first place. They should go to a library or someplace else where it is quieter. In any case, we are not going to be so inflexible as to say that you should never study while listening to music. It seems to help some students. We would, however, ask you to try to figure out if it really works for you. You might want to try a little experiment. Try studying one night with music and one night without, for the same amount of time and working with the same kind of course material. Test yourself each night to see how much you have learned. For example, you could have a friend quiz you on the readings you did for a course. See if you did better with music or without music. You may be surprised to find that you are the kind of person who studies better without music.

SEEKING HELP: MANAGING YOUR RESOURCES AMONG PEERS AND FACULTY

When you are in high school, you can usually count on parents and teachers to support your efforts to learn. In college, it is a little different; you have to be able to go out and get the help you need on your own. You have many resources, including special academic support offices set up by the college to help you with your academic problems. Colleges also usually offer counseling centers that can help you with many different problems. (We discussed these in Chapter 1.) In addition, two very good sources that all college students can use are peers and professors.

Patterns of Help Seeking

A great deal of research has studied college student help seeking, including four major issues: (a) who seeks help, (b) why students do or do not seek help, (c) what kinds of help they seek, and (d) from whom they seek help. We will highlight just a few important points that you should be aware of. We hope this review will help you decide when to get help, from whom to get help, and the kind of help that will best aid your learning. Remember, getting help is not the same as getting answers.

Who Asks for Help? First, many college students never seek help at all. They try to do it all by themselves, even if they are having difficulties. For example, Karabenick and Knapp (1988) found that the college students who were most likely to seek help had grades in the B− to C + range. It makes sense that students who are getting Bs or As are less likely to seek help. They seem to be doing well and so don't need as much help. But the fascinating discovery of this study was that students who were getting Cs, Ds, and Fs were very unlikely to seek help. Here are students who are doing poorly and yet they don't seek out help. These are the students who can use it the most, and they are the least likely to seek it.

STRATEGY SUGGESTION

Be aware of your need to seek help if you don't understand something, and don't be afraid to ask for help.

Why Don't Some Students Ask? There are many reasons why some students might not seek help. First, in many cases, students believe that if they ask, it must mean they are not smart enough. Not asking protects self-esteem, in a strange way. In our individualistic American culture, where the strong, independent person is often held up as an ideal, not asking for help is seen as virtuous. Of course, in terms of academic learning, we all need help at some time. If we could learn everything by ourselves, we would not even need formal schooling. And in other domains, such as athletics, there are coaches who help individuals learn the skills to become good athletes. The idea that you can learn without help is just not supported by the realities of development. So realize that you will probably need help at some point, and seek it out when you do.

Knowing when you need help is an important issue. Experts in a field know when they don't know something, and they know where they can find the relevant information or whom to ask to help them find it. Novices in a field often are not aware of what they know and don't know. They often think they know something when they really don't. This is another reason why students may not seek help—they may not know they really need help. Then they get their midterms back. They suddenly find out that they are not doing well and that some things they thought they understood, they really didn't. One of the difficulties in academic learning is that it can be hard to know how well you are doing. In athletics, it is easier to know: you can sink a free throw or not, you can do a backflip or not, you can hit the baseball or not, you can skate backward or not, and so on. You and your coach can easily see what you can and can't do, and you can work together to improve. In academic learning, it is harder to know because the outcomes are not as concrete as make–miss or fast–slow. This is one of the reasons why we have stressed throughout this book the importance of becoming aware of your own strengths and weaknesses. As you become aware of weaknesses, you can then try to do something about them, including seeking help.

STRATEGY SUGGESTION

Be an adaptive help seeker, not a dependent help seeker.

What Do People Ask for? In addition to knowing when you need help, you also need to know what kind of help to ask for. A lot of research has covered the different ways that students seek help in academic settings. A major distinction is between dependent help seeking and adaptive help seeking.

Dependent help seeking is when you ask someone else to do the task for you, without getting involved in learning. When you were in elementary school, we are sure you ran into other students in your classes who were always bugging you: "What is the answer to number six?" or "Tell me what to do here, I can't figure it out." These students also may have been the ones running up to the teacher all the time for constant help and reassurance. For college students, it is not quite the same, but we are sure you know students who are always just trying to get the answers for a math test or a chemistry lab, without trying to learn how to do the work. Research shows that while dependent help seeking may help students complete a task, it does not result in as much learning as adaptive help seeking does.

In contrast, in **adaptive help seeking**, the person seeking help is actually trying to learn rather than just getting the answers. The help seeker may ask for hints to help her get started on the task. Or she may ask someone to show her how to do one problem, but then go on to try the other problems on her own. Adaptive help seekers do not just ask for the answers; they want to know how to get the answers on their own. Not surprisingly, research shows that adaptive help seeking is related to better learning and achievement over the long run. Of course, adaptive help seeking is harder and takes more time than dependent help seeking, but over time the payoffs in terms of your learning and achievement are much higher.

Who Gets Asked? In classroom situations, of course, students usually go to classmates and the teacher for support. This makes sense, as they are the ones who are involved in the specific assignments and tasks for that class. When you were in high school, your parents were probably a key source of help and support, but for college students, parents are often not easily accessible and may not have the expertise to help with college-level work. Another source of help in high school may have been your friends, because you probably took the same classes. But in college, your close friends may have very different courses from you as they pursue different majors, or even if they are taking the same course as you, they may have a different section with a different instructor and different assignments and tasks. This means that you may need to seek help from your classmates and the professor, people you might not know very well and may not feel comfortable asking for help. However, it is key that you do seek out these people for help.

> STRATEGY SUGGESTION
>
> *Seek help from professors when you don't understand course material.*

Seeking Help from Faculty Members

Professors and teaching assistants are great sources of help as you try to learn and understand the course material. They are experts in their field and therefore have the knowledge to help you understand and learn the course content. Of course, class time is designed to help you learn and understand, but you have to remember that among the many students in the course are people with different levels of knowledge and skills in the area. Professors have to decide how to pace the class material so as not to go too fast or too slow for the students. They also have to decide how much depth and detail they want to present, given the diversity of student knowledge and skills in the course.

Usually, professors gear the course to the "average" student level of prior knowledge and skills, or at least what they perceive to be the average level. For some students, this average level may be too easy, and for other students, this average level may be too difficult. In most cases, the average college level is much, much higher than the average level chosen by high school teachers (who have to deal with an even greater diversity of student knowledge because their classes include students who will never go on to college). Accordingly, for many college students, the average level of a course is much more difficult than what they are used to from high school. This means that you will often not understand everything that is presented in class. When this happens, you should seek **professor support.**

Students often avoid seeking a professor's help because they think that professors don't like or are too busy to meet with undergraduates. It is true that professors are very busy, and you need to respect their time. However, most professors are open to meeting with you. There are always some who will not be very accessible, but for the most part, they will take the time to help you. The catch is that you have to take the initiative. For example, some of you attend schools with 20,000 or more undergraduates. At places like this, many classes enroll more than 500 students. It is very difficult for professors to get to know students in these large classes, and often the students actually meet with graduate student teaching assistants, rather than professors. The teaching assistants would be the first choice to go to for help in this situation. But even at these large schools, professors are usually willing to meet with undergraduates *if* the student takes the initiative by coming up after class, coming to office hours, or even just sending an e-mail. Professors are happy to help, but it is up to you to take the first step.

It is important that you respect professors' time by being prepared when you go to them for help. This means knowing what you want help with and having specific questions or problems you want to talk about. All professors have heard before and hate the question, "I missed class yesterday, was there anything important that I should know about?" For a professor—who took the time to prepare carefully for the class you missed—each and every class meeting is important. In high school, teachers may have wasted a day occasionally, since you met 5 days a week for 9 months or more, but in college, there are a limited number of class sessions per term, so every one is important.

This kind of question is not a good use of professors' time, and you will risk alienating them by asking it. In fact, if you did miss class for some good reason, before you ever go to the professor, you should get the notes and handouts from your classmates. Go over the notes yourself or with your classmate and see whether you can understand the material first yourself. If you still can't understand it, then develop a series of questions about the material and bring those to a meeting with the instructor. Then you can start off the conversation with a much more focused agenda, and the professor will be able to give you much more specific help, rather than just trying to repeat the lecture in a shorter period of time. Professors will be impressed by this approach.

You should make the same type of preparations if you are going to talk to an instructor about a topic for an upcoming paper or about your grade for an already completed exam or paper. When you want to discuss a paper topic, it is not helpful to ask a professor, "I don't know what to write my paper on; what do you think is a good topic?" One of the reasons the instructor assigned a paper (instead of an exam) was probably to give you some choice regarding the topic so that you could choose something that interests you. You should think about some possible topics and do a little research on them, then go to the instructor with your questions. For example, you may discover that there is so much research on a complex topic that you need help narrowing it down.

Professors can help you do this and point you in the right direction to find relevant literature. The same type of preparation is necessary if you are going to ask a professor about your grade on a paper or exam. It is perfectly fine to go to an instructor to point out an arithmetic error that resulted in your getting the wrong grade (e.g., the points were added up wrong, the extra-credit question wasn't added in). Professors will quickly and gladly fix this type of problem. However, it is a different situation if you think your paper or essay exam was graded improperly and you are asking the instructor to regrade it or change the grade. In this case, you need to respect the instructor's position and try to understand the grading system first, then develop a rationale for why you think your paper or answer deserves a better grade.

Professors are interested in what you have learned from the class, and to earn a better grade, you need to show them that you have learned the material and that your paper or exam reflects your knowledge. Accordingly, you need to prepare beforehand and be able to show how what you wrote represents a good understanding of the material. The best strategy is to ask how you can improve your paper or exam answer, and use the conversation to help you understand the material better. It does not work to point to a sentence or paragraph and say, "See, here is where I meant to say that (whatever the professor says you should have said). I know it only partially sounds like it, but in my head, I know that is what I meant." All professors have heard some version of this before, and while it may be true, we can grade you only on what you wrote on the page, not on what was or wasn't in your head at the time. However, if you can demonstrate that what you wrote does reflect a good understanding, then professors may be open to changing the grade. More important, regardless of the grade, at least the conversation with the professor should help you understand the material better.

© Daniel Fleck – FOTOLIA

Try to form at least one personal relationship with a professor each term.

Besides direct academic help, professors can also provide you with other kinds of help and support that will make your college career more successful. Light (2001), in his study of successful college students, found that one of the most important factors in student success was a personal relationship between the student and some professor. This professor could serve some of the functions of a parent, such as providing some emotional support, but the most important aspect was that the professor could help the student navigate the college system and act as a mentor. This mentor relationship sometimes continues after the student's graduation.

In terms of emotional support, it is always good to have some professor or other adult (such as a counselor or a dormitory director) to talk to about issues besides academic ones. College students face many different stresses, not just academic ones, including personal relationships, identity, finances, sexuality, and more. Talking to someone besides a peer about some of these issues can be helpful. Professors may be willing to talk about some of these issues, but often they are most comfortable talking with you about their area of expertise. As both of us are psychologists and teach psychology courses, students often come to us to talk about personal issues, assuming that as psychologists, we must be therapists as well. Neither of us is trained as a therapist or counselor, and if the conversation goes beyond some general advice and support, we are sure to refer the student to our university's counseling center (see Chapter 1). It is better to seek this type of help from counselors or other professionals than from your professors, who do not have the expertise you may need.

On the other hand, we are very happy to talk with students about research in psychology, how to get into graduate school, what it is like being a professor, and other aspects of college life and psychology. The same is true of most other professors. They love to talk about their discipline, what it takes to do well, how to do research, what it was like in graduate school, how to get into graduate school, how to start a career in the area, and so on. Professors chose to work in their area because of their deep interest in it. They spent many years preparing and made sacrifices to work in academia. They love to talk to undergraduates about their field and may even try to recruit you to the field. So they are usually happy to mentor and advise you about options in their field. You may find talking to them about it very useful in your own career decision making.

Another way to build a personal relationship with a professor is to volunteer to work with him or her on some project outside of class. Light (2001) reports that students often regard this type of outside class experience as one of the best learning experiences they had in college. Many colleges now offer some type of undergraduate research program that pairs students with professors to work on some research project. The professor gets research help, and the student gets experience in the field, learns what research is like, learns some skills, and also gets to know the professor a little more closely. If your school offers such a program, you should try to get involved in it.

STRATEGY SUGGESTION

Make good use of peers as a resource for learning.

Seeking Help from Peers

Your peers are an excellent source for academic help in college. We use the word *peers* or *classmates,* not *friends,* because in many cases, your friends may not be in your classes and may not be able to help you academically. Of course, friends are essential in college for emotional and social support, and you should cultivate a good set of close friends that you can rely on to support you. In this chapter, however, we are suggesting strategies to help you learn more in your classes and do well academically. **Peer support** is an important academic strategy.

First, you should develop at least one personal relationship with another student in every one of your classes. This person should be someone who knows you and would be willing to help you in the class. At a minimum, this person should be willing to share notes with you in case you miss class due to some emergency. Even better, the student might be willing to help you study. You may be able to study together for exams, or if there are group projects, you can be partners.

Getting to know someone in each of your classes can help to reduce the isolation you may feel in college. First-year college students often don't know anyone and may be in classes that are quite large and impersonal. Again, it is not like high school, where you knew some people because they grew up in the same neighborhood. You will meet other people in your dorm or elsewhere, but you also need to get to know people in your classes because they are the ones who have the same readings, assignments, exams, and papers as you. Finally, it is always good to have someone to talk to about the course. You may think you are the only one who is struggling or who didn't understand what the professor was saying in his or her lecture. Having someone to talk to about the class can help you become aware of your own knowledge and understanding. Most likely, if you did not understand something, there are others who did not as well. Not only is this reassuring, but you can also then work with them to try to improve your understanding.

You should try to develop a relationship with students who are responsible and who want to learn, just like you. It does not mean that you have to try to find the smartest people in the class and make friends with them. It just means that you should try to find people who are responsible and committed to learning, who will come to class, take good notes, and be involved in learning. You must be willing to reciprocate and go to class, take good notes, be involved, and be willing to share your work. You are not doing this so you can skip class and expect your peer to do all the work. It should be an equal partnership, with both people committed to sharing the responsibility of learning and doing the work.

STRATEGY SUGGESTION

Develop peer study groups in your classes.

Besides finding one person to work with in a class, you might want to develop a group of two or three peers who will work together. Many students have study groups, which means that they study with a few of their friends in a group. This type of group is usually just for support in terms of planning and going to study at a set time. Once they get to the library or study place, they all study individually because they are in different courses and majors, so one is studying math, the other psychology, the other Spanish, and so on. This is perfectly fine, and if it helps you manage your study time and schedule, then it is a good strategy.

But even better than this type of study group is a group of classmates who are all in the same class, who work together to help each other learn the material for that class. This type of group can be very valuable: Research has shown that it can help students do better. But these groups must be productive and work well to be successful. Many students do not like working in groups because of previous bad experiences in small groups. They found they did all the work themselves because there were "free riders" who did not do their share. Or a student took over and tried to dominate the group, not allowing anyone else to contribute ideas. These are serious problems, and you need to work hard at establishing procedures that will make your small group function well. It is worth the effort, because working in groups can be an important part of your success in college—and even more so after college, as employers are continually asking for individuals who can function effectively as part of a team. Figure 4.1 lists some of the features of constructive groups. These should help you set up your study groups.

 **FIGURE 4.** Features of constructive study groups.

SIZE

Limit the size to about three to five people. In groups larger than five, responsibility can become unclear and some people may wind up doing more of the work. Also, with more members it is much harder to find times when everyone can meet.

CLEAR GOALS AND EXPECTATIONS

Set some goals for the group's work. Is the goal to divide up the workload so that everyone has less to do? Or is the goal to help and support one another? Clarify the expectations for all individuals in the group: what each person expects to gain and will be expected to contribute. If the workload is divided up, who is responsible for what? If members will have different roles (one person is the editor, another is the researcher, another is the writer, for instance), be clear about what is involved in each role.

RULES FOR GROUP FUNCTIONING

What are the rules about missing meetings? What are the rules about not getting your part of the work done? What are the rules for group interactions during meetings? How is the group going to operate?

SELF-TESTING AND GROUP EXPLANATIONS

Group members should test each other on their understanding of the material and take turns explaining material to the other members. Explaining material to others helps the person doing the explaining the most.

CHAPTER SUMMARY

This chapter covers a number of different strategies for managing your resources. One of the most important—if not the most important—is managing your time. To do well in college (and life in general), you must be a good manager and regulator of your own time. Successful people are ones who are organized and make good use of their time. They make schedules and prioritized to-do lists that help keep them organized and on track. Various strategies can help you manage your time, and you should develop a flexible set of strategies that work for you.

Another important resource that has to be managed is your physical space for studying. It is important that you have places set aside for studying and that they be free of distractions. Your capacity for attention is limited, so you need to arrange your environment to allow you to concentrate on studying. This chapter offers a number of strategies that may help you make your study environment productive for learning.

The final important resource is other people, particularly peers and professors. In high school, you had a lot of other people who helped you manage your academic work. In college, support is not as readily available, so you have to take the initiative and seek out professors and peers to help you. Help seeking can be a very important strategy for learning, provided you seek help to learn, not just to get the answers or finish the task. Professors can help you in many ways, and you should seek them out for both academic help and mentoring and advice. Finally, peers and peer study groups can be a very good source of help, if you use them properly.

Managing Your Resources II

INTERNAL TOOLS

Chapter Goals

After reading this chapter you should be able to:

- Describe healthy living habits and why they are essential to college success

- Understand psychological strengths that are related to college success and offer an honest evaluation of yourself

- Identify your ability to communicate well with others and recognize the vital importance of valuing diversity in human experience

Key Terms

attributional complexity

automatized

Big Five

binge drinking

commitment

contextualized relativism

delay of gratification

dualism

fundamental attribution error

loneliness

optimism

personality

CHAPTER 5

n the previous chapter, we stressed the importance of being organized. Appointment books, weekly schedules, and to-do lists are all essential *external* tools needed for being organized. We have rarely met a successful student who is able to be successful in the absence of these organizing tools. But having external tools is only one piece. In this chapter we talk about the *internal* tools for college success. Specifically, we discuss the importance of healthy living, healthy relationships, and capitalizing on our virtuous traits. The main message of this chapter is that to be successful in college, one must develop certain habits and engage in certain behaviors that go beyond academics. A successful college student is successful in other areas of life as well, and in this chapter we try to paint a portrait of that successful person. College brings freedom, but also responsibility. It is important to remember that the decisions you make today will have a cumulative effect on your future. Activity 5.1 provides an initial assessment of your healthy habits. Complete this instrument before reading further.

ACTIVITY 5.1 *Assessing Well-Being*

Answer the following questions using the following scale: 1 = strongly disagree, 2 = disagree, 3 = neutral, 4 = agree, 5 = strongly agree

		Not True of Me			**Very True of Me**	
1.	I sleep 8 or more hours each day.	①	②	③	④	⑤
2.	I eat nutritionally sound meals each day.	①	②	③	④	⑤
3.	I exercise three or more times per week.	①	②	③	④	⑤
4.	I feel stressed about school on a regular basis.	⑤	④	③	②	①
5.	I get along with people most of the time.	①	②	③	④	⑤

If your total score on the five items is lower than 14, this chapter will definitely help you.

HEALTHY LIVING

We start with healthy living. The messages we give you are ones that you have heard since you were a young child. We don't write this section to insult you or to be preachy. We write this section because every semester we and our colleagues see very talented students underachieve because they do not take care of themselves. Consider Sara, an outgoing, confident, and intelligent woman. By all accounts, Sara should be on the dean's list. But after 2 years in college, she is struggling to stay off academic probation. Sara's problem is all of the issues we discuss in this chapter: she eats poorly (although she's not yet overweight), she sleeps too little, she socializes too much, she smokes, she goes to the bar or parties at least twice a week, and she has no commitment to academic excellence. These factors might not affect you, but chances are you know someone like Sara: eating difficulties, lack of fitness activities, irresponsible alcohol consumption, and undirected academic goals.

Try to exercise more times per week than you eat dessert.

Nutrition and Exercise

A major way in which healthy living is realized is by proper food and exercise. If you went to school in the United States, you have been told this since you were in grade school. The relation between exercise, nutrition, and other positive outcomes is clear. It is less clear that exercise and nutrition have a *direct* effect on school performance. However, educational researchers Herb Marsh and Sabina Kleitman (2003) found that among Australian high school students, participation in athletics was correlated with a variety of positive outcomes, including higher academic achievement and higher educational aspirations. Granted, this study is more about sports participation than exercise. But other research shows the psychological benefits of exercise: lower anxiety, depression, and test anxiety, and higher self-esteem (Pinto, Cherico, Szymanski, & Marcus, 1988). Given the many long-term positive benefits of developing healthy lifestyles, we strongly recommend regular exercise and healthy food choices. Unfortunately, many college students do not exercise. A survey of college students (Pinto et al., 1998) found that 42% of students did not engage in even moderate exercise. In researching exercise adherence, Timothy Bungum (1997) at North Texas State found those who stuck with exercise programs and those who did not were *no* different in their *attitude* toward exercise—both groups wanted to exercise equally. What separated the adherents were factors such as higher levels of self-motivation and working out with a friend.

We recommend putting an exercise schedule into your weekly calendar (Chapter 4). One of the major problems college students face is running out of time. Too often, exercise moves to the bottom of the list. Of course, homework takes priority over exercise. However, we suspect you can find several places in your day that are filled with meaningless activities, into which you could substitute a 20- to 30-minute exercise session. We also recommend that you find an exercise partner, someone who will go to the campus fitness center with you. The two of you will hold each other accountable. The time will pass more quickly and will be more enjoyable if you're with a friend.

As for nutrition, research has also demonstrated that healthy eating is correlated with academic performance. For example, children who eat a high-quality diet have better cognitive performance (Sigman, 1995). In addition, pregnant women who are given protein supplements more often give birth to infants with improved cognitive performance. Although these studies were with younger subjects, the benefits of healthy living seem self-evident. However, the goal of healthy eating can be particularly challenging for college students. Although university dining services frequently present students with healthy choices, students are just as frequently presented with unhealthy selections of high-fat entrees. Another difference from home is that desserts are also available at *every* meal (how many of you grew up with dessert choices at lunch and dinner every day?). On top of all this, it is also the case that cafeteria-style dining means that each meal is an all-you-can-eat buffet. It is common for students in their first year of college to gain weight, due to a combination of unhealthy eating, reduced activity due to hectic schedules, and reduction in school activities that involve exercise. One sample of American college students found that at the beginning of the fall semester, 79% of students had a Body Mass Index (BMI) in the normal range, but at the end of the fall semester, that number dropped to 68% (Anderson et al., 2003). All college students are well served by remembering that healthy eating is going to be more of a challenge in college than it was in high school.

STRATEGY SUGGESTION

If you have free time, try to take a short nap instead of e-mailing or IM-ing.

Sleep and Free Time

It is a painful irony that traditional-aged college students are at a time in their lives when sleep is particularly important and at the same time the pressures of college make sleep rare. Although sacrificing sleep may seem like a good idea the night before a big test, the long-term effects of limited sleep will take a toll on your performance. For example, William Kelly (2001) found that students who slept 6 hours or less per night had a lower GPA than students who slept 9 hours or more. In addition to sleep quantity, it is also crucial to get high-quality sleep. Research has shown that those who report poor-quality sleep have lower college GPAs than those who report high-quality sleep. Andrew Howell and associates (Howell, Jahrig, & Powell, 2004) found that among full-time college students, those with a high quality of sleep had a GPA of 2.86, and those with a low quality of sleep had a GPA of 2.64. We understand that sleep can be difficult to obtain amid the hustle and bustle of college life. But like other valuable commodities, we strongly urge you to see sleep as valuable (if not sacred!) and give it higher priority than partying, socializing, and watching television.

Dangerous Behaviors

College life brings freedom. But with freedom comes responsibility. Unfortunately, too many students take advantage of the freedom but forget about the responsibility. The most common dangerous behavior in which college students engage is **binge drinking,** defined by the Centers for Disease Control and Prevention as consuming four or more alcoholic beverages at one time for men and three or more for women. A recent survey by the Centers for Disease Control found that 28.1% of people age 18 to 24 engaged in binge drinking at least once in the last 30 days. Additionally, 8.4% in this age group were identified as "heavy drinkers"—two drinks per day for men and one drink per day for women (Centers for Disease Control, 2004). Not all of these young people in this national sample were necessarily college students, but with percentages like these, it is safe to conclude that research bears out what you probably already know—some college students drink too much.

We run the risk of sounding preachy in this section, but we include this discussion because the research shows that reckless behavior due to alcohol negatively affects many students. Ultimately, the decision you make about drinking is up to you. But there are several things to keep in mind about alcohol consumption. First, for many of you, simply consuming any alcohol is illegal in all 50 states. We realize that underage drinking is common on many college campuses, and professors and college personnel are not naïve. But it is worth noting that it is illegal for most of you, it is vigilantly enforced in most cases, and it has accompanying penalties that are both quite severe and long lasting. As an example, criminal background checks are now required in the state of Michigan for all those seeking employment as a teacher in a public school. Such scrutiny is present when you apply for jobs and after you have obtained them—some organizations release (fire) their employees if they are caught drunk driving. Second, excessive drinking has the potential for more immediate collateral damage to your schoolwork. Staying out late, sleeping late, evenings without studying, and hangovers all negatively impact your school performance. Whatever decision you make regarding alcohol consumption, we strongly encourage you to consider the long-term negative impact extreme behavior will have on your college experience. What seems like harmless, adolescent fun can stay with you a long time; driving while intoxicated, excessive celebrations following athletic events, and embarrassing pictures posted on the Internet could have future repercussions.

VIRTUES

The previous section discussed negative aspects of daily living. In this section, we examine positive aspects of human behavior and how these positive traits and behaviors promote human flourishing. After reading this section, you should have a good idea of what constitutes, psychologically speaking, "the good life." At first glance these traits may seem unrelated to school performance, but the fact is that those who are psychologically strong and emotionally happy are those who will do well in school. They also get sick less, suffer from depression less, and report greater life satisfaction (Bolt, 2004).

Commitment

In Chapter 2 we stressed the importance of goal setting for academic success. In this section we stress the importance of goal setting from a broad perspective. **Commitment** involves a long-term determination for achieving success. On a daily basis, you will want to make sure you are making progress toward what you hope to achieve. In an English class, maybe the goal is to achieve a B by the time you turn in your final draft of a multiple-draft paper. Being committed means having the right attitude toward the goal. It is easier to be committed to goals we enjoy or embrace. If we have a goal of getting an A in physics, it might be harder to do if we are not committed to learning physics. In this case, we may need to shift our focus to increase our commitment. In other words, instead of being committed to learning physics, you may be committed to getting into medical school. This commitment to medical school will help you set and achieve your learning goals in physics class.

Commitment stems from determination. Sometimes our determination takes the form of a drive *toward* something. The student's drive to get into medical school serves as the basis for the student's behavior in physics. Sometimes our determination takes the form of a drive *away* from something. Some students are driven by fear of failure. These students may work hard, but they work to stay away from something—getting a bad test grade, flunking a class, not succeeding in college—rather than to achieve something. Although it may be better to have a commitment to move away from something than no commitment at all, research shows that it is far better to have a commitment toward something than a commitment away from something. Those who strive toward something are psychologically healthier, including having lower anxiety (Emmons & Kaiser, 1996) and greater reported happiness (Elliot, Sheldon, & Church, 1997). They also are more likely to achieve their goals (Coats, Janoff-Bulman, & Alpert, 1996).

STRATEGY SUGGESTION

List the academic tasks you love to do. What makes you so determined?

Self-Control

Self-control is vital not just to college success but to all of human flourishing. As described by Daniel Goleman (1995) in his book *Emotional Intelligence*, imagine yourself as a 4-year-old who is given the following dilemma: An adult says that you can either eat one treat now or he will give you two treats if you can manage to wait a few minutes. Such a dilemma is what psychologists call a test of **delay of gratification,** which describes the ability to delay an immediate reward for a later reward. In the context of college learning, this would mean not going to the recreation center until you are done with your math homework, typing your paper first and using IM later, or not going out on Friday night until after you finish your reading for Monday.

The 4-year-olds alluded to above were part of Walter Mischel's research at Stanford University (described by Goleman, 1999; Bolt, 2004). The researchers made the following proposition to the children: You can have either one marshmallow now, or, if you wait, you can have two marshmallows later. Roughly two thirds

FIGURE 5. The path from commitment to goals action.

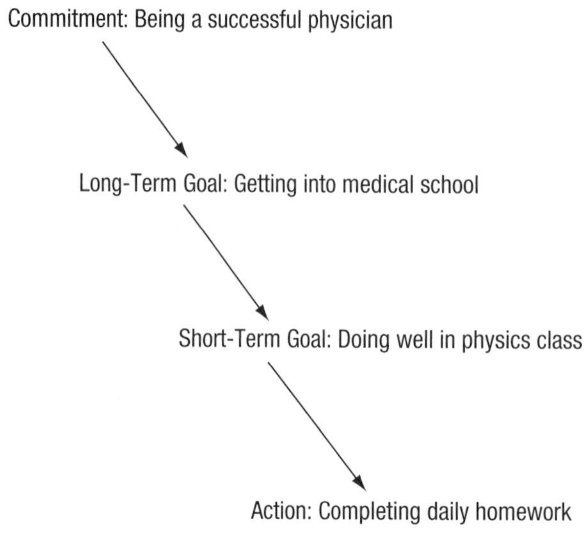

Commitment: Being a successful physician

Long-Term Goal: Getting into medical school

Short-Term Goal: Doing well in physics class

Action: Completing daily homework

of the children were able to resist temptation to get the two-treat reward. The researchers noted the strategies adopted by the resisters—trying to distract themselves by playing with their hands and feet, hiding their eyes, singing, even trying to go to sleep. What is even more interesting and more relevant to college learning is what happened to those children years later. The list of positive psychological traits among the resisters is compelling—greater social competence, more self-assertiveness, better stress management, greater ability to persevere in the face of difficulty, higher self-esteem, less stubbornness, and less tendency to become angry. Perhaps most striking is the 1262 to 1052 advantage the resisters enjoyed over the nonresisters on the SAT exam many years later. (How would you like to add 210 points to your SAT score?) We will learn later in this book, just because two events are related does not mean that one caused the other. In other words, we can't prove that self-control produced all these beneficial effects. However, finding a correlation does allow us to make predictions. So, if we know that you have self-control, we can be more confident that you will have a more positive psychological profile.

STRATEGY SUGGESTION

Don't put yourself in situations where you will be tempted.

In a study of eighth-grade students, Angela Duckworth and Martin Seligman (2005) found that students' scores on a measure of "self-discipline" were twice as powerful in determining final grades as students' IQ scores. Success is as much about perseverance as it is about inborn talent.

So self-control has many benefits, but it comes at a price. Imagine that you are a participant in one of Roy Baumeister's studies on self-control (Baumeister, Bratslavsky, Muraven, & Tice, 1998). You are given a bowl of radishes and a bowl of chocolates, which are placed on the table in front of you. You are then told either (depending on which experimental group you were assigned) to: (a) eat the radishes, with the sweets still present, or (b) eat the chocolates. After the eating portion of the experiment, the food is removed and you are asked to try to complete some unsolvable puzzles. The researchers are interested in how long you keep trying to solve the impossible problems. Do you think the radish eaters or chocolate eaters tried longer? When one of this book's authors first read this study, he predicted that the radish eaters would try longer because they had developed "mental toughness" by resisting the chocolate. Wrong. In fact, the chocolate eaters tried longer, and the researchers believe it was because the radish eaters had to spend more mental and emotional energy resisting the chocolates. Because they had to "spend" energy on avoiding the chocolate temptation, they had less diligence left over to try the problems. The chocolate eaters (besides being sugared up) had not spent any self-control energy and thus could give more energy to attempt the problems.

We identify three lessons that can be learned from the research on self-control for college learning. First, the research has led some to argue that self-control is not a *skill* but rather a *resource*. Practicing self-control is not like training for a road race, in that the more you train the farther you'll be able to go. Although practicing self-control *will* have at least one benefit: If you successfully show self-control, you will have the confidence that you can show self-control in the future. Another lesson is that self-control is not easy. If it were, everybody would have it. The moral of the story stemming from this research is that diligence and self-control are not cheap and they're not free. The more we are stressed, fatigued, sick, or otherwise weakened, it will be harder for us to have self-control. Applying this notion to your college life, we recommend avoiding situations in which you will have to exert a lot of self-control. Studying in a Greek house when there is a party going on downstairs, watching *Lost* while you are working on math homework, and having your e-mail program open while you're trying to finish a term paper are some examples of situations where you will have to spend self-control resources. That is, if you study in those settings, you'll spend self-control energy on resisting the party, the TV show, or the Internet. This will give you less diligence for your schoolwork. Finally, many books designed to improve learning (or other parts of the human experience) place a heavy emphasis on shaping the external world to fit our needs—what we discussed in the last chapter. Examples would include picking a quiet floor on which to study, choosing not to party on weekends, and choosing professors from whom you feel you can learn best. But this is not always possible, so we remind you that in situations where you can't modify your environment to fit you, it is important for you to change to fit the external environment. Examples include adapting to a professor's style, picking the times of the day when you know your residence hall will be quiet, and adjusting your sleep schedule to maximize when you will learn best (as opposed to when all your friends are awake). In other words, changing our internal world to meet the demands of the external world is just as important as trying to change the external world to fit the person we are.

How can we put off until tomorrow what we are tempted to do today? We can perhaps learn a lesson from the 4-year-old marshmallow resisters. We list some strategies for self-control in Figure 5.2.

FIGURE 5.2 | Strategies for improving self-control.

As we note in this chapter, self-control is better understood as a resource rather than a skill. Consider these strategies for maximizing this resource.

1. *Change your focus.* Think about something besides what is distracting you. The young children who avoided the marshmallows tried not to think about how delicious the marshmallows would be and would avert their gaze away from the tempting treat. So, when you are presented with something that tempts you, don't think about it.

2. *Reevaluate the situation.* Instead of focusing on all the positive aspects of what you're not doing and all the negative aspects of what you are doing, flip your thinking around. Think critically about the tempting event and generate some aspects of it that are not that appealing. Is going to the football game all that great? After all, it's crowded, cold, and there will be other games. And if you stay and study, you will be way ahead of all of your friends who are not studying, you'll be able to get a decent night's sleep, and you'll be rested for the exam.

3. *Tone down your emotions.* Impulse control is related to being able to regulate the "hot" parts of our brain and allow the "cool" parts to take over. When the son of one of the authors throws tantrums when his goals are thwarted and he perceives an injustice in how he was treated, his ability to make calm decisions is long gone. In general, when we allow our emotions to overthrow our rationality, self-control is unlikely. Stay calm.

Humility

In Chapter 3 we examined the role of self-efficacy in learning. Research on self-esteem suggests that self-esteem does not actually *cause* increased academic achievement (Baumeister, Campbell, Kruefer, & Vohs, 2003). However, abundant research also shows that high self-esteem is *correlated* with high academic achievement. As discussed in Chapter 3, one way this positive relation between self-esteem and achievement could develop is that you get a good grade on your first test, which gives you self-confidence, which leads to high self-esteem. This increased self-esteem helps you prepare for the next test and makes it more likely you will do well on it. This positive cycle (or negative cycle for poor performance) is contagious and makes the link between success and self-esteem a critical one for college success.

Although self-esteem is predictive of academic achievement, there is another side to how we view ourselves that also deserves attention. Specifically, we argue that a degree of humility is also a virtue that can improve achievement as well. Humility brings with it several advantages. First, humble people are lifelong learners. They understand that there is much to learn and that the acquisition and use of new knowledge is ongoing. Second, humble people have better personal relationships. Most of us prefer to spend time with humble people than with arrogant people. Humility will give you positive relationships with your friends and classmates and professors. Third, having humility, in a peculiar way, suggests confidence—a confidence that is enduring and not short-lived. As Martin Bolt (2004) said, "Humility reflects a sense of security in which feelings of personal worth are based on stable, reliable sources . . . rather than on more transient, external sources . . ." (p. 154).

Bolt offers several ways to promote humility, which we believe will make you a better learner and thinker. First, seek accurate feedback. Sometimes hearing honest feedback about our performance is difficult. As a friend of one of ours has said about hearing others' opinions, "Don't ask the question if you don't want to know the answer." But asking the question is the only way you'll get better. Second, keep schoolwork in perspective. Doing poorly on a test can be discouraging, but remember that it's only *one* test from *one* professor in *one* class in *one* semester. This will help temper that discouragement. Conversely, when we experience lots of success, we should avoid becoming too blustery or full of ourselves, which may be easier if we remember the times when we did not have as much success. Third, it is important to lead a balanced life. If we have multiple interests and attempt to develop multiple talents, we protect ourselves against feelings of despair. If we are interested in or good at only one thing, then our sense of self-worth may be tied solely to that activity. The first author recently received highly critical reviews regarding another textbook that he is writing. As a coping tool, it helped him to remember that he had many other aspects of his life in which he experienced success: the success of this book, a record of high-quality teaching, and a happy home and family life. Financial planners talk about having a "diversified portfolio"; that is, spreading your money out among stocks, bonds, and bank accounts. This reduces your risk—if one investment does poorly, you still have others to protect you. Just like in financial investments, having a diversified portfolio of interests and abilities protects us from the occasional bad news life inevitably brings.

Optimism

The last virtue we explore is optimism. We define **optimism** as the general belief in future positive outcomes. Activity 5.2 has a six-item measure developed by Scheier, Carver, and Bridges (1994) to measure optimism.

ACTIVITY 5.2 *Assessing Optimism*

		Not True of Me			Very True of Me	
1.	In uncertain times, I usually expect the best.	①	②	③	④	⑤
2.	If something can go wrong for me, it will.	⑤	④	③	②	①
3.	I'm always optimistic about my future.	①	②	③	④	⑤
4.	I hardly ever expect things to go my way.	⑤	④	③	②	①
5.	I rarely count on good things happening to me.	⑤	④	③	②	①
6.	Overall, I expect more good things to happen to me than bad.	①	②	③	④	⑤

Higher scores reflect greater optimism. If you scored 24 or higher, you are probably very optimistic. If you scored 12 or lower, you're probably pessimistic. We recommend you pay particular attention to this section of the book.

Source: From "Distinguishing Optimism from Neuroticism (and Trait Anxiety, Self-Mastery, and Self-Esteem). A Re-evaluation of the Life Orientation Test," by M. F. Scheier, C. S. Carver, and M. W. Bridges, 1994, *Journal of Personality and Social Psychology, 67,* pp. 1063–1078. Reprinted with permission from M. F. Scheier.

What positive benefits does optimism have? Among other things, optimism is correlated with various other positive health indicators. More importantly for our purposes, optimism is correlated with high morale, being in a good mood, and resistance to stress. Optimistic people also report less anxiety. As we will learn in Chapter 11, a moderate amount of anxiety can be good, but high amounts of anxiety tend to interfere with high performance on tests (McKeachie, 2005).

Why should optimism be better than pessimism? Could you imagine it the other way? Would it be better, especially given what we just said about humility, to be more guarded about your future prospects for success? Is it true that "pessimism is sanity," as an attorney once said on a CNN talk show? According to the research, it is not—optimism is psychologically healthier than pessimism. What are some advantages to having an optimistic attitude? Numerous studies have shown that optimism is positively correlated with resistance to stress, lower levels of depression, better physical health, faster recovery from surgery, and greater life satisfaction (see Bolt, 2004, for a review). With respect to college students, Aspinwall and Taylor (1992) found that students who entered college with an optimistic attitude better handled the emotional stress of college. These students scored lower on measures of stress, depression, and loneliness. Those who believe that "pessimism is sanity" probably want to protect themselves from disappointment. However, pessimism also brings with it a variety of unhealthy psychological and physical characteristics. Pessimists prepare for failure instead of expecting success. Be optimistic.

Is being optimistic easier said than done? Or can we teach ourselves to be optimistic? We believe that you can teach yourself to be optimistic. We offer three suggestions for teaching yourself to be optimistic. It might be cute and maybe even inspiring to listen to young children believing that they can someday grow up to be President of the United States. But, of course, almost no one does. It's probably not a good idea to tell young children that their dreams will never come true. But also, the words of the New Testament writer who said he would "put the ways of childhood behind me" resonate with us. So, the first way to teach yourself to be optimistic involves, ironically, learning to be realistic. Having a "realistic optimism" allows us to pursue reasonable goals. Disappointment will inevitably occur. Optimism will not shield you from disappointment. Your optimism should not be an illusion. If you are taking a difficult class, you need to recognize that it's difficult, and you need to realize that there is a chance that you will struggle. But such realism need not preclude approaching difficult tasks with hope and energy, believing that you will give maximum effort to achieving your goals.

The second part of teaching yourself to be optimistic is learning to rebound from failure. As we just mentioned, college life is sometimes hard. Even the most successful people in the world do not achieve all things all of the time. In fact, it's probably safe to say that most people fail most of the time. The highest batting average in Major League Baseball in 2005 belonged to Chicago Cub Derrek Lee, who was hitting .335 for the season. Impressive, indeed. But another way to think about this batting king is that he was *unsuccessful* two out of every three times he came to the plate. If you were betting on Derrek Lee to get a hit, you'd probably lose money. And he was the best. If you get discouraged in the face of failure, it will negatively affect your ability to accomplish subsequent goals. It helps to rebound from failure quickly when we keep in perspective the fact that we are not the only ones facing disappointment. Everyone gets negative results. What will separate you from other people is if you respond to the negative results with increased resolve and commitment to do better next time.

The third part of teaching yourself to be optimistic involves engaging in optimistic behavior without thinking. Research shows that if we can make optimistic attitudes and behaviors part of our **automatized** behavior, we show better psychological coping. Automatized behavior is what we do without thinking. Psychologist Susan Nolen-Hoeksema (1998) found that when people were depressed, those who were told to think about their lives (vs. those who were told to think about something else) became even more depressed. University of Kansas's Daniel Batson (Batson, Fultz, Schoenrade, & Padvano, 1987) found that when he asked students to perform acts of kindness toward other students, they felt better, but only if they were *not thinking* about why they were doing it. In other words, we can overthink our happiness. If we spend too much time analyzing ourselves, it might backfire. So teaching yourself to be optimistic involves making it an automatic part of who you are rather than constantly reminding yourself to be optimistic (Wilson, 2006). Figure 5.3 has three strategies for improving your optimism.

FIGURE 5.3   Three ways to improve your optimism.

1. *Be realistic.* Not all dreams will come true. Your optimism should be realistic optimism.

2. *Rebound from failure quickly.* Even the most successful people fail a lot of the time. The best baseball players get out two of three times they bat. What matters is not *if* failure happens, but *when* it happens, how you will respond.

3. *Make it automatic.* Thinking optimistically should be so routine that you don't even think about it. If you can get to the point that you don't worry about your optimism, you are probably in the right frame of mind.

RELATIONSHIPS

Healthy Relationships

It is important to avoid **loneliness**—"a sad or aching sense of isolation" (Parkhurst & Hopmeyer, 1999, p. 58). Loneliness should not be mistaken for not having friends. Although not having a lot of friends is correlated with loneliness, it is also the case that some people with lots of friends may still be lonely and those with only a few friends may not be lonely at all. Loneliness is a subjective experience (an opinion). Because loneliness is subjective (we are lonely if we "feel" lonely), loneliness tends to be related to the quality of friendships. Being lonely is not healthy. Friendships that are meaningful, not aggressive or manipulative, and that endure over time tend to protect us against loneliness. We all feel alone from time to time. But researchers have found that chronic loneliness is related to dropping out of school, alcoholism, depression, and other medical problems (Asher & Paquette, 2003). In short, it is vital that you stay engaged and connected with other people. Usually that connection will be with other students, because they are the people you see most often and because you share common experiences with them. But it matters less with whom you make these connections than it does that you make them at all. You don't need a lot of friends to be happy and healthy, but research shows that having solid, meaningful, and lasting friends predicts happiness and success.

STRATEGY SUGGESTION

Identify one friend you have had for more than 3 years. E-mail that person three times this semester, with a long note about the events in your life. Also ask for a return note.

Part of building healthy relationships involves understanding yourself and others. Psychologists define one's **personality** as the enduring traits of a person that stay stable over time and circumstance. A common personality theory is known as the **Big Five** personality theory (McCrae & Costa, 2003). This theory states that people's personality is made up five factors:

- Introversion/extraversion: Are you outgoing?
- Openness: Are you interested in new experiences?
- Neuroticism: Are you nervous?
- Agreeableness: Are you easy to get along with?
- Conscientiousness: Are you responsible?

© Marc Dietrich – FOTOLIA

Another part of healthy relationships involves understanding the role of the environment in shaping people's behavior. Research shows clearly that people will act differently depending on the external situation. For example, we act differently when we are at a football game than when we are at a symphony concert. This is because the power of the situation is very strong—football games bring out certain behaviors and symphonies bring out different behaviors. Unfortunately, whereas we are pretty good at recognizing the power of the situation in our own behavior (e.g., "I was drunk"), we are not as good at recognizing the power of the situation in others' behavior. If someone is gruff and mean-spirited, we assume that they are and always will be gruff and mean-spirited. This tendency to attribute other people's behavior to internal causes (personality) and our own behavior to external forces is known as the **fundamental attribution error.** This error harms relationships because we fail to recognize that forces beyond people's control are influencing them. This, in turn, leads us to be less understanding and less forgiving of others when they fall short of what we expect. So the same "I was drunk" excuse that we make for our own behavior we would not let others make for their behavior.

Interpersonal Communication

Entire books are written on the science and practice of effective interpersonal communication. Thus, we cannot cover everything here. In this short section, we suggest three strategies for effectively interacting with others.

1. *Perspective taking.* Moving from the first year to the last year of college, one cognitive change students experience is a change in perspective taking. First-year students are more likely to see learning as memorizing a set of right–wrong facts, which educators call **dualism.** Fourth-year college students see learning as constructing one's own sense of right and wrong based on evaluating multiple viewpoints. This stage is referred to by many names, but we call it **contextualized relativism** (Hofer & Pintrich, 2001). This shift from dualism to contextualized relativism occurs because of an increased ability to take the perspective of others. This allows you to understand (even if you don't agree with) a variety of viewpoints. In addition to the cognitive benefit of taking the perspective of others, there is an emotional benefit. Specifically, understanding how others feel creates mutual respect in a relationship. Mutual respect fosters healthy interaction between people. Understanding what it's like to be another person increases your intellectual and social competency. Your transition from dualism to contextualized relativism is affected by several factors, including taking classes that challenge your current way of thinking. This transition can also be enhanced by exposing yourself to people who are not like you. If you spend time with people who have had different life experiences, you will increase your ability for perspective taking.

2. *Be positive when you can, be negative when you must.* We certainly want to take advantage of the opportunity to compliment people we like. We feel good about praising others, and we certainly feel good about *receiving* praise from others. But relationships built on honesty are the healthiest. And healthy criticism is as valuable as healthy praise. Criticism is usually hard for most people to give, and certainly harder to give to people we care about. But effective interpersonal communication depends on tactful and constructive criticism when it is warranted.

3. *Be critical without being cynical.* Constantly offering compliments and praise will begin to ring hollow after a while, especially when the receiver of the messages knows that they are unwarranted. Even young children know when parents are giving praise when it is not deserved ("You're just saying that because you're my dad."). So as we mentioned above, we believe that there are times to be critical—identifying ways in which a person's performance is not satisfactory or at least not as good as it could be. But the criticism should be constructive and tactful. If criticism is not constructive and tactful, it is cynicism. Being tactful and constructive improves the feedback in two ways. First, tactful and constructive feedback has a positive tone, even if the content is negative. Second, tactful and constructive feedback offers recommendations for improvement. For example, telling a fellow student that her paper is poor will be better received if you also offer recommendations on how to make it better. Finally, highlighting the positive aspects of others' work will motivate and inspire them to continue working on their project.

Respect for Diversity

There are at least two reasons why having respect for diversity is important. The first, put simply, is that it is the right thing to do. Treating all persons with dignity and respect is vital to being an educated person. Reasonable people can disagree about political or sociological matters related to race and ethnicity, but no one can deny that equality and respect should be embraced by all educated people.

Respecting diversity because it is the right thing to do is sufficient enough reason to motivate us. But understanding and respecting diversity also is related to other positive cognitive activities. Researcher Mary Inman (2005) discovered that there is a positive correlation between those who are sensitive to concerns about racism and those who are able to see multiple causes of other people's behavior. Specifically, she found that college students who were better able to recognize instances of racial insensitivity (i.e., more often recognized "subtle racism") had greater **attributional complexity**—a preference for complex reasoning, problem solving, and analyzing multiple causes of events or behaviors—than those who were not racially sensitive.

Effective relationships also depend on effective use of language. The words we use affect people's reaction to us. One component of this is using *culturally sensitive language*. We believe strongly that educated people have a responsibility to use spoken and written language that is not hurtful and that does not denigrate a particular group of people. It is rare that people would use public language that intentionally or maliciously harms others. However, sometimes our language is unintentionally hurtful, and if we knew that it was hurtful we wouldn't have used it. In this section we list some components of culturally sensitive language. It is important to remember that guidelines for language usage change over time, so what we recommend here may not be appropriate 10 years from now. It is very important for educated people to be aware of changes in how groups of people prefer to be described. Still, the fact that such descriptions change over time does not make it unimportant to learn. Rather, it makes it more important for you as an informed citizen to stay current as you seek to use bias-free language in speaking and writing. (For further information, please consult the *Publication Manual of the American Psychological Association*, 2001.)

1. *Use labels carefully.* While labels are sometimes important as descriptors, be careful not to use them in a way that is hurtful to others. When describing people, it is important to use people-first language. Some of these differences are subtle but important. For example, when referring to senior citizens who suffer from dementia, "persons with dementia" should be used over "demented people." If the labels are important in understanding what you are describing, then use them. If they are not relevant, such labels are probably not helpful. When referring to groups, take care to use proper designations. For example, referring to the racial category of a group or person should be used only if it is relevant to the conversation. Referring to a professor by saying "I have a Black psychology professor" should be used only if that professor's race is salient to your discussion. That is, avoid using a racial designation when the person's race is not relevant to what you are saying. For example, saying "I met a nice Latino man today" is using a racial category when it is not necessary. It also suggests that you are surprised by this person's niceness, which makes it an implicitly prejudicial comment.

2. *Remember your own bias.* Remember that your own perspective brings with it certain ideas that you probably take for granted. For example, referring to certain religious practices or symbols as "strange" or "exotic" is probably offensive to those for whom these practices are standard. Referring to a certain group's clothing as a "costume" can be seen as offensive; using a term like *clothing* or *outfit* is preferable. (After all, do you wake up in the morning and put on an outfit or a costume?) Also be sure to avoid referring to the group to which you belong or the majority group as the standard. For example, describing the differences between "gay men" and "normal men" is offensive; comparing "gay men" to "heterosexual men" is preferred.

3. *Gender.* In most public discourse and written prose, the terms *men* and *women* are preferred to *gentlemen* and *ladies*. It is especially inappropriate to refer to adults (age 18 and over) as "boys" and "girls." The terms *male* and *female* are used to refer to one's biological designation (as in scientific writing), but they are not often used in everyday language. Make sure you use parallel terms. Saying "husband and wife" or "man and woman" is appropriate, but the phrase "man and wife" does not treat each person equally. Also avoid using the male pronoun to refer to all people: *firefighter* is preferable to *fireman* and *police officer* is preferable to *policeman*.

4. *Race and ethnicity.* Use as much specificity in referring to subgroups of people as you need to. Words that describe groups change over time. Currently more people use *Latino* or *Latin American* than *Hispanic* to refer to people who come from one of the 17 Latin American countries, although both are appropriate. Since the designation of "Latin American" is more general than describing someone's country of origin, using a more specific descriptor is

appropriate (e.g., *Guatemalan*). Both *Black* and *African American* are appropriate. The term *people of color* or *person of color* is a suitable term to describe someone with non-White ancestry. *White* and *Caucasian* are general terms; *European American* is more specific, but both are appropriate.

Some people may be cynical of the above discussion, thinking such statements are more about politics than student learning. We disagree. We think these issues are important to being an educated person. We want to impress upon you that labels have power, and that to use them accurately reflects a respect for the person to whom you are speaking or referring. It also demonstrates a more advanced understanding of all of the ways in which people differ. Finally, the proper use of language bears the mark of a thoughtful and sensitive person.

CHAPTER SUMMARY

The main lesson we hope you learn from this chapter is that being successful in college involves more than studying well and being motivated. There are other life skills that will affect your well-being and your performance. Perhaps in this chapter more than others, we have exposed you to facets of life that, if successfully lived out, will bring success and happiness and flourishing well beyond college. For long after the last exam is taken, a full and meaningful life awaits you.

Improving Your Attention and Memory

Chapter Goals

This chapter will help you:

- Improve your attention
- Hold information in working memory more effectively
- Use strategies for transferring information to long-term memory
- Use strategies for pulling information out of long-term memory

Key Terms

deep processing	recognition memory
encoding	schema
long-term memory	secondary task
metacognition	selective attention
mnemonics	sensory memory
primary task	shallow processing
prior knowledge	surveillance
recall memory	working memory

CHAPTER 6

Worry about things you can control. Don't worry about things you can't control. Sometimes uncontrollable factors work in your favor and sometimes they do not. One thing you can control is how you study. As you will learn in this chapter and the next, choosing how to study is very much within your control. Some students choose poor study environments where it is difficult for them to concentrate (see Chapter 4), and choose learning strategies that result in only superficial understanding. Other students choose good study environments where it is easier to concentrate and learning strategies that result in high-level understanding of course material.

The focus of this chapter is improving your attention and memory. We will provide tips to improve these skills that will make a difference in your academic performance, however fortunate or unfortunate your current situation may be. The items in Activity 6.1 will also help you assess your current levels of attention and memory.

ACTIVITY 6.1 *Assessing Your Attention and Memory*

Circle the statements that best describe your approach to college. Add the corresponding points for all items.

1. Rote memorization is my most preferred way of learning material.
   - (4) never or almost never
   - (3) rarely
   - (2) frequently
   - (1) always or almost always

2. When I have trouble remembering something, I think of things that are related to what I'm asked to remember.
   - (1) never or almost never
   - (2) rarely
   - (3) frequently
   - (4) always or almost always

3. I listen to lyrical music when I study.
   - (4) never or almost never
   - (3) rarely
   - (2) frequently
   - (1) always or almost always

4. I am easily distracted.
   - (4) never or almost never
   - (3) rarely
   - (2) frequently
   - (1) always or almost always

5. I usually study in a noisy place.
   - (4) never or almost never
   - (3) rarely
   - (2) frequently
   - (1) always or almost always

SCORING:

The following categories give a rough indication of your memory strategies:

16 and above: You probably have good memory strategies, attention, and selection of study environment. This chapter can serve as a helpful review of important memory skills.

11–15: You probably have moderately good memory strategies. However, you may need to revisit some of your strategies. This chapter will help you identify some ways you can improve your memory.

10 and below: This chapter is definitely for you. It will help you focus on some important memory strategies. We encourage you to read this chapter carefully and to use the suggestions we offer.

In this chapter we will introduce you to the building blocks of human thinking. First, to learn something, you must perceive it and pay attention to it. Then you must learn it, which means submitting the information to your mind in a way you can understand it. Then you must remember it, which means pulling up the information you previously learned at the particular time you need it. This is an extraordinarily complex process, and in some ways it's amazing that humans can do it at all. But, in fact, people generally learn and remember things with great ease and accuracy. What's more, the ability to learn and remember new material can be improved with practice. In this chapter we give an overview of how people process information, and discuss ways in which this information-processing system can be improved. We hope that by the end of this chapter, you will be familiar with ways you can improve your memory.

THE HUMAN MIND AS A PROCESSOR OF INFORMATION

© EuToch – FOTOLIA

Human beings are processors of information. Specifically, knowledge is out there in the world, and it's your job as a student to take the relevant knowledge and to make sense of it. Learning something new involves taking the information and putting it into your memory. When the time comes to use that information, you must be able to retrieve the information from your memory. Learning and remembering something involves several steps. Let's start at the beginning. You cannot learn something unless you notice it and pay attention to it. Paying attention to new information is the first step in the learning process. The next section takes a close look at how you perceive and pay attention to the many things around you.

AN OVERVIEW OF THE HUMAN MEMORY SYSTEM

To understand this discussion of learning and memory, it may help you to think of a computer. Psychologists have adopted the computer as a metaphor for how people learn new things and remember old things. The computer analogy to learning new material (psychologists call this **encoding**) is "saving" something on a computer. If you have typed some material on the screen, to have that information available later on, you must place it in the computer memory. Saving a document on a computer allows you to return to it later and use the document again. Likewise, when you are learning new information from a college course, you must commit that information to memory to be able to use it later on.

The computer analogy to remembering previously learned "saved" material is "retrieving" or "opening" a document. This allows you to access information that was stored in the computer memory (such as on the hard drive or on a zip disk) earlier. Likewise, when you take a test, you are retrieving knowledge you wrote to your memory earlier. Figure 6.1 shows the sequence of steps involved in learning and remembering. It provides a good overview of how this chapter is organized. We now turn to a specific discussion of learning; then we will discuss memory.

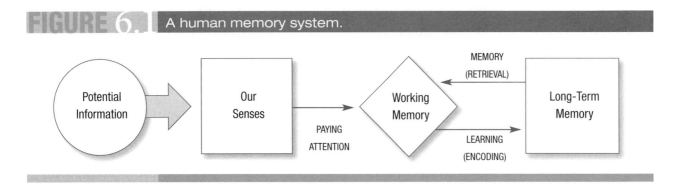

FIGURE 6.   A human memory system.

PAYING ATTENTION

To learn something, you must first have it presented to you. In college, this usually takes the form of listening to a lecture or reading a textbook. People can experience events in the world in many ways—through sight, hearing, touching, smelling, or tasting. Anytime you are awake and conscious, you are taking material from the outside world and making sense of it (processing it). The first step in the processing of information is paying attention to it.

As you read this page, there are countless stimuli in your environment that could potentially grab your attention. In addition to the words on this page, you may also hear a conversation down the hall, hear the buzz of an overhead light, and feel the seat of your chair pressing against your back. If you were constantly to notice all of these events in your environment, you would likely not get anything accomplished. There are too many stimuli in your environment to pay attention to at once, and you wouldn't be able to concentrate. So, with all of these stimuli out there, how do we manage to concentrate on anything? We do so by attending to some stimuli and blocking out others.

What does this mean for you? As a student, you are constantly bombarded with stimuli from the outside world. You could choose to pay attention to any of these. Paying attention to anything has a cost involved. One way to think about this is that you have only so much "attention money" to spend. You have only so much real money to buy things with, and once it is gone, you can't buy anything more. Likewise, once the attention money is gone, you cannot pay attention any longer. You choose the things from the outside world you will buy with your attention. Paying attention to one thing means you may not be able to pay attention to something else. Attention involves choices.

When you sit in class, you probably (we hope) listen to the professor's lecture. But you could also be paying attention to the activity going on in the seats next to you. You could also be thinking about weekend activities (college students have been known to think about them at times!). You might hear the dull roar of an air conditioner or the shuffling of bodies in their chairs. As you know, some of these inputs are important for your learning, some are not. The goal is to pay attention to the important inputs and to block out the unimportant ones.

Attention as a Pie

It may be helpful to think of attention as a pie, as shown in Figure 6.2. First, a pie is limited in size; it is not infinite. Likewise, your attentional capacity is only a limited size. Second, a pie can be cut into several pieces. Likewise, your

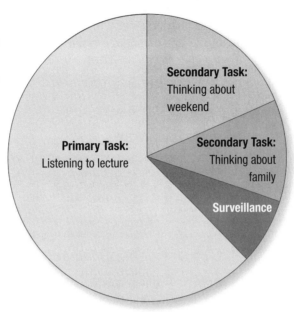

Attention as a pie.   FIGURE 6.2

When we spend our attentional resources on one thing, it reduces our ability to attend to others.

Primary Task: Listening to lecture

Secondary Task: Thinking about weekend

Secondary Task: Thinking about family

Surveillance

attention can also be cut into several pieces. While you are sitting in a lecture, your main attentional focus should be on understanding the content of the lecture. The task to which you devote most of your attention is called the **primary task.** Often other activities or thoughts may demand your attention. Perhaps you are still thinking about a telephone conversation you had with your parents before you came to class. These other tasks to which you also devote attention are called **secondary tasks.** When people tell you that they have "other things on their mind," it probably means that some secondary task is taking up a lot of attentional capacity. Another piece of the pie is called **surveillance.** This refers simply to being consciously aware of things around you: hearing background noises, feeling the back of your seat, and so forth. When you are studying, reading, or listening to lectures, the more you can reduce the distractions of other events vying for your attention, the more attention you can devote to your primary task.

Divided Attention and Selective Attention

Has anyone ever said to you, "I need your undivided attention"? This means that the person wants you to concentrate only on what she is doing or saying, and to ignore other information. As we noted above, attention is divided into tasks. The more your attention is distributed (divided) over many tasks, the harder it is for you to pay attention to any one. Try Activity 6.2 to see the difficulty of divided attention.

As Activity 6.2 illustrates, it is very hard for most people to do two tasks at once, especially if one of them is moderately difficult. The more difficult the tasks are, the more difficult they will be to perform simultaneously. College students are not always aware of this. Many of them read while their stereos are on, they

ACTIVITY 6.2 *An Attention Divided*

Try to complete the task described below. You will need a pencil and paper. Have a friend time you and record the number of words you write down in the first minute and compare it to the number of words you write down in the second minute.

What You Need: Pick a song to which you know almost all of the lyrics.

First Minute: For one minute, simply write down the words to this song.

Second Minute: Continue to write down the words to this song, but now, simultaneously, start saying (out loud) the Pledge of Allegiance (or some other speech, creed, poem, or story that you know well).

Words written per minute

First minute _____

Second minute _____

You probably noticed a decline in the words per minute written down in the second minute. This happened because the more you divide up your attentional pie, the harder it is to do any one task. Just as this task was hard for you, so will it be hard for you to read a book while listening to music, or do math problems in a noisy dorm room. The concept of divided attention has implications for several of the tips we suggest for improving your attention.

---

may try to talk on the phone while doing math problems, or they may allow conversations to go on in their dorm rooms when they are trying to study for an exam. In each of these cases, their attention is divided. The problem with dividing attention like this is that when you have to attend to multiple stimuli, you will not be able to process the information as well. You might claim that you can block out irrelevant stimuli, so a stereo or conversation won't affect you. Being able to block out distracting stimuli is referred to as **selective attention**. Some people are probably better at blocking out than others, but it still takes attentional energy to do so. The best advice, which we will reiterate later, is to minimize distractions. If you do choose to study with music on, we encourage you to consider music without lyrics. Attending to the lyrics of songs will divide your attention and reduce your ability to concentrate.

STRATEGY SUGGESTION

Read and study in a quiet environment (see Chapter 4 as well).

Automatized: Doing Without Thinking

Throughout much of this book we emphasize the concept of **metacognition**, which is mentioned in Chapter 1 as well as in later chapters. Metacognition is a thoughtful, reflective approach to learning. The premise of this book is that you can improve your learning by being thoughtful and reflective. However, in one case it doesn't necessarily pay to be reflective and metacognitive. In the case of improving your attention, metacognition may slow you down unnecessarily. Instead, what you should strive for is to automatize your behavior.

Making your behaviors **automatized** means that the behavior is so familiar that you can do it without thinking. (We discussed this in the previous chapter as well.) Think about what it was like to learn one-variable algebra. For many people, the cognitive tasks involved in algebra are quite difficult to master. Chances are you spent a good deal of time on problems such as $2x + 5 = 8$. If you have a strong math background, you probably don't struggle with such problems anymore. You can solve them, in a sense, without thinking. Such a task has become automatic for you.

Why is this important? It's important because now that you have automatized this task, you don't have to devote as much attention to it, and thus you can devote more of your attention to other cognitive activities. In mathematics, for example, if you have automatized one-variable algebra, you can devote attention to a higher level of mathematics. Since algebra is required for so many higher order mathematics topics, the students who will do the best in higher order math are the ones who have automatized the lower order skills. So, when you are learning calculus, it helps to have automatized algebra so that you can spend more time on learning derivatives and integrals. If you have to devote lots of attentional resources to the algebra portion of calculus, learning calculus is likely to be a most unpleasant experience.

Automatizing certain tasks will be very useful to you in your learning. Consider how often, as a student, you engage in the activity of reading. Think about all of the different cognitive tasks involved in reading:

1. Pronouncing/decipering the words
2. Understanding what the individual words mean
3. Understanding what the sentences mean
4. Understanding the main themes of the story
5. Identifying how this reading relates to other material

All of these tasks could require a lot of attentional resources. Here's how you can make the task easier for yourself: work to automatize the lower-level activities such as deciphering and comprehending the words and sentences so that you will have to pay less attention to them. This will allow you to pay more attention to higher level activities such as comprehending main themes and identifying how the reading relates to other course material.

> **STRATEGY SUGGESTION**
>
> *Work to automatize as many of your cognitive skills as you can.*

If you follow this strategy suggestion, greater attentional capacity will become available to you. You will be free to use this additional attentional capacity in ways that will make your learning richer and more meaningful.

Right now you may be saying, "I'm a slow reader. I always have been a slow reader. How can I survive in college if I have to devote so much of my attentional capacity to reading?" Slow reading is a cause for concern. But the good news is that you can improve your reading speed. We will discuss ways you can do this in Chapter 9. If you're a slow reader now, we hope you won't be by the end of this book.

Psychologists have shown that people's attentional power in general can be improved with practice. This is true not only of reading, but also of other cognitive activities, such as mathematics and other kinds of problem solving. Imagine yourself as a participant in an experiment by Spelke, Hirst, and Neisser (1976). They used only two volunteer participants—one graduate student and one undergraduate student—over an extended period of time. The two main cognitive activities they had the students do were (a) read short stories and (b) write down words that were dictated to them. The trick was, they had to do these tasks at the same time, just as you had to do in Activity 6.2. The main result from this study was that both students improved in their ability to read the short stories while writing down the dictated words. For example, in the first week's experimental sessions, the undergraduate student had an average of 75% comprehension of the short stories and the graduate student had an average of 83% comprehension. By the seventh week, the undergraduate student was averaging 86% comprehension and the graduate student was averaging 99% comprehension! Both students also improved their reading speed. They not only got smarter at reading, they also got faster.

How did the students manage to make such dramatic improvements? As time went on, the students were able to automatize these tasks and to perform both of them simultaneously without overloading their attention systems.

As you can imagine, we don't recommend that you do your textbook reading at the same time that your roommate has you take dictation. The major lesson to be learned from this study is that even when attentional capacity is pushed to its limits by cognitive distractions, you can improve your ability to perform difficult cognitive tasks by automatizing as many of them as you can. If you automatize tasks such as reading and simple arithmetic, you can give yourself more attentional energy and thereby improve your learning. This is why reading while listening to music is not a good idea. The attention you can pay to reading goes down. If the text is difficult, this is even worse because you need more resources.

How do you automatize such tasks as reading? We have only one simple answer: practice. You become a better reader by reading; you become better at math by doing math problems. Be patient. Automatization does not happen overnight. Just as learning to serve a tennis ball or play a guitar takes hundreds of hours of practice, so does automatization. Over time, you will notice improvement, just as you do in athletics or music. And as time goes on, you will begin to reap the rewards of the hours of work you have invested. Below, we give six strategies for improving your attention.

Tips for Improving Your Attention

Because your attentional capacity is limited, it makes sense to use the attentional resources you have as effectively as possible. We offer several suggestions below and summarize them in Figure 6.3.

1. *Practice.* It may sound silly, but the more you study, the better you will become at it, *if you do it right.* The more you concentrate and pay careful attention, the easier it will become for you. Studying with the proper strategies

is important. Just like any habit, a bad habit can also become ingrained. Practice doesn't make perfect. Practice makes permanent. Be sure to do it right.

2. *Reduce competition from secondary tasks.* When you are thinking about some other activity or problem, your studying will be hindered if you "bring it with you" to the study table. The best strategy is to address the problem or complete the activity before you study. Often this is not entirely possible. With personal problems, for example, they are not always easily or quickly resolved. However, you can still work to focus yourself on the task at hand. You may have heard athletic coaches tell their players to "stay focused." For example, a college tennis player may look out at the crowd or watch his teammate on the next court. This divides the athlete's attention and detracts from athletic performance. In a similar way, talking to friends, worrying about another course, or even being hungry (hunger can be a very powerful secondary task!) will take away from your focus and hurt your studying.

3. *Don't listen to music.* Many of you listen to music while you study. And some of you will still get along fine in college. Based on what we said about attention, you can probably see why listening to music will likely hinder your performance. At the very least, it's not likely to improve it, even though some students claim they can't study without the stereo on. As a general rule, we recommend you not listen to your iPod during study times. If you choose to anyway, we have a couple of suggestions. First, listening to instrumental music (music without lyrics) would be best. This is because if words are present, you are likely to devote attention to comprehending them. This is a secondary task that can take up a lot of capacity that should be used for concentrating on studying. Second, limit yourself to listening to music while doing tasks that require somewhat less capacity. Activities such as copying notes or assignments, doing problem sets that are fairly easy for you, or making posters or other materials are more compatible with listening to music. Attention-demanding activities such as reading difficult material or studying for a test should be done without any musical distraction.

© Marc Dietrich – FOTOLIA

4. *Find a good study environment (see also Chapter 4).* The basic message is this: Find a study environment in which you can maximize the attention you pay to your primary task (learning) and minimize the attention you pay to secondary tasks. You are the best judge of where you study best. The general rule is the quieter the better. Places with lots of people usually have lots of noise. The more attention you pay to the noise, the less you pay to studying. This means that dormitory rooms are not always the best place, particularly in the evening. Even libraries, places known for optimal studying, can be loud or distracting. In the evenings when many people congregate, the noise can sometimes rise to a frustrating level. However, large libraries usually have lots of uncharted territory. By exploring the nooks and crannies of your library, you may find a quiet, hidden place where people seldom go.

College students who live at home may face different challenges when it comes to focusing attention. In high school you may not have had to concentrate as hard on your studies as you do now. The usual distractions, such as the family television, younger siblings, and your responsibilities around the house, may make it difficult for you to pay attention to your learning. The best advice we can give to people in this situation is to set aside definite periods of time for you to be a student. This means that during these times, you should eliminate all distractions around you. If it means leaving for a few hours every evening or staying at school after your last class in the afternoon, do it. If you can separate the time you spend studying from the time you spend with your family, you will increase the quality of both.

5. *Take breaks when your attention wanders.* No one can maintain the high degree of concentration needed for successful learning forever. Everybody needs to take breaks, and how long a person can go without taking a break depends on the individual. When you feel your concentration drifting, walk away. Do something else. Different activities will work for different people. You must figure out what the most effective break-time activities will be for you. Brisk walks and short naps are popular diversions that usually work. Other popular diversions for college students—long e-mail or IM sessions, snacks with high sugar content, and watching TV for a long time—are things you may wish to do, but we don't recommend that you do them as study breaks. IM tends to drag on because there is always someone to message, and sugary snacks can make you lethargic. And TV? Television can tire your eyes and make you lethargic, with even less energy than you had before the break. Furthermore, you may have trouble walking away once you start watching. Most important: *Do not consume alcohol on a study break.* Alcohol, a depressant, slows the rate of activity of your central nervous system (i.e., your brain) and will make studying more difficult. Whatever you do, pick something that will bring you back to your learning refreshed and able to pay attention.

Some students just take breaks whenever they feel they need one. Another strategy is to schedule breaks for yourself as rewards for prolonged concentration. For example, you can promise yourself to take a 15-minute break if you do quality work for 45 minutes. Many students report such scheduling to be effective.

6. *Stay rested and healthy.* It's a lot easier to pay attention if you have had enough sleep. Being tired severely limits your attentional capacity. We understand the occasional necessity of staying up late to finish pressing assignments. With advanced planning, however, you avoid many of these last-minute, late-night preparations. Stay rested. It will pay immense dividends over the long haul of an entire semester.

It's also a lot easier to pay attention if you are not sick. Illness is physically draining, and it drains valuable attentional resources that you need for learning. Rest and health go hand in hand. Getting enough rest decreases the probability that you will get sick. You can't control whether your roommate gets sick or some other issues related to health. But you can control how much you rest. We realize that sometimes you may feel that college forces you to choose between success and sleep—if you sleep, you don't have time to study, and if you study, you have to forsake sleep. But that's a false choice. Truth is, the rested person is the best learner.

We remind you of a few important tips discussed in Chapter 5. Engage in behaviors that will help you avoid illness. Consider a few: (a) don't smoke—smokers get sick more often than nonsmokers do, (b) minimize alcohol intake—excessive drinking often occurs at the expense of sleep (i.e., staying out late instead of sleeping), and (c) exercise—those who exercise have better physical and mental health. The importance of personal health cannot be overstated (see Chapter 5).

1. *Practice.*

   You will get better at paying attention the more often you pay attention. Practice keeping your mind focused on your schoolwork.

2. *Reduce competition from secondary tasks.*

   To study well you must have a clear head. Leave all other concerns (either deal with them first or decide to handle them later) when you tackle academic tasks.

3. *Don't listen to music.*

   One of the biggest myths on college campuses is the belief that music facilitates learning. With the possible exception of classical music, this is not so. Music is a distraction that should be avoided.

4. *Find a good study environment.*

   A quiet, comfortable room with minimal distractions is the best.

5. *Take breaks when your attention wanders.*

   Short rests will refresh you. A short nap or brisk exercise will help recharge your attentional battery.

6. *Stay rested and healthy.*

   Get enough sleep, do things that will reduce the chance of illness, and engage in healthy life habits.

LEARNING: BRINGING IN INFORMATION

Learning something involves several steps. We just described the first step—you must pay attention to what you want to learn. In this section, we describe the steps involved in bringing information into your memory so that you can use it later. You will get an overview of how psychologists understand learning and memory, and see the parts of the learning and memory process. We start with what your mind does with information as soon as you experience it—what psychologists call **sensory memory**.

Sensory Memory

Imagine sitting in a political science class listening to a professor lecture on the branches of government. You hear what is said about the branches of government, but when you drop your head to write it down, you can't remember what she said. This has probably happened to you before. This phenomenon illustrates what underlies sensory memory—information that is held for a very brief period of time. Sensory memory stores information from the outside world very briefly—about 2–3 seconds for spoken material. So it is important to be metacognitively aware if something did not enter sensory memory. If that happens, and it happens to everyone, make sure you speak to a classmate or the professor to review the material that slipped by your sensory memory. Information must first go into sensory memory or it won't be learned. We now look at the next step on the road to learning, something called **working memory**.

Working Memory

Ask a friend from another area code for his cell-phone number. After he repeats the whole number, try to dial without it being repeated. Without writing it down, go to the phone and dial the number. Did you remember all 10 digits? This activity illustrates the memory system known as working memory.

Working memory is the next step in the learning and memory process. It has two important features. First, it stores only a limited amount of information; working memory has limited capacity. A second important feature to remember about working memory is that it stores this limited amount of information for only a limited period of time; it has limited duration. So working memory can hold a little bit for a short time.

In one of the most well-known articles on learning, psychologist George Miller (1956) argued that humans can understand between five and nine pieces of information. (He said, "Seven, plus or minus two.")

Not only does working memory have limited capacity, it's also the case that information cannot stay in working memory forever. If you don't transfer the information from working memory to **long-term memory**—the final repository of learned information—you will forget it. Just like the phone number that you will have to look up again, you won't remember things in working memory forever. Psychologists interested in learning and memory generally agree that information can stay in working memory for approximately 30 seconds before it is either (a) transferred to long-term memory or (b) forgotten.

Since a 10-digit phone number exceeds "seven, plus or minus two," how are we able to remember 10-digit phone numbers? (A contact list, of course!) We do this by putting individual digits into pieces or chunks. For example, you will likely combine the three numbers of the area code into one chunk (734). You might then chunk the three numbers of the prefix together (764), and then chunk the last four digits into two groups of two (4–2–5–3 becomes 42, 53). As you can see, even though there are 10 numbers to remember, the number of chunks is within the range of seven plus or minus two. Activity 6.3 gives another example of grouping.

STRATEGY SUGGESTION

When learning new material, break the information into pieces that make sense to you.

Long-Term Memory: The Mind's Permanent Warehouse

Long-term memory holds information that you will need to retrieve later. Unlike working memory, which has a limited capacity and holds information for a limited period of time, long-term memory (in theory) can hold an infinite amount of information and can hold it for your entire lifetime.

A discussion of long-term memory reminds us of a cartoon showing a student in a classroom who raises his hand to say, "Sorry, teacher, I can't learn any more. My brain is full!" Actually, the opposite is true. Human beings can store a limitless amount of information, so our brains will never get full. As we will learn later in this chapter, the more you know, the easier it is to learn. Also, there appears to be no limit to the amount of time that information will stay in long-term memory.

Grouping Information and the Limits
of Short-TermMemory

Read the numbers listed below aloud to one friend under Condition 1 and to another friend under Condition 2, then compare their performance.

Condition 1: With 1-second spacing between the digits, read each of the following digits to a friend (read across, one at a time):

1	7	7	6	1	9
4	5	1	8	1	2
1	9	9	4	1	4
9	2	1	8	6	5

Wait 10 seconds, then ask the person to recall as many digits as possible (in order).

Number of digits correctly recalled: _____ Percentage: _____/24 = _____% of digits.

Condition 2: Now read the digits to a friend as they appear below:

1776   1945   1812   1994   1492   1865

Wait 10 seconds, then ask the person to recall as many digits as possible (in order).

Number of dates correctly recalled: (_____ x 4)/24 = _____% of digits.

Invariably, people remember a greater percentage of digits in Condition 2. The reason is simple: Our working memory capacity is exceeded in Condition 1. However, when the 24 unrelated digits are combined into familiar pieces, they become 6 well-known, easy-to-remember chunks. The implication for learning is this: We can handle only so much information at a time, and the more we can put knowledge together into meaningful pieces, the more we will remember.

For example, research studies have found that people can recognize faces from their high school yearbook decades after graduating (Bahrick, Bahrick, & Wittlinger, 1975). Although you won't remember everything that ever happens in your life, you still will keep some very old memories far into your elderly years. You might have forgotten what you had for lunch last Saturday, but you may remember who your date to the senior prom was or what your street address was when you were growing up, decades later. As we will see in this chapter and throughout this book, if you learn something well enough and if it's important to you, your memory can be very powerful.

Long-term memory has an organization and a structure—a "look" to it. Psychologists usually refer to this look as a **schema**—the way in which knowledge is organized in memory. Learners build schemas in their memory as they study. It is important for schemas to be well developed and make sense to the learner. The better ordered your schemas are, the more likely it is that you will remember the material when you need it. Figure 6.4 shows a schema for the material in this chapter. In the next section, we will show you ways to build organized schemas. The learning strategies we suggest will help you build rich and orderly knowledge schemas.

FIGURE 6.4   A schema of the human memory system.

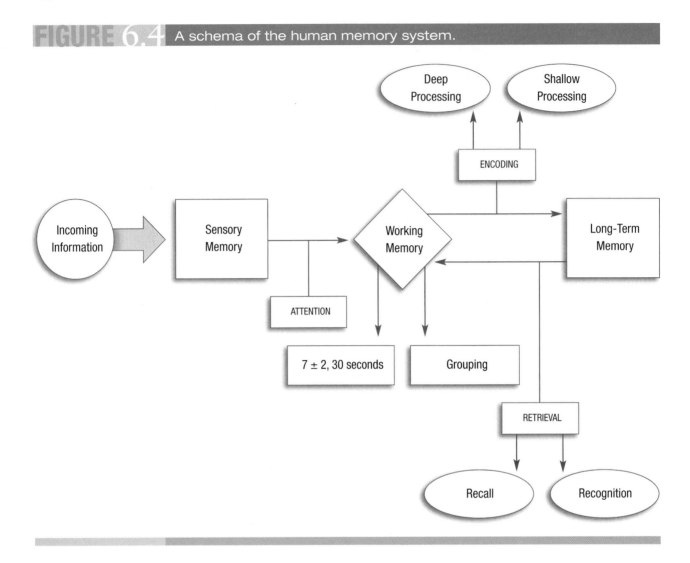

Putting Information into Long-Term Memory

As we have seen, information cannot stay in working memory very long. It must be either (a) transferred to long-term memory or (b) forgotten. In this section, we describe the process by which information is transferred from working memory to long-term memory. Psychologists have a fancy word for this—*encoding*—but most people just call it learning.

Encoding can take place in two ways. We can encode information using **shallow processing** or **deep processing.** When you encode information using shallow processing, you are paying minimal attention to what you are learning. For example, suppose you are studying brain anatomy in your psychology class. An example of shallow processing of this material would be simply to memorize the names for the different parts of the brain. For example, if you were learning the four lobes of the brain, you would simply repeat to yourself "frontal, parietal, occipital, temporal" over and over. This activity will likely help you remember the names of the four lobes, but it will do very little for helping you to remember more complex and meaningful information about brain anatomy.

An example of deep processing of this material would be to learn the different parts of the brain, identify any specific activities that are associated with those parts, and learn how the different parts of the brain interact and are related to each other. Listen to how a student who is engaging in deep processing might study this material: "Occipital, that's where vision first gets processed. It comes from the optic nerve to the back of the brain—that's where the occipital lobe is located. This is where the visual image is processed. Then the visual information gets sent to the frontal cortex through a visual relay center in the midbrain. The frontal cortex is responsible for higher level visual activity like recognizing what an object is. A lot of the frontal cortex is called association cortex, because it integrates information from various parts of the brain. That means that it associates information of various types. A lot of complex activities are performed in the frontal cortex. Things like planning, problem solving, and reasoning."

As you can probably guess, you are more likely to remember something when you use deep processing than when you use shallow processing. Now we want you to try an example of deep processing and shallow processing. In Activity 6.4, we give two lists of 10 nouns. Study each list for roughly the same amount of time, then close your book and test yourself on the second list.

Deep processing is an umbrella term used to refer to a variety of high-level cognitive strategies that lead to a sophisticated understanding of material. In Chapter 7, we look at deep processing under a microscope and explore several strategies that are considered deep processing.

Shallow and Deep Processing

This exercise illustrates the benefits of deep processing. Study each list for 2 minutes, according to the following guidelines.

Shallow Processing: List 1

For the list on the left-hand side, simply try to memorize the list of words by repeating the information several times to yourself. In other words, engage in shallow processing. After 2 minutes, close your book, wait 5 minutes (don't think about the words), then test yourself. Write down as many words as you can remember.

Deep Processing: List 2

For the list on the right-hand side, we want you to engage in deep processing. For example, think of a definition of the word. Imagine a place where you find this object. Think of features of the object or think of other objects that might be associated with the thing you are trying to remember. After 2 minutes, close your book, wait 5 minutes without thinking about the list, then write down as many words as you can.

List 1: Shallow Processing	List 2: Deep Processing
Salmon	Bookcase
Lightbulb	Can opener
Coffee	Acorn
Hubcap	Wicket
Scooter	Fishing pole
Flashlight	Lamp shade
Handkerchief	Shingle
Underwear	Mailbox
Phone book	Blanket
Swing set	Computer

(continued)

Number Recalled (List 1): _____   Number Recalled (List 2): _____

You will remember more from deep processing because you have created a richer, more elaborate memory. Maybe you thought of a very vivid image of a word, or maybe a memorable scene involving the object. Whatever the case, deep processing results in more detailed thinking about the object, and therefore greater recall. This principle is also true for items that are more complex than just a list of words. In fact, with complex material, it is probably even more important to go beyond simply memorizing the material to gaining a sophisticated understanding of the concepts.

Deep processing is even more helpful when the material you are learning is more complex than a simple word list. Think about it: The things you learn in college are complex; the concepts have multiple ideas attached to them, and the ideas are interrelated. If the only thing a professor asks you to do is to memorize a list of terms and their definitions, then shallow processing may be a sufficient strategy. However, college is rarely this easy or straightforward. More than likely, the professor will require you to go beyond simply knowing definitions. In these cases, deep processing becomes essential.

STRATEGY SUGGESTION

As course material becomes more complex, make an effort to use more deep processing.

Along with its greater benefits, deep processing has a greater cost associated with it. Namely, it takes more time and effort to do deep processing than it does to do shallow processing. In fact, many of the techniques we describe in this book have the same kind of cost–benefit element. In general, higher quality learning requires more effort and commitment on your part. Processing information at a shallow, superficial level may not require a lot of work, and processing information at a deep level takes more effort. Think of the time you spend in deep processing as an investment. When you put in the necessary effort, your investment will be rewarded with handsome dividends come test time. The dividends will be in the form of a thorough understanding of the material. And good grades will follow.

Now that you've seen how we bring information into memory, the next logical question is, How do we get information out? As you will see, there is a strong link between how well you originally put information in and how well you will be able to pull it out.

GETTING INFORMATION OUT OF LONG-TERM MEMORY

Let's return to our computer metaphor. Earlier, we said that encoding information in long-term memory is like saving information on a computer disk. Similarly, getting information out of long-term memory, commonly referred to as remembering, is a lot like bringing information back from your flash drive. However, our ability to remember information is not as accurate as the computer's ability to bring information back from a flash drive. Instead, the ability to remember information depends a lot on how well you learned it originally. A computer will "remember" a paper you wrote exactly as you last saved it. Human memory is not that accurate. You usually won't be able to remember things verbatim. Still, your memory can be quite accurate. Let's explore different ways you can remember old information.

Retrieval: How Does Information Get out of Long-Term Memory?

People can remember in two basic ways. One is called **recognition memory**, and the other is called **recall memory**.

Recognition. Recognition memory is identifying the concept you are trying to remember when you are given a set of possibilities. If this sounds something like a multiple-choice test, you are exactly right. When your professor gives you a multiple-choice test, he is testing your recognition memory. He wants to know whether you can identify the relevant principle of fact from a list of four or five alternatives. In theory, the retrieval process for recognition memory is fairly simple (even though we all know some multiple-choice questions can be quite difficult). Recognition is just a matter of comparing the alternatives you have been given to what you have in your memory (Ross, Ryan, & Tenpenny, 1989). If you have encoded the information well to begin with, it should be easy for you to match your memory up with the correct alternative. Here we see the main principle of this section coming through: The better you learn something, the easier it will be to remember. A lot of school learning involves recognition memory. However, you need to use recall memory to succeed in school as well.

Recall. Recall memory is generating a portion of your memory on your own, without a list of alternatives. Answering the question, What is the capital of Vermont? requires recall memory. Notice how this memory process differs from the process required to answer the following question:

Which is the capital of Vermont?
   a. Dover
   b. Bennington
   c. Montpelier
   d. Wilmington

In the latter case, as we pointed out above, you need only compare the four alternatives to information you have in memory. In the former case, however, you need to search your memory for relevant information, then determine how appropriate it is (Eysenck, 1990). This process leaves a lot of room for error. For example, you might search your memory and come up with the city of Hartford or Providence. As you can see, the process of recognition is easier, because the mistakes that come from searching your memory and coming up with inappropriate responses generally will not occur.

If you know your professor is going to give multiple-choice tests, you may not have to work as hard to learn the information as you would if you were preparing for a fill-in-the-blank or essay test. One of the features of becoming a self-regulated learner is learning to recognize that different school tasks require different types of learning. Thus, if a test is going to be multiple choice, you should prepare by making sure that you can recognize terms that are given to you and recognize when they apply. If you decide to process the information deeply and strive to be able to recall the information as well, you will probably be better off. However, recall from Chapter 2 that a good student allocates time wisely. If you have one test for which you will have to know the material extremely well, and another that will be multiple choice (and by your estimation, the easier test), then you should allocate your learning (encoding) time appropriately.

The difference between recognition memory and recall memory is an important one to understand. Not all memory requirements are the same. After a bit of studying, you might be able to recognize a concept on a multiple-choice test. However, you might not be able to recall it or to write a very coherent essay about that concept. To be able to do that, you will have to spend more time encoding the material.

STRATEGY SUGGESTION

Find out from your professor whether tests in the class will require recognition or recall memory. Plan your study strategies and study time accordingly.

The Importance of Prior Knowledge

Before you read any further, try out Activity 6.5 on your friends. When psychologists John Bransford and Marcia Johnson (1972) gave students this task, they found that those who were told the passage was about washing clothes remembered significantly more of the passage than those who were not. Why is it easier when people know the passage is about washing clothes? It is easier because their **prior knowledge** about washing clothes aids their encoding and retrieval of the information. This prior knowledge helps them to organize the information when they are encoding it. That is, they already know the sequence of washing clothes, and, since this matches the sequence in the passage, it is easy to learn. Then, when it is time to recall the passage, it is easy for them to recall the sequence because they are familiar with it and it makes sense to them in the clothes-washing context. Without this prior knowledge, the information is hard to understand. The lesson to be learned is this: The more you know, the easier it is for you to remember.

ACTIVITY 6.5 *Prior Knowledge in Memory*

This activity demonstrates that the more you know, the easier it is for you to remember.

Condition 1: Read the passage in italics to a group of friends (or at least one). Wait 1 minute after you've read it. During that time, you should talk about something else. Then, ask them to write down as much as they can remember from the passage.

Condition 2: Read the same passage to a different person, but this time say the following *before* you read it: "The following passage is about washing clothes."

The procedure is quite simple. First, you arrange things into different groups. Of course, one pile may be sufficient depending on how much there is to do . . . . After the procedure is completed one arranges the materials into different groups again. They then can be put into their appropriate places. Eventually, they will be used once more and the whole cycle will then have to be repeated. However, that is part of life.
(Bransford & Johnson, 1972)

Condition 1   Condition 2

Number of Sentences Recalled (out of 7):   _____   _____

The more you know, the easier it is to learn. Think about situations in which you have encountered difficulty in your own learning. It was probably because you couldn't relate the material to things you knew. Whenever you are having trouble understanding something, put it in terms that are familiar.

This example also illustrates the importance of schemas, discussed earlier in this chapter. We already have an organized knowledge structure in our head—a schema—and when it is "activated" by the hint that the passage is about washing clothes, all of the relevant knowledge attached to that schema becomes easier to remember. Look back at Figure 6.4, which shows the schema for our memory system. If you were to have trouble remembering the concepts in that schema, being reminded of some part of the schema will help you remember the other parts of it. Prior knowledge serves to activate the relevant schema, which in turn improves memory for that schema.

Introductory classes are hard for various reasons, and one of the reasons they are hard is that you don't have much prior knowledge about the field. As you learn more, you develop a context for understanding the material, and therefore your learning becomes much easier.

STRATEGY SUGGESTION

When learning new material, put it in familiar terms.

Use Many Memory Cues

Have you ever seen an actor in a movie and recognized him from another movie but can't remember which one? For example, did you notice that the groom in *The Wedding Planner* is one of the doctors on *Grey's Anatomy*? The same thing can happen when you are taking a test, and it can be very frustrating. How can you deal with memory failures? One way is to use cues to facilitate your recall. Cues are items that are associated with the thing you are trying to recall. The more cues you can generate, the more likely it is you will be able to remember. When you are trying to remember that actor, you might try to activate cues: You try to picture him in the other movie, you try to remember what the movie was about, you try to remember other actors in the movie, and you listen carefully to his voice in hopes it will prompt your recall. The reason it is probably difficult to recognize the doctor in *Grey's Anatomy* and the groom in *The Wedding Planner* is that there are very few cues—the roles are not the same in terms of mannerisms or voice. Figure 6.5 gives strategies for unblocking failed memories by generating cues.

Based on research on human memory, we can identify four general principles that you can use to improve your memory. Figure 6.6 lists these principles. We can't guarantee that they will always improve your memory, or that all of them will be practical for all learning situations. However, the research on memory is clear: It is not a fixed ability. You can help yourself remember more, and thereby make yourself smarter. We encourage you to keep these principles in mind as you study.

FIGURE 6.5 Curing a memory block.

What can you do when you are taking a test and you have a memory block? The following techniques might be helpful.

1. *What are related concepts?*

   Try to remember concepts that are related to the one you are trying to recall. This will activate knowledge that is psychologically "near" the term you want to remember. If you can, start writing down all the concepts that you think are related. On a biology test, for example, a fill-in-the-blank question might ask, "Damage to the _____ will result in impairment of balance and motor coordination." If you can't remember, start listing items that are closely related. For example, lower brain region, diencephalon, hypothalamus, etc. Eventually, by asking yourself what each of these structures does (and determining whether one of them correctly answers the question), you may eventually end up at the correct answer, which is cerebellum. The alternatives are "near" the cerebellum, and saying these to yourself will provide good memory cues for cerebellum.

2. *Where have I seen that?*

   When you are trying to recall something from your experience, such as an actor's previous movie, try to imagine where you saw it. Was it in the theater? If so, with whom did you go? Was it at home on video? On television? Who was with you? You can do the same thing with course material. Ask yourself: Where in the text was this written? What chapter? Was there a memorable picture accompanying it? Did we learn this in lecture? What were the circumstances? These questions may provide enough cues to unleash your memory.

3. *Where was I?*

   Try to remember where you were when you read this portion of the book, or where you were sitting in lecture when it was presented. Imagining where you were when you learned material will also provide important memory cues.

FIGURE 6.6 General principles of memory improvement.

Apply these general rules for improving your memory in appropriate situations to help you remember more.

1. *Group.*

   Put pieces of information into meaningful units. Treat related material as similar pieces.

2. *Use deep processing.*

   Encode information at a deep level, not a shallow level. Don't settle for memorization. Push yourself to understand the material at a higher cognitive level. When you do so, your memories will be more durable and accurate.

3. *Use prior knowledge.*

   Take advantage of your prior knowledge to help you learn and remember. If you are having trouble remembering something, put it in terms you can understand and know a lot about. For example, if you know a lot about music, think of how the material relates to music. If you are knowledgeable about athletics, use athletics. The principle is clear: The more you know, the easier it is to learn (and remember).

4. *Use cues.*

   Use as many cues as you can from the context of what you have studied to help you remember it. Think of related material and other information that will trigger your memory. For example: Where were you when you learned this? What part of the text explained this information?

MNEMONICS: SPECIFIC TRICKS TO IMPROVE YOUR MEMORY

Memory shortcuts can help you remember certain things in very specific circumstances. These shortcuts are called **mnemonics** (pronounced "nee-mon-iks"—the first *m* is silent). Here are a few of these tricks.

First-Letter Technique

To use the first-letter technique, take the first letter of each of the items you want to remember and make a word or phrase out of them. For example, you may have learned to remember three important trigonometric formulas by the nonsense word *soh-cah-toa* (pronounced "soak-ah-toe-ah"). This helps you remember that in a right triangle, the *s*ine of an angle is equal to the *o*pposite side divided by the *h*ypotenuse (*soh*), the *c*osine is equal to the *a*djacent side divided by the *h*ypotenuse (*cah*), and the *t*angent is equal to the *o*pposite side divided by the *a*djacent side (*toa*). One of us once knew a chemistry student who remembered the common gas equation $PV = nRT$ by inventing the word *pivvnert*.

A variation of this technique is to use the first letter of each of the items of the list to make new words that form a memorable sentence. For example, another way to remember the trigonometric formulas is with the sentence "*Some Old Horse Caught Another Horse Taking Oats Away.*" You may have learned the lines of the music staff (EGBDF) with the sentence "*Every Good Boy Deserves Fudge*" or "*Every Girl's Bonnet Does Fit.*" You also might have learned the names and order of the planets in the solar system by remembering the sentence "*My Very Excited Mother Just Sat Upon Nine Pins*" (or some variant of this). These memory tricks will ensure that you can always remember certain important pieces of information, thus freeing up your cognitive capacity for other important learning and thinking activities.

Imagery

When you think of your childhood, you may have clear, vivid memories. Our most memorable experiences usually have clear visual images associated with them. In general, information that has vivid images associated with it is much easier to remember. Psychologist Mark Marschark (1985) found that when students were asked to remember random lists of sentences, the ones they best recalled were the ones with vivid images. For example, in "His size and good speed helped to improve opinions of his college's players," the reference to the person's size and good speed helped students to form a vivid picture of this person. This image made the entire sentence more memorable. An example of a low-imagery sentence is "His keen interest and tactful personality helped to improve opinions of his college's students." This sentence does not offer much to grab hold of in terms of vivid pictures. It's hard to visualize a "keen interest" or a "tactful personality."

STRATEGY SUGGESTION

When you want to remember something, try to create a vivid image of it.

Psychologists Gordon Bower and David Winzenz (1970) used a similar activity to study the effects of imagery. They asked people to remember a pair of words by thinking of an image of two objects interacting. For example, for the word pair *cigar–piano*, a person might imagine a lit cigar being smoked by the keys of a piano. (Yes, it's weird, but it's also memorable.) Participants were then given one word from the word pair and asked to recall the other word.

When participants learned the words by just repeating them over and over, they recalled an average of only 5 words out of 15 total. When participants formed images of the two objects, they remembered, on average, almost 13 words. This technique is similar to a process discussed earlier—shallow processing versus deep processing.

Imagery can be a useful tool in your school learning. For instance, you will probably have to take a foreign language in college. Imagery might be a good way to remember vocabulary words in the new language. One student who was taking Spanish had trouble remembering the Spanish word for dining room—*comedor*. She solved the problem by visualizing the Commodores (a popular musical group of the 1970s and 1980s) coming over to her apartment for dinner. After forming that image, she had little trouble remembering this new word. Activity 6.6 lists 10 pairs of words (the same words used in Activity 6.4) with which you can practice the imagery mnemonic.

ACTIVITY 6.6 *Forming an Image*

You can remember associations between words and concepts by vividly imagining them interacting.

For this activity, form an image for each of the 10 word pairs listed below. Have a friend test your memory for these pairs by reading you one of the words, then you try to recall its partner.

Salmon—Bookcase	Lightbulb—Can opener
Coffee—Acorn	Hubcap—Wicket
Scooter—Fishing pole	Flashlight—Lamp shade
Handkerchief—Shingle	Underwear—Mailbox
Phone book—Blanket	Swing set—Computer

The more imagery you can associate with words, the better you will be able to remember them. This technique, however, is limited in at least two ways. First, it works only for words, not for complicated concepts. Second, the words have to be concrete objects. How would you form an image of agreeableness? This technique (along with other mnemonics) is limited to concrete kinds of memorization.

Peg-Word Technique

The peg-word technique is a variant on imagery. It uses imagery in combination with a preset list of rhyming words to help you form associations between the rhymes and the objects that you need to remember. The list of rhymes itself is very easy to remember and requires no extra attentional capacity. Activity 6.7 allows you to try the peg-word technique.

The principle behind the peg-word technique is that each rhyme serves as a "peg" on which you can "hang" the word you need to remember. The way you do this is to form a visual association between the object in the rhyme and the

Peg-Word Mnemonic

The peg-word technique can help you memorize a list of concrete objects for a test or quiz.

Procedure: Learn the 10 rhymes listed below, then associate those objects (e.g., bun) with the 10 words. For example, imagine the candle resting in a hot-dog bun. Close your book for 5 minutes, then try to remember the list of words.

One–Bun Six–Stick

Two–Shoe Seven–Heaven

Three–Tree Eight–Gate

Four–Door Nine–Wine

Five–Hive Ten–Hen

Words to Remember:

Candle Compact disc

Television Scissors

Barbell Swing set

Cake Doorknob

Toaster Hose Number Recalled:_____

---

word you're remembering. Let's take an example from Kenneth Higbee's (2001) book, *Your Memory: How It Works and How to Improve It* (2nd ed.). Suppose you want to remember these five items: paper, tire, doctor, rose, ball. To use the peg-word method, you would form a visual association between paper and bun (the first word in the rhyme—see Activity 6.7). For example, you could imagine eating a bun made out of paper. Second, associate tire and shoe: visualize a car that has four shoes where the tires should be. Third, visualize a doctor and tree: perhaps a doctor (white coat and all) climbing a tree. Fourth, rose and door: visualize a rosebush hanging in the middle of a door. Fifth, ball and hive: visualize balls instead of bees flying into and out of the hive.

These visual pegs should help you remember the list when you need to. Let's test whether this method worked for you. What was the third item? Three is a tree. What was the image associated with tree?

Method of Loci

The loci method is another mnemonic that relies on the principle of imagery. It is similar to the peg-word method, but instead of using a list of rhymes, you use a set of familiar locations, such as landmarks you pass on the way from your dorm to a classroom. This mnemonic gets its name from the word *loci* (plural of *locus*), which means "place" or "location." This method pairs up words you're learning with a set of loci.

Let's say you are trying to memorize the same five items from the peg-word example: paper, tire, doctor, rose, ball. Pick five locations on your walk to one of your classes. The landmarks should be very familiar to you so that you don't use up extra capacity remembering them. Otherwise, the loci method would make your task harder, because you would need to remember two lists. Let's say you pass a tall oak tree, a flagpole, a statue, a fire hydrant, and a stop sign. As with the peg-word method, you simply associate your word list with your landmarks. First, visualize an association between paper and the oak tree; for example, a sheet of paper hanging from one of the branches. Next, visualize an association between a tire and a flagpole, such as a tire being run up the flagpole instead of a flag. Continue this for the rest of the words.

When you need to recall the list, you simply imagine starting on your journey to class. What is the first landmark on your journey? This should be easy to remember, because you have selected a well-learned sequence of objects. You first come across a tall oak tree. Do you remember what object is associated with the oak tree? Next, you pass the flagpole. What object is associated with the flagpole? If you have developed vivid images of the objects interacting with your loci, you should have no trouble remembering them.

You're probably thinking that this is an extraordinary amount of work to remember just five words. We agree. But the principle can be extended to many more words. Theoretically, you can remember as many words as you have locations on your path. If you're a golfer, you can think of one landmark per hole at your favorite course, so you can remember 18 items. In general, the principle operates the same for 50 items as it does for 5 items.

Having a good memory is crucial to college success. If you know how the memory system works—including attention, short-term memory, encoding, retrieval, and mnemonics—you will be better able to "fix" memory problems when they arise, because you will know where your memory system is failing.

The main limitation of most memory techniques is that they are effective only for memorizing simple things such as word lists. Keep in mind the limitations of these methods and use them appropriately. A self-regulated learner will recognize when using these mnemonics would be helpful and when they do not apply. In college, most of the learning you will engage in will be high-level, complex learning, in which you need to develop a sophisticated understanding. The tasks you will encounter in college require more than just a good memory. They require skills like organization and thinking, which are generally thought of as higher level cognitive processes. It is to these more sophisticated learning strategies that we now turn in Chapter 7.

CHAPTER SUMMARY

If you are going to remember something, you first have to pay attention to it. We don't attend to all the information in our world; much of it we choose to ignore. It is vital that you focus attention exclusively on your class lectures and textbook and screen out other inputs. Studying in a quiet environment will make this possible. Our working memory system has a limited capacity, with less than 10 pieces of information available to process to long-term memory at any one time. Our long-term memory system has limitless storage capacity, but accessing long-term memories is not always successful. Your ability to remember long-term memories is directly related to how well you learned it in the first place. Particularly with complex material, you must do more than just memorize it, so that you have a richer understanding of the material (deep processing). During tests, questions that require you simply to recognize information from a list of possible choices are usually easier than ones that require you to recall information. Certain memory shortcuts (mnemonics) can be helpful for remembering lists and similar tasks.

Improving Your Cognition and Metacognition

Chapter Goals

This chapter will help you:

- Memorize better
- Identify when you should and should not use memorization
- Build deep understanding for course material
- Better organize course material in your notes and in your mind
- Identify which strategies are required for each of your courses

Key Terms

association learning	metacognition
deep rehearsal	organization
distributed practice	rehearsal
elaboration	shallow rehearsal
massed practice	task analysis

CHAPTER 7

This chapter is about learning strategies. It might be the most important chapter of the book, because learning strategies form the foundation for completing college work well. We consider four learning strategies in this chapter: rehearsal, elaboration, organization, and metacognition. These four skills are the foundation of college success.

Why is this chapter so important? Because research shows clearly that one of the major distinctions between good college students and poor ones is that the good ones have better strategies. Good students are not born with better strategies; they have learned them. We hope this chapter goes a long way toward helping you develop these absolutely essential strategies. Activity 7.1 offers an additional assessment of your cognitive and metacognitive strategies.

ACTIVITY 7.1   *Assessing Your Cognitive and Metacognitive Skills*

Circle the statements that best describe your approach to learning. When you are finished, add the corresponding points for all items.

1. I generate questions to help me understand class material.
   - (1) never or almost never
   - (2) rarely
   - (3) frequently
   - (4) always or almost always

2. I notice or look for examples of what I'm learning in one class in other classes or in my life outside of school.
   - (1) never or almost never
   - (2) rarely
   - (3) frequently
   - (4) always or almost always

3. I try to make comparisons and note similarities between what I read in textbooks and what I hear in lectures.
   - (1) never or almost never
   - (2) rarely
   - (3) frequently
   - (4) always or almost always

4. I monitor my progress to assess whether I am learning what I set out to learn.
   - (1) never or almost never
   - (2) rarely
   - (3) frequently
   - (4) always or almost always

5. I vary my approach to learning depending on the class and type of assignment.
   - (1) never or almost never
   - (2) rarely
   - (3) frequently
   - (4) always or almost always

SCORING:

The following categories can provide a rough indication of your current cognitive and metacognitive strategies.

16 and above: You probably have good cognitive and metacognitive skills. This chapter can serve as a helpful review of important skills.

11–15: You probably have moderately good cognitive and metacognitive skills. However, you may wish to develop them further. This chapter will help you identify some ways you can improve your thinking strategies.

10 and below: This chapter is definitely for you. This chapter will help you focus on some of the important cognitive and metacognitive skills. We encourage you to read this chapter carefully and to use the suggestions we offer.

LOW-LEVEL STRATEGY: REHEARSAL

You can think of each learning strategy as belonging to one of two types: low-level or high-level. This is similar to the distinction we made in the last chapter between deep processing and shallow processing. The low-level strategy we will discuss is **rehearsal.** Rehearsal, as its name implies, involves repeating information you want to remember over and over until you have memorized it. In this section, we will identify ways in which rehearsal might work best for you and consider situations in which rehearsal will and will not be effective. Figure 7.1 lists different ways of rehearsal from another learning inventory.

How to Do Rehearsal

You already have some idea of what rehearsal is like from times when you have had to memorize something for school. In its most basic form, rehearsal involves saying things repeatedly to yourself. Below we list some aspects of rehearsal that are worth considering.

Part versus Whole. Suppose a section of your biology class requires you to memorize body parts from a cat dissection. One question you must ask yourself is whether it is best to study the entire dissection at once or to break it up into parts, maybe learning the digestive system completely, then moving on to the circulatory system, and so on. The answer to this question depends on several factors. First, the sheer size of the project will predict which method is better. Obviously, the larger the set of body parts you need to learn, the more likely it is that partial learning will work better. If the task is manageable in one piece, then learning the terms all at once may be better.

A second important aspect is the degree of interrelation between the parts. Psychologists generally have found that if the parts of a system are highly interrelated, it may be best to learn the entire system as a whole. For example, in a cat dissection, learning the parts together may be useful since the internal organs are interrelated. At the very least, it would be helpful to learn all of one system (e.g., digestive) as a unit because the components all work together. Learning how one component is related to another will help you learn both more easily.

As another example, many colleges and universities offer sports-officiating classes in which, among other things, you learn the rules of certain sports. A sports rule book is divided into different sections, called Rules. Although there is

---

Sample rehearsal items.	**FIGURE 7.1**

1. When I study for this class, I practice saying the material to myself over and over.
2. When studying for this class, I read my class notes and the course readings over and over.
3. I memorize key words to remind me of important concepts in this class.
4. I make lists of important terms for this course and memorize the lists.

Keep in mind that whether rehearsal is effective depends partly on what the demands of the class are and also on how much of the other strategies you use in combination with it. We discuss this in this chapter.

Source: From *A Manual for the Use of the Motivated Strategies for Learning Questionnaire* (MSLQ), by P. R. Pintrich, D. Smith, T. Garcia, and W. J. McKeachie, 1993, Ann Arbor, MI: NCRIPTAL, School of Education, The University of Michigan. Reprinted with permission of W. J. McKeachie.

some overlap, these Rules are fairly distinct from one another. For example, in the basketball rule book, Rule 1 is "Court and Equipment" and Rule 10 is "Fouls and Penalties." These two rules have no obvious relation, so it would not be helpful to study them as a whole. In this case, learning in parts is better.

Cramming versus Dispersing. A generation ago, psychologists asked one of the classic questions, Is it better to learn all at once, or to spread learning out over a long period of time? Psychologists call learning all at once **massed practice** and learning that is spread out **distributed practice.** The classroom analogy is studying during several evenings before an exam versus staying up late to cram the night before. On this question, the research is abundantly clear: Cramming before an exam results in poorer learning than spreading out your studying. If this is the case, why do students so often cram? One reason may be poor time management. Another may be that some students perform better when faced with deadlines. Although these reasons may be valid, the fact remains that you will remember more when you distribute your learning over several sessions.

This is true both for studying and for course preparation in general. For example, if your class will cover four textbook chapters in a 4-week period leading up to an exam, it is important that you spread out your reading fairly evenly over those 4 weeks. Similarly, when the time comes for studying, you should begin several days before the test. (And remember, reading your textbook for the first time is not studying for the test!) If your test will cover four chapters, then when you are reading the last chapter, you would probably want to start reviewing the other three chapters. By the time you have finished, your reading of the last chapter will be done and you can review it.

Sometimes time constraints prevent such well-planned studying. We suspect that everyone has crammed from time to time. (We both have.) The timing of assignments sometimes can prevent you from spacing out your studying. In these extreme cases, clearly, cramming is better than no studying at all. But we strongly encourage you to avoid these situations. Proper planning and scheduling will go a long way toward allowing you to distribute your rehearsal over longer periods of time. Activity 7.2 gives you a chance to try cramming versus spreading.

Deep versus Shallow Rehearsal. This issue was discussed in the previous chapter, but it is worth repeating in the context of learning strategies. College students often choose memorization as their preferred study method. We don't necessarily think this is a good idea, but given that students do it, it's important that they do it in a way that makes their memory of the material as rich as possible. Toward this end, we stress the importance of **deep rehearsal** over **shallow rehearsal.** Activity 6.4 gave an example of shallow versus deep processing. We encourage you to try this activity again to see the importance of deep processing.

One of the best ways to do rehearsal is to associate the material you are trying to learn with material that you have already learned. This is called **association learning.** Association learning means identifying a relation between two pieces of information. Although you may not be aware of it, you probably remember many things because of association. For example, you probably learned to tell the difference between *principle* and *principal* by remembering that a school principal is your "pal." Spelling *separate* correctly is easier if you remember that you "separate the *a*'s." The association principle holds for visual information as well. For example, we remember that Italy looks like a boot, and that Michigan looks like a mitten.

According to Kenneth Higbee (2001), using association helps because it provides more "memory tags" for the new information. The more information you can

Massed versus Distributed Practice

Try to memorize this list of words one group at a time. After completing the first group, take a break before moving on to the second group. After the second group, take a break. On returning, redo both of the first two groups before moving on to the third. Continue this procedure for the fourth and fifth groups. Have a friend test you on your recall, to see if this method gives good results.

plate	roach	nurse	orange	dock
wish	floor	pizza	fruit	door
table	brush	child	store	dust
heater	mark	mild	telephone	ball
chair	fence	floor	apple	plane
carnival	sharp	garage	pummel	slave
truck	cheek	grass	drill	haze
mallard	spice	bird	hallway	money
shirt	honey	couch	trout	drum
hose	sunny	data	shaft	dice
glove	sheep	hammer	book	game
shark	dolphin	school	color	cake
steel	daisy	heart	soup	spine
farm	monograph	disk	mope	starfish
horse	miner	flame	beach	nail
frank	coal	explosion	circle	whale
paper	clove	skunk	cottage	tank
business	shell	food	robe	sunk
milk	brake	wood	shore	bass
flower	gateway	dough	shoe	party
witch	juice	stone	wool	hair
dust	gross	door	lock	steer

Number of Words Recalled: _____/110 = _____%

relate to the material you are trying to learn, the more possibilities exist for triggering the correct memory. For example, you can remember the difference between port and starboard by remembering first that *port* and *left* both have four letters. Then you can remember which side of the boat has a red light and which side has a green light by remembering what color port wine is—red. When returning from sea, you always come in with the red lane-marker buoys on your right side—red, right, returning. These associations have helped many sailors remember simple nautical rules. Of course, to remember different information will require different associations, but the basic association principle is the same for all learning.

Association learning also makes material more meaningful. If you associate information with material that is personally relevant to you, it will, of course, have more meaning. For example, you probably have to remember passwords and PINs for your ATM card, computer accounts, and voice mail. Many people use numbers (birthdays or anniversaries) and words (family names) for passwords so that they are easier to remember.

Making material more meaningful to you is part of the learning strategy called **elaboration.** We will discuss elaboration in the next section on high-level learning strategies, but we are discussing it here as well because the point where rehearsal leaves off and elaboration picks up is not clear cut. Rehearsal in its more sophisticated forms could be viewed as elaboration. We tell you this because it may not always be clear exactly what strategy you are using. In fact, during an evening of studying, you may use a combination of strategies. The important point is to find the right combination of strategies that works best for you.

When to Use Rehearsal

As with all the study strategies we've discussed so far, rehearsal is appropriate at some times and not at other times. For three learning situations, rehearsal works very well.

1. *Classes that require lots of memorization.* For example, in a medical terminology class, you could use association learning to pair the symptoms of an illness with the term used to describe it. You could remember that roseola infantum is a rash babies get by first pairing the word *infantum* with baby, then remembering that rashes are red like roses (as in roseola).

2. *Tests that are mostly multiple choice.* Rehearsal works especially well if the multiple-choice items ask you to recall definitions. For example, in a history of psychology class, your knowledge of dates, schools of thought, and famous psychologists may be tested with factual multiple-choice questions. This is a good candidate for rehearsal.

3. *Tests that ask other kinds of objective questions.* For example, you can score better on matching items and fill-in-the-blank questions by using rehearsal. A flash-card rehearsal technique would be effective for learning definitions, for instance. Simply write the definition on one side of the flash card and the name of the concept on the other. You might also use *oral rehearsal*, that is, simply repeating the concepts to yourself until you have memorized them. A third technique is called *cover-half*. To use this technique, list all the concepts you need to learn on the left side of a sheet of paper, and the definitions on the right. Cover the definitions with a piece of paper. Read the first concept and try to think of the definition. Slide the piece of paper down so you can see the first definition, and check off each concept you define correctly. Next, cover the left-hand side and work the other way; see if you can identify the concepts by reading the definitions. You will probably find this part easier. (Remember the difference between recognition and recall memory from Chapter 6? Recognition is easier. Covering the concepts requires recognition; covering the definitions demands recall.) Figure 7.2 describes these three rehearsal techniques.

When Not to Use Rehearsal

In some situations rehearsal will probably not work. One is if the test will involve large, integrative essay questions. For example, a test for a literature class will probably require you to make connections across different works of the same author, or to identify themes in a particular type of literature. Rehearsal will not help you with this kind of task. Even if the test questions are not essays, certain multiple-choice questions are more conceptual and require more critical thinking and problem solving. (In Chapter 11 we discuss these and other types of test questions.) For example, if you must understand the difference between two theories to select the right choice, rehearsal will probably not help. This type of question will require more thinking.

These techniques for rehearsal can help you memorize objective facts.

1. Flash Cards: Write the definition on one side of an index card and the name of the concept on the other. Look at the concept and try to think of the proper definition. Go through all the cards. Place the cards you got right in one pile and the ones you got wrong in another. After completing all of them, redo the ones you got wrong until they are all in the "right" pile.

2. Oral Rehearsal: This requires less preparation time than flash cards do. Simply go through your notes, and when you come across a definition, repeat the definition to yourself. Do this until you have memorized all the terms. This technique may not be as helpful as the others, because flash cards and cover-half involve writing down the concepts and the definitions to prepare for studying. The act of writing them down probably improves learning by itself.

3. Cover-Half: List the concepts on the left side of a piece of paper and the corresponding definitions on the right side. Cover the right side and try to think of the correct response for each concept. After you complete this, cover the left half and read the definitions. Try to recall the terms that match the definitions.

Rehearsal has its limits. In fact, research suggests that it is the least effective learning strategy when compared to high-level strategies. Of course, rehearsal is better than nothing, and good rehearsal is better than poor rehearsal (which is why we give you advice about how to do it better). Still, we encourage students to engage in the higher level learning strategies of elaboration, organization, and metacognition. We now turn to those strategies.

HIGH-LEVEL STRATEGIES

We now explore more sophisticated ways to engage your course material. High-level strategies go beyond simple memorization. The goal of these strategies is to help you develop a conceptually rich understanding of the course material. For example, when you use elaboration, you add information that was not in the original learning material. Thus, you come away with a more developed conceptualization than what is in the text. Three high-level strategies are most important for you to know. The three strategies are elaboration, organization, and metacognition.

Elaboration

Elaboration will help you improve your understanding of course material by building conceptually rich connections among the concepts you are learning. The goal is to go beyond simply memorizing to understanding. Figure 7.3 lists the six questions measuring elaboration from another learning inventory. The goal of this section is to help you become more effective in your elaboration. Toward that end, here are four specific techniques for elaboration.

Summarizing. One way you can elaborate on course material is to summarize the main points of a lecture or textbook section. You might sit down with your notebook after a class lecture and write down the most important points the

FIGURE 7.3　Sample elaboration items.

1. When I study for this class, I pull together information from different sources, such as lectures, readings, and discussions.
2. I try to relate ideas in this subject to those in other courses whenever possible.
3. When reading for this class, I try to relate the material to what I already know.
4. When I study for this course, I write brief summaries of the main ideas from the readings and the concepts from the lectures.
5. I try to understand the material in this class by making connections between the readings and the concepts from the lectures.
6. I try to apply ideas from course readings in other class activities such as lecture and discussion.

Source: From *A Manual for the Use of the Motivated Strategies for Learning Questionnaire* (MSLQ), by P. R. Pintrich, D. Smith, T. Garcia, and W. J. McKeachie, 1993, Ann Arbor, MI: NCRIPTAL, School of Education, The University of Michigan. Reprinted with permission of W. J. McKeachie.

professor covered that day. Summarizing requires that you reduce a large amount of material into a small amount by recognizing what is most important. The ability to do this is one thing that separates good students from poor students. You can get better at it with practice. In general, we recommend that after you read each textbook section, you write a brief summary of the main points. Likewise, after lectures, write down the main points. Activity 7.3 lists some questions that will help you summarize the information from the previous chapter.

ACTIVITY 7.3　*Summarizing*

The following questions will prompt you to summarize the main points of Chapter 6.

1. Describe how attention is like a pie.

2. What does *automatized* mean?

3. What are two features of working memory?

4. Define shallow processing and deep processing.

Paraphrasing. Another way to elaborate on course material is to restate what you are learning in your own words. Being able to listen to and understand a professor's lecture, or read and understand a textbook, represents a certain degree of learning. However, being able to explain what you heard or read is clearly more difficult and represents more sophisticated understanding. Here is one way to do paraphrasing and summarizing that researchers have found effective: work with a partner who is also in your class, and ask questions of each other (e.g., King, 1992). By doing this, you will force each other to paraphrase. Activity 7.4 lists questions about the previous chapter. Try out your paraphrasing skills by answering them in writing or aloud.

Paraphrasing

The following questions about Chapter 6 will help you develop the ability to paraphrase. Write your answer in the space below or tell your answers to a classmate.

1. In what way is the human mind like a computer?

   _____

   _____

2. Why is it hard to do two difficult cognitive tasks at the same time?

   _____

   _____

3. What are two ways to improve your attention? Why do they help?

   _____

   _____

4. Why is recall memory better than recognition memory?

   _____

   _____

5. What is one type of learning for which mnemonics will work well? What is one for which they will not work well?

   _____

   _____

Analogies and Generalizations. A third way you can elaborate on course material is to think about how the material relates to other things you know or other things you are learning. How is what you are learning like something you already know? In Chapter 6, for example, we likened the human mind to a computer. The mind is analogous to a computer because it receives inputs (information), saves portions of the input to its memory, and retrieves that information when the user calls it up, much like a computer does. Although the analogy is not perfect, we used it in hopes that it would help you remember the components of the human information-processing system.

Once you have found two concepts that form an analogy, you can then develop a generalization about them. A generalization is a statement that is true of all of the elements you are considering. Think for a moment about how soccer and basketball are the same. In other words, think of analogies between them. The object of both is to score more points than your opponent (as opposed to golf), in both the offensive team has control of the ball (as opposed to baseball), a team scores in both by placing the ball in a goal in the midst of defensive opposition (as opposed to swimming). These are generalizations that identify how the two sports are the same. Activity 7.5 provides two stories. Your task is to identify how they are analogous—what generalizations can be made across the two stories. When undergraduates read these two stories, often only a minority of readers recognize the analogy. If you can recognize it, you probably have a more sophisticated understanding of the underlying principle (described at the bottom of Activity 7.5).

ACTIVITY 7.5 *Analogies and Generalizations*

Read the following two stories and identify how they are similar.

Story 1: A small country was ruled from a strong fortress by a dictator. The fortress was situated in the middle of the country, surrounded by farms and villages. Many roads led to the fortress through the countryside. A rebel general vowed to capture the fortress. The general knew that an attack by his entire army would capture the fortress. He gathered his army at the head of one of the roads, ready to launch a full-scale direct attack. However, the general learned that the dictator had planted mines on each of the roads. The mines were set so that small bodies of men could pass over them safely, since the dictator needed to move his troops and workers to and from the fortress. However, any large force would detonate the mines. Not only would this blow up the road, but it would also destroy many neighboring villages. It therefore seemed impossible to capture the fortress. However, the general devised a simple plan. He divided his army into small groups and dispatched each group to the head of a different road. When all was ready he gave the signal and each group marched down a different road to the fortress at the same time. In this way, the general captured the dictator.

Use your summarizing skills to state the main point of this story:

_____

_____

_____

Story 2: Suppose you are a doctor faced with a patient who has a malignant tumor in his stomach. It is impossible to operate on the patient, but unless the tumor is destroyed, the patient will die. There is a kind of ray that can be used to destroy the tumor. If the rays reach the tumor all at once at a sufficiently high intensity, the tumor will be destroyed. Unfortunately, at this high intensity, the healthy tissue that the rays pass through will also be destroyed. At lower intensities the rays are harmless to the healthy tissue, but they will not affect the tumor either. What type of procedure could you use to destroy the tumor with the rays and at the same time avoid destroying the healthy tissue?

The main point of this story is:

_____

_____

Do you recognize any similarity between these two stories?

_____

_____

_____

Answer: Small, simultaneous forces converging from multiple directions can destroy an enemy within.

Analogy:	Fortress Story	Radiation Story
Small, simultaneous forces	Troops	Radiation
Converging	Going down different roads	Shot from different locations around body
Enemy within	Rebel dictator	Cancer

Source: From "Schema Induction and Analogical Transfer," by M. L. Gick and K. J. Holyoak, 1983, *Cognitive Psychology, 15.*

Generative Note Taking. The last strategy is much like summarizing and paraphrasing, but it applies particularly to your notes. (Chapter 8 discusses note taking in detail, but this strategy is also worth mentioning here.) You will improve your learning if you do more than simply write down what the professor says. Generative note taking involves expanding on what the professor says. The basic approach is to expand your notes, after class, with examples, questions, analogies, and so forth. An effective way to do this is to think of your own examples and insert them in your notes at the appropriate time (probably after class, which is why in Chapter 8, we will tell you to leave plenty of blank lines as you take notes in class). You can also do generative note taking by thinking of questions that were not answered in class. You might ask these questions of the professor either at the beginning of the next class or during office hours. Choose the generative activity that works best to improve your learning. This strategy, in conjunction with the other three described above, will help you form a rich, elaborative understanding of course material.

Organization

The second of the high-level learning strategies is **organization.** Organization helps you to identify important information, to see relations within course material, and to make connections from one part of the course material to another or from one course to another. Figure 7.4 has items that measure organization from another learning inventory.

The strategy of organization that we are describing goes beyond simply keeping all of your notes from different classes organized (preferably in different ring binders)

Sample organization items. **FIGURE 7.4**

1. When I study the readings for this course, I outline the material to help me organize my thoughts.
2. When I study for this course, I go through the readings and my class notes and try to find the most important ideas.
3. I make simple charts, diagrams, or tables to help me organize course material.
4. When I study for this course, I go over my class notes and make an outline of important concepts.

Source: From *A Manual for the Use of the Motivated Strategies for Learning Questionnaire* (MSLQ), by P. R. Pintrich, D. Smith, T. Garcia, and W. J. McKeachie, 1993, Ann Arbor, MI: NCRIPTAL, School of Education, The University of Michigan. Reprinted with permission of W. J. McKeachie.

and making sure your notes are in chronological order. This is clearly the beginning of organization. But the type of organization we are talking about goes much deeper. It is a demanding endeavor that will take time and require you to become familiar with what you are learning. Below we suggest three specific ways to use organization in your learning.

Outlines. We encourage you to make outlines of lectures, either before the lecture begins or afterward. Some professors help by providing an outline before the class starts. Be sure to keep this outline with your notes. If the teacher does not provide an outline, then review your notes after class and make an outline of the topics discussed, using headings and subheadings. Figure 7.5 is an outline from the first day of an introductory psychology class.

We suggest that you outline your textbook readings too. Most textbooks have chapter outlines or a table of contents that can serve as an outline. Copy that outline on a sheet of lined paper, with space between each heading so that you can fill in the details as you read. An outline can make material from your textbook much easier to study come test time.

FIGURE 7.5   Outlining.

An outline of your text can help you see how topics are related.

I. What is psychology?
    A. Defined as the science of behavior and mental processes
    B. Subfields
        1. Biological Psychology
        2. Developmental Psychology
        3. Cognitive Psychology
        4. Abnormal Psychology

II. Brief History of Psychology
    A. Wilhelm Wundt: established first psychology lab in Leipzig, Germany
    B. G. Stanley Hall: established first American psychology lab at Johns Hopkins
    C. Freud (Austria): founder of study of behavior disorders *(Interpretation of Dreams)*

III. Perspectives on Behavior
    A. All events are interpreted from a perspective
    B. Perspectives in Psychology
        1. Biological Perspective
        2. Behavioral Perspective
        3. Sociocultural Perspective

IV. Psychology's Big Questions
    A. Nature versus Nurture
        1. Plato
        2. Aristotle
        3. John Locke
    B. Role of Culture

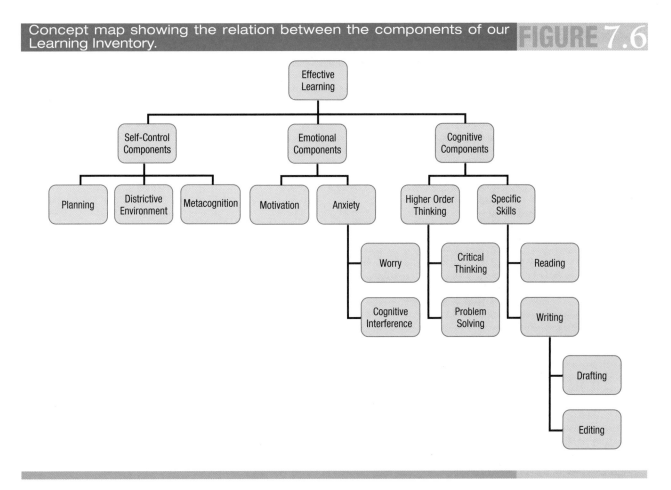

Tables and Charts. Like outlines, tables and charts can help you see relations between concepts. They can be particularly helpful if you will be asked to compare and contrast concepts on a test. They can also aid you in writing a composition that involves compiling multiple sources. Putting all of the information from the various sources on the same page will allow you to identify the different types of information or perspective that each source provides.

Concept Maps. A concept map is a pictorial representation of a set of concepts that shows the relations among those concepts. A concept map helps you to see how the elements of a topic fit together. Like outlines, tables, and charts, you can create concept maps for both lectures and readings. Figure 7.6 is a concept map of the Learning Inventory you completed in Chapter 1.

Metacognition

Metacognition is the awareness and control of your own learning. In other words, people who are metacognitive know when they know. A crucial difference between good learners and poor learners is that good learners understand their own study habits, they know their limits (what they can and cannot accomplish with given task requirements and time constraints), and they adjust their learning to accomplish their goal in the most efficient and effective way. Figure 7.7 lists 12 questions measuring metacognition from another learning inventory. You can think of metacognition as consisting of three activities: planning, monitoring, and modifying.

FIGURE 7.7 Sample metacognition items.

1. During class time I often miss important points because I'm thinking of other things.

2. When reading for this course, I make up questions to help focus my reading.

3. When I become confused about something I'm reading for this class, I go back and try to figure it out.

4. If course materials are difficult to understand, I change the way I read the material.

5. Before I study new course material thoroughly, I often skim it to see how it is organized.

6. I ask myself questions to make sure I understand the material I have been studying in class.

7. I try to change the way I study in order to fit the course requirements and instructor's teaching style.

8. I often find that I have been reading for class but don't know what it was all about.

9. I try to think through a topic and decide what I am supposed to learn from it rather than just reading it over when studying.

10. When studying for this course I try to determine which concepts I don't understand well.

11. When I study for this class, I set goals for myself in order to direct my activities in each study period.

12. If I get confused taking notes in class, I make sure I sort it out afterward.

Source: From *A Manual for the Use of the Motivated Strategies for Learning Questionnaire* (MSLQ), by P. R. Pintrich, D. Smith, T. Garcia, and W. J. McKeachie, 1993, Ann Arbor, MI: NCRIPTAL, School of Education, The University of Michigan. Reprinted with permission of W. J. McKeachie.

1. *Planning.* Planning serves both a motivational and a cognitive function. As we discussed in Chapter 2, planning is important because it forces you to set goals, and goals motivate. Planning also helps you understand the cognitive tasks involved in completing your work. One way to identify the cognitive requirements of your learning is to conduct a **task analysis:** Figure out the steps required to complete the task and the strategies or skills you will have to employ to complete each step. Items 5, 9, and 11 in Figure 7.7 measure planning, as do Items 2, 3, 4, 12, 13, and 14 from this book's Learning Inventory. Look at those items again and ask yourself to what extent you engage in those particular activities when you study. Activity 7.6 provides an example of a task analysis and asks you to complete one for one of your courses.

ACTIVITY 7.6 *Task Analysis*

A task analysis identifies the tasks that need to be done and how you can go about doing them. The following task analysis is for an assignment in an industrial–organizational psychology course.

Job Diagnostic Survey (JDS) Project: Baxter Community Center

Task	Requirements	Goals
1. Meet with other group members	1 hour on campus; need someone to take initiative in meeting	make list of project goals; find time to meet with Melanie at Baxter CC

2. Meet with Melanie at Baxter Community Center	need transportation downtown; need a good showing—as many group members as possible; read section of text on Job Diagnostic Survey and portion from technical manual of JDS so that we can answer any questions Melanie has about JDS	decide on time of questionnaire administration; decide on format—will workers complete them during staff meeting, take them home, or take them back to their office?; decide on questions of confidentiality—how can employees be assured?
3. Attend staff meeting and distribute JDS to employees	be very familiar with JDS administration procedure; be prepared to answer any questions employees might have; check with professor before going to clear up any confusion—be sure to write them down to keep track of them	collect data for project
4. Meet as a group and decide when/how to code/analyze data	read scoring portion of JDS technical manual and bring to meeting; figure out how to enter data in computer for work with SPSS	get data coded, entered, and analyzed for write-up
5. Meet as a group and divide up writing assignments	must be familiar with JDS background; familiar with how to write methods section to be understood by lay audience; build tables of averages and interpret them in terms of national norms	provide a written report to Baxter Center
6. Meet with Professor VanderStoep after turning in draft of report	take his suggestions into account; check with him on technical aspects of project that are still not clear	work toward finished product
7. Deliver final report to Melanie	practice a short oral presentation that walks her through various aspects of report	FINISHED!

Now work on your own task analysis for a course you are currently taking.

Task	**Requirements**	**Goals**
1. _____	_____	_____
2. _____	_____	_____
3. _____	_____	_____
4. _____	_____	_____

2. *Monitoring.* As we noted in Chapter 2, planning and setting goals are only part of the equation for college success. If you do not monitor your progress toward those goals, then the goal setting will not be effective. As an example, imagine having a goal of being able to draw a 3-foot-long line on a chalkboard. You draw a line, but you have no way to know how long the line is or even whether it is shorter or longer than 3 feet. You have a goal, but it is not helpful because you are not able to monitor your progress toward that goal. The ability to monitor progress is vital. In studying, you may have a goal of getting 80% of your answers correct on an upcoming exam. Of course, it's impossible to monitor your progress on the exam before you actually take it, but by taking practice tests, studying with friends, and the like, you can have a good idea of how well you are achieving your goal.

We offer two specific suggestions for monitoring your studying. The first is *attention tracking.* One way to do this is to place a check mark in your textbook every time you feel your attention wandering. This is a form of attention tracking—keeping track of your attention. You may find by using this technique that, over time, the number of check marks goes down, a sign that you are increasing your attention. You can do attention tracking during lectures, as well. By placing a check mark in your notes every time you feel your attention drifting away from the lecture, you can stay focused in class.

A second way to monitor your learning is by self-questioning. Quizzing yourself at the end of readings or after lectures is a good way to monitor your learning. Some textbooks provide review questions at the end of a text. We find that very few students use these, unfortunately. From the perspective of monitoring, being provided with the questions is even better than generating questions yourself, because if you generate them yourself, you may just focus on what you know, and not force yourself to answer questions about what you don't know. Another option is to work with a classmate and ask questions of each other. Whatever method you choose, some form of self-questioning is important.

3. *Modifying.* The final aspect of metacognition is adjusting your studying to meet the needs of the task. After you have set goals for yourself and monitored your progress toward those goals, you must now use the information about how well you are achieving your goals to change your studying as necessary. If you are progressing toward your goal and things are going well for you in a class, no regulating will be needed. But if learning is not going as you planned, you will need to make changes. For example, if your grade on your first biology test is poor, you should ask yourself why. Once you determine why you didn't do well, you will need to make adjustments to your current strategies. Perhaps you need to spend more time on the class. (It would be convenient if you also found by monitoring your progress that you didn't need to spend as much time in another class, and thus you could "borrow" time from that class and "spend" that time in the class where you are struggling.) Perhaps it's not a matter of spending more time, but rather spending better quality time. Finding a better study environment (see Chapter 4), choosing a better time of the day to study (avoiding late nights), and so forth are part of the constant adjustments that successful learners make in response to the feedback they receive from monitoring their progress. The specific adjustments will ultimately be up to you and will be based on your individual circumstances. What is important is that you do make these adjustments in response to feedback you receive on your learning.

DIFFERENT STRATEGIES FOR DIFFERENT COURSES?

In this chapter we have given you the tools we think are necessary to develop effective cognitive and metacognitive learning strategies. The extent to which you develop these strategies will depend on your motivation to use them and how often you practice them.

Although we think these strategies are important, we also want to advise you that they may not work equally effectively under all learning conditions. For example, in our study of college students' use of learning strategies (VanderStoep, Pintrich, & Fagerlin, 1996), we found that these strategies made more difference in the final course grade in some subjects than in others. We asked students taking psychology, English, and biology classes to fill out a learning inventory similar to the one you completed in Chapter 1. We then divided the students into three groups based on their final grade in the course: high, medium, and low grades. We examined the relation between the students' final grades and their scores on the learning inventory. What we expected to find was that the students with high final course grades would score higher on the learning strategies scales. For example, students with As would have a higher score on elaboration than students with Cs would. We did find this to be true—but only for students taking psychology (social science) and biology (natural science) classes. We did not find any relation between learning strategies scores and the final grade for students taking English (humanities) classes.

What does this mean? One thing we think it does *not* mean is that if you are an English, history, or other humanities major, you should ignore this chapter. What it does mean is that it's worth your time to think carefully about your use of each strategy (which is basically metacognition and something we would advocate anyway). Consider two examples where your learning strategies will differ.

A Class Involving Mostly Discussion and Writing Papers

You may find that arts and humanities courses, as well as upper level courses in all disciplines, involve far less lecture and far more group discussion. Grades in these courses may depend on writing papers much more than on objective tests. In a class that emphasizes paper writing and class discussions with very little memorization or lecture, the strategies of rehearsal and elaboration may not be helpful. In this case, strategies such as keeping a journal of what you read and discussing the course content with peers would be most helpful. Preparing for take-home projects, essay tests, and papers will involve collecting information from multiple sources (such as group discussions and course readings) and integrating these sources into your writing assignments. For these tasks, strategies that focus on memorizing course material will not be as helpful. Strategies that force you to organize and reflect on what you are learning will be the most helpful. (Chapter 10 offers many suggestions for improving your writing, which will also help you in this type of course.)

A Class Involving Mostly Lecture and Objective Tests

You may find that social science and natural science courses, as well as most introductory courses in many disciplines, involve a large amount of lecture. Grades in these courses may depend largely on multiple-choice tests or other objective assessments. In a course consisting mostly of lectures and objective tests, a steady diet of rehearsal and other ways to improve your memory would be helpful.

Recognizing the applicability of cognitive strategies to different learning situations is an important part of being able to use them effectively. Keep in mind that their applicability may depend in part on what type of course you are taking.

CHAPTER SUMMARY

We believe this chapter more than others provides the foundation on which successful learning is built. Your ability to use these strategies effectively is the basis for applying many other concepts in this book. For example, the chapters on reading (Chapter 9) and writing (Chapter 10) are in many ways applications of these strategies to those two particular activities. If you finish this book knowing nothing else, at least try to become familiar with the components of effective cognitive and metacognitive learning strategies.

Now that we have laid the cognitive and motivational building blocks of successful learning, we spend the rest of the book addressing specific activities you will likely encounter in college. We start with an inescapable part of the college experience: note taking.

Taking Notes

Chapter Goals

This chapter will help you:

- Take notes so that the note-taking activity itself will improve your learning

- Take notes so that you can use them later for review

- Identify the major pitfalls that keep students from taking good notes

- Use note taking as a high-level learning strategy to build rich knowledge structures

Key Terms

elaboration
generative note taking

CHAPTER 8

Ever have trouble understanding a professor's lecture? Professors know. Although in our minds we are always crystal clear, sometimes we professors do not succeed in making our thoughts appear organized and comprehensible. It's hard for students to change the professor, so we recommend that you focus on trying to understand the ideas in the lectures and to find better ways to take notes. We hope that this chapter will improve your note-taking techniques and make note taking more profitable for you, even in the face of unclear professors. To start, take the brief assessment of your note-taking habits in Activity 8.1.

ACTIVITY 8.1 *Assessing Your Note-Taking Skills*

Circle the statements that best describe your note-taking habits. When you have finished, add the corresponding points for all items.

1. I miss class:
   - (4) never
   - (3) once or twice a semester
   - (2) once or twice a month (4–8 times a semester)
   - (1) once or twice a week (over 15 times a semester)

2. I find it hard to concentrate:
   - (1) at least once per class period
   - (2) at least once a week
   - (3) only one or two times a month
   - (4) I almost never have trouble concentrating in class (my mind wanders only once or twice a semester during class)

3. I ask questions or provide a comment in class:
   - (4) once a week or more
   - (3) once a month or more
   - (2) only once or twice a semester
   - (1) I do not participate in class unless called on by the professor

4. Positive features of my note-taking habits (add a point for each of these that applies to you):
   - (1) I look over my notes after class.
   - (1) I go back and expand and/or clarify my notes after class.
   - (1) I review my notes with the professor or with a classmate.
   - (1) People who have borrowed my notes have commented on how organized and easy to understand they are.

5. Negative features of my note-taking habits (subtract a point for each of these that applies to you):
   - (−1) I try to write down what the professor says verbatim.
   - (−1) I lose track of what the professor is saying because I am trying to write down as much as possible.
   - (−1) The only time I look at my notes is a day or two before the test to review.
   - (−1) I have a hard time understanding my notes when I go back to them because I can't read the writing or understand the abbreviations, or there are parts missing.

SCORING: The following categories provide a rough indication of your current note-taking performance:

16 and above: You are probably a good note taker. This chapter can serve as a helpful review, although we suspect you have learned some good note-taking habits already.

11–15: You are probably a good note taker at times. However, you may have some bad habits (how many parts of Question 5 applied to you?), or you may sometimes be a good note taker but perhaps not all the time. This chapter will help you identify some of the occasional problems you have with your note taking.

10 and below: This chapter is definitely for you. It will help you focus on some of the important aspects of effective note taking. We encourage you to read this chapter carefully and to use the suggestions we offer for improving your note-taking skills.

As a college student, you will find that note taking is one of the most useful study skills to have. You will find yourself taking lots of notes in class. Most professors will encourage you to think and discuss during class and not simply take notes the whole time. Still, professors spend a lot of time lecturing during class time, and the expectation is very clear: *I want you to write this down. You will need to know this information to do well on tests.* You cannot expect to remember material if you don't write it down: Good note taking is essential to college success.

In this chapter, we will discuss two basic functions that note taking serves.

1. Note taking serves as a way to help you store or encode the material (recall encoding from Chapter 6).
2. Note taking is a way to keep the information in written form until you need it for later reference.

After discussing these two functions, we will present 12 strategies for effective note taking. We encourage you to adopt as many of them as you see fit.

In this chapter we will focus on strategies (process) instead of style (what your notes look like). The strategies will help you think about the process of taking notes in class: What should you pay attention to? What should you write down? How should your notes be organized? These are important issues for improving your note taking. We will avoid suggesting a specific style for your notes. For example, we won't discuss whether you should use one column or two columns, use Roman numerals or Arabic numerals, or take notes in pen or pencil. (We've had students ask these questions previously.) Instead, we let you decide what your notes should look like, based on what feels most comfortable. Instead of talking about styles of note taking, we will focus on how you can improve the *process* of taking notes.

We strongly believe that good note taking techniques are related to good school performance. Figure 8.1 gives examples of notes taken by an "A" student and by a "D/F" student. Using these notes, complete Activity 8.2 before you read on.

What Makes Good Notes Good?

Identify what distinguishes the good notes from the bad notes in Figure 8.1.

1. Which are the good notes? (A)   (B)

2. Which are the bad notes? (A)   (B)

3. The best feature of the good notes is:

_____

4. The biggest weakness of the bad notes is:

_____

If you don't take good notes, you probably won't perform as well as you could. Of course, we have also said this with respect to other topics in this book, such as memory. It is no less true of note taking. If you don't believe us, the differences in the notes in Figure 8.1 should convince you. We suspect that the difference in quality is compelling. Now, we can't guarantee that good notes will always lead to good grades, but it's a pretty good bet.

FIGURE 8.1   Good notes vs. less effective notes.

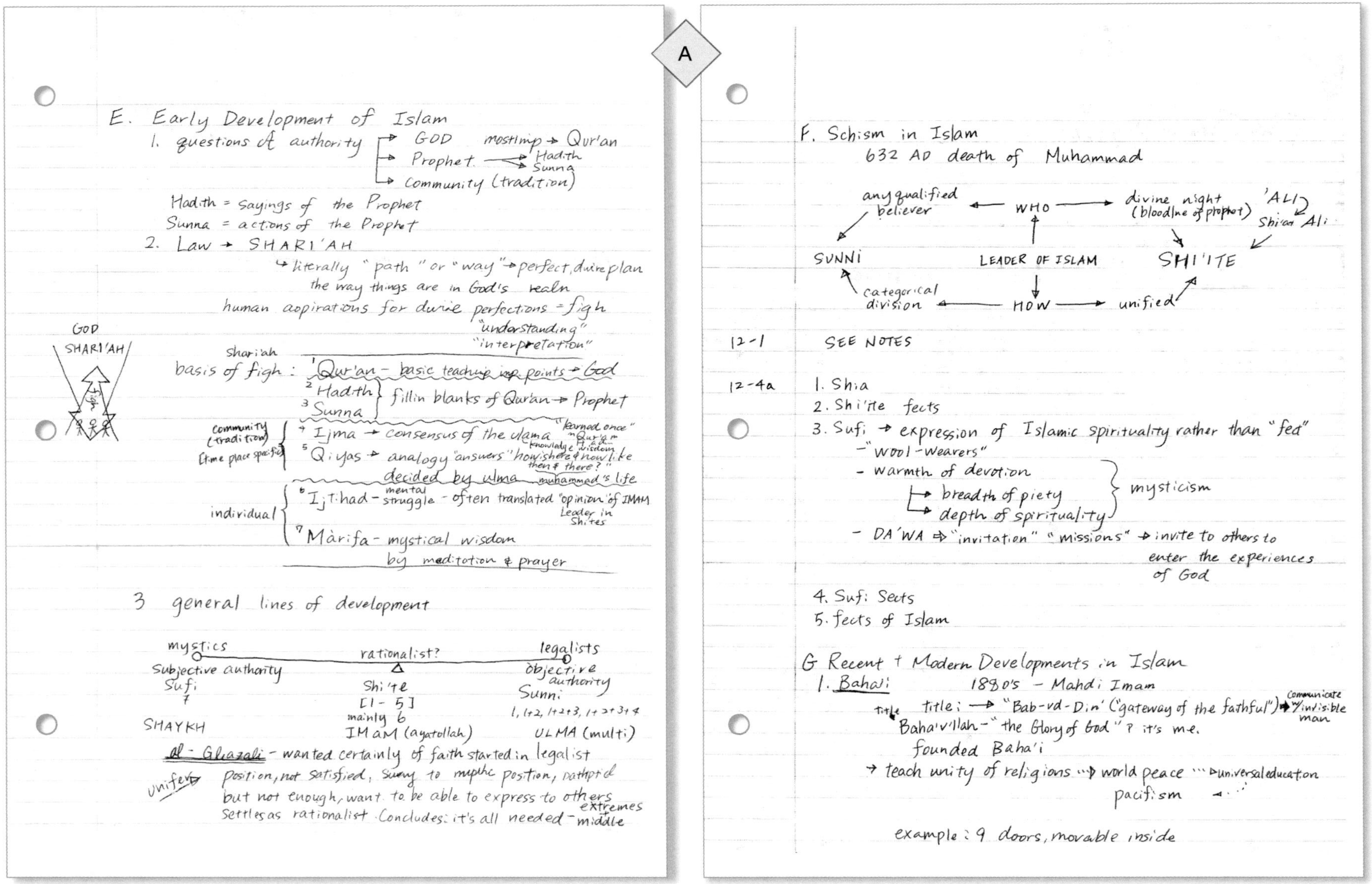

A

Right sheet:

F. Schism in Islam
632 AD death of Muhammad

any/qualified believer → WHO → divine right (bloodline of prophet) Shi'as Ali

SUNNI ← categorical division → unified → SHI'ITE

LEADER OF ISLAM → HOW → unified

SEE NOTES

12-1

12-4a

1. Shia
2. Shi'ite sects
3. Sufi → expression of Islamic spirituality rather than "fed"
- wool - weavers
- warmth of devotion
  breadth of piety
  depth of spirituality } mysticism
- DA'WA → "invitation" "missions" → invite to others to enter the experiences of God

4. Sufi Sects
5. Sects of Islam

G. Recent + Modern Developments in Islam
1. Baha'i: 1890's - Mahdi Iman
title: → "Bab-ud-Din" ("gateway of the faithful") → communicate / invisible man
Baha'u'llah - "the Glory of God"? it's me.
founded Baha'i
→ teach unity of religions → world peace → universal education → pacifism

example: 9 doors, movable inside

Left sheet:

E. Early Development of Islam
1. Questions of authority
GOD → mostim/ip → Qur'an
Prophet → Hadith
Community → Sunna (tradition)

Hadith = sayings of the Prophet
Sunna = actions of the Prophet

2. Law → SHARI'AH
→ literally "path" or "way" → perfect, divine plan
the way things are in God's realm
human aspirations for divine perfections → fiqh "understanding" "interpretation"

GOD
SHARI'AH

Shari'ah basis of fiqh:
1. Qur'an - basic teaching up points → God
2. Hadith } fill in blanks of Qur'an → Prophet
3. Sunna
4. Ijma → consensus of the ulama "eternal ones" knowing Muslim "truth" most there?
5. Qiyas - analogy "answers "how shari'ah would be"
  decided by ulama   Muhammad's life
  Ijtihad - mental struggle - often translated opinion of IMAM Leader in Shi'ites
  individual
  Ma'rifa - mystical wisdom by meditation & prayer

3. general lines of development

mystics   rationalist?   legalists
Subjective authority   objective authority
Sufi   Shi'te   Sunni
SHAYKH   El - 51   1, 1+2, 1+2+3, 1+2+3+4
                 mainly 6
                 IMAM (ayatollah)   ULMA (multi)

Al-Ghazali - wanted certainty of faith started in legalist position, not satisfied, swung to mystic position, not happy but not enough, want to be able to express to others extremes unifies as rationalist Concludes: it's all needed middle

FIGURE 8.   continued

I Piaget's   Infants
- Six substages
  ① reflexes (0-1)   sucking
  ② primary? reactions (0-4)
  own body
  ③ 2ndary reactions (4-8)
  actions on objects?
  ④ ??
  ⑤ tertiary (?) reactions (12-?)
  repeating stuff (e.g. in high-chair w/food)
  ⑥ representation thought
  delayed imitation

- Object Permanence
stages:
1,2 : out of sight, won't look
3 : ?
missed   4 : look for hidden objects
ages?   5 : A not B error   [B] ?
              [A]
6 : Has object perm

II Memory
① recognition
② recall
③ infant amnesia

[B]

III Perception
① affordances: graspability
② cross-modal } what's the difference
③ intermodal

Slow down!

IV language
?
→ Babbling   (6-10 months)
cooing
1st words   12 months
2-word sent   18 m

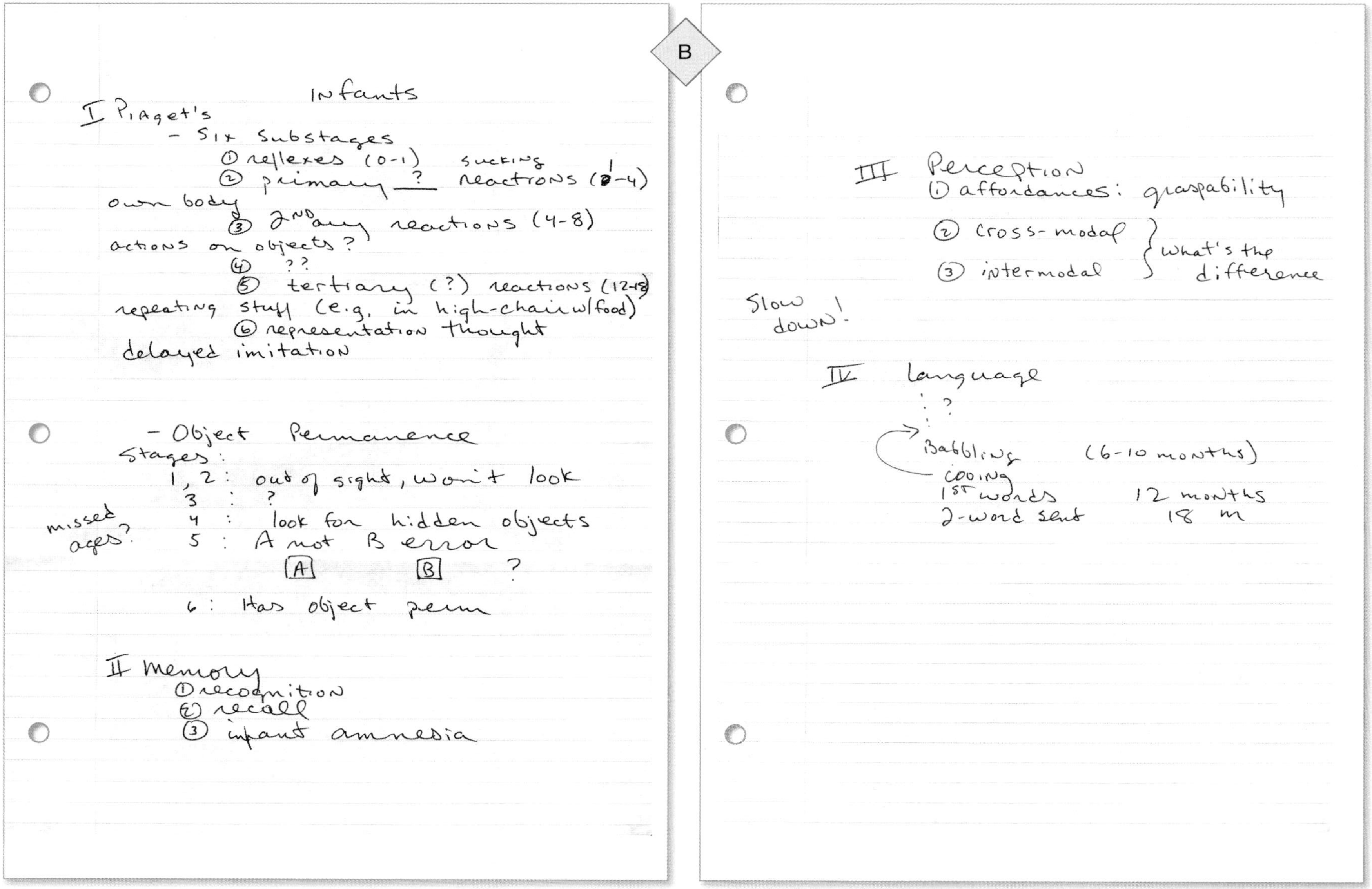

The focus of this chapter is on taking class notes during traditional lectures. Certainly that is the most common situation for note taking. However, we encourage you to think broadly about note taking from other sources. Consider taking notes from textbooks (see Chapter 9), distance-learning courses, group discussions, and videos. Too often students confine their note taking to traditional lectures. One of the authors shows short video clips in his courses. Students rarely take notes on these videos, even though test questions frequently come from the material in the videos. Some students have expressed dismay when they are tested on the video. The author politely reminds them that video time is not a time to tune out. The general note-taking principles we discuss in this chapter apply equally to taking notes from sources other than lectures.

THE TWO FUNCTIONS OF NOTE TAKING

It's best to think of note taking as both a process and a structure (Kiewra et al., 1991). The process of note taking itself includes absorbing the material better as you listen to (or read or watch) the source. The structure of note taking involves the actual end product—the notes themselves—and using these notes as a review tool. Let's look at these two different functions.

Storing Information Mentally

What would you do during a lecture if you were going to be tested on it immediately afterward? Would you take notes on the lecture, or would you just listen without taking notes? If you would take notes, you are probably a person for whom note taking improves the learning (what we called in Chapter 6 *encoding*) of class material. After all, if you have to take the test right after the lecture, it's not as though the notes are going to be useful to you for studying. We encourage you to complete Activity 8.3 with a classmate to see the importance of the actual activity of note taking for learning.

ACTIVITY 8.3 *Note Taking as a Way to Encode Information*

The following activity will help you see the importance of note taking in learning new material.

Task 1: Immediately after one of your classes, write a short quiz on the material and give it to a classmate. Have your classmate take the quiz right away, without looking over any notes.

Task 2: In the next class period, switch roles. Have your classmate prepare a quiz for you. Again, take the quiz immediately.

The act of taking notes itself probably helped your performance on this quiz. This chapter explains why note taking is a valuable learning process. To test whether note taking actually improves learning, you could take another quiz from another class session *without* taking notes in class, but we are so sure that good note taking helps learning that we don't encourage you to try this! A version of this experiment was conducted by Shrager and Mayer (1989).

In an experiment conducted by educational psychologists, some students took notes during a videotaped lecture and some students did not (Shrager & Mayer, 1989). The researchers tested the students right after the lecture, before the students had time to study their notes. In both groups they had two types of students: one type had no knowledge of the lecture topic (low prior knowledge) and one type had a lot of knowledge (high prior knowledge). Those who had low prior knowledge did better if they took notes during the lecture than if they did not, but this was not true for those with high prior knowledge. What this demonstrates is that note taking can serve a vital learning-improvement function if you don't know much about the material beforehand. Other studies have shown less impressive "encoding effects" of note taking. Kenneth Kiewra (1985) reviewed the studies to date and found that far more studies showed a positive effect of note taking on learning than showed no effect (and almost none showed detrimental effects). Of this much we can be fairly sure: If done properly, note taking serves to improve learning. This is one reason why note taking is important. The act of taking notes makes you work harder to understand what is being said in class. Read over the suggestions in Figure 8.2 and then try them out in Activity 8.4.

Suggestions for taking effective notes.   FIGURE 8.2

These suggestions will help you improve your understanding and memory of information from lectures in class.

1. *Think about what the professor is saying.* If you don't take notes (and we've all been guilty of this at one time or another), it is very easy to let your mind wander and to lose track of what is being said. Note taking keeps your mind focused on the topic and forces you to try to understand it.

2. *Write down what is important and leave out what is unimportant.* Not everything said during a lecture is worth writing down. When you take notes, you must decide what is important enough to write down and what can be left out. This will improve your learning, because you must process the information at a deep level. (Do you remember the difference between "deep processing" and "shallow processing" from Chapter 6?) By deciding what is important and what is unimportant, you are improving your learning.

3. *Use your own words.* No one is fast enough to write down everything a professor says, and even if you are, you will learn later in this chapter that this is not a good idea. When you take notes, you must condense a sometimes long-winded explanation given by your professor into a one- or two-sentence description for your notes. That requires sophisticated work on your part. You must decide how best to record what the professor says, using your own words.

Identifying the Main Points from a Lecture

This exercise will help you see whether you are catching on to the most important aspects of a lecture.

1. What is your most difficult class this semester (in which you take a fair amount of notes)?

   _____

2. Look at your notes from one day of that class. What are the three main points the instructor was trying to make?

   a. _____

   _____

   b. _____

   _____

   c. _____

   _____

(continued)

3. Now go to your professor's office during office hours. Ask her to look at what you have written above. Does your professor think those were the most important points of the lecture? If not, ask her if she would be willing to write down what she thinks were the most important points.

a. _____

b. _____

c. _____

We hope it is clear that the actual process of taking notes will improve your learning from the lecture you are listening to. We next discuss the more common conception of note taking, that of external storage.

Storing Information in Writing

In addition to being a good way to improve your learning, notes provide a way to store all of the information you will need for the exam. An exam in college usually covers several weeks of classes. You may hear a lecture in the first week of September but not be tested on it until the first week of October. It is impossible for you to remember all the important ideas and facts from lectures over such a long period of time without writing them down. Your notes serve as an external storage place. They are where you will go to find the information you need. Read Figure 8.3, then complete Activity 8.5 to see how to apply the information in the figure.

FIGURE 8.3   Notes as an external storage device.

Your notes will serve as an effective storage device if you follow these suggestions.

1. *Use your notes.*

If you go to all the trouble of taking good notes, use them in studying for tests. The point of storing course information is very simple: You will need the information to review for exams. Therefore, if you take notes, you should use them. If you find that your notes are not that helpful when you are studying for tests, maybe the kind of information you're writing down is not the kind that's being tested. Maybe you are taking notes on unimportant information. To check yourself, compare your notes with someone else's who is doing well. This may give you an idea of what is important in the lectures and what is not.

2. *Organize your notes.*

If your notes are going to serve as your file of important information, it is important that you keep them organized. First, make sure that the notes are in correct order. A loose-leaf three-ring binder may be best for this purpose. Binders allow you to add pages in case you miss class, so you can still keep your notes in proper order. This practice will also allow you to go back and expand on the information. Also make sure that you put a date on all of your lecture notes and that you have some kind of outline system (we'll talk about outlining again later in this chapter). Use separate notebooks for each class—this will also help with your organization.

Making a Good Storage Place

This exercise will give you an idea of whether your notes are effective as a storage site.

Step 1: A good test of whether your notes have stored information effectively is if someone else can figure out what your notes mean. Pick a class in which you take a lot of notes. For this assignment you will need the help of a friend who is not in the class. Give one day's notes to your friend and ask him to answer the questions below:

1. Based on the notes, what do you think were the main points of this lecture?

   a. _____

   b. _____

   c. _____

2. What things were unclear in the notes?

   a. _____

   b. _____

   c. _____

3. Were the notes well organized?   YES   NO
4. Do you think you could study from these notes?   YES   NO

   If no, why not?

   _____

Step 2: Read your friend's responses, and refer to your notes to answer the following questions:

1. Was your friend correct, in your estimation, about what the main points of the lecture were?   YES   NO
   If not, what were the main points?

   a. _____

   b. _____

   c. _____

2. How could you improve the clarity of the things your friend found to be unclear?

   _____

   _____

(continued)

ACTIVITY 8.5 *continued*

3. If your friend said the notes were unorganized, how could you organize them better?

_____

_____

4. If your friend said he couldn't study from these notes, how could you make them more user-friendly?

_____

_____

Now let's look at specific ways to improve your note taking. You don't necessarily need to adopt all of these strategies to be a successful note taker, but if you are using very few of these strategies—or even doing the opposite of what we suggest—changes could be very beneficial for you. We recommend that you compare your notes to the strategies listed in Figure 8.4 and the descriptions below and consider how you could improve your note taking.

FIGURE 8.4 Thirteen note-taking strategies.

1. Go to class.
2. Pay attention.
3. Write neatly.
4. Make your notes attractive.
5. Don't write too much or too little.
6. Avoid unnecessary or long words.
7. Take notes in your own words.
8. Be organized.
9. Pick out the main points.
10. Don't use a tape recorder.
11. Form connections between concepts.
12. Compare your notes with a classmate's.
13. Review and clarify your notes after class.

A BAKER'S DOZEN NOTE-TAKING STRATEGIES

Being a good note taker requires many skills and habits. We believe that the strategies described in this section can help you improve your characteristics as a note taker and learn to take good notes. Figure 8.4 summarizes them for you so you can refer to them as needed.

1. Go to Class. This was so important we mentioned it already in Chapter 1. If you must miss class, we encourage you to borrow notes from someone and copy them into your notebook. Bear in mind that not attending class will be very harmful to your performance. There is tremendous advantage to hearing the professor's lecture yourself, rather than getting it secondhand from a classmate. The biggest reason has to do with the first function of note taking, mentioned at the beginning of the chapter: note taking improves encoding. If you are not in class to process the information, notes won't help your encoding. Another disadvantage of copying notes rather than taking them is that you may lose information. Your classmate may not have written down all of the important points, she might not have understood everything the professor said, she may use a different note-taking style, or she may use different abbreviations or terminology. All of these things will interfere with your comprehension. The bottom line is simple: Go to class and your notes will be better.

We recognize that you may not be able to attend every session of every class in every semester. A few things to keep in mind on those rare occasions when you must borrow someone else's notes are:

- Ask to borrow the notes of someone who is doing well in the class. Chances are, that person takes pretty good notes.
- Copy the notes by hand, don't photocopy them. By writing the notes out, you will be more likely to think about what is in your classmate's notes. (Remember, note taking is an aid to encoding.) If you simply photocopy them, you may not even look at them, and you will not be able to ask your classmate for clarification—which is our next tip.
- Copy the notes with your classmate by your side. He can help you with anything that you don't understand.
- Go to the professor during office hours and ask for clarification of anything you still do not understand.
- Notify professors in advance if you know you will not be in class. If that is not possible, e-mail them that day and let them know you will be absent. This is simply common courtesy, and it also may increase the chances that they will spend time with you to go over anything you don't understand. (When you notify the professor that you will be missing class, please don't ask, "Are we going to do anything important today?")

2. Pay Attention. Remember when we talked about attention in Chapter 6? We said that attention is like a pie that has limited capacity and is difficult to divide up; the more you divide it up, the harder it is to concentrate on one thing. Make sure that when you are in class, the thing to which you are paying the most attention is the lecture. If you let your mind wander, you will miss what is said. If you miss what is said, you will spend time either trying to remember what the professor said (which you won't be able to do, if you never encoded it) or asking a classmate what the professor said. You will then likely miss the next thing the professor says, and this unhealthy cycle of playing catch-up will continue. Pay attention and avoid this problem.

© andresr – FOTOLIA

Sometimes even the most attentive student can get lost in a fast or unorganized lecture. As a student, you should feel empowered to ask your professor to slow down. This is easier in small classes or on campuses where students and professors are acquainted to some degree. Regardless of your situation, professors will not find it unreasonable if you occasionally ask them to clarify or slow down.

3. Write Neatly. Nothing is more frustrating than not being able to read your own writing. The more time you have to spend figuring out your own handwriting, the less time you will have for reviewing your notes. If you often ask yourself "What does this say?" when you are looking at your own notes, then your writing needs improvement.

4. Make Your Notes Attractive. This is similar to Number 3. In general, we want your notes to look good. It sounds shallow, but here's our reasoning. People who work to have clear notes will more likely have a clear head. If you take pride in how your notes look, you will have a better organized sense of the course. Notes that have an attractive appearance also look good to others. If your notes look good, you will develop a positive reputation among professors and fellow students as someone who attends class, is organized, understands the material, and takes pride in his or her work. We hope this doesn't sound like we are promoting style over substance. We would prefer sloppy notes with good content over neat notes with poor content. Still, we believe that if you work to have notes that *look* good, your notes will *be* good.

5. Don't Write Too Much or Too Little. This may sound like a no-win proposition, but we don't think it is. It is important to strike a balance between writing so much that you get behind during the lecture and writing so little that you don't understand what you meant when you go back to review. It is not wise to try to write down everything the professor says. In the first place, you won't be able to do it. In the second place, not everything that the professor says is worth writing down (you may have already figured that out). When you write down the main points, try to be brief and to use some abbreviations. Use abbreviations that are familiar to you and with which you feel comfortable. If you haven't developed any abbreviations in your note-taking style, here are some common ones:

ABBREVIATION	MEANING
w/	with
w/o	without
b/c	because
s.t.	such that (used frequently in math classes)
w.r.t.	with respect to (also used in math classes)
↑	increases
↓	decreases
→	leads to, causes
↔	is related to
e.g.	for example
i.e.	in other words

Abbreviations can be valuable, because they free up time for you to write down more information and to think more carefully about what the professor is saying. However, if you abbreviate too much, you may find yourself having trouble figuring out what all of the abbreviations mean. Your notes need to make sense on their own. For example, consider the following sentence from notes on a course in introductory psychology:

T. a. many fn. of the hypo: f, f, f, s.

You may not be able to decipher this sentence without spending a lot of time nosing through your textbook. Your notes should be clear enough that you don't need to consult your textbook to make sense of them. The above sentence will not be very helpful to you in your studying, whereas the next sentence, which still uses abbreviations, is much better:

Many funcs. of hypothalamus. e.g., feed, fight, flight, sex.

This sentence does not contain much information, but at least it will be understandable when you go back to it at test time. The professor probably said something like:

One of the structures in the limbic system is the hypothalamus. It is located just below the thalamus, which is what the word "hypo" means. By electrically stimulating or by destroying portions of it, biological psychologists have identified different survival functions that are located in the hypothalamus. In other words, different sets of neurons in the hypothalamus fire when different bodily functions are activated. The four most common functions are: (a) hunger motivation, or feeding; (b) the ability to defend one's self, or fighting; (c) the ability to escape enemies when the species deems it necessary, or fleeing; and (d) also sexual desire is located in the hypothalamus."

The one-line summary effectively covers everything the professor said.

The best policy is not to abbreviate important concepts until they have become familiar to you. Save your abbreviations for words that are not an essential part of the sentences or phrases that you write. For example, in anatomy class, don't abbreviate different body parts until you are very familiar with them. Since knowing body parts is such an important part of an anatomy course, you should write them out fully. It may be helpful to develop abbreviations for phrases such as "is located near," "is contained in," or "functions as." The abbreviations you use will depend on what works for you and the type of course it is. Just remember, too many abbreviations may save you time in the short run but will cost you time in the long run.

6. Avoid Unnecessary or Long Words. Phrases like "there is" and "there are" take time to write and add very little to your notes. You will understand the sentence just fine if you leave out these phrases. Try to notice which phrases you can eliminate as you take notes. (If you understand Spanish, you may want to use the much shorter *hay*, which means both "there is" and "there are.")

Furthermore, a short word that means the same as a long word is always preferable, unless the long word is important in the course. It may be hard to come up with a synonym for something like "left main artery" (although after a while you may start to use "l.m.a."), but you can often shorten conventional words. Write "very" instead of "extremely," and "use" instead of "utilize." (Can you think of others?) That will save you some time and possibly avoid some hand cramps.

7. Take Notes in Your Own Words. When you take verbatim notes, you spend a great deal of energy trying to write down everything the professor says word for word. When you take notes in your own words (what are called generative notes), you think about the notes and begin to elaborate on them during the lecture.

Why are generative notes better? They are better because the cognitive process of taking generative notes requires more thinking on your part than does taking verbatim notes. Generative notes require listening carefully to what the instructor says, then mentally summarizing the main points. You must comprehend the professor, then put the ideas into your own words. This is where the term *generative* comes from. You are generating notes from your own thinking, as opposed to copying what the professor says. Research has found that **generative note taking** enhances students' comprehension of the lecture topic (Kiewra et al., 1991).

STRATEGY SUGGESTION

Don't be a sponge when you take notes. Be active. Think about what the professor says, and try to put the lecture into your own words.

---

8. Be Organized. We talked about the importance of being organized in Chapter 7 when we covered learning strategies. An organized note-taking system is part of being cognitively organized. Here are some ways you can make your notes more organized:

- *Use a hierarchical structure.* This usually requires an outline, which professors sometimes provide before lectures. If the professor puts an outline on the course Web site or computer projector, write it down. If he goes to the trouble of writing it down, he must think it's worthwhile, and you should too.

- *Leave plenty of blank space in your notes.* Don't feel a need to cram as much as you can on one page. Leave space between concepts, and leave even more space between major section headings and subheadings. This will allow you to go back later and fill in any information that you missed (this is related to Strategy 13).

- *Use indentation to indicate the organization of ideas.* Don't line all your notes up on the same left margin. Indent when a particular topic falls under another. This will help you see how the course concepts relate and which topics are more or less important.

- *Don't feel obliged to adopt someone else's method of note taking.* The specific manner in which you write your notes should be up to you. Some people have developed particular systems of taking notes. Our recommendation is to adopt a note-taking system with which you feel comfortable. If your current system is working—if your notes are organized and they are serving you well in studying for tests—stick with it. On the other hand, don't feel obligated to stick to a system simply because you have been using it for a long time.

■ *Don't turn your computer into your own printing press.* Many professors post their lectures on Moodle, WebCT, or other course management software prior to class. When the first author started doing this, many students came in with lecture notes already printed off. He subsequently observed far less generative note taking. He now posts the notes on Moodle only after the lecture period. Course management software is great for both students and professors, but it can breed laziness in note taking. Remember that notes are more than just external storage. If done properly, they can help you learn.

Work to keep your notes as organized as possible. If they are jumbled, messy, unconnected, or incomplete, find ways to organize them. Note taking is an important tool. If it's broken, you had better fix it. Activity 8.6 will help you see areas where your note-taking habits could be improved.

Taking Organized and Complete Notes

Are your notes organized and complete? The more "no" responses you have to the following questions, the more you need to work on organization and completeness. Compare your scores to others in your class.

1. Do you have notes from all class days you have missed?
   (If you didn't miss any classes, answer yes.)   YES   NO

2. Are all your notes in order?   YES   NO

3. Are all your notes hand-written (not photocopied)?   YES   NO

4. Have you been to a professor's office to ask questions?   YES   NO

5. Do your notes have an outline form or other hierarchy?   YES   NO

6. Did you leave blank spaces for filling in?   YES   NO

7. Do you indent your notes with headings and subheadings as opposed to having
   them all line up along the left margin?   YES   NO

Being an organized note taker, unfortunately, is not entirely within your control. The extent to which your notes are organized depends partly on the organization of the professor. Sometimes professors are very organized in their lecture presentations. They may have very clear outlines, they may stop and review at the end of major topics, and they may make connections between important points. However, fate will not always be that kind. When you have a disorganized professor, you must work even harder to make your notes organized. This may involve doing the reading before class so you have some idea of where he is going. You also might have to spend more time in his office asking for clarification.

9. Pick Out the Main Points. This strategy is related to the strategy of taking generative notes. You will be able to pick out the main points of a lecture better if you are taking generative notes. Why? Because the process of taking generative notes means that you are thinking about what is being said. If you are thinking about the lecture, the main points should become apparent to you.

Picking out the main points really involves figuring out what is important and what is not. Good students are better able to identify the important points than poorer students are. They likely do this by thinking about what they read or hear in class, putting things into their own words, and, as a result, identifying the main points.

10. Don't Use a Tape Recorder. George, a doctoral student in public health, was taking an advanced statistics course. He sat in the front row, never missed a class, and took what appeared to be magnificent notes. He also carried a tape recorder to class with him every day, and he recorded every minute of the 4 hours of weekly lectures. One of the authors, a classmate of George's, once asked him whether he ever went back and listened to the tapes. He said he didn't. The author asked him if he erased the tapes a week or so later, or after the test, when he (presumably) wasn't going to need them anymore. Again, he said no, that he kept them all and planned to do so even after he completed his Ph.D. The author's wife, a classmate of George's in a different class, reported that George also recorded every minute of this class as well. George was an excellent student, but we wonder whether the tape recorder was important to George's success.

Students sometimes wonder if it's a good idea to tape-record lectures. Occasionally they ask if we mind being tape-recorded in class. In fact, some universities now have the capacity to podcast professors' lectures so that students can download them to their media player. Whether it is recording yourself or downloading podcasts, we do not recommend recording lectures, for several reasons. First, knowing that you have a taped or downloaded version of the class may lull you into complacency during class, which could make you less likely to process the information well. (Or in the case of podcasting, it might prompt you to skip class altogether. Of course, the problem is that you may not return to the podcast.) Second, assuming you have gone to class, it is a waste of time to go back and listen to something you have already heard. If you are paying attention in class, there should be no need for a recording. If there are parts of the lecture you miss, instead of listening to a podcast, we recommend e-mailing your professor with your specific question. In addition, since the cost of tapes can be quite high, tape-recording is not a good use of your money either.

All indications suggested that George was an excellent student, and maybe students who are conscientious enough to bring a tape recorder tend to be strong students. Although the tapes probably did not hurt George's performance, we doubt they helped him much. He was left with hundreds of hours of taped statistics lectures that probably cost quite a bit of money to make and to which he probably never listened.

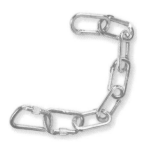

11. Form Connections Between Concepts. In Chapter 7, we talked about the importance of seeing relations between the things you are studying. Through the learning strategy of **elaboration,** you can build connections among the various course topics. One way to do this is to make connections in your notes. Without connections, your notes are just an unorganized array of facts. However, if you do form connections between the concepts in your notes, you will have an integrated and rich body of knowledge with conceptual coherence.

What does it mean to form connections? How should you go about forming connections? Here are two techniques that we recommend:

■ *Identify relations between your lecture notes and your course readings.* This will enrich your knowledge structure by illustrating how the lecture material complements, overlaps, or diverges from course readings. Lectures often include further examples of concepts covered in the text. For example, Figure 8.5 shows material on learning theory from an introductory psychology course. You can see that the text outline and lecture notes are not identical, but they do overlap. You can build connections in your knowledge if you study how the lecture notes compare to the text outline. For example, the notes don't talk specifically about Skinner, so your text must be your source for this topic. Your lecture notes seem to have richer examples of the schedules of reinforcement, and they also may define the principles of reinforcement and punishment better. If you combined these two pieces of material into a larger framework, you would have a much more thorough understanding of learning theory.

■ *Generate questions about what you hear in lecture.* You can do this either in class or after class. If you think of questions in class, ask them right then. If you think of them as you are going back over your notes, e-mail your professor or ask your teaching assistant in the discussion section. Formulating questions will require more thought on your part and will help you form additional connections between concepts.

12. Compare Your Notes with a Classmate's. Whether it's after class or while you're studying for an exam, looking at someone else's notes can be helpful. We recommend that you compare notes with someone who attends class regularly,

---

Comparison of notes from lecture and notes from textbook.   FIGURE 8.5

Class Notes

I. Classical Conditioning

   A. Pavlov

   B. Updating Pavlov

   C. Pavlov's Legacy

II. Operant Conditioning

   A. Skinner's Experiments

   B. Updating Skinner's Understanding

   C. Skinner's Legacy

III. Learning by Observation

   A. Bandura's Experiment

   B. Applications

Textbook Notes

I. Classical Conditioning

   A. Basic Principles

   B. Applications

   C. Cognitive Perspective

II. Operant Conditioning

   A. Basic Principles

   B. Schedules of Reinforcement

   C. Critique

III. Learning by Observation

IV. Philosophical Critique of Learning Research

   A. Public Policy

   B. Religious and Moral Implications

has a neat and organized method for note taking, and does well on tests. Comparing notes helps you evaluate the quality of your own notes. It will also allow you to fill in any gaps in your notes.

Of course, this should be a two-way street. Comparing notes can help both people. Most of the time, two people taking notes from the same lecture will come away with different things, so comparing notes allows you to pool information. It also helps each person develop a new perspective on the material. Maybe you had one interpretation of the topics covered and your classmate had a different one. The two of you can then work toward the best understanding of the material, thus improving your course comprehension. In general, comparing notes allows you to increase the quality and quantity of your notes.

13. Review and Clarify Your Notes After Class. If you take your notes during lecture and then do not look at them until you start studying for tests, you are not using them as well as you could. After class, you should do several things to review and clarify your notes:

- *Go over notes after class.* This will help you remember things and fill in gaps. You probably didn't get a chance to write down everything, so after class—when you are more relaxed and have more time—you can elaborate and clarify sections of your notes. You could go as far as to recopy them. This is usually not necessary unless you can't read your handwriting.

- *E-mail or visit your professor to ask questions.* Do this if you still do not understand something after you have clarified and elaborated on your notes and compared your notes with a classmate's. Have specific questions in mind; don't simply say, "I didn't understand yesterday's lecture. Could you explain it to me?" Identify what you had problems with, and ask for help. You will get much more cooperation if you are organized and to the point. Often, the best time to talk to professors is right after class, when the material is fresh in both of your minds. If this is inconvenient for you or your professor, go to office hours, make an appointment, or send an e-mail.

Now that you have read about strategies for improving your notes, we invite you to consider your current level of note-taking skill. Activity 8.7 asks you to evaluate your own note taking and identify three ways in which your note taking can get better.

ACTIVITY 8.7 *Evaluating Your Note-Taking Performance*

Determine the extent to which each statement applies to you. Use your answers to identify your strengths and weaknesses, then suggest ideas for self-improvement below.

1.	Go to class	①	②	③	④	⑤
2.	Pay attention	①	②	③	④	⑤
3.	Write neatly	①	②	③	④	⑤
4.	Make notes attractive	①	②	③	④	⑤

5.	Use proper amount of writing	①	②	③	④	⑤
6.	No long/unnecessary words	①	②	③	④	⑤
7.	Take notes in own words	①	②	③	④	⑤
8.	Organized notes	①	②	③	④	⑤
	Hierarchical notes	①	②	③	④	⑤
	Blank spaces in notes	①	②	③	④	⑤
9.	Pick out the main points	①	②	③	④	⑤
10.	No tape recorder	①	②	③	④	⑤
11.	Form connections between concepts	①	②	③	④	⑤
	Integrate text and lecture	①	②	③	④	⑤
	Generate questions in lecture	①	②	③	④	⑤
12.	Compare notes with classmate's	①	②	③	④	⑤
13.	Review/clarify notes	①	②	③	④	⑤
	Ask professor for help	①	②	③	④	⑤

Total Note-Taking Score (out of 85): _____

Based on your responses, identify three ways you could improve your notes.

a. _____

_____

b. _____

_____

c. _____

_____

CHAPTER SUMMARY

This chapter has given you some specific dos and don'ts for note taking. In the end, the best notes are the ones that help you learn. Developing a useful note-taking system may take some trial and error on your part. Keep in mind that your time is limited, so you may not be able to do everything you want in every class. On the other hand, if you don't take good notes, you are much less likely to do well.

Some professors emphasize material in class notes when constructing exams. A test may depend exclusively on what was presented in class lectures. So, if your notes are similar to your professor's, you will do just fine. Other professors may use questions from a test bank developed for the textbook. In this case, it is important that you do the reading carefully. If the professor covers the same things in class that are in the text, then your notes will also be helpful. In general, it is almost always true that your notes will serve as a valuable resource come test time.

As one final piece of advice in this chapter, to encapsulate the many tips we have given so far, we urge you: *Take your note taking seriously*. In many ways, note taking represents the essence of college student learning. The process of taking notes is a valuable endeavor, so do it well.

Improving Your Reading

Chapter Goals

This chapter will help you:

- Learn what expert readers do, and how to use that information to become more of an expert yourself

- Take full advantage of all the features of a book, not just the text in the book's main body

- Identify some activities to do *before* you start reading a text

- Develop ways to be active rather than passive when you read

- Identify some activities to do *after* you are done reading a text

Key Terms

bibliography	index
decode	narrative text
expository text	preface
front matter	table of contents
glossary	

CHAPTER 9

Reading is one of the most important skills for learning, both in college and in life. If you can't read well, you will not do well in college or in life. It is as simple as that. However, by reading well, we do not mean just being able to decode words and know what the words mean. This is the foundation of reading, and it is hard to learn from reading if you can't **decode**—translate letters and sounds to words. But there is much more to reading than just decoding. In college, professors assume you know the words you are reading. What they want you to do is to extract the meaning from the text to learn about and comprehend the important ideas, theories, principles, models, and other aspects of the content area they are teaching. They want you to come to understand and be able to use these important ideas in your own thinking. It is not enough to just know the words; you must be able to comprehend the larger meaning of the ideas in the text. Accordingly, your main goal when reading should be comprehension and understanding, not just decoding the words or trying to memorize the words that are in boldface or italics. Some students equate reading with just decoding the words. Others take a more active approach to reading. What kind of reader are you? Before you read further, complete Activity 9.1 to find out.

ACTIVITY 9.1   *Initial Assessment of Reading Strategies*

Indicate the extent to which you do the activities listed while reading.

	Never or almost never	Rarely	Frequently	Always or almost always
Set a goal before you begin.	①	②	③	④
Ask yourself questions about the text.	①	②	③	④
Change your strategy based on the difficulty of the text.	①	②	③	④
Take notes during the reading.	①	②	③	④
Reread when you don't understand.	①	②	③	④
Listen to music.	④	③	②	①
Fall asleep.	④	③	②	①

SCORING:

The following categories give a rough indiction of your reading strategies:

24 and above: You probably have good reading strategies. This chapter can serve as a helpful review of important reading skills.

17–23: You probably use good reading strategies some of the time. This chapter will help you identify ways you can improve your reading.

16 and below: This chapter is definitely for you. It will help you focus on some important reading strategies. We encourage you to read this chapter carefully and to use the suggestions we offer.

PROFILE OF A GOOD READER

What do good readers do when they read? As you might imagine, psychologists and educators have done a great deal of research on reading and comprehension. This research has investigated the behavior of very young children as they begin to learn to read as well as examined older readers and the strategies they use when they try to comprehend various kinds of text. The research has often compared good readers to poor readers and investigated the different strategies of these two types of readers.

Research on the good or expert readers shows that they are "active" readers. They don't just read the text passively, word for word, but they constantly think about what they are reading and try to make sense out of it. In other words, they are self-regulated when they read. They are readers who set goals for their reading, monitor their comprehension and progress toward their goals, and try different strategies to make sure they are reaching their goals. They try to increase their comprehension by relating what they are reading to what they already know; in other words, they link new material to their prior knowledge on the topic. Other ways good readers are active and self-regulatory: They ask themselves questions as they read, they try to monitor their comprehension, and they repair their understanding if they discover they don't understand something. This repairing can involve, at the simplest level, rereading the text, but active and good readers use a host of other self-regulatory strategies to help them understand what they read. We discuss many of these strategies in this chapter.

Besides being active and self-regulated, good readers also know a lot about strategies for reading. They have a lot of metacognitive knowledge about texts, reading, and reading strategies. They know about different types of texts. They know strategies they can use for reading comprehension; they know how to use these strategies; and most important, they know when and why to use them. In this chapter, we provide some of this metacognitive knowledge about reading strategies, but it is up to you to use them in your own reading. This chapter presents strategies focusing on three phases in reading: (a) prereading strategies, or those to consider before you start reading; (b) strategies to use while you are reading; and (c) strategies to use after you finish reading.

PHASE 1: PREREADING STRATEGIES

Research on reading shows that expert readers think about their goals for reading before they start. They don't just pick up a textbook and start reading it; they think about how the text material is organized and how best to approach reading it. They also think about what they know about the topic before they start reading. In this section, we will discuss strategies for setting goals for reading and other strategies for "prereading" a text.

Parts of a Book

One of the first components of effective reading is knowledge of different parts of a book. Everyone is familiar with the main body of the book; it contains the main text that most people read. But there are other components of a book that are interesting and can aid comprehension. First, there is the **front matter.** This portion of the book contains notes from the authors to the readers, information on what motivated the authors to write the book, and other introductory information. Most students skip the front matter, but it often has interesting material. Although you can get away with skipping the front matter, we recommend you do *not* skip the **table of contents.** The table of contents shows the order of chapters and the different sections of each chapter. (Sometimes there is a section called "contents in brief," which will not have the sections of the chapters, but all textbooks will have a full table of contents.) It is vital that you look at the table of contents. Much like a well-planned trip needs a resource like Mapquest, so too a well-planned trip through a book requires knowing the direction of the book. Oftentimes, each chapter will have a list of its subheadings at the beginning. Or (as is the case in this book) the chapter will begin with chapter goals. These goals usually correspond to the main parts of the chapter.

In the main body of the book, there are other parts besides just the text. In this book, for example, we have activities and figures. Many students see these features of the book as a way to speed up their reading, with the logic being that these sections can be skipped and thus they can finish sooner. This is a bad idea. Set-off items like activities and figures contain *very* important information that should *not* be skipped. The information in figures, tables, and insets is often a summary of what the authors spent several paragraphs discussing. So if a writer is going to give you built-in review material, by all means use it. Another way this information is valuable is that professors and test-bank writers often use these boxes to prepare test questions. They use them because the boxes provide good summaries and also because they know students often skip these and they want to reward students for reading them. So don't ignore the parts of the book that are not "text" per se.

At the end of the book (called the end matter), there are two other important parts of the book. The first is the **bibliography.** Just like a bibliography you prepare for a research paper, a book's bibliography is a list of all of the works cited by the authors. This can be helpful if you are using the book for research purposes. For example, if you are doing a research paper on constructionist interpretations of the U.S. Constitution, the first book you use will likely have other valuable references in its bibliography. From this first book, you may decide to narrow your research to the 17th Amendment—the direct election of U.S. Senators by voters. The first book may have good citations on the 17th Amendment. Another important part of the end matter is the **index.** The index contains all of the concepts used in the book and page numbers where the concept is discussed. Larger books may have an *author index* and a *subject index*. The index is extremely helpful when you are reviewing for exams. For example, if your class notes from organic chemistry make reference to ketones but you didn't quite understand what you wrote, you can use the index to find the material in the book rather than flipping through dozens of pages. A third component of the end matter is the **glossary.** Similar to the index, the glossary contains all of the main concepts from the book and their accompanying definitions.

Set Goals for Your Reading

Many students approach a reading session with a goal of just completing the reading within a certain time: "I have two hours to study tonight, so I can read the three chapters in my sociology textbook." This is certainly reasonable in terms of time management and your study schedule, but expert readers have different goals in mind when they read.

The most important goal for reading is to achieve understanding. This means you always try to be an active reader and always search for meaning (comprehension) in the text. Expert readers do this for everything they read, but especially for textbooks or other books that they are studying. So before you start to read, remind yourself that your goal will be comprehension.

Another important goal to set before you start to read is to understand why you will be reading this text. Will you be reading it to study for a midterm exam? Will you read the text so you can contribute to a discussion in a seminar? Are you going to write a paper about the material it covers? These questions will help you guide and direct your reading, because how you read the text should change depending on your purposes and goals.

Activate Your Prior Knowledge

One of the most stable findings in research on reading is that prior knowledge has a great influence on reading comprehension. In other words, what you already know about the topic has a huge impact on what you can learn from reading a text. When you have prior knowledge, it is easier for you to absorb the text because you can integrate any new information into what you already know. On the other hand, if you don't know very much about the topic, then you will be confronting more new information in the text and won't necessarily have the schemas (see Chapter 6) in place to integrate the new material. Creating these schemas takes time, so reading will be more difficult when you don't have much prior knowledge. (The importance of prior knowledge is also discussed in Chapter 6 on memory and Chapter 13 on problem solving.)

One strategy for activating prior knowledge is to ask yourself questions about the topic in the text before you start to read. What do you know about this topic already? What have you heard about it? Do you have any experiences with it? For example, in a history course, the topic of the text might be the Vietnam War. This event in American history happened some time ago, and you probably have no direct recall or experience of it. But you may have heard about it from your parents or grandparents. You may have seen a popular movie about it or read other textbooks or novels that referred to this topic. What can you recall about it now? Jot down these ideas on a sheet of paper. It does not matter if what you recall are facts, opinions, or vague recollections of something someone told you about the war. Look at what you jotted down. What sense can you make of these notes? Given what you have written, what questions do you now have about the Vietnam War? Write down these questions and try to answer them as you now go on to read the text. For example, you may have noted questions such as, When did it start and end? What happened there and why were we there? Where is Vietnam? How many people died in the war? What is the status of the United States' relations with Vietnam now? What happened to Vietnam after the war? Why did Vietnamese refugees come to the United States? These questions can guide your reading and help you take a more active role in reading the text.

Examine the Structure of the Text

Besides activating their prior knowledge about the topic, expert readers also know about different types of text and the different parts of a text. Different kinds of texts are organized in different ways. Different disciplines have different ways of thinking about knowledge in their field, so textbooks in different subject areas may not be organized in the same fashion. In addition, general textbooks obviously are not organized in the same way as novels or specialized books on a topic. It is important that you try to understand this organization of knowledge and the structure of the books that you will read for your courses. Here are some ways you can look at key aspects of the text before you begin reading.

© homestudio – FOTOLIA

Examine the Table of Contents. What is the overall organization of the book? The chapter headings in a textbook indicate important general areas within the book, and by implication within the field. These chapter headings most likely will reflect how the instructor organizes the course as well. For example, an introductory psychology book will have chapters for biological psychology (brain and behavior), learning/cognitive psychology (learning, memory, thinking), social psychology (person in a social world), personality (traits and individual differences), developmental psychology (psychology across the life span), and clinical psychology (behavior disorders and treatment). These are the main subfields in psychology, and the chapter headings are a clue to important differences in how psychologists study different psychological phenomena. In more specialized books (not general textbooks), the chapter divisions signal different parts of the "story" or argument the author is trying to develop. For example, an art history book may have a chronological structure, with chapters corresponding to time periods (e.g., Middle Ages, Renaissance), and the author discussing how the art in each period differs from art in other periods. In novels, the chapter breaks may be less informative as they may serve very different roles, such as signifying a lapse in time (a chapter may occur several days, weeks, months, or years later than the previous one) or a different character's point of view (the husband's perspective in one chapter, the wife's perspective in the next).

Survey Headings Within Chapters. Most textbooks have headings within chapters. These headings are not just randomly put in to break up the writing; they are there for a purpose. The author is trying to communicate something through the headings and their placement. In general, most authors organize chapters into topics, and they signal a change in the topic with a chapter heading. That is, within the same chapter, all the material refers to the same general topic, but within that topic, the author identifies different subtopics with chapter headings. For example, this chapter has three main headings: "Phase 1: Prereading Strategies," "Phase 2: Strategies to Use While You Are Reading," and "Phase 3: Strategies to Use After Reading." These headings reflect the importance of these three phases in the process of reading. Most general textbooks use main headings in similar ways. They signal important distinctions that you should pay attention to in your reading and studying.

In addition, within these three main headings, the subheadings also signal important distinctions. So, this section on prereading has four subheadings: on parts of a book, setting goals for your reading, activating prior knowledge, and examining the structure of the text. This means that within the phase of prereading, there are four important general activities. Again, most textbooks use subheadings in a similar fashion. These subheadings will help you keep track of where you are in your reading and also help you understand the structure of the argument or information the author is trying to convey to you.

Read the Preface, Chapter Overviews, and Chapter Summaries. Your main goal in reading is to understand the author's main points or ideas. All authors have an argument they are trying to present, and they want you to comprehend their ideas. Of course, some authors are better than others at conveying their ideas, making it easier for you to extract the meaning from the text. To help you understand their books, most authors include a **preface** in the front matter where they discuss their general goals and reasons for writing the book, their perspective on the issues, how they have organized the book, and perhaps even a statement of their main theme. As we mentioned at the beginning of this section, reading the front matter will help you understand the authors' goals and what they would like you to learn from the book. In addition, in some disciplines, particularly the social sciences, different authors have different general theoretical perspectives on issues. The authors might mention their perspective in the preface, which will help you understand how they interpret and discuss the ideas in the discipline. For example, in economics, some perspectives stress the role of the government, and other perspectives stress the role of the market in addressing economic problems. Depending on their perspective, authors will have different views of the problems, different interpretations of the data, and different suggestions for how to solve economic problems. Knowing the authors' perspective ahead of time may help you in reading and understanding the text.

In addition, most textbooks offer an introductory section at the beginning of each chapter. The purpose of this section is to give you an overview of the material in the chapter. Besides telling you what will be covered in the chapter, it may also tell you the goals of the chapter or what your goals should be in reading it. Studying the overview can help you set your goals and activate your prior knowledge for the chapter.

Finally, many textbooks close each chapter with a summary or review section that restates the general ideas or conclusions of the chapter. It may be a good idea to read the review or summary *before* reading the rest of the text, so that you will know where the author is going to end up. In addition, sometimes you can get lost in the detail in the rest of the chapter, but this final summary section usually restates the main ideas of the chapter without all the details. By reading the last section first, you will know what the big ideas are so you can focus on them as you read the chapter. If the authors go off on some side roads or tangents from the main argument, you can spot these digressions and try to maintain your focus on the main ideas.

STRATEGY SUGGESTION

Read the chapter review at the end of the chapter first.

Understand Expository and Narrative Texts. Texts are often structured in different ways depending on their content and substance. An important general distinction is the difference between expository and narrative texts. **Expository texts** focus on conveying information, whereas **narrative texts** tell a story. General textbooks are the classic expository text, and short stories and novels are good examples of narrative texts. Some nonfiction books are organized with a narrative structure more than an expository structure. For example, the popular book *A Civil Action* tells the story of an environmental pollution case and the lawyers who tried the case, as well as the families who were affected by the pollution. This is not a novel; it is nonfiction, but the text is structured and written very much in a narrative style.

Figure 9.1 lists some ways expository texts may be structured (see Wood, Woloshyn, & Willoughby, 1995). Knowing these general types of texts may help your comprehension. For example, if you realize that the book you are reading is a compare/contrast text, then you will be ready to take notes or write a summary that reflects this general organization. Figure 9.2 lists some features of narrative texts and provides a general set of questions that you might want to think about as you read a novel, a short story, or even a nonfiction book that is told in a narrative structure (Wood et al., 1995). This metacognitive knowledge about text structures will help guide your use of strategies in Phase 2—the strategies to use while you are actually reading.

FIGURE 9.1   Expository text structures.

1. **Classification.** The text is designed to convey the categories in an area as well as the relations among the categories. Often these reflections are hierarchical.

    Examples:

    - A biology text that discusses the classification systems for plants and animals and the levels of categories and classes
    - A psychology textbook that summarizes the classification of mental health disorders, from psychotic to neurotic problems

2. **Illustration.** The text focuses on an example or a case study to convey a general idea.

    Examples:

    - An anthropology text that gives an in-depth description of a remote tribe and culture to illustrate the role of kinship relations
    - A business textbook that uses a case study of a company to show the problems of management–union relations

3. **Comparison/contrast.** The text makes distinctions between two or more categories or events.

    Examples:

    - A philosophy text that compares four different philosophers in terms of their theories about the nature of knowledge
    - A chemistry text that compares two different models for describing a chemical reaction

4. **Causal.** The text develops a causal argument for why something occurs or happened.

    Examples:

    - A history text that describes a sequence of events that caused a war
    - A biology text that explains how smoking causes cancer

5. **Problem/solution.** The text presents a problem, then discusses a solution to it, or several potential solutions.

    Examples:

    - An engineering text that describes the problem of increasing gas mileage in cars and several potential solutions to the problem
    - An economic text that discusses the problem of a recession and economic and political solutions to the problem

6. **Procedural description.** The text describes in some detail how to do something, such as the steps and the order in which they must be performed.

    Examples:

    - A math textbook that describes the steps to solve quadratic equations
    - An accounting textbook that describes how to set up an accounts payable/receivable system

Narrative text structures. FIGURE 9.2

Main Features of Narrative Text

1. A main character who has goals, needs, motives, beliefs, thoughts, and emotions
2. A time period or specific setting in which the story takes place
3. A major goal that the main character is trying to achieve, which is usually blocked in some way
4. A plot that describes how the main character overcomes the barriers to the goal or resolves a conflict to reach the goal
5. An ending that details the outcome: whether the main character was successful or unsuccessful in reaching the goal
6. Some type of moral or theme (such as loyalty, cooperation, or persistence)

Questions to Ask Yourself While Reading a Narrative Text (adapted from Wood et al., 1995)

1. Who is the main character/protagonist? What is this character's main goal?
2. How would you describe this character in terms of personality, behavior, and so forth? What clues lead you to these descriptions? Why do you think this about the character?
3. Who are some of the other characters in the story? What are their roles? Why are they in the story? What are their relationships to the protagonist?
4. What is the main problem/conflict that prevents the protagonist from reaching the goal?
5. How do the characters try to solve the problem or conflict?
6. How is the problem eventually resolved? If it is not resolved, why not?
7. What are the important events in the story? Why are they important?
8. What is the main theme or moral? What is the author trying to say in this story?

PHASE 2: STRATEGIES TO USE WHILE YOU ARE READING

After you have done some of the prereading activities, you will be in a better position to begin reading the chapter. You now have some ideas about your goals for reading, the authors' goals and the main ideas in the chapter, and what you already know or don't know about the topic. This prepares you to be a more active reader. To control and regulate your reading as you read, you can use a number of different strategies. These strategies are most helpful for textbooks or specialized topical nonfiction books, rather than novels. They will help you extract the meaning from the text, find the main ideas, and remember them so that you can use them not just for tests, but in your thinking and in your life.

Recall our discussion of attention and memory in Chapter 6, where we explained the operation of the general information-processing system of the mind. One of the key aspects of this system is the way it moves information from working memory (your consciousness, what you are currently attending to or thinking about) to your long-term memory. Your long-term memory already has a great deal of knowledge stored in it, and what you are trying to do is connect the new information from the texts to this prior knowledge. In some cases, you may have to restructure your prior knowledge to fit the new information. This can happen when the new information is so different that it changes the way you think about the topic. In other cases, it is just a matter of adding the new information to your prior knowledge, without doing much restructuring. In all cases, however, you need to be active in your reading, using a number of strategies that will help you connect the new information to your prior knowledge and keep it in long-term memory. We will discuss two general families of active reading strategies: elaboration strategies and organizational strategies.

Elaborate and expand on the text while you are reading.

Elaboration Strategies

Elaboration strategies help you elaborate on the text material to see how the text is related to your prior knowledge. This elaboration is similar to the elaboration discussed in Chapter 7. It often involves putting the text information into your own words, because using your own words reflects your own prior knowledge. The following elaboration strategies will help keep you active as you read your text.

Mark up Your Text While Reading. Look around in any college library at students who are reading and it is very likely that you will see many of them using bright yellow, pink, or blue highlighters to mark up their texts. Pick up any used college textbook—it will probably be highlighted in some parts. This may or may not be a useful strategy. In many cases it is *not* useful, such as when students highlight too much text, in a rather thoughtless and repetitive manner, without really thinking about what they are reading. They are not picking out important ideas and not really actively reading as they highlight.

One of the authors of this text made this mistake in college. He did quite well in college except for one course, in which he got a C. It was a course in physiological psychology, and he did not have much prior knowledge, especially of the biological information. He spent many, many hours reading for this course because he knew he did not have as much prior knowledge as many of the other students, who were premed majors, not psychology majors. Despite all his effort, he still did not do as well as he wanted in the course. When he attended graduate school and learned some of the ideas of cognitive psychology and active reading, he went back to look at his physiology textbook. He found that it was almost all highlighted—page after page of underlining and highlighting. There were almost no sentences or words that were not highlighted. Although he was embarrassed to see what he had done wrong, it explained why he got a bad grade, even though he had spent hours studying and highlighting the text. He had not really been reading strategically. He could not separate the important information from the less important information, so he highlighted it all. This gave him comfort—he had felt that he was really studying the text, but it was clear that he really did not understand the material very well, and his overall course grade reflected his lack of understanding. Highlighting your text thoughtlessly, without trying to find the big and important ideas, will not help you learn and understand the material. There are better strategies than highlighting your text.

A useful way to mark your text is to jot down notes to yourself in the margins. Note how the text complements or conflicts with what the professor has said in lecture. Make comments about whether you agree or disagree with the text. These comments may help you think about how the material in the text fits with your prior knowledge. Another good strategy is to write down examples, in your own words, of what the author is saying. For example, in a sociology text about racial prejudice, think of an example of racial prejudice that you have witnessed in your own life.

Texts often give lists of points or categories (e.g., "The three reasons for the failure of the banks during the Depression were . . . "). These reasons or points may be spread out across a lot of text. To make them clearer, copy these points into the margin, near where they appear. For the first point, write "1" and copy the point. At the next appropriate place in the text, write "2," and list the second point, and so on. This helps you concentrate on the main points as you read, and when you later review for an exam, you will be able to find the main points easily. This way of marking text is much more active than just highlighting the text.

Write Summaries of What You Are Reading. Research shows that good readers often create summaries of what they read. This can be as simple as summarizing out loud or in your head what you have just read, putting the ideas into your own words. Even better is to write down your summaries as you read. These written records will be very useful to you when you want to review for an exam. You also can share your written summaries with classmates. Discussing the differences in your summaries will be helpful to all of you as you study for an exam.

Brown and Day (1983) suggested six rules for making summaries. These include:

1. *Delete trivial information.* For example, a biology text on cells may include a lot of detailed information on the mechanisms in cells that is not important if your main goal is to understand the functioning of the cell in general.

2. *Delete redundant information.* For example, a history text on the Civil War may repeat general information about politics in Washington as the author switches from describing the war in the East (e.g., Virginia) to the war in West (e.g., Tennessee).

3. *Substitute a general (superordinate) term for a list of subterms.* If you are summarizing a physics text that lists the many different subatomic particles, you might just list the three main larger particles. (The general term is sometimes called the "superordinate" term, which means the one that is above or at a higher level. For example, *mammal* is superordinate to *human.*)

4. *Integrate a series of events with a superordinate action term.* For a geology text, in a long description of how a volcano eventually erupts, just summarize the basic pattern of events, leaving out all the subprocesses.

5. *Select a topic sentence.* Many texts use topic sentences. Sometimes this is the first sentence in a paragraph or a section, but often you have to look more closely for the main topic sentence. It summarizes the main point of the section of text.

6. *Invent a topic sentence if there is not one in the text.* If a topic sentence is not provided, then write one yourself. In fact, trying to write your own topic sentence will probably be very useful to testing your understanding of the text.

Develop Mental Images of the Text. Another elaboration strategy is to build mental images of what you are reading. Although some types of text make it easy to develop mental pictures, this strategy can be particularly useful for abstract material. The basic idea is that our memory stores some knowledge in a part of the brain that deals with verbal information and other information in a part of the brain that deals with visual information. (Did that sentence create a mental image for you?) The verbal system will help you remember information that you learn verbally, such as words. If you also use imagery to encode information in a visual system, you will have two ways to recall the information—one verbal and one visual. Two ways of encoding are always better than one.

Mental images should be fairly simple but memorable. You may include some significant details that will help clue you in to important information. For example, in chemistry, mental images of the parts of an atom or molecule and how these parts relate to one another should help you recall the information. In psychology, an image of a computer, including its various parts, may help you remember the parts of the mind's information-processing system (sensory memory, working memory, long-term memory) and their functions. In cell biology, imagining a picture of the parts of the cell will help you more than simply learning the definitions of *mitochondria* and *nucleus*.

Make Questions and Predictions About the Text as You Read. One of the best elaboration strategies is to ask yourself questions as you read. Asking questions, including making predictions about what will happen next, will keep you actively involved in your reading. One way to generate questions is to look at the main subheadings in a text and make questions out of them. For example, in this chapter, the three main headings are the three phases of reading. You might ask yourself questions such as, What happens in Phase 1 versus Phase 2 versus Phase 3? and How are the strategies different in each phase? In addition to helping you stay actively involved in your reading, these questions also serve as short-term goals for your reading. As you read, you will try to find the answers.

Asking yourself questions also helps you monitor your comprehension. Even simple questions such as, What was the main idea of that last section I just read?, will help you be aware of whether you are paying attention and how well you are understanding what you read. One of the authors of this book can still recall sitting in the college library, reading a textbook, and being aware of reading the words and of the passage of time—but when he got to the end of the chapter, he could not recall what the chapter was about, even though he had read every word. Can anyone relate to this? Of course. All of us have had an experience like that. When this happens, we are decoding the words, but we are not really attending to the material. We may be daydreaming, thinking about what we will do after studying. We may be thinking of the professor and the other students in the class. Whatever we are paying attention to, it is obviously not the meaning of the ideas. Asking questions and searching for the answers will help you to avoid this problem.

Figure 9.3 (adapted from Pressley & Woloshyn, 1995) lists *question frames* that might help you generate questions for your reading. A reader uses the question frame to insert information learned from the text. You can use these question frames for many types of texts, but they are most useful for expository texts. See Figure 9.2 for questions that are useful for narrative texts.

STRATEGY SUGGESTION

Use organizational strategies to help you read actively.

Question frames.   FIGURE 9.3

Describe _____ in your own words.

What does _____ mean?

Why is _____ important?

Explain why _____.

Explain how _____.

How are _____ and _____ similar?

What is the difference between _____ and _____?

How does _____ affect/influence _____?

What are the strengths and weaknesses of _____?

What causes _____?

How could _____ be used to _____?

What would happen if _____?

How does _____ tie in with what was said in class?

How does _____ relate to _____?

Source: From *Coginitive Strategy That Really Improves Children's Academic Performance,*
by M. Pressley and V. Woloshyn, 1995, Cambridge, MA: Brookline Books.

Organizational Strategies

Organizational strategies involve organizing the material in a text by making a
map, a diagram, an outline, a matrix, or a chart. Like elaboration strategies, organizational strategies help you connect the new ideas with your prior knowledge,
but they also help you organize the new information into a form where the
relations between ideas are clear.

Develop And Use Concept Maps To Organize Ideas. Concept maps allow you to
diagram the relations between different concepts and ideas. Nowak and Gowin
(1984) developed the strategy of concept mapping to help individuals "see" the
meaning of materials. The technique has a number of steps, but the basic idea is really
simple. It involves selecting the main ideas, concepts, terms, and so forth from a text
(or a lecture) and drawing a diagram that illustrates their relations. Figure 9.4
provides some examples of concept maps to show you what they can look like.

Don't worry if your concept map for a selection of text differs from a classmate's. The same information may be mapped in many different ways. A concept
map is "correct" if it represents the way you think the terms are related to one
another. Of course, when the text specifies relations among the terms, you should
try to capture those relations. Drawing a concept map helps you draw a mental
picture of the text. You can share your concept map with classmates, compare
and contrast the maps, and discuss how your understanding differs from theirs.
Activity 9.2 asks you to draw a concept map of this chapter. You can start now
and build it as you finish reading the chapter.

FIGURE 9.4 Concept maps.

Example 1: Concept map of some constructs from Chapter 3.

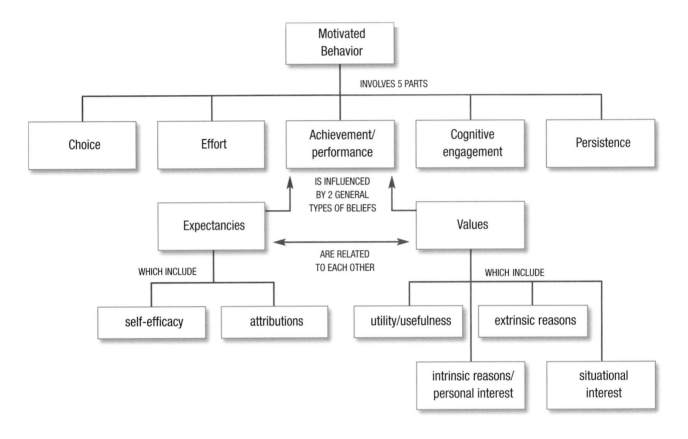

Example 2: Function and structure of a memory system.

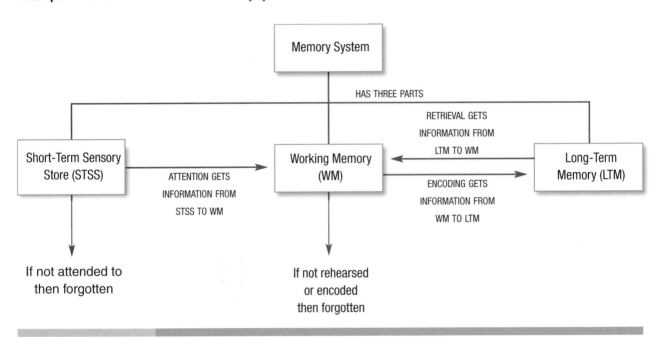

Concept Map of Chapter 9

Draw a concept map of this chapter. Use lines or arrows to show the relations among concepts.

Here are some ideas for constructing concept maps that researchers have suggested (Nowak, 1998; Nowak & Gowin, 1984):

1. Develop a list of terms, ideas, concepts, and so forth from the text selection you are reading.

2. Arrange the terms in this list into a hierarchy, with more inclusive or broader terms at the top of the hierarchy, more narrow or specialized terms near the bottom.

3. Start to draw your map by placing the more inclusive terms near the top of the map. Write the more specific terms lower on the page, and link the terms at the top to those below with lines or arrows (see Figure 9.4).

4. After you have sketched the basic framework of your map, label the lines that connect the terms or concepts. You might label them with "linking" words that describe the relations between the items at each end of the line (*are a part of; depends on; is caused by; determines;* and so on). The map should illustrate the relations among the terms and among the various levels of the terms.

5. At some point you may realize that your map is not quite turning out the way you thought it would. It is perfectly fine to start over and redraw the map. This happens often, and it is often a sign of your growing understanding. It makes sense that as you construct the map and are actively thinking about the meaning of the terms and their relations, you might reconceptualize how the terms fit together.

6. Share your map with others in the course. Comparing your map with other students' maps can lead to a discussion about the ideas and terms and how they are related.

Develop and Use Matrices or Charts. Sometimes information lends itself to a more structured representation. Matrices allow you to organize information that has two general "dimensions." Write the dimensions in the top row and first column, then fill in the cells with specific information. Example 1 in Figure 9.5 is a matrix that organizes information about the parts of the brain and the functions these different parts perform. Example 2 is a matrix for the human memory system.

Charts and other diagrams that display the relations among ideas or constructs also may help you organize information. Concept maps and matrices may be best for information that has a hierarchical arrangement, but with charts or other diagrams, you can display the relations among any types of terms. For example, one of the authors of this book almost always draws a little chart or diagram for any psychology article he reads that has statistics in it. This diagram helps him understand the causal relations among the variables in the study. For example, for a study of how student motivation relates to achievement, he drew a little diagram (see Figure 9.6) showing that this study investigated how self-efficacy (a "will" variable) influences the use of cognitive strategy (a "skill" variable), which, in turn, leads to better grades (achievement). Under each of the three main columns, he lists the actual measures used in the study and notes whether the data and results actually support the cause-and-effect hypothesis. A simple diagram like this really helps him organize his thinking. Of course, many psychological studies are much more complicated, which means a diagram can be that much more helpful. Studies in the natural sciences and other social sciences that investigate causal sequence of variables or events may also lend themselves to this kind of diagram.

Example of matrix organizers.

FIGURE 9.5

Example 1: Brain Areas

	Hindbrain	**Midbrain**	**Forebrain**
Parts	Pons Cerebellum Medulla		Cortex Limbic system Thalamus Hypothalamus
Functions	Controls basic physiological pro-cesses (breathing, blood pressure, balance)	Relay or connecting pathway between hindbrain & forebrain	Complex thinking Emotional responding Motivation

Example 2: Memory Structures

	Short-Term Sensory Store	**Working Memory**	**Long-Term Memory**
Function	Perception	Action on information	Storage of information
Duration	A few seconds	Less than a minute	Very long
Capacity	Limited	Very limited (7 ± 2) chunks	Unlimited
Cognitive Processes	Attention	Rehearsal Elaboration Encoding	Retrieval

Simple causal diagram.

FIGURE 9.6

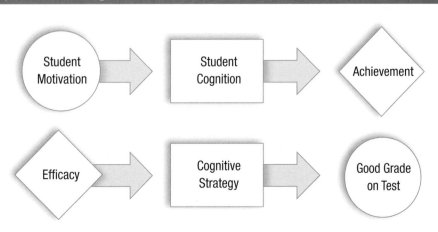

Develop and Use Outlines. At some point in your life as a student, you probably have had at least one teacher who discussed the importance of outlining. He or she was probably referring to using an outline for writing a paper. We will discuss that strategy in the next chapter, on writing. Here, we are referring to the strategy of making an outline of text material that you are reading. Of course, many textbooks now provide an outline at the beginning of each chapter. This outline can be useful as you look over the chapter (see the previous section on prereading strategies), and it may also serve as a good starting point for your own outline. Even when an outline is provided, you will want to make your own so that you can add detail that helps you comprehend the text. More important, creating your own outline will help you to be an active reader. You will be thinking about the text and how its ideas fit together, rather than just passively following the provided outline.

Include in your outline details in the text that aid your comprehension. If you are starting with the general outline provided by the textbook, you should be adding significant amounts of material to it. You don't have to follow the formal rules of outlining (such as using Roman numerals followed by capital letters and so forth), but your outline should have a general hierarchical structure with headings and subheadings. You should not copy the text word for word, but you should paraphrase the important ideas and see how they fit together. An outline can be very useful later when you review for an exam. You may not have to go back and reread the text, but just review your outline and refer to the text if there is something in your outline that you don't understand.

Finally, you might want to create an integrated outline of material from the text readings, course lecture notes, and any notes from a discussion section. One of the authors used to do this quite frequently in college, and it helped him see the connections between the lecture and text materials. He would usually start with his lecture notes (also kept in an outline format—see Chapter 8, on note taking) and then go to his text to see how the material in the text could fit into or supplement the lecture-note materials. He rewrote the lecture notes onto new pages, adding the new material from the text to this new outline. He started with the lecture notes because he figured that was the more important material, since the professor was taking time to discuss it in class. The textbook almost always covers more material than is covered in class, but generally a professor will stress the most important material in lecture. On the other hand, creating the new combined outline revealed what parts of the text were not discussed in class, which allowed him to review that specific material. Finally, in the process of creating this integrative outline, he was reviewing all the lecture and text materials, and he could monitor his understanding of all of it. If he did not understand something, he could go back to his original lecture notes or the textbook to figure it out. Creating an integrative outline is more work than just reviewing lecture notes and the text, but it provides benefits that often are worth the effort.

PHASE 3: STRATEGIES TO USE AFTER READING
Ask Yourself Some General Questions

If you have been an active reader, you will have been asking yourself questions all along. Now that you have read the entire text, ask yourself a few more questions. What was the main idea or theme of the reading? What are the important points to remember? How does this chapter relate to other chapters in the book? How does what you read relate to what was said in lecture or in discussion sections? Is there anything you don't quite understand?

Another strategy for asking questions is to pair up with a classmate, read the material, and ask each other questions about the text. This will help you see what other students think were the important points. You might also enjoy the competition of trying to answer questions from someone else and challenging them with questions they may not be able to answer. (Medical students often engage in this, quizzing each other on obscure diagnoses and treatments.) Exchanging questions and answers may prompt you to discuss the ideas in the text and become more actively engaged in trying to understand the material.

Write a Final Summary

After you have read the text and asked questions about it, go back over your summaries of the text and write a final summary. You can update the summaries you have been writing all along, or you can create a new one that integrates all the other summaries. By creating one final summary, you force yourself to try to distill the overall main idea of the text. This process will help you recall the big idea of the reading, and the summary will be useful when you review the reading for an exam.

All of the strategies in this chapter can be helpful. You do not have to use all of them. You should find strategies that you like to use and that you feel comfortable using, and refine and improve them to fit your material and your study style. If some strategies do not appeal to you, don't force yourself to use them. The important point is that you use some of these strategies to become and stay an active reader. These strategies will help you plan, monitor, and control your reading, allowing you to become a strategic reader and one who will certainly learn more and do better in school.

CHAPTER SUMMARY

Reading is an essential skill for life, not just college, so it is important that you become good at it. Good readers do well in college and learn more than poor readers do. One of the characteristics of good readers is that they read actively. You can approach each of the three general phases in reading with a number of different strategies. First, in the prereading phase, you should set goals for your reading and ask yourself what you know about the topic (assess your prior knowledge). You should also preview the text to get a sense of its structure and content.

In the second phase, during your actual reading of the text, you should try to stay as active as possible. This means using elaboration and organizational strategies to help you understand and remember what you are reading. Finally, in the last phase of reading, when you are done reading the text, you should go back and test yourself on your understanding of the material. You may also want to write a general summary of what you just read. These strategies will help you to become an active reader and aid your comprehension. You will not necessarily use all of them, but you should develop a set of reading strategies that work for you and use them in all your reading tasks.

© Galerie André – FOTOLIA

Improving Your Writing

Chapter Goals

This chapter will help you:

- Learn what expert writers do, and use that information to become more of an expert yourself

- Identify some activities to do *before* you start writing

- Understand how to evaluate source material, especially from the Web

- Identify strategies for generating high-quality text

- Identify some activities to do *after* you are done writing a draft

Key Terms

audience	planning
knowledge generation	revising
knowledge telling	translating
peer-reviewed journals	

CHAPTER 10

Writing is a difficult task for most people. It doesn't matter if you are a freshman just starting college, an accomplished senior, or even a college professor writing a book about writing, most of us find that putting words on the computer screen is difficult. While there may be many reasons for the difficulty, there is one basic solution: you need to be a self-regulated writer.

Because the task is difficult, many students wait until the last minute to write their papers. As the deadline for the paper approaches, they find that writing becomes easier. This is partially because as the deadline gets closer, they stop "editing" their text and just let the words flow out. However, by waiting until the very end, they leave themselves with almost no time to revise their writing. And, as we will see, revision is the key to good writing. Very, very few people are able to write a polished first draft. In fact, most people who say they can write something perfectly the first time and do not need to revise probably are not judging their writing accurately. All of us can improve our writing by revising.

In addition, as we have noted previously, procrastinating until right up to the deadline can serve a self-protective function. If the paper earns a poor grade, the writer can attribute the grade to the lack of time and effort, thereby protecting his or her self-worth (remember *attributions* from Chapter 3). In this case, the writer does not have to conclude that lack of ability caused the poor grade. On the other hand, if the paper receives a good grade, then the writer can attribute the success to good writing ability or general intelligence or ability. This increases the writer's sense of self-worth.

How to write well is the subject of many, many books by English scholars, teachers, and professional writers. The diversity of authors has given us many different perspectives on the writing process and ways to improve your writing. This chapter does not attempt to summarize all the points and perspectives from these books. Our perspective is a psychological one: we focus on how to self-regulate your writing process. We do not focus on the details of grammar or the mechanics of writing good sentences. You can go to lots of other books for those issues. We will present a general research-based model of the writing process, then discuss the three phases of writing and the strategies that will help you master each of these phases. Activity 10.1 has the writing items from the Learning Inventory. It will give you an initial assessment of the extent to which you engage in self-regulated writing. Keep in mind that all writers, including textbook authors, can always improve their skills. The advice we provide in this chapter is advice we simultaneously give ourselves.

ACTIVITY 10.1   *Assessment of Your Writing*

Indicate the extent to which you engage in the following behaviors when you are writing.

When I write I:	Never or almost never	Rarely	Frequently	Always or almost always
Make an outline	①	②	③	④
Feel rushed	④	③	②	①
Proofread	①	②	③	④

Allow a friend to read it	①	②	③	④
Turn in the first version I print out	④	③	②	①
Have multiple pieces of information open when sitting at the computer, such as a textbook, Web sites, and note cards	①	②	③	④

SCORING:

The following categories give a rough indication of your writing strategies:

20 and above: You probably have good writing strategies. This chapter can serve as a helpful review of important writing skills.

15–19: You probably use good writing strategies some of the time. This chapter will help you identify ways you can improve your writing.

14 and below: This chapter is definitely for you. It will help you focus on some important writing strategies. We encourage you to read this chapter carefully and to use the suggestions we offer.

Just like reading, writing involves several different learning strategies. In Figure 10.1 we list several learning strategies that we believe are related to effective writing. If these phrases describe what you usually do when you write, you should be encouraged—they comprise the foundation of effective writing. If not, keep these phrases in the front of your mind as you read this chapter. We encourage all students to develop the habits reflected in Figure 10.1 and to adopt the strategies described in this chapter.

OVERVIEW OF THE WRITING PROCESS

As with reading, the psychological processes involved in writing have been the subject of a great deal of research. Just as the research on reading has compared good readers with poor ones, the research on writing has often compared good or expert writers with poor or novice writers. Often, researchers gather data by giving these two groups of writers a writing task, asking them to "think aloud" while they are writing, then comparing what the writers in the two groups said

Strategies associated with effective writing.   FIGURE 10.1

- Outlining material to keep it organized

- Finding the most important ideas in written material

- Making charts, diagrams, or tables to organize material

- Going back to review difficult or confusing material

- Setting goals to direct your writing

FIGURE 10.2 Model of the writing process.

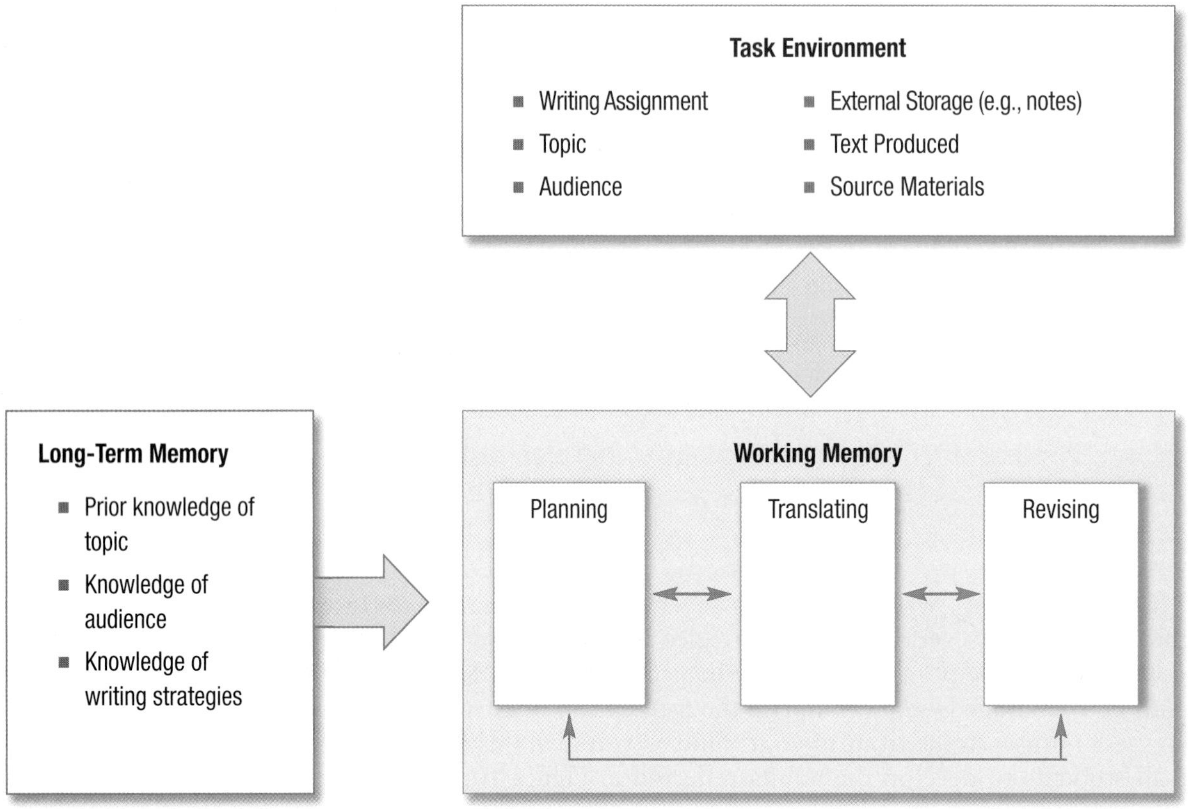

Task Environment

- Writing Assignment
- Topic
- Audience
- External Storage (e.g., notes)
- Text Produced
- Source Materials

Long-Term Memory

- Prior knowledge of topic
- Knowledge of audience
- Knowledge of writing strategies

Working Memory

| Planning | Translating | Revising |

Source: From *Cognitive Psychology and Instruction* by R. Bruning, G. Schraw, and R. Ronning, 1995, Englewood Cliffs, NJ: Merrill/Prentice Hall.

and the quality of the written product. This so-called "think-aloud" data provides some evidence of what goes on in the minds of students when they write.

Based on this type of research, psychologists have developed a general model of writing that describes the processes writers engage in as they write. Figure 10.2 gives the general model of writing that has guided much of the research on writing (Bruning, Schraw, & Ronning, 1995; Flower & Hayes, 1984; Hayes & Flower, 1986). As you can see in Figure 10.2, the task environment (the external environment) includes the writing assignment and any external notes, text, or materials that you have collected or generated. These external factors influence the writing process by affecting what is going on in your working memory. Recall that the working memory is limited in space. The fact that three general processes go on at once in working memory shows the demands that writing makes on the cognitive system.

As you can see in Figure 10.2, working memory is the site of three general phases or processes that all writers go through: planning, translating, and revising. These phases are listed in the order they often take place, but, in fact, they can go on simultaneously. We will discuss them in order, but you should be aware that they can and do happen together.

Planning involves setting goals for your paper. Recall Chapter 2 on setting goals for studying and life. Goals are also important for your writing. You might set goals for the content of your paper as well as for how you will manage the writing process (such as writing a little bit every day, completing one section in a sitting, and so forth). Planning also includes generating ideas and content. Finally, planning includes organizing these ideas into an outline or structure that will serve as a general blueprint or plan for your paper.

Translating involves the actual writing of text. In this phase you create text that translates your ideas into the actual words, sentences, and paragraphs of your paper.

Finally, in the **revising** phase, you read over your text and improve it to make it communicate better with the audience. Revising means more than just correcting grammatical mistakes and spelling errors. It also involves adding, deleting, and rearranging the text to create more meaning for the reader. Many writers think revision is just fixing simple errors, when, in fact, it involves much more than simple corrections.

As noted in Figure 10.2, long-term memory contributes three types of knowledge to the writing process: knowledge of the topic, of the audience, and of writing strategies. You will draw on all this knowledge in long-term memory as you engage in the writing process. Just as in reading, you need to activate this knowledge so that it will be available as you write your paper.

Now that you have a general overview of the writing process, we turn to some strategies that will help you in your writing.

PHASE 1: PREWRITING AND PLANNING

Just as with reading, the first phase of writing involves planning and developing an approach to the writing task. Several aspects of writing are similar to the reading process.

STRATEGY SUGGESTION

Set specific and short-term goals for your writing.

Set Specific Goals

Setting goals is one of the most important aspects of writing. Expert writers always have a general goal for the text they are trying to produce. They also have a number of specific and short-term goals. For example, a writer who is writing a book does not set one single goal of writing the book in 1 day or even 1 week or 1 month. The expert writer breaks up the task into smaller, more specific and manageable parts that can guide his or her writing. For example, as was mentioned earlier in this book, one of the authors of this book tries to write every Monday through Friday morning from 9:00 until noon. He usually has an outline and decides each day to write a specific section of the outline that day. Some days he is successful in completing the section, some days he is not. The important point is that he has a specific and short-term goal that could be accomplished in the 3-hour time block. He knows he is not going to finish a whole chapter in one

3-hour session. Furthermore, he knows he can usually generate about four to five pages a day, so he plans accordingly. Having a goal allows him to feel good when he reaches it, and this accomplishment motivates him to continue to write the next day. If he set a goal of writing a whole chapter in 1 day, he would not reach the goal and would feel frustrated and angry. Specific, short-term goals help guide the writing process, and they also help to motivate you by letting you feel a sense of accomplishment.

Some writers don't set goals for completing a specific section but plan on writing a specific number of pages in each writing session. This is often the case with writers who are not writing expository text (like this book) but more creative fiction such as short stories or novels. Once they have written the specific number of pages for the day, they may reward themselves by doing something enjoyable. Other writers set a specific goal of writing for a certain amount of time each day. Ernest Hemingway often set a goal of writing 6 hours a day (Zimmerman, 1998). He would get up early in the morning and write for 6 hours, then in the afternoons he'd go fishing or to his favorite bar. Hemingway's behavior here is a good example of how to use rewards. Hemingway rewarded himself for writing by doing other activities he found pleasurable, but only after he did the writing (recall this suggestion from Chapter 3). For other writers, even a small goal can still produce great results. The American novelist John Updike reportedly has a goal of two pages a day. It doesn't seem like a lot, but if repeated every day, it will add up very quickly. Imagine a 10-page English paper. Instead of writing all 10 pages the night (and morning) before it is due, wouldn't it be better to write 2 pages a day for 5 days? The quality would be much higher, your stress will be lower, and you will be showing the first characteristic of a self-regulated writer.

The important point is that expert writers set specific goals for their writing and work hard to manage their time and lives so they can accomplish those goals. The goal could be anything from 6 hours a day to 60 minutes to six paragraphs. When you have a writing task, setting specific and short-term goals will help you complete the work.

STRATEGY SUGGESTION

Activate your prior knowledge.

Activate Prior Knowledge

In the chapter on reading, we discussed how activating your prior knowledge before reading a text can help you understand the material. In the same way, activating your prior knowledge before you begin writing can be helpful. In reading, activating your prior knowledge will help you understand other people's text. In writing, activating your prior knowledge will help you generate your own text. Activity 10.2 will help you assess your prior knowledge about a writing topic.

As you plan your writing, you will want to activate several kinds of prior knowledge: knowledge about the topic, knowledge about your audience, and knowledge about the writing process.

Prior Knowledge

Choose a paper you need to write this semester. Use this worksheet to activate your prior knowledge for this particular assignment.

Topic: _____

1. What do you know about the topic at this point?

   _____

   _____

2. Where did you learn what you know, and where can you document that information?

   _____

   _____

3. What has the professor said?

   _____

   _____

4. What have you read in the text?

   _____

   _____

5. For whom will this paper be written? (Circle all that apply.)

   a. Classmates/peer review   c. A service-learning paper for an organization outside of the university

   b. Professor   d. A case file for a social service agency

6. How much prior knowledge of the topic does the audience have?

   a. None   c. High

   b. Low

7. Which type of writing is required?

   a. Expository   c. Mixed

   b. Narrative   d. Other

8. If expository, what strategies will you use? (Circle all that apply.)

   a. Classification   d. Problem/solution

   b. Illustration   e. Procedural description

   c. Compare/contrast

Prior Knowledge of the Topic Area. Think about what you already know about your topic. Most likely, you are writing the paper for a course. What have you learned about the topic in the course so far? What has the professor said about the topic in lectures or discussion? What information do you recall from the course readings? Do you have ideas or information about the topic from any other sources?

Jot all of these ideas down on sheets of paper, on note cards, or on the computer. Don't worry about putting the ideas in order yet, just try to write down what you already know about the topic.

Prior Knowledge of the Audience. One of the most important strategies of expert writers is that they always keep their audience in mind as they write. This helps to focus and guide their writing. Ask yourself the following questions: For whom am I writing this? What do they know about the topic? How can I write my paper in such a way that the audience will understand my point? Try to put yourself in the place of your future readers and try to imagine what they know and don't know. Then, as you write, you can be more explicit about aspects of the topic that the audience may not know, explaining these areas in more detail. On the other hand, if the audience already has a pretty good idea of certain aspects of the topic, you don't have to go over these areas as thoroughly.

In college, your professors, who will read and grade your papers, are your main audience. Of course, your instructors will have quite a bit of content knowledge in the general discipline, although they may know more or less about your specific topic. For example, both of the authors of this book are psychologists, so we have a great deal of knowledge about psychological topics in general. However, we are not specialists in all areas of psychology, so if you were a student writing a paper on some topic in clinical psychology, such as autism or borderline personality disorders, we would not have as much specific knowledge on those topics. Regardless of the topic, it is important to remember that your professor or instructor is your main audience. So keep in mind what this individual knows or doesn't know about the topic, and try to prepare your paper accordingly.

In some writing classes, the instructor may ask you to write a paper for a particular audience. For example, you might write a short article that could be published in the student newspaper on some topic of interest to students at your college. In this case, the instructor will want you to write your paper with other students in mind as the audience, rather than the instructor. In addition, you may sometimes write for an audience of other students in your class. This will be the case in courses that use peer review of papers. Peer review means students share their papers with their classmates. These peer reviewers read your paper and give you feedback. In this case, you have to think about the other students in the course as your audience and keep in mind what they may or may not know about the topic.

Prior Knowledge About the Genres of Writing. The genres for reading that we discussed in the last chapter apply to writing as well. There are different types of texts to read, so there are different types of texts to write as well. In some English or creative writing classes, you may be asked to write narrative texts. For these assignments you should try to fill in the story grammar for narrative texts. However, in almost all of your college courses that require papers, you will usually be writing expository texts. In Chapter 9 we discussed some of the types of expository texts (see Figure 9.1), such as classification, illustration, comparison/contrast, causal, problem/solution, and procedural description. To structure your paper, you will want to choose one (or a combination) of these types of expository texts. For example, your paper may focus on comparing and contrasting three different approaches to solving an economic problem. In this case, you might include parts of both a problem/solution text and a compare/contrast text. Another example of combining genres could be a psychological paper in which you describe a particular psychological problem (problem/solution) and also explain the causal factors that lead to the problem (causal), then conclude with some suggestions for solution (problem/solution again) based on your analysis of the causes.

The important point is that different genres require different types of structure as well as different kinds of content. If you are writing a compare/contrast paper, then you know you have to organize your content knowledge according to dimensions against which you will compare perspectives, models, or theories. If you are writing a causal paper, then you know you have to organize your material in a sequence that builds the causal relations you want to convey. Knowing about genres will help you structure your paper and make decisions about what you need to include in the paper.

Make an Outline

Now that you have activated your prior knowledge about the content, the audience, and genres, you need to organize it in some fashion before you actually start writing. Most writers organize by developing some form of an outline. Again, as we noted in the chapter on reading, you don't need to follow the formal rules for outlining (numbering, indentation, and so forth). What is important is that you try to place your ideas in some organizational framework. Activity 10.3 provides guidelines for preparing an outline.

Making an Outline

Choose a paper you will have to write this semester (preferably one that is five or more pages long). Use these questions to guide your development of an outline.

1. What are the main points of this paper? Select no more than three. If you have more than three, try to summarize some of them into a larger point.

2. What is the relation among the three points?

3. Is there a necessary order to the points? For example, is one point necessary to understand the next point, or do the points have a chronological order?

4. For each of the three points, identify subpoints. Are these subpoints related in any way? For example, does one subpoint fall under another in terms of hierarchy?

5. Based on this work, can you identify a flow or outline for your paper?

One way to organize your paper is to have your notes on cards or sheets of computer paper so you can shuffle them around and see what order makes sense for presenting them. As you move the content around, you start to develop a sense of how best to present the material. You should then sketch out a general outline. This outline may change as you actually write, but at least it will give you a starting point. In addition, the outline will break the work into sections that can become your short-term goals. Thus, an outline will make the task more manageable in several ways.

Another way to organize your paper is to draw a concept map or diagram of your paper, rather than an outline. You could use concept mapping, which was discussed in the last chapter, to sketch the relations between ideas and concepts, and use this map to organize your writing. The visual representation of the ideas also may help you organize your thoughts more than a simple outline would. Figure out which type of organizational strategy works best for you. The most important point is that you should have some kind of structure for your paper before you begin writing.

SOURCE MATERIALS

Finding Sources

One of the important parts of planning your paper is collecting various source materials. Of course, your textbooks are a good place to start; they often provide lists of related books and articles. In fact, many textbooks now include, at the end of chapters or the end of the book, a list of suggested readings that provide more detail and information about the topics of the course. In addition, the reference list can direct you to related articles and books. Since these sources have been selected by the authors of your book, they are almost guaranteed to be of good quality and to be relevant. The authors of your textbooks are experts in their field, so you can probably trust their judgment as to the quality of their sources.

STRATEGY SUGGESTION

Evaluate your source materials carefully and thoughtfully.

You can find material for your topic in many sources. An excellent source is the books and journals published by scholarly organizations in the field. For example, in psychology, the American Psychological Association (APA) publishes many journals in various subfields of psychology, such as developmental, educational, cognitive, clinical, organizational, social, personality, and many others. These are **peer-reviewed journals,** which means that the articles contained in the journal have been evaluated by other researchers in the field. Peer researchers review the research, pointing out any errors or deficiencies. Often the articles are revised several times before the journal finally accepts them for publication. These journals represent the best knowledge in the field because of this rigorous peer-review process. In almost all fields of research, from the humanities to the natural sciences to engineering and education, you can find the same kind of peer-reviewed journals. These are very good sources for a paper.

At the same time, because these journals are aimed at professionals in the field, they can be somewhat technical and difficult for a novice to understand. We recommend that you look for summary and review articles published in these journals, which summarize a particular area or research topic (some fields have whole journals devoted to review articles). A good review article for your paper topic can be a gold mine because it will review the main aspects of the research, summarize studies and draw conclusions, and point out the issues and directions for future research. In psychology, the two main general journals that publish review articles are *Psychological Review* and *Psychological Bulletin*. In addition, the bibliography will give you dozens of other articles that you can read to build your knowledge base. Most university libraries subscribe to these review journals. If you are wondering which journals are review journals in a field, we recommend that you ask your professor.

The Web as a Resource

For most students, the World Wide Web is the main means of finding source material. The Web makes volumes of material easily accessible, and it allows you to access material from around the world. Moreover, via the Web, you can gain access to this material instantly, on your own computer. You don't need to go to the library and wander through paper copies looking for the material, then take notes on it or copy the relevant parts. With the Web, you can often download the material right to your own computer and save it in files that you can easily use afterward. The Web is truly a revolution in the access and use of information.

© Daniel Gilbey – FOTOLIA

However, one of the disadvantages of the Web is that anyone in the world can put anything at all on the Web. It is important to know the source of the material and to determine its credibility. Some Web materials are simply electronic versions of paper copies, such as full-text versions of peer-reviewed journals. In this case, there is no concern over credibility or accuracy.

However, other Web materials undergo no quality control. No one reviews these Web sites for accuracy. There are no peer reviewers and editors for much of the material on the Web. Anyone can start a Web site on a topic and put whatever he or she wants on it. This means that you have to evaluate the quality of the information. How can you judge the quality and accuracy of the information you find? It is crucial to be able to answer this question, as there is so much information out on the Web and so many different sources, people, and institutions providing it. It is a difficult task, but it is essential to the quality of your paper.

Alexander and Tate, in their book *Web Wisdom: How to Evaluate and Create Information Quality on the Web* (1999), provided some guidelines and criteria to use in evaluating source material from the Web. These criteria are simple and general enough that they are relevant to all topics and areas that you might be working on as you use the Web. Alexander and Tate (1999) suggested you think about five general criteria as you examine and use information from Web sites. We will briefly describe each of the five criteria. Figure 10.3 summarizes these five criteria and lists specific questions to help you evaluate each criterion.

Evaluate the Authority of the Web site. Web sites are developed and maintained by many different institutions, companies, organizations, and even individuals. The extent to which the entity that created the Web site has definitive knowledge on the topic defines its authority (Alexander & Tate, 1999). For example, the APA, a professional organization of psychologists, monitors and maintains the quality of its journals. On the Web, however, anyone can "publish"

FIGURE 10.3   Criteria and questions to consider when evaluating a Web site.

1. Authority: Does the person/organization that created the Web site have definitive knowledge or expertise in the area?

   a. Who has developed the Web site and information on it—an individual, a company, an organization, an institution?

   b. What are their qualifications, credentials, or expertise in this area? How long have they been in business or how long has the Web site been operating? What is their business or their organization's goals?

   c. Is there a way to contact the individual or organization? Is there a way to get information about their expertise and credentials?

   d. Is the material on the site copyrighted? Where does the material come from—from other reports, internal research, outside experts, newspaper accounts, or some other source? How was the material obtained?

2. Accuracy: Is the information on the site reliable, valid, and free of errors?

   a. Is the information free of grammatical, spelling, and typographical errors?

   b. Are the sources of the information cited, so you can check for yourself the original source of the material?

   c. Is the work original research by the author, and is it clearly stated?

   d. Is there any indication that the information or work has been checked or reviewed by outside reviewers or editors? Some online journals follow the usual peer-review process, though they don't publish hard copies of the articles. This type of peer-reviewed online journal would be much better than a blog that lets anyone post an article without review.

3. Objectivity: Can you determine the objectivity of the information? Is it free of bias as much as possible?

   a. Is the point of view of the organization or individual clear to you?

   b. Is the page or site free of advertising?

   c. Is it clear what the relation is between the information on the site, the organization or individual responsible for the site content, and any advertising on the site?

   d. Is there any explanation of how the site differentiates advertising from information? What are the policies of the site in regard to taking advertising?

   e. Are editorial and opinion material clearly marked as such, as opposed to factual or research material? Are both of these distinguished from ads, entertainment, and other information on the site?

   f. Does the site include any statement regarding the goals or mission of the organization? How would these goals influence their presentation of information? (e.g., a tobacco lobby site would presumably have a goal of selling tobacco products, which could influence the presentation of information.)

4. Currency: How current is the information on the site?

   a. Does the site provide a date indicating when the material was first created or written?

   b. Does the site indicate when the material was first posted to the site or when the site was last updated?

   c. If the information includes statistics, polling data, or other opinion data, does the site indicate when it was collected?

5. Coverage and intended audience: What topics does the site cover and who is the target audience?

   a. Does the site include a listing of its topics or a table of contents?

   b. Is a print version of the material available? Does the Web site include the complete version of the printed material or just some excerpts or an abridged version?

   c. Who is the target audience for the site? Is the target audience composed of novices, experts, the general population, or some other segment?

Source: From *Web Wisdom: How to Evaluate and Create Information Quality on the Web*, by J. Alexander and M. Tate, 1999, Mahwah, NJ: Lawrence Erlbaum Associates.

material simply by posting it. You should expect that material on the Web site maintained by the APA would be more reliable and of higher quality than the content of Bob's Psychological Web site, developed by an individual with no training or background in psychology. In the same way, the American Medical Association's (AMA) Web site would be a much better source of medical information than a Web site developed by Sally the Faith Healer, who has no medical background and no medical degrees. These may seem like silly and trivial examples, but there are many, many individuals who develop and maintain Web sites on any number of topics, and you need to be able to judge their qualifications and expertise to evaluate the quality of the information they provide. See Figure 10.3 for some questions to consider when evaluating the authority of a Web site.

Evaluate the Accuracy of the Material on the Site. Alexander and Tate (1999) defined accuracy in terms of the reliability and validity of the information. Errors of any kind, from simple typographical errors to errors of fact, throw a source's accuracy into doubt. Regularly published journals benefit from a rigorous review process that helps maintain the accuracy of their articles. Good newspapers and magazines employ fact-checkers who work to make sure that articles contain accurate information. For example, as Alexander and Tate (1999) pointed out, if you read two articles, one from the *New York Times* newspaper and one from a tabloid that you see at the grocery store checkout counter, which source would you trust more for accuracy of reporting? It seems clear that some sources are much better at maintaining their accuracy than others are, and in this case, it is well known that the *New York Times* has extremely high standards for accuracy of reporting, whereas tabloids are notorious for unreliable and invalid stories on all kinds of topics. When you are dealing with Web sites, you cannot rely on such common knowledge of the accuracy of different sites. You have to try to evaluate the accuracy of the sites on your own. Refer to Figure 10.3 as you try to determine the accuracy of the information on a Web site.

Evaluate the Objectivity of the Web site. Alexander and Tate (1999) defined objectivity as the extent to which the material on the site is free of distortions due to personal feelings or other sources of bias. Of course, most information has some bias built into it, given that any author has personal beliefs and theories. However, the goal is that written articles and books are as free as they can be from bias and distortions. One of the reasons that peer review is so important is that it allows the reviewers to point out the biases or distortions in research or an article that the author had not been able to see.

In addition, organizations, companies, and institutions often have significant economic interest or other concerns that can lead them to distort information in written reports, articles, or Web sites. Alexander and Tate (1999) pointed out that tobacco companies might not be completely objective in their reporting on the effects of cigarette smoking, whereas the AMA probably would. In the same way, a pharmaceutical company that has invested in a specific drug to treat attention deficit disorder might not present information on the effectiveness of the drug with the same level of objectivity as the AMA or the APA would. Figure 10.3 lists some questions to consider when you evaluate the objectivity of a Web site.

Determine if the Material Is Up-to-date. In both the social and the natural sciences, it often takes quite some time for data to be collected, analyzed, written up, and then submitted for review. Then the review process adds even more time as other researchers read it and write comments. Next, the authors have to revise the article to address the reviewers' concerns and questions. Finally, after several rounds of this, the article may be published. The length of this process can make the information in regularly published journal articles somewhat less current than might be desired. In contrast, researchers can post their work to the Web almost as soon as they collect the information. For example, scientists who study the human genome can post their results to Web sites so that other researchers can use them almost immediately, greatly speeding up the process of scientific discovery. The Web has made the posting of information almost simultaneous with the production of information or knowledge.

In social and natural sciences, recent reports are more highly respected (all other things being equal) than older studies. In the humanities, written works that have stood the test of time might be more highly regarded. So if you are doing a research article on schizophrenia and find an article from 1975 compared to 2005, the older paper will have a completely different approach and will not have the wisdom of all 30 years of research on the neurochemistry of mental illness. See Figure 10.3 for some questions to consider when you evaluate the currency of information on a Web page.

Evaluate the Coverage and the Intended Audience for the Site. The last criterion suggested by Alexander and Tate (1999) is to examine the coverage (the range and depth of topics that the site includes) as well as the target audience for the Web site. Printed books and journals are developed for different audiences: some are for novices to the field (e.g., introductory textbooks in chemistry, biology, sociology, psychology); others are for more advanced undergraduates. Then there are books designed for graduate students or professionals in the field. And, of course, some books are for a general audience, not necessarily college students or graduates. The target audience will determine the depth and sophistication of the material covered in the book. Introductory textbooks in a subject are designed to cover the main topics and areas in a field, but they do so at a relatively superficial level. They can't go into much detail and still be readable by a novice. Other books, designed for professionals in the field, will have much more depth, much more technical language, and a level of sophistication that makes them very difficult for novices to read. They also may cover only a few topics, or even just one topic in great detail, in contrast to introductory textbooks.

Web pages and Web sites have similar characteristics. Some may be designed for use by novices who have some interest in an area but little prior knowledge. These sites may offer lots of help and easy navigation. Other sites may be designed for use by professionals in the field (e.g., the Web site for researchers working on the human genome project) and may not be as user-friendly as sites for novices. Some sites may offer information on many topics, whereas others specialize in one particular topic. It is important for you to determine the coverage and target audience of a Web site to see if it matches your needs and background knowledge. Figure 10.3 lists some questions to consider when evaluating a Web site's coverage and intended audience.

These five criteria and the general questions listed in Figure 10.3 are useful for evaluating any source, not just Web sites. It is always important to evaluate the quality of your source material as you gather information for a paper. Happy surfing, and remember to have a critical eye when you are on the Web. We now move on to the next phase of the writing process: the actual generation of text.

PHASE 2: GENERATING TEXT

One of the hardest parts of writing is the actual production of the words, sentences, and paragraphs that become the text of your paper. It is also one of the most mysterious processes of human cognition. The psychological research has not been as revealing about how ideas become sentences and paragraphs as it has been about how we generate ideas (Phase 1) or how we go about revising our text (Phase 3). However, research on young writers (Bereiter & Scardamalia, 1987) has shown that very often novice writers employ a general **knowledge-telling** strategy when they try to produce text. In other words, young writers tell everything they know about the topic. This approach is somewhat useful, but research also has shown that expert writers use a more general strategy called **knowledge generation.** Knowledge generation is when writers go beyond just telling their knowledge and actually create new meaning as they write their text.

© bluestocking – FOTOLIA

Of course, one of the biggest differences between knowledge telling versus knowledge generation is that young children (those in elementary and middle school) often use knowledge telling, whereas older and more experienced writers try to do more than just tell the audience what they know. Perhaps you can recall a time in middle school when you had to write a report for school. If you were operating with a knowledge-telling strategy, you probably went to some source, like a Web site, took some notes about the topic, then wrote up those notes for your paper. You did not do much more than just repeat what was in the Web site, but you did put it in your own words.

One of the authors of this book can recall doing exactly this for an elementary school social studies report on Sierra Leone, a country in Africa. He went to the library, got the *World Book Encyclopedia*, took some notes about the flora, fauna, economy, and history of Sierra Leone, and wrote this information for his paper. However, the reason he remembers this paper so well is that while he was looking at the *World Book Encyclopedia*, he noticed the much bigger *Encyclopedia Britannica* on the shelf. He looked up Sierra Leone in there and was amazed at how much more information and detail was in this book, compared to what he had found in the *World Book*. Before this he had not realized that there were different levels of encyclopedias; he had thought they were all the same and had basically the same information. But the *Britannica* volume had much more information, and it was written in a much denser style with much bigger words. He did put some of this *Britannica* material in his paper as well because it sounded so authoritative compared to the simple *World Book*. The main point he learned from this exercise was that it was possible to use more than one source, and that it was a good idea to integrate material from several different sources into a paper. Nevertheless, he still used a basic knowledge-telling strategy—get some information and repeat it in your paper with citation (but in your own words, so you are not engaged in plagiarism!).

Although college students are older and have more experience with writing, many college students still use the basic knowledge-telling strategy. They don't use encyclopedias (or shouldn't), but they use articles from journals, textbooks, other books on the topic, and information from various Web sites. They often just copy material out of these sources and then repeat it in some fashion, using their own words. Professors, as experts in the field, can recognize the basic strategy of knowledge telling, and they are not interested in that kind of paper. They already know the information (or know where to get it); they don't need you to tell it to them again.

What the professor would like to see is that you actually *did* something with the information you collected from your sources. Just as in Chapter 9, where we encouraged you to be an active reader, when you write, you need to be an active writer. Your job is not just to repeat in your own words what you have found out from your sources. It is to take that information and transform it in some way to make a point, perhaps even a new point. You can develop an argument by presenting the information in such a way that you actually express some new meaning. You can create a new way of looking at or thinking about the material. Of course, it is not expected that you create something completely new and unique, but rather that you take the existing information and combine it in a new way. Combining sources is actually how you create new meaning. This is not an easy task and it requires thinking and revising—that is why good writing takes time. The suggestions below can help you move from knowledge telling to knowledge generation.

Translate Your Outline into Paragraphs and Sentences

Depending on how detailed your outline is, you can work directly from your outline to craft paragraphs and perhaps even sentences. The major headings in your outline should be the major sections of your paper. Then, under those major sections, there should be single points in your outline (or parts of your concept map) that deserve separate paragraphs. Finally, if you have a very detailed outline, within those separate sections or paragraphs you may have points in your outline that can form the sentences.

Write One Main Idea to a Paragraph

A paragraph should express only one main idea. You probably learned about topic sentences in previous English classes: the topic sentence expresses a paragraph's main idea. Each paragraph should have only one topic sentence. It is usually the first or second sentence in the paragraph, and then the remaining sentences elaborate on this idea. In this paragraph, the topic sentence is the first sentence, and the other sentences elaborate and flesh out the basic idea.

Most paragraphs, especially in expository texts, will have one idea per paragraph. Most paragraphs are usually about three to six sentences long, although some writing coaches think this restricts writers' freedom. The three-to-six rule is a good guideline, but there may be exceptions. If your paragraphs are much longer than that, it is likely that you are trying to express more than one idea in the paragraph. One of the authors of this text uses a simple strategy to check the paragraph lengths in his own writing as well as in all his students' papers. If the paragraph takes up most of one whole page of text (or one computer screen), it is probably too long. Look at your paragraphs. If there are not two or three per page, then your paragraphs are probably too long and need to be broken up into smaller paragraphs that express only one main idea.

Connect Paragraphs with Transitions

As you translate your outline into paragraphs, you need to help the reader see the connections between the paragraphs. You have the outline of your ideas in front of you, and you see how they are linked to one another. Or, if you are using a concept

Connecting words.		FIGURE 10.4
Accordingly	Conversely	
As noted above	For the same reason	
As previously noted	In summary	
At the same time	Similarly	
Because	Therefore	
Consequently	Whereas	

map, you have an even better visual representation of how the ideas are connected. The reader, however, does not have access to these outlines and structures. All he or she has is a very linear set of sentences and paragraphs. You need to help the reader see how the idea from one paragraph leads to the next idea in the next paragraph, and so on. This will help the reader see your argument and the development of your ideas.

An effective way to make transitions between paragraphs is to use connecting words such as those listed in Figure 10.4. You can also use a simple sentence that tells the reader what you are going to do next. For example, you could describe the three phases of writing, then indicate that you will move to describe the first phase in detail. These sentences may seem awkward in some cases, but they can help signal the reader that you are moving from one section to the next section of the paper. We are now moving to the next section!

Use Headings and Subheadings

Most expository texts do not just start up and then continue on and on from one paragraph to another until the end. They use headings and subheadings to signal to the reader how the paper is structured—where the sections begin. As in Chapter 9, when we discussed the use of subheadings to help you understand a text as a reader, you should use subheadings as a writer to make your text more reader-friendly. Have you noticed that this book uses many headings and subheadings? Do they help you as a reader?

Many college students do not use subheadings in their papers, making it difficult for readers to follow the flow of their argument. This also signals to the professor that you may not be a good writer, as most good writers do use headings and subheadings. Of course, if you are only writing a three- to five-page paper, you may not need headings and subheadings. However, anything longer than five pages probably could benefit from headings that break up the text and identify the different sections of the paper. We believe these four strategies (summarized in Figure 10.5) will help you move from knowledge telling to knowledge generation.

FIGURE 10.5   From knowledge telling to knowledge generation: Making meaning from your writing.

We believe the four strategies below will help you move from being a knowledge teller to a knowledge generator. Competent writers do more than simply rehash already-written facts. Competent writers take existing written material and present it in a new way.

1. *Move from outline to text.* The major headings of your outline should become your paper sections. The next level of your outline should be paragraphs within sections. And, if your outline is very detailed, the next level of your outline should be the basis for your sentences within paragraphs.

2. *Feature one idea per paragraph.* Each paragraph should have one controlling idea. This is particularly true in expository text. If you find your paragraph has more than one idea in it, consider dividing the paragraph into two smaller ones and then beefing up each paragraph with more information to support your case.

3. *Use transitions.* Through your outline or concept map, you have developed (knowledge generation) a flow of ideas. This line of reasoning may not be as apparent to others who aren't as familiar with the topic. Transitions will help the reader see the connections that you have made in your head.

4. *Use headings and subheadings.* Having an outline in the form of headings and subheadings will also help the reader understand your text. Too many college papers have a title page and then simply paragraph after paragraph with no obvious aids to the reader. Especially in expository text, headings are helpful to you as you create the text and helpful to readers as they consume the text.

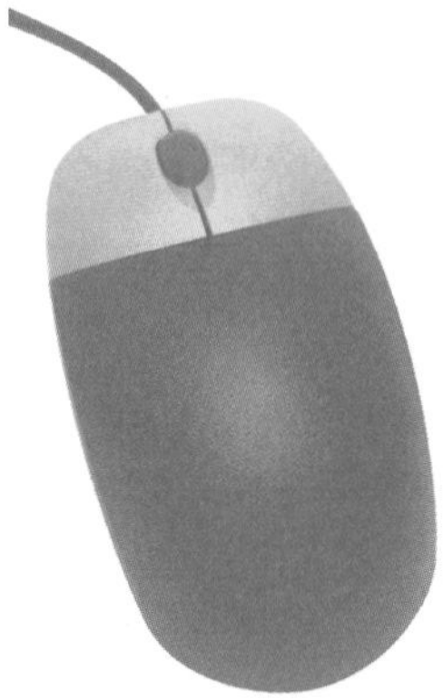

PHASE 3: REVISING YOUR TEXT

The single most important phase of writing is revising. Expert writers revise their texts all the time. They plan for it and make time for it in their writing schedule. The psychological research on writing shows that the revision of text is the key factor that distinguishes between expert and novice writers. Research on younger children finds that these novice writers do very little, if any, revision. Moreover, if they do revise their text, the revision focuses mainly on more technical aspects of writing such as spelling, grammar, and punctuation. When one of this book's authors tries to assist his middle school daughter in revising her class papers, it is difficult to move beyond checking for spelling and other superficial matters. Any suggestions that deal with the content or style of the writing are met with resistance and irritation. As authors mature, they realize that suggestions for revision are not indictments on one's writing quality, but rather a great opportunity to improve.

Expert writers have automatized much of the technical aspects of writing, so they do not worry so much about spelling and grammar. They worry about editing their text for meaning and readability. Does the text make sense? Will the reader be able to understand the ideas and argument? Does the argument flow in a logical manner? Does the text say what I wanted it to say? These are the types of questions you need to ask yourself as you edit your text.

Fix Technical Problems

The technical level of revision is important, as your papers need to be technically correct. Professors do not enjoy reading papers that are filled with spelling and grammatical errors. With all the spelling and grammar checkers available in word-processing programs, fixing these problems is relatively easy. When professors read papers with spelling errors now, they assume, rightly or wrongly, that you did not have time to run the spell checker because you were finishing the paper a few minutes before it was due for class. More important, if you did not have time to correct basic technical problems, professors will assume you had no time to revise your paper for more substantive issues.

Beware: some spell checkers will flag words they don't recognize, but that doesn't mean the alternate spelling they offer is correct or that you have not used the correct word in the first place. Sometimes the recommended alternatives are different words that change the sentence's meaning. Using a spell checker clearly cuts down on spelling errors, but it should not lull you into false security. You still need to know how to spell the word in question (or look it up in the dictionary) and to know its proper meaning. As a simple example, a spell checker will recognize both *compliment* and *complement* as spelled correctly, but they mean different things. (Do you know the difference?)

Reread Your Paper for Meaning

After you have completed your first draft, read your paper over for meaning, checking to see if the paper makes sense to you. Look for how the argument flows, how the paragraphs are connected. You may want to print it out and read it over in a hard copy so you can mark it up. It is hard to read the whole paper when it is on a computer screen and you can see only part of a page at a time. Also, a hard copy lets you make notes about the parts of the paper that don't make sense to you or that need work.

Outline the Text You Have Written

One of the authors of this book uses a strategy of trying to re-outline the text he has written to see if it matches his original outline. He goes through the text paragraph by paragraph, and for each paragraph he tries to determine the main idea. He keeps these main ideas for each paragraph in an outline, which he can examine to see if it matches the original outline. This strategy also helps him see the flow of his argument and how each paragraph contributes to the overall argument. He also uses this strategy to examine student papers. It helps him understand what the student is trying to say (just as we pointed out in Chapter 9—outlining a text can aid understanding).

Get Feedback from a Peer or Friend

Most expert writers share their text with someone to help them see the text in a new light. After spending a great deal of time and effort writing something, most authors are attached to their words, sentences, and paragraphs. This can make it difficult to reread your own text and figure out what needs to be revised. Another person, however, has no emotional attachment to the text and so can read it and give you unbiased feedback. This feedback can be very helpful to you in writing more clearly and persuasively. It is sometimes difficult to listen to this feedback (as it is for this author's middle school daughter), but over time you will develop a thicker skin and recognize that the feedback is actually very valuable.

Ask yourself the questions in Activity 10.4 as you reread your own text. Your peer editor might also use these questions to develop feedback for you. We encourage you to give this list to your peers when they read your papers.

ACTIVITY 10.4 *Questions to Ask in Editing a Paper*

1. What is the paper about? What is its main theme?
2. What are the goals of the paper? Does it accomplish them?
3. Who is the audience for the paper? Will they understand it?
4. What are the best parts of the paper? Why?
5. What parts are unclear or weak? Why?
6. What would you change about the paper?
7. Are the technical parts of the paper correct (spelling, grammar, punctuation, etc.)?

Go Back and Make Changes to Your Text

Before computers, it was not easy to make changes in text. If papers were written by hand, then whole sections had to be recopied. If they were done on typewriters (an "ancient" technology that you might have heard of), then whole pages had to be retyped, or parts had to be "whited" out with a special liquid that covered up the typing and then could be typed over when it dried. Or the writer could literally cut and then paste paragraphs or sections onto new sheets of paper to move parts of the text around. (The terms *cutting* and *pasting* on computer word-processing software are left over from the era of typewriters.) The authors of this text can remember doing all of these things in their own college days, but you are spared such drudgery. Computers make the editing process much, much easier. Given this ease, there is no excuse for not editing your papers.

The computer is just a tool. It will not do the revision for you, but it will make the task easier. You should make use of this tool to write better papers. It is also possible that the computer can create some other types of errors—pasting in the wrong spot, laziness in proofreading, and overlooking spelling errors. Some of these oversights can be reduced by editing the printed page rather than editing on-screen. Both of us edit on-screen as well, but we think it increases the chance for mistakes.

OTHER WRITING TIPS

Descriptive Writing Strategies

A lot of students play it safe with their writing. Students take a "just the facts" approach to writing, not giving the reader much more than a bare-bones account of the event they are describing. This is more appropriate in certain subject areas, such as natural and social sciences, than others (see the next section, on writing in different disciplines). But particularly in humanities writing, we encourage you to be descriptive in your writing. Figure 10.6 lists four strategies that will enhance your writing and challenge your skills. First, using specific words is better than using general words. Saying "The refs called a bad game" says nothing about the referees, the game, or your definition of *bad*. Saying that the refs were out of shape, out of position, or appeared arrogant gives more detail. Saying that the game was overly physical or that the crowd was unruly describes details about the

Strategies for making writing more descriptive.

1. *Use specific words.* Specific words are more powerful than general words. More specific words will more accurately convey to your reader what you are trying to say.
2. *Show, don't tell.* Describe scenes with action and detail.
3. *Use your senses.* Activate the reader's sense of sight, smell, touch, sound, and body awareness.
4. *Create a focus.* Select the one impression you want to create in a paragraph, and use all of the information in that paragraph to support that focus.

Source: Writing Assistance Center, University of Nebraska (www.unl.edu/english/wac)

game. And saying that the refs wrongly administered a double-foul situation describes how you defined *bad*. Second, using action words will add life to your text. Passively telling about an event will not engage the reader in the same way that an active account of it will. Third, use your senses so that the readers will use theirs. Instead of simply saying it was a "snowy Michigan day," describe the snow (amount, color, texture, how it fell, how it felt on your body), describe Michigan (specific location, who else was there), and describe the day (time, temperature, surroundings). Fourth, identify the controlling idea (main point, focus) of each section of your writing. Then gather all of your writing strategies around "making the case" for that main point. (We mentioned this earlier when discussing strategies for generating text—Phase 2.)

Writing in Different Subject Areas

As we alluded to in the previous section, professors in different subject areas will expect different kinds of writing. We encourage you to consult your professor directly if you have questions. Most of the time, professors will pass out guidelines for course writing. This will help with specific recommendations. We offer general advice here. First, writing in natural science and social science is generally more expository than narrative. It is also more economical. The emphasis is on detail and precision, especially in the section of a paper that describes research methodology. The reason for this emphasis on detail is because if a subsequent writer wants to replicate your methodology, he or she will need to know exactly how you defined your terms (e.g., "loneliness is defined as . . . ") and what equipment you used (e.g., male albino rats) to conduct your research. The style is straightforward, without a lot of sensory detail or long narrative. Striving to be direct and to-the-point will usually serve you well in the natural and social sciences.

In the humanities, precision and detail are also highly regarded, but the focus is more on analysis. The analysis could be of a particular text (as in English), an event (as in history), or a ritual (as in cultural anthropology). You will also be asked to draw some conclusions based on your research and writing. For example, a paper in political science might require you to consider the question of whether the U.S. Constitution has attached to it only those rights found in the actual document or whether it has penumbral rights—certain rights not stated but that emanate from the original text. As you do your research, you will likely be asked to state a position and form an argument defending that position.

Although there are many common elements of successful writing that cut across all writing demands, it is important to know these differences. This section does not address all of the differences. The more you become acquainted with a particular subject area, the better your writing in that area will become. So getting familiar with a subject area is a key to developing writing expertise. And the way to become familiar with a subject area is reading material from that subject area. Reading in a subject area exposes you to how experts in the field write. This is a good long-term strategy. In the meantime, a short-term strategy for improving your writing in a subject area is to ask your professor for tips. Your professor is an expert in the field and can give you good advice. Furthermore, the professor, at least for class papers, is the **audience** of your writing—the person for whom the writing is intended. When you know your audience, the specific needs of your writing become easier to meet.

Writing a Blog

Estimates vary as to how many blogs (short for "Web log") exist on the Internet, but it's easily in the millions. Many of you may already have your own blog. The blog's purpose may be a personal journal you share with friends, a diary of your athletic team, or a political or social commentary. We are not crazy about students' spending too much time blogging, but we do recognize that this activity may have one beneficial by-product—it provides writing practice. Some advice on blog writing may contradict what we've said in this chapter. For example, the site http://problogger.net encourages bloggers to use catchy headlines and bullet lists. More formal writing usually does not include these as much. However, other tips (found at the same Web site) are very similar to advice that we would give you for formal writing. For example, making your opinion known (focus), editing your text (Phase 3), and using as few words as needed to get your point across are general strategies that will aid you in formal writing as well (see Figure 10.7).

FIGURE 10.7 Tips on writing a blog.

1. Make your opinion known.
2. Provide lots of links.
3. Less is more.
4. 250 words is a sufficient post.
5. Make snappy headlines.
6. Be passionate in your writing.
7. Use bullet points.
8. Edit your work.
9. Make your posts easy to scan.
10. Be consistent in your style.
11. Litter the post with keywords.

Source: http://Problogger.net

CHAPTER SUMMARY

This chapter has discussed the writing process. Writing is a difficult task for just about everyone. It is important that you plan and set goals for your writing. If you want to become a better writer than you are now, you need to work at it, engage in planning, set goals, and monitor your progress toward those goals. Besides goal setting, one important aspect of planning is the collection of information that you will use. Many sources are available to you, and you must be careful in your use of them. It is important to evaluate the authority, the accuracy, the objectivity, the currency, the coverage, and the intended audience of all your sources, but especially the sources and material you find on the Web.

After your planning, goal setting, and information collecting, it is time to begin translating your ideas into actual text or prose. Although this is a difficult task, the strategies in this book should be helpful to you. In particular, you should try to go beyond the general strategy of knowledge telling and really try to generate new knowledge as you write.

The final step in the general writing process, and one of the most important, is the revision of your text. One of the major factors distinguishing good writers from poor writers is that good writers revise their text and poor writers do not. Or, when poor writers do revise, they tend to focus on technical aspects such as spelling, grammar, and punctuation, not the logic of the argument, the clarity of the writing, or the organization of the text. These larger issues are more important to consider in revising your text than are the technical aspects, although you should make sure that you use computer tools (e.g., spelling and grammar checkers) and proofread carefully to ensure that your text is readable and technically correct as well.

Taking Tests

Chapter Goals

This chapter will help you:

- Learn general test-taking strategies
- Learn specific strategies for studying for multiple-choice tests
- Learn specific strategies for studying for essay tests
- Identify strategies for writing good answers to essay questions
- Adopt coping skills for handling test anxiety

Key Terms

cognitive interference	norm referenced
criterion referenced	recall memory
emotionality	recognition memory
multiple choice	test anxiety

CHAPTER 11

Tests in college are like death and taxes: You can't avoid them. So instead of playing defense and helplessly waiting for tests to occur, it's better to play offense and anticipate what kinds of tests you will have and determine how best to study for them. In this chapter, we teach you to go on offense.

We start with a distinction that many professors make between two different types of tests: *norm referenced* versus *criterion referenced*. The distinction really lies in how the tests are graded and scored. Although you don't have any control over the type of tests your professors give, you can benefit from knowing how they are graded. We then turn to strategy. First, we give some general test-taking tips. Then, we suggest ways to study for and take objective tests. *Objective tests* are tests for which a question has only one correct answer. Essay tests require different strategies, and we will cover these as well. Essay tests are not likely to have only one correct answer. Furthermore, the quality of the presentation of your answer may be as important as the content of your answer.

We then examine the issue of test anxiety. Many students find that they get very nervous when they take tests. We will suggest ways you can reduce this anxiety. We conclude this chapter by urging you to consider tests not simply as high-stakes evaluations that will comprise a major part of your course grade. Rather, we hope you will view tests as a learning tool, an opportunity for you to get important feedback about what you have learned in this course in particular, and how well your learning strategies are working in general. Tests provide you with valuable information that can make you a better student in the long run.

Activity 11.1 contains the five items from the Learning Inventory that assess test taking. Please complete these items again before you read further.

ACTIVITY 11.1 *Assessing Your Test-Taking Skills*

Circle the statements that best describe your approach to taking tests. When you are finished, add the corresponding points for all items.

1. After I get a multiple-choice test back, I look at the ones I got wrong and realize I made a "stupid mistake".
   - (4) never or almost never
   - (3) rarely
   - (2) frequently
   - (1) always or almost always

2. I study the same way for essay and multiple-choice tests.
   - (4) never or almost never
   - (3) rarely
   - (2) frequently
   - (1) always or almost always

3. I try to make comparisons and note similarities between what I read in textbooks and what I hear in lectures.
   - (1) never or almost never
   - (2) rarely
   - (3) frequently
   - (4) always or almost always

4. My nervousness distracts me from clear thinking during tests.
   - (4) never or almost never
   - (3) rarely
   - (2) frequently
   - (1) always or almost always

5. I jot down an outline for an essay answer before I begin writing.

   ① never or almost never   ③ frequently

   ② rarely   ④ always or almost always

SCORING:

The following categories provide an indication of your current test-taking strategies. The guide below will help you classify yourself.

16 and above: You are probably pretty good at taking tests. This chapter can serve as a helpful review of important strategies and skills.

11–15: You probably are pretty good at taking tests. However, you may want to revisit some of your strategies. This chapter will help you identify some ways you can improve your test taking.

10 and below: This chapter is definitely for you. It will help you focus on some important test-taking tips. We encourage you to read this chapter carefully and to use the suggestions we offer.

NORM-REFERENCED VERSUS CRITERION-REFERENCED TESTS

We start this chapter with a brief description of how professors might grade your tests. One type of grading is called **norm referenced.** When a test is norm referenced, it means that your score is determined (at least in part) by the performance of others in the class. This is colloquially referred to as "grading on a curve." It is not uncommon for professors to use some form of test curving. This could help students, because the grading scale can be less rigid than the professor's usual one. For example, if the professor uses a grading scale in which 94% and above is an A, 90% to 93% is an A−, and so on, when he "curves" the grades, those ranges may be less stringent. So, 90% and above might be an A, and 86% to 89% might be an A−. Of course, this could work against you if the professor decided that too many people got high grades, and therefore made the grading scale more stringent.

The second type of test grading is called **criterion referenced.** When a test is criterion referenced, your score is simply a measure of how well you performed on the test. Your score is not determined by its relation to other people's scores; it is simply a reflection of how well you as an individual did on the test—presumably how much you learned. If all of the students in the class scored above 90%, all students would get As or A–s.

Although you have no control over how professors grade tests, it is important that you are aware of the difference. If the professor does not tell you at the beginning of the semester how he or she grades (i.e., if it is not stated or implied on the syllabus), make sure you ask. The more you know about the evaluation procedures, the better.

GENERAL TEST-TAKING TIPS

In this section, we give basic advice for improving your test taking. Many of these tips you have probably heard before, and in fact, we mentioned some of them in Chapter 5 as suggestions for general life skills. But even so, they bear repeating in the context of test taking. This advice is good for any kind of test. In the subsequent sections, we offer specific advice for different kinds of tests. But first, the basics. We offer six ways to make your test taking a more positive and effective experience.

Before the Test

Sleep. All-nighters are a bad idea. If given the choice between not studying and studying all night, an all-nighter is better. But if given a choice between staying up all night and studying, or spreading out your studying and getting a good night's sleep, take the good night's sleep every time. Sleep before the test is vital. If you're fatigued, you can't perform as well. If you are a musician, athlete, or actor, you know this. It is just as true in mental activities as it is in physical activities.

We understand that college sometimes makes you feel like a hamster on a wheel and there's no way to jump off. But the biggest way to avoid late-night studying right before a test is to work ahead. Keeping pace with your assignments and reading will make it so much easier for you to get a reasonable night's sleep prior to the exam. We are not so naïve to think that college students are not going to fall behind, or that success in college can be achieved without some sleep deprivation. We both pulled all-nighters in college and lived to tell about it. And even when you become established in your career, late-night work will still be required. But staying up late is not a long-term solution that will work for you. You will get tired more often, sick more often, and fall behind even more. We recommend at least 8 hours of high-quality sleep at night, paired with a brief nap early in the afternoon, as the best strategy for staying rested and avoiding all-nighters.

Eat. If your test is in the morning, eat breakfast before you go. Even if it's just a glass of juice and dry cereal in your room, you will do better if you eat before your test. Long-term healthy eating is also a must. If your diet regularly lacks basic nutrients, your ability to function at your highest level will eventually suffer.

During the Test

Relax. In the final section of this chapter we will discuss test anxiety. But it's worth mentioning here as well. The bottom line is that when you are nervous, you don't perform as well. If you encounter a tough question that is worth a lot of points, you might start to panic. Panicking creates distraction, distraction creates poor performance, and poor performance creates even more panicking. It is crucial to stay calm during a test. You will do better.

Pick Your Spot. Find a spot in the classroom that makes you comfortable. When he was in graduate school, one of the authors was taking a course in probability theory and saw a student stumble in a drunklike state toward the front of the classroom, test in hand, his shirt dripping with sweat. The professor took the test from him and assisted him to the door. He was never seen in the class again. He was probably having a panic attack. Before he left the room, his panic attack caused a great deal of commotion, no doubt a distraction to those around him. Of course, you can never know who among your classmates might be afflicted with such a condition. However, you can control, to a certain extent, where you sit. It should be a spot that is familiar and comfortable. Drippy noses, coughing, and loud paper shuffling are irritating. And sitting near friends is distracting. Do your best your best to find a place where you can devote an entire hour to uninterrupted work.

Every semester one of the book's authors receives requests from students to take tests in a private work space. The private work space is supposed to help students with ADHD achieve better concentration. If a student has a documented disability, colleges are required to provide optimal accommodations to assist that student. Fortunately, the building where this professor teaches has several lab rooms near his classroom that allow students who need extra quiet to receive it. Let the testing environment work for you, not against you. If you are helped by quiet spaces, ask your professor or your academic support center if you can have one. This author is skeptical that quiet places produce large improvements in test scores, but what is most important is that it relaxes the student and gives him or her greater attentional capacity to take the test.

Preview the Whole Test. Before you begin writing or bubbling, look through each page of the test. We recommend four stages to completing a test. First, find parts of the test that you know well and can answer easily. Do those first. This will guarantee you some points and give you some early confidence. Second, we recommend that you look back through the test and identify what parts will be the most difficult. Plan to answer them *last*. This will prevent you from getting discouraged. Furthermore, by completing the other parts of the test, it may activate some *schemas* (Chapter 6) that will aid you in answering the hard parts. Third, after you have answered the easy parts and identified the difficult parts, attack the rest of the test—the items of medium difficulty. Finally, do your best to complete the difficult parts. This approach may not work for everyone, but we believe most of you will be well served by following this sequence. It will particularly help those who struggle with taking tests.

Pace Yourself. In addition to helping you sequence the test—answer the easy stuff, identify the hard stuff, answer the medium stuff, answer the hard stuff—previewing the test also allows you to figure out how long the test will take to finish. Your estimate will determine how quickly you need to finish the easy stuff and how much time you think you need to budget for the difficult stuff. Also make sure you have clarified with the professor whether extra time will be allowed and factor any extra time into your pacing.

ANSWERING OBJECTIVE QUESTIONS

Objective questions are questions for which there exists one correct answer—at least in theory. The most common form of objective question is **multiple choice.** "MCs," as they are often called, require you to select the correct answer from a group of alternatives provided on the test. Activity 11.2 gives examples of multiple-choice questions from earlier portions of this book.

Sample Multiple-Choice Questions

Test your ability to answer multiple-choice questions and your memory of earlier chapters of this book. Below each question, write down your reasons for your choice. Compare your thinking to the suggestions in Figure 11.1.

1. According to Chapter 1, which of the following is *not* a characteristic of a self-regulated learner?

   a. strategic   c. controlling

   b. organized   d. effortful

Explain how you arrived at this answer:

_____

_____

2. According to Chapter 6, multiple-choice questions test the type of memory psychologists refer to as:

a. recognition   c. working

b. recall   d. long-term

Explain how you arrived at this answer:

_____

_____

3. Chapter 8 suggests that you do not borrow someone else's notes (except in an emergency) because:

a. note taking improves encoding   c. you can't trust others in your class

b. professors may not approve   d. you will lose all your friends

Explain how you arrived at this answer:

_____

_____

4. Which of the following are elements from the Big Five personality theory described in Chapter 5?

A. control   a. A and B

B. monitoring   b. C and D

C. agreeableness   c. A and D

D. openness   d. B and C

Explain how you arrived at this answer:

_____

_____

What makes a multiple-choice question hard? In general, the greater the conceptual similarity between the correct answer and the distracters (the incorrect answers), the more difficult the question. Try Activity 11.3 before you read further.

This question serves to illustrate the following point: The more similar the incorrect alternatives are to each other, the harder a multiple-choice question will be. (You could probably find non-Texans who think any of those four alternatives are correct.) Also, the more plausible the incorrect alternatives are, the harder the question is. (Isn't it more plausible to think that Dallas or Houston is the capital rather than Van Horn or Mule Shoe?) Of course, you have no control over the choices. Certainly after taking the first test or quiz in a course you will get an idea of the difficulty level for that course. Professors often want to know if you can identify the definition of a concept or can recognize an example of the concept. Multiple-choice questions are an efficient way of measuring students' memory for course concepts.

Conceptual Similarity and Test Difficulty

Compare the difficulty level of these two questions.

1. What is the capital of Texas?
    a. Dallas
    b. Houston
    c. Austin
    d. Fort Worth

2. What is the capital of Texas?
    a. Austin
    b. San Marcos
    c. Van Horn
    d. Mule Shoe

Which question was harder (circle one)?   Question 1   Question 2

Why do you think so?

_____

_____

Strategies for Taking Multiple-Choice Tests

What are some strategies for doing well on multiple-choice questions? Some of the suggestions below may seem straightforward and obvious, but too many students have indicated to us that they missed multiple-choice questions because they made some of these errors. Figure 11.1 gives five strategies for answering multiple-choice questions. The suggestions combine to form the acronym READY—which is what these suggestions will make you for multiple-choice tests.

These strategies might be overkill for easy questions, but for more difficult questions taking these steps will produce better results.

Some Questions About Multiple-Choice Tests

Student folklore has developed some interesting theories about how to take multiple-choice tests. Some of the folklore is probably correct, some is probably not. In an attempt to separate fact from fiction, we offer our opinion (based on experience and research) on some of these theories. Figure 11.2 summarizes this section.

1. *When in doubt, should I always answer "c"?* Members of the military may be familiar with the phrase "When in doubt, Charlie out." (Civilian translation: Pick "c" if you're unsure.) But the answer to the question is no. Even if it is true that one answer alternative appears more often than others, it would simply be due to randomness, and there is no reason to expect "c" to be most common. If you have no idea of the answer, choose the response that seems most plausible.

FIGURE ▮ ▮ ▮ ▮ | Strategies for taking multiple choice tests.

Follow these suggestions to be **READY** to take multiple-choice tests.

1. **R**ead the entire question. You may think you know what the question is saying, but if you don't read it all the way through, you may miss something. Here's a favorite question of ours (but not of our students) from Introductory Psychology that a lot of people get wrong:

    Joshua is 5 years old and has the intellectual capacity of a 4-year-old. Intelligence testers would say that Joshua's mental age is:

    a. 4   d. 120
    b. 5   e. 125
    c. 80

    Many students give "c" (80) as the answer. The reason is that they do not read the entire question. Traditionally IQ has been defined as mental age (the age at which someone performs intellectual tasks) divided by chronological age (a person's actual age), multiplied by 100. When students see the mental age and the chronological age in the question, they assume they need to compute IQ. Thus, they divide 5 into 4, multiply by 100, and get 80. The problem is the question didn't ask for IQ, it simply asked for mental age, which was stated right in the question—4. If they had read the whole question carefully, they would have avoided this mistake. (Incidentally, we have now started to underline the words *mental age* in this question, and the error rate has gone down. We conclude that people obviously know the answer, but they aren't paying attention. If we point out the important information by underlining it, students get it right. But don't count on the kindness of professors; test taker beware.)

2. **E**xamine all answer choices. Beware of questions that have an intuitively appealing answer that is incorrect. If that answer is one of the first choices, you may select it without considering all of the answers, and thus will miss reading the correct one. Consider this question based on Chapter 3:

    Briana wants to do well in her biology classes because she values getting good grades, out-performing others, and getting into medical school. Briana is said to be motivated by:

    a. external rewards
    b. greed
    c. intrinsic rewards
    d. extrinsic rewards

    Although the difference is subtle, the correct answer (we hope you will recall) is "d"—extrinsic rewards. Professors with a penchant for detail may include distracters that are similar to the correct answer in many ways. If you didn't read all the choices, you might have selected "a"—external rewards—because it looked like the correct answer. Be careful.

3. **A**lternative interpretations? OK, so you think you understand the question? That's good. But before you go on, make sure that the question is really asking what you think it is asking. Do this by (a) checking all the relevant terms and concepts and (b) making sure that you're not thinking of something else from another part of the course. The following is an example of a question that students might interpret incorrectly.

    What is MOST important about the fact that humans can remember things?

    a. It is the foundation of success in college.
    b. It helps us remember people's names.
    c. It defines our existence, anchors us in the past, and interprets our future.

continued

This is a difficult question. We first read the question completely (Step 1) and consider the choices (Step 2). Now we need to make sure we are interpreting the question correctly. This is why this problem is hard; we don't know what the professor is thinking. Does she mean the MOST important thing for this course? If you are reading this book, the best answer might be "a." After all, the focus of the discussion of memory (Chapter 6) was on its applications to school settings. The other two do not deal with this. However, in a cognitive psychology or philosophy class, the best answer might be "c." After all, there is more to memory than simply school tasks. Without it, our existence would literally be moment to moment, no past to anchor us and no future to look toward. Make sure you are clear on what the professor is asking, and if you are unsure, don't be afraid to ask.

4. **D**elete nonplausible choices. Once you understand the question correctly, you are ready to narrow down the choices. This can make questions that look difficult at first much easier. You may want to cross out those you are not considering to cut down on the amount of information you have to process (remember Chapter 6's discussion of the limited capacity of our attentional system). Consider this question:

    Which of the following characterizes the "will" component of academic success?

    a.   self-efficacy

    b.   organization

    c.   memory

    d.   taking good notes

    Remember that the "will" component refers to motivational beliefs. If you know the material, you will recognize that "b" and "c" are examples of the "skill" component of academic success (cognitive and metacognitive strategies), so you can eliminate them. Alternative "d" is a possibility, since motivated people will probably take good notes. However, note taking is viewed more as a cognitive activity, and self-efficacy is a more clear reference to will, so "a" is the better answer. Answering this question may be easier if you eliminate "b" and "c" quickly so you can focus more attention on deciding between "a" and "d."

5. **Y**ield: Did you miss something? *Slow down!* Take one last look at the question to make sure you have not underestimated the difficulty of the question or made the question more difficult than it is. Step 1 above gives an example of a question that looks more difficult than it is. If you pause briefly, you are more likely to avoid an error. The word *not* in a question poses another type of challenge. Many professors make an effort to bring the word to your attention by underlining it, putting it in CAPITALS, or typing it in **bold face.** Whether your professor does so or not, beware of the word's presence in a sentence. It's frustrating to miss such a question because you simply misread it.

A similar misconception is that you should give the same answer on all questions you don't know. There is no reason to do so. Assuming that the letters of correct answers are randomly (evenly) distributed among the four or five answer alternatives, the chance that you will get a question right when you know absolutely nothing about the concept being tested is either 25% (with four alternatives) or 20% (with five alternatives). This will be true regardless of which alternative you choose.

FIGURE 11.2   Summary of common questions about multiple-choice tests.

1. *When in doubt, should I always answer "c"?*

   No. Presumably the answers are randomly distributed, but even if they weren't, there's no evidence that "c" is most common.

2. *If I get a string of the same letter, should I assume that I made a mistake and change one of them?*

   No. Although some professors may try to avoid letter strings, some may be inclined to use them just to have fun. Most, we suspect, pay no attention at all to such matters. Thus, change an answer only because you think it's wrong, not because the answer sheet looks too orderly.

3. *Is it true that you should trust your "first instinct" and avoiding changing your answer?*

   No. Go with what you believe is correct. Don't worry about whether it was your first choice or not.

4. *Are multiple-choice tests easier than essay tests?*

   For some students, perhaps so. But this may have more to do with a student's level of writing skill than with the nature of multiple-choice tests. Beware: Professors can make multiple-choice questions very difficult if they want to.

---

   2. *If I get a string of the same letter, should I assume that I made a mistake and change one of them?* Probably not. It's important for you to know that the instructor's manuals of many textbooks come with test-item banks. Although the writers of these test banks probably make an effort to have equal amounts of each letter as the correct answer, your professor will not select the order of the questions based on the letters of correct answers. Professors select only some of the test questions and pay no attention to which letter is the correct answer. Therefore, you can't expect the answers in a given test to have an even mix of answer letters. One of the authors of this book gives multiple-choice exams in Introductory Psychology and Developmental Psychology and uses items from the test bank. Since questions are selected without attention to the letter of the correct answer, on one test there were *seven* questions in a row with "b" as the correct answer. The professor noted that very few students got the whole string of seven correct. He concluded that even the most successful students were swayed by self-doubt and changed some of their answers. Indeed, some students have reported to us that they have actually gone back to change answers because the string of answers didn't look right. Don't do that. Pay no attention to the letter sequence. The letter sequence that "looks good" will be the one that has the correct answers!

   If professors don't use test banks, they may be more likely to avoid using a consecutive string of the same letter. But even in this case, if you change an answer just because it is part of a string, you run the risk of switching a right answer to a wrong answer. Don't be led into temptation; go with what you think is right.

   3. *Is it true that you should trust your "first instinct" and avoid changing your answer?* No. Perhaps this seems to be true because you more often remember the times when changing your answers cost you points, and less often remember the

times when changing your answers gained you points. In fact, research suggests that changing your answers, on average, is a pretty good idea. (Provided, of course, you have a good reason to do so.) Marshall Geiger (1991), of the University of Maine, examined the effect of answer changes on student test performance. Using tests from business administration courses, he identified erasure marks on multiple-choice tests with a high illumination light. He found that students picked up approximately three points by changing their answers for every one point they lost. Don't take this to mean that you should go back and change a lot of your answers. But the point is clear: If you are undecided, go with what you believe is correct, whether it is your first choice or whether you go back and change it. As you work through the test, you may recall some information that is relevant to an earlier question.

4. *Are multiple-choice tests easier than essay tests?* This is an interesting question. Most students would probably say yes. Many students also report that they study longer for essay tests. Further, you will recall from Chapter 6 the difference between recognition and recall: recognition is identifying something once it is presented to you, and recall is actually being able to access the piece of information. Recall, which essay tests require, is more difficult. We will offer some suggestions for studying for essay tests later in the chapter.

We urge you, however, not to be lulled into false security about multiple-choice tests. They can be difficult for two reasons. First, a multiple-choice question can ask about the reading at a very high level of detail. A professor would probably feel justified in asking what many students would consider a very picky question from the reading in a multiple-choice test. It is not practical to ask such detailed questions in essay tests. Second, complex ideas can be tested with any kind of question. It is true that multiple-choice questions are often factual or definitional in nature, and thus not too difficult if you know the facts. However, it is also true that multiple-choice questions can test complex ideas very efficiently and effectively.

Other Types of Objective Questions

Matching Questions. Matching questions list a set of definitions or examples for course concepts in one column and the corresponding concepts in another and ask the student to pair up the definitions or examples with the proper concepts. A matching question essentially consists of lots of multiple-choice questions rolled together. The correct answer for one concept serves as a distracter for all the others.

Two factors determine the difficulty of matching questions. First, "extra" or "leftover" definitions in the list add to the difficulty. If there are 10 concepts and 10 definitions, you know that each definition must be used. This type of matching exercise will probably not be any more difficult than multiple-choice questions are. However, a question with 10 concepts and 20 definitions is more difficult. You will have to consider 10 extra definitions. In this case, a matching exercise will likely be more difficult than multiple-choice questions.

The second factor determining the difficulty of matching questions is the degree of similarity of the items. For example, students in psychology often get the concepts of proactive interference and retroactive interference confused. Proactive interference is when old information interferes with the recall of new information. For example, suppose you take French in high school and take

Spanish in college. If you have trouble on your college Spanish exam because you confuse French words with the new Spanish you are learning, this is proactive interference. Conversely, retroactive interference is when new information interferes with the recall of old information. Again, if you took French in high school and Spanish in college, then traveled to France, the extent to which you had trouble remembering your French because you were confusing it with your newly learned Spanish reflects retroactive interference. You can see how these concepts could easily be confused. A matching task would be more difficult if it included both of those concepts (or both of those definitions). For example, this part of a matching test may be difficult:

1. proactive interference   a. old information interferes with new
2. retroactive interference   b. new information interferes with old

In general, the more similar (and thus confusing) the items are on a test, the more difficult the test will be. This is true regardless of the type of test.

STRATEGY SUGGESTION

Try to identify possible areas of confusion and anticipate them when you study. Make extra effort to distinguish between such difficult items.

Fill-in-the-Blank Questions. Questions that require you to complete a sentence by filling in a missing word can be more difficult than multiple-choice questions. Fill-in-the-blank questions are similar to multiple-choice questions: Through the sentence descriptions, they both provide ample memory cues to help you access the answer. However, fill-in-the-blank questions may be more difficult because the answer is not provided among a list of alternatives. Rather, you must generate the answer on your own. Do you remember the types of memory we talked about in Chapter 6? Multiple-choice questions require **recognition memory** and fill-in-the-blank questions require **recall memory.** Memory is usually better for recognition than for recall.

Definitional Questions. For definitional questions, professors simply list a variety of concepts along the left-hand side of the paper and ask you to provide definitions. These are similar to fill-in-the-blank questions in that they both require recall memory. However, definitional questions are more difficult because they lack the memory cues that fill-in-the-blank questions give. When the professor supplies you with only the concept, your memory doesn't receive any "jump start" to start it thinking along the right lines. If you know a test is going to have definitional questions, make sure you study accordingly.

Definitional Multiple-Choice Questions. You will be able to answer definitional multiple-choice questions correctly if you know the definitions of the concepts being tested. They do not require application of principles. Although it is possible to score well on tests made up of definitional multiple-choice questions by studying with rehearsal, we caution you not to rely solely on the rehearsal

For definitional tests, make sure you are able to formulate definitions for terms. It is not enough that you are able to recognize concepts; you must come up with the answers yourself.

learning strategy (Chapter 7). If you do, you will likely develop only a low-level factual understanding of the material. See Activity 11.2 for examples of definitional multiple-choice items.

Conceptual Multiple-Choice Questions. A more difficult type of multiple-choice question is one that involves the application of a course concept. This type of question requires two things. First, you must be familiar enough with the concept to be able to define it. Second, you must be able to recognize when that concept is being applied. This will require a higher level of comprehension of the course material. Professors are fond of this type of question because it is an effective way to see which students simply know the definitions of concepts and which ones know how to apply the concepts. If you cannot do the latter, you will not score well on conceptual multiple-choice questions.

Activity 11.4 summarizes research on the human brain and gives examples of the five kinds of objective questions. This will give you an idea of the range of difficulty these questions can pose. Do Activity 11.4 before you read further. Figure 11.3 gives answers to the questions.

As you can see, objective questions vary in type and difficulty. Although multiple-choice questions may sometimes be easy, we hope Question 5 in Activity 11.4 shows you that they can also require some sophisticated thinking and high-level comprehension of the course material.

Examples of Objective Questions

ACTIVITY 11.4

Read the following passage and answer the questions below.

Our brain is divided into two hemispheres—left and right—that are connected by a band of fibrous tissue known as the corpus callosum. In most people, the left hemisphere is the dominant hemisphere for speech production. The right hemisphere, on the other hand, is responsible for other tasks such as spatial reasoning. Also, the two hemispheres control the opposite sides of the body; the left hemisphere controls the right side, and the right hemisphere controls the left side. We also have two different fields of vision—left and right. When information is presented to our right visual field, it gets crossed over to our left hemisphere. When information is presented to our left visual field, it gets crossed over to our right hemisphere. When the picture of an object is presented to our left visual field, and then sent to our right hemisphere, most people have no trouble identifying the object, even though it is not sent to the left hemisphere where language is processed. The reason is that the information gets transferred across the corpus callosum, the brain's interhemispheric communication link. However, some people have had this link surgically cut, eliminating this communication. In these people we see a very interesting phenomenon when we flash a picture of the object to the left visual field. The information goes from the left visual field to the right hemisphere. But, because

(continued)

ACTIVITY 11-4 *continued*

the left hemisphere is responsible for language, the person is unable to say the name of the object out loud. Even though the information gets sent to the brain (right hemisphere), these people are unable to say the name of the object. Remember though, the information is in the right hemisphere, the person just can't name it.

1. *Matching*

   _____ right visual field   a. tissue connecting two hemispheres

   _____ left visual field   b. right hemisphere

   _____ corpus callosum   c. left hemisphere

                                     d. spatial ability

2. *Fill-in-the-blank*

   * The information from the left visual field is processed in the _____.

   * The information from the right visual field gets transferred from the _____
   by way of the _____.

3. *Definitions*

   corpus callosum: _____

   left hemisphere: _____

4. *Definitional multiple-choice*

   The right hemisphere is most responsible for skills such as:

   a. speech production

   b. processing information from the right visual field

   c. spatial reasoning

   d. all of the above

5. *Conceptual multiple-choice*

   A patient whose corpus callosum is severed participates in a visual-field experiment. In the right visual field the experimenter briefly displays a picture of a dog. In the left visual field the experimenter briefly displays a picture of a cat. This individual will be able to use his _____ hand to indicate he saw a _____.

   a. right; cat

   b. left; dog

   c. left; cat

   d. right or left; dog

   e. right or left; cat

TAKING ESSAY TESTS

The other major type of test question is the essay question. Essays differ in the length and breadth of material they are designed to test. Essays that require knowledge of only a small set of concepts might be called "short answer." Other questions, which are more genuinely called essay questions, ask for information covering a broad range of concepts. Below we discuss two basic kinds of essay questions: those that require thinking and those that do not require thinking. This

FIGURE 11.3

Answers to Activity 11.4.

See how well you did on the questions in Activity 11.4.

1. c, b, a

2. right hemisphere; left hemisphere; corpus callosum

3. fibrous band of tissues that connects the two hemispheres place in the brain where language ability is housed in most people

4. c

5. This question requires a conceptual understanding of the principle of hemispheric specialization. You might have memorized what the hemispheres do and what happens to information from the two visual fields. This will allow you to answer the first four types of questions. However, answering a conceptual multiple-choice question will be difficult unless you are able to apply your knowledge to this particular situation. In fact, many students have trouble with this question.

How would you solve this problem? First, using Strategy 3 mentioned earlier, we can safely eliminate "d" and "e". Because the information is only in one hemisphere (since the person's corpus callosum is severed), we know the information cannot be in both hemispheres. Next, ask yourself if a person could draw a cat with the right hand (answer "a"). This would mean that the word *cat* was being processed in the left hemisphere, therefore coming from the right visual field. This is not the case. Next, could a person draw a dog with the left hand (answer "b")? This would mean that the word *dog* was being processed in the right hemisphere, therefore coming from the left visual field. This is also not the case. Finally, could a person use the left hand to draw a cat (answer "c")? This would mean that the word *cat* was being processed in the right hemisphere, therefore coming from the left visual field. As the question indicates, this is the case, and therefore the answer must be "c".

---

distinction is not a strict dichotomy, but rather a matter of degree. Some questions simply require rote recall of facts, and in that way are more like objective questions, except that they test recall memory instead of recognition memory. Other questions are very abstract and conceptual and require much more than rote recall. Still others lie somewhere in between.

Essay Questions That Do Not Require Thinking

In some cases, the only thing that distinguishes an essay question from an objective question is the type of memory that is required. Multiple-choice questions, for example, require recognition memory. Some essay questions, on the other hand, require recall memory, but not any higher order thinking. In such cases, the professor simply wants to test whether you can remember a theory or concept.

Consider, for example, the following multiple-choice questions based on material from Chapter 7:

1. James studies for tests by repeating concepts over and over to himself and by studying flash cards with the name of the concept on one side and the definition on the other side. What type of cognitive strategy is James using?

   a. rehearsal

   b. elaboration

   c. organization

   d. metacognition

2. Bethany studies for tests by developing diagrams that illustrate the relations between course concepts and by explaining what she has learned to a friend. What type of cognitive strategy is Bethany using?

   a. rehearsal   c. organization

   b. elaboration   d. metacognition

3. Ashanti studies for tests by making outlines of class lectures and textbook readings. What type of cognitive strategy is Ashanti using?

   a. rehearsal   c. organization

   b. elaboration   d. metacognition

Now consider the following essay question:

Identify the three different cognitive strategies discussed in Chapter 7. Give an example of each one.

The three multiple-choice questions and the essay question tap the same knowledge, but you would probably consider the essay question harder than the multiple-choice questions. The essay requires you to recall the strategies without any memory cues (except for indicating that they are found in Chapter 7), whereas the multiple-choice questions provide ample cues. Also, the essay question requires you to generate examples, whereas the multiple-choice questions provide those examples for you. Still, despite the difference in difficulty, you would probably admit that this is not the most difficult essay question you have seen. It requires only recall, and a small amount of higher order thinking.

In graduate school, one of us was a teaching assistant (TA) for a class in child psychology. The tests had essay questions worth 6 to 10 points each. After administering the test, the professor gathered all of the TAs to describe the grading scheme. He would instruct us by saying something like, "This is an eight-point question. Students must define four concepts: A, B, C, and D. For each concept they define correctly, they get two points. If any definition is incomplete, give them one point. If they don't mention it at all, give them zero."

Such questions are easy for professors to write. The professor simply decides what content she is interested in testing, and designs a question that will require students to access that concept from memory. These questions are also easy to grade. On a question like this, professors often set very clear grading guidelines (as our story illustrates). Very straightforward, but, we also think, very dull!

Questions and grading criteria like this eliminate ambiguity about testing. The objectives are very clear, and thus the grading is easy. The problem with this approach to essay questions is that it doesn't require much beyond memorization of course concepts. Since objective questions effectively test your memory for course concepts, essay questions should go beyond that and require more higher level cognitive activity. To that end, many professors write essays that do require you to think.

Essay Questions That Do Require Thinking

The more demanding type of essay question may require you to do some of the following:

1. *Apply.* You will likely have to use your knowledge of the course concepts to apply what you know to a particular situation. You may have to think of examples of particular concepts (although even the "nonthinking" essay often

required this), or you may be asked to identify when a course concept is being used. For example, you might be asked to apply your knowledge of penumbral rights found in the Constitution to the Griswold privacy decision and the Roe abortion decision. It is very important for professors to know whether students can apply knowledge. Alfred North Whitehead (1929) called knowledge that cannot be used "inert knowledge." Essay questions are a good way to test whether knowledge is inert or whether it can be accessed and used in meaningful ways.

2. *Integrate.* A question may ask you to integrate across several concepts or course themes. You must demonstrate that you have done more than just memorize definitions, that you also have learned the interrelations between the concepts. How does A relate to B? What are the components of A? Having a good "outline in your head" will help you write integrative essay questions. You can prepare for these questions by using the organizational rehearsal strategy discussed in Chapter 7. For example, a professor in developmental psychology might ask, "Explain how the cognitive development concept of object permanence relates to the social development concept of separation anxiety in infancy."

3. *Analyze.* Sometimes essay questions ask you to analyze a particular situation based on what you have learned in the course. Professors want to see whether you will use information from the course to analyze the problem. Maybe you could have analyzed the problem without ever having taken the course. However, it is very important for you to "show off" for your professor by demonstrating to him or her that you can use what you have learned to analyze problems.

This kind of essay question can be difficult because it may ask you to go well beyond definitional knowledge of the course material and to use that knowledge in a flexible and meaningful way. To recognize whether the professor is trying to make you think in this way, look for the following "marker" or "trigger" words:

Compare/contrast

Defend

Describe

Activity 11.5 gives examples of each of these three types of questions, and Figure 11.4 has sample answers. Try Activity 11.5 now, then compare your answers to the sample answers.

Writing a Good Answer to an Essay Question

In Figure 11.5 we list four characteristics of students who write good essay answers. Developing these characteristics will help you do well on these questions. Notice that the first letters of the characteristics make the acronym WORK. This is appropriate because studying for tests—especially essay tests—takes hard work.

The activities suggested in Figure 11.5 would fall under the cognitive strategy of elaboration (discussed in Chapter 7). We think elaboration will work for most kinds of tests, especially tests that require you to think. However, these elaborative strategies may be especially effective for essay questions because writing an answer to an essay question is, in itself, a form of elaboration. So, since you will have to elaborate on the exam, it will be helpful to use elaboration during your studying.

ACTIVITY 11.5   *"Thinking" Essay Questions*

You should be able to answer the following questions with what you have learned in this course.

1. *Apply.* MacKenzie studies for exams by repeating definitions of concepts over and over to herself. Lucinda studies for exams by generating examples of concepts, explaining what she has learned to her roommate, and making charts and outlines of how concepts relate to each other. Identify the learning strategies being used by each student, and note the strengths and weaknesses of each.

2. *Integrate.* The local school board in your hometown has discovered that you recently read a book on learning to learn. The instructional subcommittee of the school board is interested in ways they can improve students' learning, thinking, and motivation. They call on you for your expertise. They ask you to give a workshop entitled "The Keys to Successful Learning." Please identify the important points you will make in your presentation, and indicate why they are important.

3. *Analyze.* You are in your first year of coaching a high school athletic team. After the first 2 weeks of practice, you feel that the players have quite a bit of athletic talent, but they seem unmotivated to succeed. They treat practice with contempt and do not put forth their maximal effort. In an attempt to remedy the situation, you draw on your knowledge from your *Learning to Learn* book. What are some ways in which your knowledge about motivation for learning can inform your thinking on how to motivate your athletes?

FIGURE 11.4   Answers to sample essay questions.

Compare your answers in Activity 11.5 to these sample answers.

1. *Apply.* MacKenzie is using a rehearsal strategy, which is a low-level strategy. Lucinda is using organization and elaboration, which are high-level learning strategies. MacKenzie will do satisfactorily if the exams require only memorization of definitions. If they require higher level comprehension like critical thinking, problem solving, or application of course concepts, she will have trouble. Lucinda will be well prepared for any type of test but may be particularly strong on an essay test that requires organization and thinking.

2. *Integrate.* It takes two basic things to survive in college: "skill" and "will." The skill components include memory-improvement techniques. There are several ways you can improve your memory. (Here you would list those ways.)

    There's more to college learning than memory, though. You also have to study using good learning strategies. The learning strategies are broken down into two main types: cognitive and metacognitive/resource management. The best cognitive strategies to employ are organization and elaboration. Rehearsal is OK if you have exams that require only memorization. Tests that require high-level understanding are best studied for using the high-level strategies. Metacognitive/resource management strategies involve checking the effectiveness of your learning strategies and adjusting them based on how well they are working. They also deal with knowing when and how best to get assistance from professors and classmates, how to conduct effective study groups (peer learning), and how to manage your time and study environment effectively.

    The best "skill" won't do any good without the appropriate "will." This means setting goals for yourself, both short term and long term. Your goals should be difficult and specific. It also involves being motivated; college students are motivated by either intrinsic rewards—learning for its own

sake—or extrinsic rewards—learning to get a good grade or do better than others. Will also involves believing in yourself and your competencies, having a sense of self-efficacy. What the mind can conceive and believe, the mind can achieve.

3. *Analyze.* It's important for athletes, just like students, to plan, set goals, and monitor progress toward those goals. The coach should ask the athletes what they hope to accomplish this season. These goals should be difficult and specific, such as win over 50 percent of their games, or win the conference championship—whatever they think is reasonable. Athletes must also have a sense of self-efficacy, or a belief that they are competent enough to accomplish their goals. If they don't believe in themselves, then they won't do well. As the saying goes, whether you believe you can or whether you believe you can't, you are probably right. Finally, it takes two things to be good at athletics, just as in academics: "skill" and "will." You can't have one without the other. If you don't practice your skills, it won't matter how motivated you are. Likewise, no matter how talented you are, it will mean nothing if you aren't motivated to achieve.

Four characteristics of a good essay writer: WORK. FIGURE 5

Developing these characteristics will make your essay answers better.

1. **W**rites well. Although professors are not likely to grade the quality of writing per se, poorly written answers will not receive much sympathy. Nothing is more frustrating for a professor than to try to wade through a poorly written essay answer (or a poorly written *anything* for that matter!). Make sure your answer is organized and your sentences are clear. Write neatly—it is excruciating to read poor handwriting. This may not cost you points on the test, but rest assured it is far more likely to hurt you than to help you.

2. **O**utlines. Think before you write. Maybe you want to jot down an outline at the top of the page or in the margin, or maybe you can simply form a "mental outline." Whichever you choose, make sure you have a clear sense of what you want to say in your answer. This is especially true of long essays. If you don't have an outline in your head, your thoughts will appear random and disjointed and will suggest to the professor that your course knowledge is not integrated or coherent.

3. **R**eady for all questions. The best way to be ready for an essay test is to practice writing. When you know a test will contain essay questions, you will want to be sure that you get practice in writing. If the teacher gives you questions that "might" be on the exam, practice writing responses to those items. You and your classmates can also think about what might be on the exam and write responses to questions you make up yourselves. It also might be helpful to make outlines of course material (remember Chapter 7's discussion of the importance of elaboration?), to draw charts and figures showing relations between course themes (remember Chapter 7's discussion of the importance of organization?), and to do other exercises that will help you when you actually write essay answers.

4. **K**een responses. Good essay writers give answers that are keen; that is, they are sharp, to the point, and, most important, *they use information from the course.* This probably sounds silly and obvious.

(continued)

FIGURE 11.5   continued

We wouldn't mention it if it weren't for the fact that in our experience, students often answer essays based on intuition and common sense and not on what they learned in the course. On a test, the professors want you to use your new knowledge. You can presume professors will ask themselves a question something like this when they are grading: "Could this student have answered this question the way she did without even taking this course?" If the answer is yes, then the professor assumes that the student has not learned the material very well. The moral for you: Make sure you show off to your professor by using information from the course.

TEST ANXIETY

Too often, students do not do as well as they could on tests because they are overly worried about their performance. This is called **test anxiety,** and it plagues many students. The word *anxiety* has negative connotations for most people. Anxiety is seen as something to be avoided. However, what if we used the word *arousal*? Arousal probably has positive connotations for you. In fact, arousal and anxiety are very similar. Anxiety is best understood as too much arousal, and whereas some arousal has been shown to be good, too much arousal (anxiety) can be debilitating.

Psychologists have explored the relation between arousal and performance. Research suggests that if you graph the relation between arousal and performance, it will look like an upside-down *U*, as shown in Figure 11.6. This relation, known as the Yerkes-Dodson law (Yerkes & Dodson, 1908), means that anxiety that is either too low or too high hinders performance. Moderate anxiety, however, results in the best performance. You probably have personal experience with this, perhaps in athletics, music, or academics. When you really don't care about something, and therefore your anxiety is low, your performance is likely to be poor because you don't put much effort into it. When your anxiety is high, your performance is also low, because the anxiety interferes.

Perhaps the best cure for anxiety is to prepare fully. You can use certain strategies (mentioned later) to combat test anxiety once you enter the exam room. However, to reduce the chance that you will experience test anxiety in the first place, we recommend being as prepared as you possibly can be. You've probably already noticed this relation—the more you study, the less nervous you feel. You start to feel nervous when you have a feeling that you won't know something. The best way to avoid that feeling is to know as much as you can.

We break test anxiety down into two parts: emotionality and cognitive interference. Both can cause you difficulty, but they do so for different reasons.

Emotionality

The **emotionality** component of test anxiety refers mostly to the physiological aspect of anxiety. This includes sweating, tenseness in your muscles, increased heart rate, and so forth. (Recall the story from earlier in this chapter about the student in Probability Theory?) This kind of anxiety can occur with any activity,

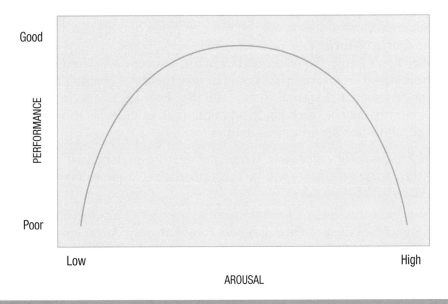

FIGURE 11.6

Arousal and performance.

Anxiety may not be bad. In fact, a moderate amount of anxiety may be helpful.

not just test taking. You may have experienced these effects before a performance in athletics or music or before giving a public presentation.

If you tend to experience these symptoms, it is important that you try to alleviate them. Psychologist Herbert Benson (Benson, Greenwood, & Klemchuk, 1975) suggested ways we can produce what he called a "relaxation response." These are listed in Figure 11.7.

Such techniques may not be practical to do for too long a time during a test. Still, if your physiological symptoms of stress become debilitating, it may be worth the time to take a couple of minutes to try to slow yourself down. Close your eyes and relax. After you have calmed down, return to the test.

If you don't feel comfortable doing the relaxation response during the test, you should try to relax before you walk in to take the test. Negative physical responses to stress will likely decrease your performance. So relax.

FIGURE 11.7

Responding to anxiety.

The "relaxation response," described by Herbert Benson, MD, can help you during a high-stress testing situation.

1. **Sit quietly.** Find a comfortable position and close your eyes.
2. **Relax your muscles.** Start at the bottom of your body and work up. First imagine your feet becoming relaxed, then imagine that feeling moving all the way to the top of your head.
3. **Breathe through your nose.** Focus on breathing and concentrate on a simple word (e.g., one) or phrase each time you breathe out.

Cognitive Interference

Another way in which anxiety can affect your test performance negatively is by interfering with your thinking. **Cognitive interference** occurs when anxiety disrupts your ability to process information.

Unfortunately, some students may go through much of college without realizing that the source of their poor performance is actually test anxiety and not the fact that they don't know the material. If you are someone who frequently says, "I knew the material, but as soon as I got in to take the test, I couldn't think of the answers" or "As soon as I started to take the test, I couldn't concentrate," your level of test anxiety may be too high. In addition to using the relaxation technique we described, consider two other possibilities:

1. *Ask the professor for extra time.* Removing the time pressure will reduce your stress. Some professors will be accommodating, some will not. You won't know unless you ask.

2. *Ask the professor to let you take the test in the college's academic support center.* Sometimes the presence of others causes anxiety. A less crowded room may help you relax.

Activity 11.6 will help you evaluate your level of anxiety. If you answer "yes" or "sometimes" to three or more of these items, you may be able to improve your academic performance just by finding ways to relax during tests.

ACTIVITY 11.6   *Are You Test Anxious?*

Ask yourself these questions to evaluate your level of test anxiety.

When you take a test, do you:	YES	NO	SOMETIMES
Emotionality			
1. Get an uneasy, upset feeling in your body?	○	○	○
2. Feel your heart beating faster?	○	○	○
3. Have emotional responses, such as sadness or anger?	○	○	○
Cognitive Interference			
4. Worry about how other students are doing?	○	○	○
5. Worry about the questions you can't answer?	○	○	○
6. Think about the bad things that could happen if you do poorly?	○	○	○

TESTS AS LEARNING TOOLS

In most courses, professors give about three to five tests. For the most part, students see them as necessary evils. We hope that you will adopt a different understanding of testing and come to regard test taking as a chance for you to demonstrate what you know, both to yourself and your professors. Testing gives you feedback. Without feedback, you would never know how well you are doing.

If you didn't know how well you were doing, you could never improve. So, testing is an important aid to your learning. We hope that you view it as such.

In addition to the few times your professor tests you, we encourage you to *test yourself* as well. Test yourself frequently. Test yourself at your desk, or have your roommate ask you questions. The more you know about your progress, the more likely it is that you will be able to improve.

Finally, we recognize that taking tests is stressful. We are glad we are no longer students; we do not miss that pressure. But we would like to point out that just because we are not students doesn't mean we are not being evaluated constantly, just like you are (including being graded by reviewers and editors on the quality of this book). Keep in mind that you will be evaluated your whole life. You will be evaluated in college (through tests), you will be evaluated in graduate school if you choose to go, and you will be evaluated in your job by your coworkers and supervisors. Taking tests in college prepares you for what lies ahead in your professional life—evaluation. Get used to it, and look forward to it. It gives you important information that will help you improve and succeed.

CHAPTER SUMMARY

Life during college has both similarities to and differences from life after college. Both in college and after college you get evaluated. You will spend your whole life being evaluated, especially in your vocation. For this reason, taking tests is a good activity to prepare you for the future. On the other hand, college is different in that it requires you to take so many tests. Few vocational performance reviews involve in-class examinations. So, while it is important to do well on tests in college, the good news is that after you complete college, you will probably not have to worry about them anymore.

But for now you are in college, and it is important to have the proper strategies. In addition to employing general test-taking strategies such as sleeping enough, eating properly, and staying relaxed, there are also specific strategies that apply to different kinds of tests. These strategies vary based on the type of question (objective vs. essay) and the degree to which higher level learning is required. In general, factual, objective questions can be successfully accomplished with low-level learning strategies, but complex questions requiring critical thinking require high-level learning strategies. You should know as much as you can about the type of test you will take so you can vary your strategies accordingly. While you are taking tests, a moderate level of arousal/anxiety is adaptive, because it serves to motivate and focus you. High levels of anxiety, however, cause worry and cognitive distraction that will lower your performance. An energized yet focused approach maximizes performance and minimizes distraction and worry.

Critical Thinking

Chapter Goals

This chapter will help you:

- Identify the characteristics of critical thinkers
- Develop specific strategies for evaluating complex arguments
- Recognize some common errors people commit in making decisions, and ways to avoid them
- Evaluate a problem from more than one point of view

Key Terms

anchoring error

availability error

contextualized relativism

critical thinking

dualism

multilogical thinking

PMI

quasi-reflective thinking/relativism

reflective judgment

representativeness error

CHAPTER 12

W e'd be shocked if you hadn't heard the term critical thinking before. Everyone agrees that it's a good thing to do, but not everyone agrees on what it is or how to do it. Although definitions will vary greatly among writers and educators, we identify critical thinking as consisting of four components:

- Understanding the problem or issue at hand
- Evaluating the evidence presented and being curious about evidence not presented
- Considering multiple perspectives that people could have on an issue
- Taking a position in light of the evidence, while recognizing that others may disagree

We set these criteria in contrast to "uncritical thinking," which is poor and sloppy thinking. Figure 12.1 compares the activities of critical thinkers with the activities of uncritical thinkers. Look at Figure 12.1 and ask yourself in which activities you currently engage. Are you more like a critical thinker or more like an uncritical thinker? Throughout this chapter, we will give you exercises that will help you test your ability to think critically.

Activity 12.1 lists the five items of the Critical Thinking scale. These questions are taken from the Motivated Strategies for Learning Questionnaire (Pintrich et al., 1991). Although you completed the entire scale in Chapter 1, we encourage you to answer these questions again now. You should not only notice how your score compares to the overall mean (2.58), but also look at the behaviors described in the questions. These are the behaviors that typify a critical thinker. Ask yourself if you:

1. Question/challenge things you hear or read about
2. Look for evidence to support or refute people's claims
3. Come up with your own theories and evidence for them

FIGURE 12.1 Features of critical versus uncritical thinking.

How does your approach to thinking match the characteristics listed below?

	THINKING TYPE	
Characteristic	**Critical**	**Uncritical**
General Approach	Motivated	Unmotivated
Attitude	Skeptical, desires evidence	Accepting, gullible
Approach to Evidence and Conclusions	Considers carefully, is open to alternate interpretations	Does not question validity
Ability to Deal with Complexity	Recognizes that many problems have complex solutions	Solutions tend to be simplistic
Approach to Disagreement	Understands that not everyone will agree, forms opinion based on the evidence	May believe that there is only one right answer and the goal is to get the answer/ opinion from those who are smarter

We hope that by the end of this chapter, you will be doing these things even more than you're doing them now.

Critical Thinking Scale

These items from the Learning Inventory provide a measure of critical thinking. Mark how true each of the following statements is of you.

	None of the time	Some of the time	Most of the time	All of the time
1. I often find myself questioning things I hear or read in this course to decide if I find them convincing.	①	②	③	④
2. When a theory, interpretation, or conclusion is presented in class or in readings, I try to decide if there is good supporting evidence.	①	②	③	④
3. I treat the course material as a starting point and try to develop my own ideas about it.	①	②	③	④
4. I try to play around with ideas of my own related to what I am learning in this course.	①	②	③	④
5. Whenever I read or hear an assertion or conclusion in this class, I think about possible alternatives.	①	②	③	④

If your score is less than 10, this chapter is definitely for you.

Source: From *A Manual for the Use of the Motivated Strategies for Learning Questionnaire* (MSLQ), by P. R. Pintrich, D. Smith, T. Garcia, and W. J. McKeachie, 1993, Ann Arbor, MI: NCRIPTAL, School of Education, The University of Michigan. Reprinted with permission of W. J. McKeachie.

CHARACTERISTICS OF GOOD THINKERS

Edward de Bono (1971, 1985), who has written extensively on critical thinking, identified several characteristics of an effective thinker. In this chapter, we will explore how you might be able to adopt some of these characteristics. We also want you to notice that some of the features of critical thinking that de Bono identifies are topics that we have already discussed. Not only will you learn elements of critical thinking in this chapter, but we hope many of the previous chapters have also taught you to be a critical thinker.

Consider some of the features that de Bono says make up a critical thinker, listed in Figure 12.2. Read this list and identify ways your approach to critical thinking matches the characteristics given. We encourage you to refer back to this list after reading this chapter. We hope by then you will have improved your critical thinking, and your behavior will more closely match the characteristics listed.

FIGURE 12.2   Characteristics of a critical thinker.

Critical thinkers:

1. *Are confident in their thinking.* Not confident that they will necessarily find an answer, but rather confident that they can activate their thinking when they need to.

2. *Are in control of their thinking.* Remember our discussion of metacognition in Chapter 7? Your success in college will very much hinge on the degree to which you can control and correct your own learning (what we have called metacognition). This is as true of thinking as of the other skills we cover. By being metacognitive in your thinking, you will be able to identify the weaknesses in your thinking (if you don't, someone else is sure to do so) and improve on them.

3. *Are clear about what they want to do.* Critical thinkers set goals for themselves and then identify how to accomplish them. If this sounds like self-regulation, you're right. Self-regulated learning is, as you know, the key concept that cuts across this entire book. If you don't adopt goals for your thinking, you will never be a good thinker.

4. *Enjoy thinking even when the outcome is not necessarily successful.* Put simply, this is intrinsic motivation. If you don't want to be a critical thinker, you won't be. People who are good thinkers enjoy thinking. They enjoy the challenge of solving problems, of playing (mentally) with ideas, and of articulating those ideas either through writing or speaking. If you get frustrated easily, enjoy only those problems that have easy solutions, or don't enjoy the mental challenge of working through a difficult situation you probably won't be a critical thinker. We encourage you to go back to Chapter 3 and consider some of the ways in which your motivation can be improved.

5. *Treat thinking as a skill that can be improved with practice.* We have tried to stress that all of the skills in this book can be improved by practice, and critical thinking is no exception. You will become a better thinker the more you do it.

6. *Don't draw hasty conclusions.* Thinking too quickly results in more errors than thinking too slowly. Slow thinking should not be equated with lacking intelligence. De Bono blamed our educational system for encouraging quickness over thorough thinking. Unfortunately, students have time limits on their exams, so thorough thinking is not possible. Although timed tests are common in college, there are also opportunities (we hope) for you to demonstrate your thinking skills by way of activities such as take-home exams, papers, and group projects.

Source: From *De Bono's Thinking Course,* by E. de Bono, 1985, New York: Facts on File.

EVALUATING ARGUMENTS: PMI

One thing you will do more in college than in high school is to evaluate the merits of different arguments. One way to evaluate arguments is to list the advantages and disadvantages. Edward de Bono (1985) proposed a simple but effective way to do this. He called it the **PMI** technique. The *P* stands for the "plus" or the good aspects of a position. The *M* stands for the "minus" or the bad aspects. The *I* stands for "interesting" aspects of a position.

When presented with an argument, you may have an opinion about the argument right away. The PMI method forces you to slow down, step back, and evaluate whether this is really the best position to take. Suppose we were to suggest to you that your college or university should pay students for good grades: $50 for each A, $25 for each B. You might immediately think that this is a good idea. However, if you evaluate the argument using the PMI method, your position may change. Consider some of the plus (positive) aspects of implementing a pay-for-grades system:

1. It would increase students' motivation to get good grades.
2. It would raise most students' grade-point average.
3. It would give students more disposable income.
4. It would serve as an attractive recruiting tool for prospective students.

Now consider some of the potential minus (negative) aspects of implementing such a system:

1. Although extrinsic motivation would increase, intrinsic motivation would probably decrease.
2. Students would work just hard enough to do well on the tests, but not any harder.
3. Cheating would increase.
4. Animosity and competitiveness between students would increase, resulting in a very unfriendly environment.
5. Tuition would increase.

Now consider some of the interesting aspects of implementing such a system:

1. It would be interesting to see how professors respond.
2. It would be interesting to see how parents respond.
3. It would be interesting to see if professors' expectations for grades changed.

This PMI system is very simple and represents a good first step in the critical-thinking process. You cannot be an effective thinker until you realize that not all problems have simple solutions. The PMI method is effective for problems that don't have easily identifiable answers.

Activity 12.2 gives you some issues with which to practice the PMI. For each of the issues, think of positive, negative, and interesting aspects of the position. The more you practice PMI, the better you will become at it. Eventually, this technique will become second nature to you, and you probably won't have to think about doing it.

Practice Topics for the PMI Technique

Identify the *plus*, *minus*, and *interesting* aspects of the following issues:

1. Should English be adopted as the national language of the United States?
2. Should the federal government pay for the health care of senior citizens?
3. Should public schools teach in their sex-education classes that abstinence is the best approach to premarital sexual relations?

CRITICAL THINKING IN MAKING DECISIONS

So far, we have tried to identify ways you can improve your thinking ability. In this section, we examine how thinking critically can improve the decisions you make. In most cases, the unwritten rules we use to make decisions are quite good. So, most of the time, we make good decisions. Sometimes, however, we make bad decisions because our mind plays tricks on us. That is, it looks like we're making the right decision but we're not. We next discuss three of the most common errors that occur when people make decisions. We describe these to you because if you are aware of them, then you will be able to make more accurate judgments. Before you read any further, answer the questions in Activity 12.3.

ACTIVITY 12.3 *Critical Thinking in Making Decisions*

Answer the following questions, then read the explanation in the text to see how you did.

1. Bill is 34 years old. He is intelligent but unimaginative, compulsive, and generally lifeless. In school, he was strong in mathematics but weak in social studies and humanities. Which is more likely?

    a. Bill plays jazz for a hobby.

    b. Bill is an accountant who plays jazz for a hobby.

2. Linda is 31, single, outspoken, and very bright. She majored in philosophy in college. As a student, she was deeply concerned about discrimination and other social issues, and she participated in antinuclear demonstrations. Which is more likely?

    a. Linda is a bank teller.

    b. Linda is a bank teller and active in the feminist movement.

3. Does the letter *K* appear more often as the first letter of words or as the third letter?

    a. The first letter.

    b. The third letter.

4. Which is the more common cause of death?

    a. homicide

    b. diabetes

These problems were taken from Tversky and Kahneman (1983).

For the next two, ask Question 5 of one friend and Question 6 of another.

5. Do you think the Mississippi River is longer or shorter than 500 miles?_____

    How long do you think it is?_____

6. Do you think the Mississippi River is longer or shorter than 5,000 miles?_____

    How long do you think it is?_____

Representativeness Error

The first two problems in Activity 12.3 address the **representativeness error**. If you are like most college students (and the authors of this text, the first time we saw this problem), you probably chose "b" for questions 1 and 2. In fact, the correct answer to both questions is "a." The reason it isn't "b," according to laws of probability, is that a more narrow event cannot be more likely than a broader event. Ask yourself this question: Are there more people with red hair or more people with red hair and glasses? This seems easy. Since red hair and glasses is more limiting than just having red hair, of course there must be more people with just red hair. Now consider the first question about Bill. In the same way that there can't be more people with red hair and glasses than just red hair alone, there can't be more people who are accountants who play jazz for a hobby than people who just play jazz for a hobby (jazz > accountant and jazz).

Why is the red hair example easy and the jazz player/accountant example hard? Because people make a representativeness error, which means that they base judgments on how likely, how "normal," or how representative the descriptions they hear are of descriptions of people in general. The description of Bill sounds very much like the stereotype of someone who would be an accountant. This description is so powerful that it overrides our ability to consider the statistical impossibility of that conclusion.

The same is true of Linda the bank teller. There are more people who are just bank tellers than there are feminist bank tellers, so it must be more likely that Linda is just a bank teller. The representativeness error occurs fairly frequently, particularly when questions deal with judgments about people. By knowing this simple law of probability—that the combination of two events is never more likely than either of the two events separately—you avoid this thinking pitfall. Figure 12.3 gives a graphic representation of this principle.

Availability Error

Questions 3 and 4 in Activity 12.3 are examples of the **availability error**. A lot of people answer that K is more often the first letter, but in fact it's more often the third letter. People make this error because of the availability heuristic, which means that we make judgments about the frequency of events based on how easily they are recalled (that is, how *available* they are in our memories). Our memories are encoded around first letters of words, not third letters. Since we can remember more words that begin with the letter K (*king, knife, kitchen*) than we can remember words with K as the third letter (*Viking, like, poke*), we tend to think words that start with K are higher in frequency.

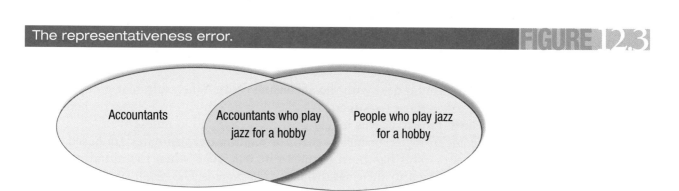

The representativeness error.   FIGURE 12.3

As this figure illustrates, the likelihood of two events occurring together can never be greater than that of either single event occurring alone. This is true no matter how much overlap there is between the circles.

Question 4 on causes of death also illustrates the availability error. A "quiet" form of death such as diabetes does not get the attention of the media. Thus, we usually don't notice it, unless it happens to friends or family. Certain types of death, however, like homicide, are often well publicized. Because of this fact and because of the availability heuristic, we tend to think that homicide is a more common cause of death than diabetes is. In fact, more than four times as many people die of diabetes as die of homicide (72,815 vs. 17,096 in 2004), according to the National Center for Health Statistics Web site.

Since the memorability of events can be a useful way to gauge their importance, the availability heuristic is often helpful. However, it can lead to thinking errors if we don't recognize when we are using it. It may, for example, lead us to believe that if we are traveling in the Middle East, we are more likely to be killed by a terrorist than killed in a traffic accident. This is because we hear much more about Middle East terrorist attacks than about Middle East traffic accidents, so they become more memorable. In fact, you are at far greater risk of being in a traffic accident than a terrorist attack if you travel to the Middle East. (In 2007, downtown Baghdad may be an exception.)

The availability heuristic may also lead us to believe that flying in an airplane is less safe than driving a car. In fact, far more people die in traffic accidents in the United States than in water, air, sea, and other nonland transport accidents combined (46,933 vs. 1,855 in 2004). However, just by watching the national news, you would have no way of knowing that, because plane crashes get reported and traffic accidents usually do not. Thus, plane crashes become more memorable.

The availability heuristic can also lead to stereotypes and prejudice, perhaps the two most painful social outcomes of poor thinking. If portrayals on the local news of ethnic minorities committing crimes are all people see or remember, the availability heuristic will cause people to overestimate the amount of crime committed by ethnic minorities. Law enforcement agencies that adopt racial profiling as a strategy use memorable features of previous crimes, specifically race, to draw conclusions about current members of that racial group who haven't committed a crime.

The simplest way to avoid falling victim to this thinking error is to look at the evidence. We have mentioned this already in this chapter, but it's worth repeating. Looking at the empirical, quantitative information is the best way to determine the actual state of affairs. Knowledge is the only cure for ignorance. Don't let your prejudices guide your thinking. Make judgments based on evidence, not on intuition, hearsay, or stereotypes.

Anchoring Error

Questions 5 and 6 deal with the **anchoring error**. When different groups of people were asked those two questions, the average estimate was longer when people were asked if the river was longer or shorter than 5,000 miles.

The anchoring error means that our quantitative estimates are based on initial estimates. This has been found to be true even when the initial numerical value is unrelated to the quantity being estimated. The result of this anchoring effect is poor thinking. Salespeople sometimes exploit it to convince us to buy. For example, the list price of an item might be $199.95, and the sale price might be $149.95. "Wow," we say to ourselves or our parents, "look at how much money I'm saving." The $199.95 becomes the anchor from which we make estimates of how good a deal we're getting. Or you might hear on TV, "Order now, operators are standing by. Remember, limit two." Although we may have planned to order only one, two now becomes our anchor, and we may be more inclined to order two than we would have been if we hadn't been given this psychological anchor. (This latter technique also takes advantage of another psychological tool: When resources appear scarce, they appear to be more valuable. Hearing that we are limited in how many we can buy leads us to believe that a lot of people want this item, and therefore it must be valuable—because how could so many people be wrong?)

Salespeople also use this technique to get people to buy a little more than they originally planned. Suppose you buy a $100 pair of shoes. Shoe salespeople might now get you to buy shoe cleaner for $5.95, polish for $3.95, and water protector for $4.95. The extra $14.85 you are spending doesn't seem like that much more in the context of a $100 purchase (the anchor). You might be less likely to spend that money without any other purchase (in which case your anchor would be $0).

So beware of the anchoring effect. When making quantitative judgments, we can be influenced by other, often meaningless, quantitative information. As with the other thinking errors, awareness is the best antidote. Knowing the pitfalls in human thinking will make you a better thinker.

THINKING FROM MULTIPLE PERSPECTIVES

Perhaps more than anything else, critical thinking involves an ability (and willingness) to consider multiple points of view. Educator Richard Paul (Paul & Elder, 1995) refered to thinking that takes place from only one point of view or perspective as monological thinking. Of course, many problems you encounter in school need only one perspective. For example, in many mathematics classes, most people agree that a lot of problems can be solved correctly with one technique. If people know that certain functions in calculus should be integrated with the "chain rule," there is little to debate. Monological thinking works just fine for such problems, where there is no need to consider multiple perspectives. Such is the case for some of what happens in school.

However, not all issues can be resolved so nicely with only one method and one clear-cut answer. Paul referred to thinking that requires the consideration of more than one perspective as **multilogical thinking**. This means that not everyone will look at an issue in the same way. A critical thinker is someone who can both identify and appreciate multiple perspectives. Even though she might hold one opinion, a critical thinker is someone who holds her position up to the same scrutiny as she holds the positions of others. Figure 12.4 lists the characteristics of multilogical thinking.

The willingness to consider multiple perspectives should not be confused with being wishy-washy. Considering other perspectives doesn't mean that you don't have a mind of your own or that you think one opinion is as good as any other or that you are unable to take a position on something. Thinking from multiple perspectives means that you are willing to recognize that the solution to a problem may not be immediately apparent, that you might not have the answer "right now," and that, in fact, more than one answer (perspective) may exist. Still, recognizing that more than one perspective exists on an issue certainly doesn't preclude you from believing that one perspective is better than another.

FIGURE 12.4   Characteristics of multilogical thinking.

Thinking from multiple perspectives means recognizing that some problems are complex and that people may differ in their opinions.

What multilogical thinking is *not*:

1. You don't have opinions of your own.
2. Your opinions are simply parroting of other opinions you hear.
3. Since people hardly ever agree, believing that one opinion is as good as any other.
4. Having one opinion and failing to recognize others.

What multilogical thinking *is*:

1. Recognizing that people's opinions will differ.
2. Recognizing that an answer might not be immediately apparent; some reflection may be required.
3. Not all opinions are created equal. You can still believe strongly that you are correct, while recognizing other views.
4. Being able to recognize and reason from different points of view.

However, your belief that Perspective A is better than Perspective B should be based on careful examination of both A and B. So, both critical thinkers and uncritical thinkers are likely to have opinions. The difference is that a critical thinker will have an opinion only after careful consideration of many perspectives.

Consider the role of critical thinking in an issue that divides Americans more than just about any other: the issue of abortion. There are people who are ambivalent about abortion, people who strongly believe that it should be illegal, and people who strongly believe it should be legal. It might be nice simply to say everyone who agrees with us is right and everyone who disagrees with us is wrong, but a critical thinker would not respond that way. A critical thinker would recognize that there are at least two different positions on this issue, self-described as either "pro-life" or "pro-choice." An uncritical thinker who is pro-life would say simply, "Life begins at conception, abortion is murder." An uncritical thinker who is pro-choice would say simply, "A women's right to choose is all that matters." A critical thinker will recognize the complexity of this issue. Consider what a critical thinker who is pro-life might say:

I understand that a woman has a constitutional right to control her own body, but that right must be tempered under circumstances in which the rights of others are involved. When a woman is pregnant is one of those circumstances. In such a case a woman's decision no longer affects only her, but also her unborn child. Furthermore, the decision about whether to allow abortion to be legal must begin with a discussion of life. Regardless of one's religious or political beliefs, medically and biologically speaking, there is life inside the pregnant woman. All discussion of whether to terminate a pregnancy must begin at this premise. Any prenatal differences are developmental distinctions not species distinctions. Since we don't treat humans of different ages differently under the law, we should not do so prenatally.

Now consider what a critical thinker who is pro-choice might say:

There is no question that what lives inside a pregnant woman from the time of conception is a developing human being. There is also no doubt that abortion is an extremely difficult choice, and that women would prefer not to have to make it. However, even though it may not be an attractive alternative for anyone, our

Constitution still provides a right to privacy for all. This is true for all matters, but it is especially important that privacy be protected regarding matters of one's own body. People are entitled to freedom from government intrusion. This right must take priority in such situations. Furthermore, I don't believe society is really ready to punish mothers and doctors criminally if they violate a ban on abortions. So, although the decision is a painful one, it is still a choice that must be kept legal.

We hope these examples illustrate that even on a very divisive and emotional issue such as abortion, critical thinking can still take place. People need not resort to name-calling or pretending that an issue is not complicated. Such reasonableness in considering different perspectives is a hallmark of critical thinking, and something we can all strive for. Activity 12.4 provides some sample issues on which to practice critical, multilogical thinking.

Multilogical Thinking

ACTIVITY
12.4

Try to identify several perspectives that might be taken on each of these issues, then articulate your own perspectives. Do this in writing or by talking to a friend.

1. What should be the position of the government on the relation between preserving the environment and promoting economic growth?

2. Should Nativity scenes (Christmas scenes depicting the birth of Jesus) be allowed in public places such as city halls or courthouses?

3. Should pregnant women who use illegal drugs during the last stages of their pregnancy be arrested for delivering controlled substances to a minor? For child abuse? If the child dies because of the mother's drug use, should she be arrested for manslaughter or murder?

REFLECTIVE JUDGMENT

In Patricia King and Karen Kitchener's book entitled *Developing Reflective Judgment* (1994), the authors highlighted a progression that college students often make as their critical-thinking skills develop. King and Kitchener studied how college students respond to problems for which one correct answer is not identifiable. You may find yourself engaged in problems like this in class or in the dormitory. Examples include the question of why prisoners return to crime, creation versus evolution, and whether capital punishment deters violent crime. Unlike calculus problems, people do not agree on one correct answer to this kind of problem.

King and Kitchener (1994), along with others (Hofer and Pintrich, 1999), believed that college students' critical thinking (what they call **reflective judgment**) develops in college in the following way (we mentioned the first and third stages in Chapter 5):

1. **Dualism.** College students arrive on campus believing (aided by 12 years of formal schooling) that there are right and wrong answers. Experts have the right answers, and the job of a college student is to listen carefully to the experts so that the student can also obtain the right answers. There is very little room for

ambiguity at this stage. Responsible students take copious notes and listen carefully to the professor. Of course, we recommend these strategies, but the strategies during this stage are rooted in the belief that the goal of college is to obtain knowledge, not to develop thinking skills.

2. **Quasi-reflective thinking/relativism.** Sometime during college (some researchers have speculated that it occurs during the sophomore year), students are hit with a knowledge crisis. Students learn that college is not like high school, that taking notes and listening carefully are not all that is important. Professors want to know students' opinions, and students are required to state their opinions on tests—and they get graded on their opinion. Students also encounter people with different beliefs, cultures, and understandings of "the truth." This sends some students spinning into a belief that all knowledge is opinion, and that all opinions are equally valid. Some students convince themselves that as long as they have opinions, they can succeed in college. When they arrive at the final stage (below), they recognize that opinions must be substantiated with evidence and a convincing defense of one's position based on critical thinking.

3. **Contextualized relativism.** During the last 2 years of college, most students recognize that life is complex and knowledge is ambiguous. We learn that the problems we face in adulthood are difficult—probably filled with (among others) ethical, religious, and economic complexities. At the same time, we don't simply throw up our hands and cognitively surrender. We recognize that we have to make commitments and choices, and those choices require critical thinking. So, we stake out our ground, we make decisions, and we recognize the tentative nature of those decisions. We must continually evaluate our positions using the same critical-thinking skills that brought us to our beliefs in the first place. This is the essence of a happy and healthy cognitive life.

EVALUATING INFORMATION ON THE WORLD WIDE WEB AS A CRITICAL-THINKING SKILL

© James Isbell – FOTOLIA

The necessity to think from multiple perspectives is illustrated well by the challenge of evaluating information found on the World Wide Web. Not since the printing press has access to knowledge been so democratized. Although only a very small percentage of people worldwide have access to the Internet, almost all American college students are online. The power of the World Wide Web is obvious. The interesting feature of it with respect to critical thinking is how the consumer cognitively processes its information. When the authors of this book were in college, we completed our research papers with textbooks and journal articles as sources. There was comfort in that approach, because text and journal articles had built-in quality-control mechanisms—checks on the validity and accuracy of their information. We suspect most students now research their papers using Internet resources (as we did most of the time for the second edition of this book). With this new technology, being a good critical thinker is even more crucial than it was just 15 years ago.

How should a student critically evaluate Web resources? The good news is that much of what is available online is the same information that used to be available in paper form. For example, the two of us wrote papers in undergrad and in graduate school using *Psych Lit*, the old paper version of psychology's database.

Today, that same information is available in an electronic version called *Psych Info*. Likewise, www.nytimes.com has the same quality-control standards as the paper version (although not all materials available in the print version are available online, unless the user pays a fee). That is not to say critical thinking is not important when you are reading the *New York Times* or psychological journals. But it is rather to say that the skills required are roughly the same as they have been in the past.

Evaluating Web sources is different for materials that do not have quality-control mechanisms in place. These materials appear on Web sites that simply put forth information as truth and require the consumer to do all the critical-thinking work. Thus, we stress the importance of carefully evaluating what you read on the Internet, paying particular attention to the skills and pitfalls presented in this chapter. Because of the democratization of knowledge that the Internet has created, much more information is now available. Evaluating truth claims found on the Internet is a task that we encourage you to take seriously. Knowledge is power, and critical thinking is the lever that you must use to lift accurate information from among the dreck and dross you will read on the Web. Recall the discussion in Chapter 10 on evaluating information on the Web.

In her book *Exploring the Internet Using Critical Thinking Skills* (1998), Debra Jones offers several suggestions for being a good thinker in cyberspace. First, you must think critically about the source of the information you find on the Web. Critical thinking involves asking a variety of questions about the credibility of the information's source. Is the author of the page unambiguous—does the creator identify himself or herself? Are the credentials and background of the author respectable? From what type of Web site does the material come—educational, research, government, entertainment, for-profit, blog? What is the purpose of the Web site—to inform, to persuade, to make money?

Second, Jones notes that Web pages differ widely in the amount of research that is used in producing the site. Web surfers should ask whether the Web site was produced using reputable research, such as those sites from science, education, or government agencies. Are there specific references to experiments, literature reviews, or other works that have quality control built into them? If so, these other sources can be used to validate the claims on the Web. For example, there is a very small group of people who believe that children should not receive immunizations for diseases such as measles, mumps, or whooping cough (or that the government should not mandate that parents immunize their children). When you encounter claims like this, it is important to review carefully the claims that are being made and weigh them against the evidence in favor of childhood immunizations. The scientific evidence that supports the claim that immunizations are harmful should be weighed against the evidence that immunizations are helpful. Are those who oppose immunizations reputable, and do they have the same degree of professional training as those who support immunizations?

Third, is the evidence presented timely? Web sites can stay online for as long as the authors are willing to pay Web-hosting fees. So consumers of the Web site must ask whether the information covers a topic of current interest. More important, the reader must ask whether the evidence is current and up-to-date. For example, returning to our example of childhood immunizations, say you are reading a Web site claiming that it is a bad idea to immunize a child against chickenpox and instead the child should simply contract chickenpox as the way to get immunized. These people may make their claim that there is not enough data to validate the effectiveness of the vaccine or that most children do not suffer a great deal from contracting chickenpox. To be a good critical thinker, you must ask yourself how current these claims are. In fact, virtually every health professional agrees that the most recent evidence shows that the vaccine is very effective and that some children suffer very negative consequences of chickenpox.

Finally, consumers of Web sites must consider carefully the assumptions of the authors. Claims of life on other planets, radiation dangers of cell towers, and government conspiracies are all based on certain assumptions about the world (or beyond). It is advisable neither to dismiss claims out of hand without considering their merits nor to accept the claims without any critical thinking. Understanding the authors' assumptions and worldview will help you make critically informed decisions about the virtually limitless truth claims that you will find in cyberspace.

LEARNING BY DOING

Certainly, as much as any other skill we have taught in this text, you cannot learn critical thinking simply by reading about it or talking about it. You will not become a good thinker unless you engage in thinking. Athletes, musicians, and artists are made, not born. So it goes with critical thinking: those who practice thinking will get better at it. We have given you some exercises with which to practice your critical thinking. We conclude with a few more general tips for improving your critical thinking.

1. Don't Sit Passively in Class. As we have mentioned before with respect to memory and learning strategies, you must be actively engaged if you're going to be successful. You won't develop your thinking skills by being passive. Ask yourself questions while you sit in class. Or better yet, ask questions of your professors while you are in class.

2. Engage in Discussion and Debate with Professors and Fellow Students. Professors are not always right. However, they have more knowledge and have thought more about their discipline than you have, and that means they are better critical thinkers about their field. One way to become a better critical thinker is to engage in dialogue with people who are good thinkers themselves, such as professors. Another way to improve your thinking skills is to engage in dialogue with people who are also learning a new field. By talking with fellow students, you can learn more about important course issues, and practice taking positions, presenting arguments, and refuting counterarguments. This is part and parcel of what it means to be a critical thinker.

This is not to say that the best critical thinkers are the ones who talk the most. On the contrary, some people who are very sloppy thinkers talk all the time, and often we would like them to stop! It is sometimes true that still waters tend to run deep. But you can be assured that those people listen very carefully to other people's perspectives on issues. You can also be assured that those people who are quiet yet effective critical thinkers are constantly engaged in a kind of "self-talk" in which they debate, discuss, and dialogue with themselves. This self-talk also can hone thinking skills. There is nothing magic about engaging in audible dialogue with others, although in general we think it will have a positive effect on your thinking skills. What is important is that you think through ideas and develop your own perspective; you can do this either through dialogue with others or through self-talk. If you never discuss issues (either with others or with yourself) and always sit passively and nonreflectively, you will never become a good critical thinker.

3. Critical Thinking Is Hard Work; It Requires Skill and Will. Here, we repeat one of the main themes of this book: Academic success, in this case in the form of critical thinking, is a function of both cognitive and motivational factors. Differences in inborn intellectual ability dictate that some people will start with more initial cognitive skill in critical thinking than others will. However, as Daniel Goleman (1995) pointed out in his book *Emotional Intelligence*, the ability to motivate yourself to accomplish difficult tasks is as important as any intellectual advantage a person might have in critical thinking. In other words, how "smart" you are only makes a small difference in determining how good you will be as a critical thinker. What is important is that you are motivated to use your cognitive skills to tackle difficult problems. If you are motivated to think about difficult issues, to wrestle with the complexities of problems, and to articulate your position, you can become a good critical thinker.

4. Be Willing to Criticize Your Own Thinking as Well as That of Others. It's easy to criticize the thinking of others, and clearly that is part of being a good thinker. However, the other part of critical thinking is being able to recognize the weaknesses in your own thinking. Recall from Chapter 7 the concept of metacognition, or thinking about your own thinking. By being metacognitive, you look at your own thinking processes. You question your assumptions and identify other perspectives and goals. You can ask yourself, "Do I really understand this problem?" or "Am I being objective?" or at least "Do I recognize my biases?" Self-criticism is the best kind of criticism, because it will make your arguments more sophisticated. It will also reduce your embarrassment when someone else (like a professor) tries to punch holes in your thinking.

5. Know the Difference Between Being Critical and Being Cynical. Cynical means simply "bashing" an idea without recognizing any potential value in it. It is a kind of knee-jerk response that many people think is synonymous with critical thinking. The idea seems to be that if you can bash other ideas, and therefore make them look dumb, then you'll somehow become smarter. That is not critical thinking. "Critical" means making constructive observations about the weaknesses of evidence. It means seeing both what is positive about the evidence and what is negative about it. Furthermore, it goes beyond simply highlighting the negative to identifying ways in which the proposal can be improved. That is, taking the idea and making it better. Cynical people operate from a perspective of hypernegativity; they assume that there must be something wrong with absolutely everything. Seeing only negative in others' proposals does not validate your own thinking. Being a critical thinker also involves offering plausible proposals that are better than the proposal you find insufficient. The world has lots of cynical people, and we hope this book does not create more of them. But the world doesn't have enough critical people—people who can think critically—and we hope this book helps you develop this skill.

CHAPTER SUMMARY

Just reading about critical thinking won't do you much good. Critical thinking is not a spectator sport, and if you don't practice it, you won't get better at it. Please use this chapter as a beginning and not an end, as a jumping-off point in a lifelong quest to make yourself a better thinker. We hope that the more you think critically, the more you'll recognize how often people engage in sloppy thinking. Seeing bad thinking in yourself and others will be the best incentive for improving your own thinking.

Problem Solving

Chapter Goals

This chapter will help you:

- Find ways to present problems with pictures, words, diagrams, or symbols

- Identify strategies for solving different types of problems

- Break problems into manageable parts

- Put problems that you don't understand into terms that are familiar to you

- Think using statistical reasoning and rules of formal logic

Key Terms

affirming the consequent

biconditional problems

creativity

denying the antecedent

escape method

functional fixedness

goal state

law of large numbers

mental set

original state

population

random simulation method

regression to the mean

sample

stepping-stone method

structural analogy

surface analogy

CHAPTER 13

n the last chapter, we gave you suggestions for how to improve your critical thinking. We suggested ways to evaluate evidence and encouraged you to keep an open mind as you do so. This chapter is a bit more specific: it deals with how to handle problems that are in need of completion. Solving problems involves mentally "going someplace." A problem solver is someone who moves from a "mental place" where the answer is not available (usually called the **original state**) to a "mental place" where the answer is available (usually called the **goal state**). In doing this, the problem solver must adhere to a set of "rules of the road" for accomplishing the task. For example, the rules in mathematics include properties of numbers, procedures of division and multiplication, and so on.

The goal of this chapter is to make you a more proficient problem solver. At one level, the best way to become a better problem solver in some area is to practice a lot. For example, to become a better mathematician, you should do a lot of math problems. However, there are also some general strategies for solving problems that are applicable to many different areas. Although both aspects of problem solving are important, the focus of this chapter is on the more general strategies for problem solving. Throughout the chapter, we will be giving you problems to solve. We ask that you try to solve them before you look at the answers (located at the end of the chapter). A brief assessment of problem solving appears in Activity 13.1.

ACTIVITY 13.1 *Assessing Your Problem-Solving Skills*

Circle the statements that best describe your approach to problem solving. When you are finished, add the corresponding points for all items.

1. I enjoy puzzles, problems, and brainteasers:
   - (1) never or almost never
   - (2) rarely
   - (3) frequently
   - (4) always or almost always

2. When faced with difficult problems, I have a hard time deciding how to begin:
   - (4) never or almost never
   - (3) rarely
   - (2) frequently
   - (1) always or almost always

3. When I hear someone state a position or argument, I skeptically try to think of alternative explanations:
   - (1) never or almost never
   - (2) rarely
   - (3) frequently
   - (4) always or almost always

4. I am good at thinking "outside the box":
   - (1) never or almost never
   - (2) rarely
   - (3) frequently
   - (4) always or almost always

5. I find personal testimonials on TV commercials convincing:
   - (4) never or almost never
   - (3) rarely
   - (2) frequently
   - (1) always or almost always

SCORING:

The following categories provide a rough indication of your current problem-solving strategies.

16 and above: You probably have good problem-solving strategies. This chapter can serve as a helpful review of important skills.

11–15: You probably have moderately good problem-solving strategies. However, you may have to revisit some of your strategies. This chapter will help you identify some ways you can improve your problem solving.

10 and below: This chapter is definitely for you. It will help you focus on some of the important problem-solving strategies. We encourage you to read this chapter carefully and to use the suggestions we offer.

HAVING THE RIGHT PICTURE IN YOUR MIND

To solve problems, we engage in certain kinds of mental activity. Unconsciously, we create "mental pictures" of things we think about, including problems we solve. Crucial to successful problem solving is creating the proper mental picture. Activity 13.2 presents what is often called the Monk Problem. Read this story and answer the two questions.

The Monk Problem

Read the following story and answer the questions.

A monk began to climb a mountain at sunrise. He reached the top as the sun was setting and meditated all night. At sunrise the next day, he came down the mountain, following the same path, but moving at a faster rate of course. When he reached the bottom, he proclaimed, "There is one spot along this path that I passed at exactly the same time of day on my way up the mountain as on my way down."

1. Can you prove that the monk is correct?

_____

_____

_____

2. What mental image (picture) comes to your mind when you think of this problem? Can you draw this image?

_____

_____

_____

WAYS TO REPRESENT PROBLEMS

Any given problem can be represented in a variety of ways. The picture you form in your mind partially determines whether you will understand the problem. Since understanding is the first step toward solution, having a good mental picture is important. Let's consider some ways to represent problems.

Pictures

How would you solve the following problem?

Andrew is taller than Bob. Bob is not shorter than Charles. Is Charles taller than Andrew?

When we ask students this question in class, only a small percentage can answer the question quickly and correctly without writing anything down. However, if forced to form the right mental representation, most students can easily see the correct answer. A pictorial representation is a good way to represent a problem like this. Forming the picture in your head will be easier if you write down the pictures as you go through the problem. Figure 13.1 gives the pictorial representation of this problem. Drawing the pictures in this way makes it clear that the answer to the problem is no.

Pictorial representations will not work in all cases. But if you get stuck, drawing a picture of the problem can often help. Look at the picture provided at the end of this chapter in the answer to the Monk Problem. A picture that represents time on the x-axis and height of the mountain on the y-axis makes the problem easier to solve.

Symbols

Sometimes it helps to think in pictures, and sometimes it helps to think using symbols. Figure 13.2 shows how we can use symbolic representation to solve the previous height problem. Notice that although the representation is different, the answer is still the same.

Both of these approaches may be helpful with a wide range of problems. Both work by allowing you to keep track of all of the elements of the problem. Using

FIGURE 13.1 | Pictorial representation.

Representing some problems with symbols can make them easier to solve.

1. Andrew is taller than Bob.

2. Bob is not shorter than Charles.

3. Is Charles taller than Andrew?

Comparing the pictures shows quite clearly that Charles *cannot* be taller than Andrew. The tallest Charles can be is *as tall* as Bob, but no taller, which is still shorter than Andrew.

FIGURE 13.2

Symbolic representation.

Sometimes it helps to allow symbols to stand for problem elements. In this case the symbols are the first letters of the names and the "greater than" and "less than" operators from mathematics.

1. Andrew is taller than Bob.

$$A > B$$

The "greater than" symbol shows that Andrew is taller than Bob.

2. Bob is not shorter than Charles.

$$B \geq C$$

Another way to say "not shorter" is to say "as tall or taller." This is best represented by the "greater than or equal to" sign. This means that the shortest Bob could be is as tall as Charles.

3. Linking these two expressions, one can ask: Is Charles taller than Andrew?

You can now solve the problem by comparing the symbolic representations in #1 and #2:

$$C > A?$$

This clearly cannot be the case, since A is greater than B and C is less than or equal to B. The symbolic representation gives us a clear answer.

---

symbols to stand for elements of the problem simplifies the situation, thus freeing up your attentional capacity (remember Chapter 6) so you can use it in understanding how to solve the problem.

Matrices

A matrix or a grid is useful when you need to identify all possible solutions to a problem or when the solution involves many steps. Consider this scheduling problem:

The following eight teams have entered a softball tournament:

Gators	Black Knights	Grey Sox	Ravens
Explorers	Bombers	River Sharks	Bandits

The structure of the tournament is round-robin, which means each team will play each other exactly one time, and the winner is determined by the best overall record. The games will be played two hours apart, with the first game starting at 9 A.M. and the last game starting at 9 P.M. (seven time slots) on two different fields (two games can be played simultaneously). Games will be played on Saturday and Sunday. Design a schedule for this round-robin tournament adhering to the following restrictions:

1. No team plays more than five games in one day.
2. No team plays more than five games on the same field.

An efficient way to solve this problem is by constructing a matrix with the team names as the row and column headings. Figure 13.3 gives an example. The cells in the lower half (below the x's) of the matrix should contain the day and time of the game. The cells of the upper half (above the x's) should contain the field number. The matrix is important because it tells you whether you have completed all of the games of the tournament, and it also helps you check all of the restrictions. For example, the matrix makes it easy to identify whether one team has accidentally been scheduled to play two games at the same time (check the columns in the lower half of the matrix and make sure the times do not conflict).

Tree Diagrams

A tree diagram is another way to represent a problem for which an entire set of solutions needs to be laid out. Tree diagrams are particularly helpful when the solution will be one of two outcomes (what are called *dichotomous* or *binary* outcomes). Suppose the National Basketball Association championship series is played between the Miami Heat and the Dallas Mavericks. Although the winner is determined by the first team to win four games, for this example, the winner will be the team that wins two out of three games. If you wanted to enumerate (list) all the possible ways in which the series could transpire, a tree diagram is most helpful. From this diagram you could answer questions such as: What is the probability that the series will last only two games (presuming each team has a 50−50 chance to win)? You would do this by counting the number of "tree branches" that involve only two endpoints and dividing by the total number of tree branches. Figure 13.4 shows how.

FIGURE 13.3 Matrix representation.

	Gators	Explorers	Black Knights	Bombers	Grey Sox	River Sharks	Ravens	Bandits
Gators	X	1						
Explorers	SAT 9A	X						
Black Knights			X					
Bombers								
Grey Sox								
River Sharks								
Ravens								
Bandits								

A matrix can help you solve problems that have multiple solutions or are best solved by identifying all possible alternatives.

Note: The cells of the matrix indicate the day of the game (SAT = Saturday, SUN = Sunday), the time of the game (9A = 9 A.M.), and the field (1 or 2). To read a team's schedule, start at the left-hand side and follow across until you get to the x, then move down that column. As an example, the Explorers play the Gators on Saturday at 9 A.M. on Field 1. This allows you to check how many games each team plays on each day and on which fields they play them. By checking the individual cells of the matrix, you can confirm that there are no conflicts in the scheduling (i.e., only one game is scheduled on each field for each time slot, and no team is scheduled for two games in one time slot).

Tree diagram.

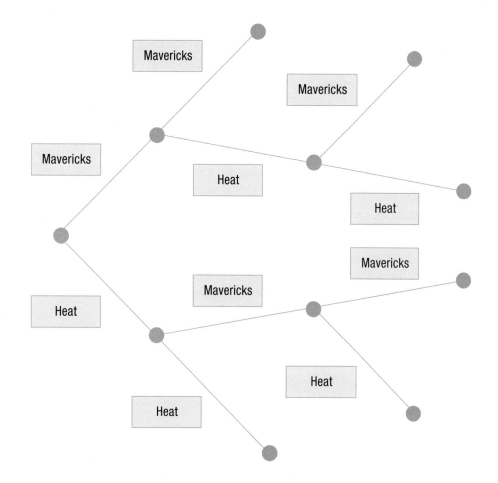

Note: The probability that the series will last only two games is 2/6 = .33. This strategy can be easily extended to larger numbers of games or to different domains with dichotomous outcomes.

Now that we have given you some ideas about how to represent problems, you can try some yourself. Activity 13.3 contains problems that will let you try using the representations we have covered.

Representing Problems

While you solve these problems, pay attention to the mental picture you form. Having the right picture in your mind is key to problem solving. Answers to these problems are found at the end of this chapter.

1. **Hobbits and Orcs:** Three Hobbits and three Orcs arrive at a riverbank, and they all wish to cross to the other side. Fortunately, there is a boat, but unfortunately, the boat can hold only two creatures at a time. Also, Orcs are vicious, and if there are ever more Orcs than Hobbits on one side of the river, the Orcs will attack and eat the Hobbits. Thus, there must never be more Orcs than Hobbits on either riverbank.

(continued)

ACTIVITY 13.3 *continued*

2. *Nine-Number Game:* This is a game in which there are nine numbers (1–9), and two people take turns picking those numbers until (a) all of the numbers are gone or (b) one person has any three numbers that sum to exactly 15. A player can have more than three numbers in all, but some subset of three must total 15. Having only two numbers (e.g., 7 and 8 or 9 and 6) adding to 15 does not count; it has to be exactly three numbers. The game starts with one person picking a number between 1 and 9. The second person then picks a number (but can't pick the one previously picked). So the game goes until one player picks exactly three numbers adding to exactly 15, or until all the numbers are picked (at which point the game is declared a tie).

3. *How Old Are You?:* Mary is 10 years younger than twice Susan's age. Five years from now, Mary will be 8 years older than Susan's age at that time. How old are Mary and Susan?

4. *International Relations:* Six delegates are seated around a table discussing international trade. The countries are Ireland, England, United States, South Korea, China, and Canada. The seating has the following restrictions:

   a. Ireland and England will not sit next to each other.

   b. South Korea and China will not sit next to each other.

   c. The United States and China will not sit next to each other.

   d. England and the United States want to sit directly across from each other.

   e. The United States and Canada want to sit next to each other.

   Construct a seating arrangement that will follow these rules.

5. *Parking Privileges:* Six parking spots are reserved for the top executives of a company: DeVos, VanAndel, Gates, Prince, DuPree, and Trump. The rules for parking are as follows:

   a. DeVos can park anywhere except in 5 or 6.

   b. VanAndel can park in 4 or 5 only.

   c. Gates can park in 3 or 6 only.

   d. Prince can park in 2 or 6 only.

   e. DuPree can park in 1 or 3 only.

   f. Trump can park anywhere except in 1 or 3.

   Construct a parking arrangement that will fit these specifications.

6. *Coin Flipping:* Suppose you flip a coin five times. What is the probability that four of the flips will be all the same (i.e., either four heads and one tail or four tails and one head)?

PROBLEM-SOLVING STRATEGIES

In the previous section, we presented some ways to visualize problems in your mind and on paper. We hope you now see that the right representation is crucial to successful problem solving. In this section, we discuss specific *strategies* for solving problems. A "strategy" is a method of operating on a problem. Strategies help to decrease the distance between where you are (the current state) and where you want to go (the goal state).

Breaking Problems into Subproblems

The rationale behind breaking a problem into subproblems is to turn one hard problem into several easier problems. This is also called *subgoaling*. (Chapter 2 also discussed short-term and long-term goals.) We sometimes do a simplified version of subgoaling when we travel. If you want to go from Point A to Point B, the most direct route on the map might involve taking a lot of turns, driving on streets with lots of stop signs, and so on. Instead, you might take the freeway—but this would require driving in a different direction at first to get on the freeway. Although the freeway might not be the most direct route, it will be faster in the end. Your strategy has three steps: to drive to the freeway, travel on the freeway, and drive from the freeway to your final destination. For example, if you need to travel west across town, you might first go east to get on the freeway. So your first subgoal is to get on the freeway. Your second subgoal is to get to the correct exit. The third subgoal is to go to your final destination. (If you've used Internet mapping sites before, you may have noticed the solution algorithm built by the software might give you the most direct route, but not the fastest or the one with the best roads.)

Working Backward

Perhaps the most common example of working backward is when people try to solve math problems by looking at the answer in the back of the book. Having the answer provides a feeling of comfort, because you know where you are supposed to end up, and all you have to do is figure out how to get there. This strategy is advisable when there is one clear-cut answer to the problem (which includes most math problems). Having one uniquely specified correct answer allows you to start at that point and weave your way back through the solution steps. This strategy will not work, however, for problems that have more than one possible correct answer. The two problems in Activity 13.4 are best solved by working backward.

Working Backward

Try the following problems, starting at the end of the problem and working backward until you find the solution. (Be advised that the first problem is easier than the second.) Solutions are found at the end of this chapter.

1. *Water Lilies:* Water lilies double in area every 24 hours. It takes 60 days for the lake to become completely covered with water lilies. On which day is the lake half covered?

2. *Gambling:* Three people play a game in which one person loses and two people win each game. The one who loses must double the amount of money that each of the other two players has at that time. The three players agree to play three games. At the end of the three games, each player has lost one game and each person has $8. How much money did each player have at the beginning of the game?

Problem Solving by Analogy

You solve problems by analogy when you use information learned in a previous problem to solve a current problem. Recognizing the relevance of previously learned knowledge to a new situation is a powerful problem-solving strategy. The ability to use analogy is also predictive of high intelligence and achievement

(Novick, 1988). The ability to recognize analogies is an important component of competent cognitive functioning. Unfortunately, students do not use analogy as effectively as they could. We hope to give you some ideas about how to improve this ability.

Recognizing the Structural Features. An analogy is not helpful unless you can understand its meaning. For example, noticing that two problems from math class both involve taxicabs and drivers will not be a very useful analogy. This is what is known as a **surface analogy**, because it is based on superficial features that are not relevant to solving the problem. One of the taxi problems could be a probability problem and the other could be a rate–distance problem. Seeing the superficial similarity of problems won't help you.

A helpful analogy is a **structural analogy.** You are making a structural analogy when you recognize the abstract similarities between two problems. For example, look at the problems in Activity 13.5. If you know how to solve the first problem, and you can identify the structural similarities between it and the second problem, then the solution to the second problem should be easy. The key to successful problem solving with analogies is peeling away the irrelevant, superficial features of the problems and recognizing the abstract, structural similarities that can help you solve the problem.

ACTIVITY 13.5 *Solving Problems by Analogy*

Try to identify the structural similarities of these two problems.

1. The college yearbook staff is trying to compile the pages of their book. The photo editor would like the student pictures in rows of 10. The layout editor would like them in rows of four. The faculty sponsor would like them in rows of five. The editor notices that with these layouts there will be two empty spots at the bottom of each page. She proposes rows of six, which will fill the page completely, with no blank spaces. Given that the number of pictures per page is between 20 and 100, how many pictures get placed on one page?

2. A high school principal is planning the graduation procession. She proposes that students march in rows of 12, but this leaves one student walking by himself. She then proposes rows of eight, but one is still left walking alone. The same is true with rows of three. Finally, she discovers that marching in rows of five fills all the rows. The graduation class is between 50 and 200 students. How many students are there?

Source: These problems are from "Analogical Transfer, Problem Similarity, and Expertise," by L. R. Novick, 1988, *Journal of Experimental Psychology: Learning, Memory, and Cognition, 14*, 510–520.

Mapping the Structural Features. Once you have identified the structural similarities of the two problems, now you need to "map" (match) the features from the first problem onto the elements of the second problem. The two problems in Activity 13.5 provide an example of mapping. (If you haven't done so already, try to solve these problems before reading further.) The principle underlying both problems (the structural similarity) is that of least common multiple (LCM). The first problem asks for the LCM of 4, 5, and 10, which is 20. But the rows of length 4, 5, and 10 all exceed the LCM by 2. This means that the answer to the problem will be two greater than a multiple of 20 (22, 42, 62, 82, and so on). Knowing this, you can solve the problem by looking for one of these numbers that is also a multiple of 6. The answer is now quite easy: 42.

After solving the first problem, you can solve the second one by analogy. First, look for the LCM, this time of 3, 8, and 12. It is 24. This time, the answer is one more than a multiple of the LCM (25, 49, etc.), it must be divisible by 5, and it must be between 50 and 200. Working the multiples of 24x + 1, you will find the answer to be 145.

Analogies can be a powerful tool for problem solving. Remember, analogies are helpful only when they are based on structural characteristics of the problems. We stress to you the importance of figuring out the abstract principle of problems when you solve by analogy. This skill will make you better able to solve a wide range of problems.

THE IMPORTANCE OF PRIOR KNOWLEDGE (REVISITED)

In Chapter 6 we explained a fundamental principle of human memory: The more you know, the easier it is to learn and remember. A corollary to that principle holds for this chapter: *The more you know, the easier it is to solve problems.* Try to answer the question in Activity 13.6 before you read further.

The Importance of Prior Knowledge

Try to solve the following problem:

Suppose you have an 8 × 8 checkerboard and 32 dominoes. Each domino covers exactly two adjacent squares, one red and one black (32 dominoes = 64 squares). Now suppose two squares are cut off the board at diagonally opposite corners. Is it possible to place 31 dominoes on the board so that all 62 remaining squares are covered? If so, how? If not, why not?

Now that you have tried the problem in Activity 13.6, notice the similarity between it and the following problem:

A tennis tournament attracts 64 participants. Thirty-two were invited from Florida, and 32 were invited from Georgia. The tournament director promised the players that they would each get to play a person from a different state in the first round of the tournament. He devises a tournament bracket in which all 32 of the first-round matches involve Florida players against Georgia players. The night before the tournament, two Florida players injure themselves and cannot compete. Can the tournament director reconfigure the bracket so that there are 31 Florida–Georgia matches?

You will notice that this tennis problem is much easier than the checkerboard problem in Activity 13.6. This example illustrates the importance of prior knowledge. Because 32 Georgians cannot play against 30 Floridians, the goal of all cross-state matches is not possible. Our knowledge of checkerboards is not so clear. It is hard to conceptualize that "diagonally opposite corners" must mean two squares of the same color, which is analogous to cross-state tennis matches.

Let's reconsider the height problem that is illustrated in Figure 13.2. We solved this problem with symbols. You could also solve it by using your prior knowledge; that is, by putting the problem in terms you can understand. Instead of Andrew, Bob, and Charles (three hypothetical people who have no meaning to you), you could use different names. For example, a basketball fan could say:

Shaquille O'Neal is taller than Tayshaun Prince. Tayshaun Prince is not shorter than Dwyane Wade. Is Dwyane Wade taller than Shaquille O'Neal?

Anyone who knows about basketball will recognize that the answer is clearly no. Thus, we encourage you to take advantage of what you already know as you try to solve problems in areas that you don't yet know.

TESTING HYPOTHESES

Sometimes problem solving takes the form of testing the validity of your claims or beliefs. This is the hallmark of scientific problem solving, and scientists do it all the time in their laboratories. A pharmacologist may believe that a certain drug will help control cholesterol. She compares the cholesterol level of those who are taking the drug to those who are not taking the drug to determine the drug's effectiveness. The pharmacologist might believe that cholesterol is affected by this drug (a hypothesis), but until she tests the prediction with an experiment, she will not know for sure.

We do hypothesis testing in our everyday life as well, although in a much less controlled manner than a scientist does. When we become acquainted with people, we try to make inferences about their personality—for example, if they are friendly or not. The best way to determine a person's friendliness is roughly the same way the pharmacologist determines a drug's effectiveness: You should put your hypothesis to the test. Thus, you look for evidence that the person is friendly or not.

However, the strategy of solving problems by testing hypotheses is often flawed for one reason: *People fail to look for information that will disconfirm their hypotheses.* Consider the following example: Suppose we present you with three numbers and ask you to figure out (by making guesses) what rule describes the sequence of numbers. After you make the hypothesis, you then select your own triplet of numbers that also follows the rule. This is how you test your hypothesis. We then tell you whether the triplet of numbers you selected is an example of the rule or not. This process of hypothesis generation and evidence gathering continues for several trials. Figure 13.5 gives an example of this kind of problem solving.

Looking at Figure 13.5, ask yourself whether you think the hypothesis that the rule is "even ascending numbers" is correct. Certainly all of the evidence you gathered (all of the triplets you selected) is consistent with this hypothesis. In fact, the hypothesis may not be correct. The rule could be just "even numbers." The rule "even numbers" cannot be eliminated, because you never tried a triplet that wasn't ascending—that didn't match your initial hypothesis. Thus the current

Testing hypotheses.

FIGURE 3.5

Suppose you are given the three numbers 2–4–6 and told that his triplet of numbers follows a rule, and your job is to figure out that rule. The table below lists your hypotheses and the triplet you selected to test the hypothesis. The right column lists the result of the tests; that is, whether the triplet of numbers was or was not an example of the rule.

Hypothesis	Number Triplet	Example of Rule?
2–4–6		
Even Ascending Numbers	4–6–8	Yes
Even Ascending Numbers	6–8–10	Yes
Even Ascending Numbers	8–12–16	Yes
Even Ascending Numbers	10–20–30	Yes

hypothesis was never disconfirmed. All of the evidence you gathered was consistent with your hypothesis because that is the only kind of evidence asked for. You need to present a number triplet that would disconfirm the hypothesis. For example, if you selected the triplet 6–4–2, this would have been inconsistent with the hypothesis "even ascending numbers." Would the evidence have been an example of the rule? Yes! What would you learn? You would learn that your current hypothesis is wrong—it is too narrow. The next step would be to try to disconfirm the new hypothesis of "even numbers." To do this, you would include an odd number. You would then see that such a triplet is not an example of the rule, so you can rule out odd numbers.

This strategy of disconfirmation will help you considerably narrow the universe of possibilities in this kind of problem. With this type of problem solving (referred to as *induction*—drawing generalizations from evidence), you can never *guarantee* that your hypothesis is correct. After all, there are an infinite number of possibilities in a problem like this. However, if you never try to disconfirm your hypothesis, you will never be able to demonstrate that your hypothesis has more claim to correctness than other hypotheses. When you look for disconfirming evidence, you will either find that your hypothesis is not supported by the evidence (in which case you can move on to other hypotheses), or reinforce the confidence you have in the validity of your current hypothesis.

STRATEGY SUGGESTION

In everyday problem solving, do not search only for information that will confirm your hypotheses, suspicions, and expectations, but rather seek out evidence that can falsify your beliefs.

Try to apply hypothesis testing in your daily life. If you think your professor is unkind, don't seek out and pay attention to only information that confirms that hypothesis. If you think your roommate is angry with you, don't seek out and pay attention to only information that confirms that hypothesis. This strategy of seeking disconfirmation will make you a much better problem solver, in school and in life.

LOGICAL REASONING

Rules for "If–Then" Problem Solving

If–then problem solving involves reasoning by logical rules. The goal is to determine whether a logical rule is being followed or violated. In this type of problem, just one exception to the rule proves that the rule is being violated. For example, in the United States, it is a rule that you must be 21 years old to drink alcohol. This rule is based on if–then logic: If you walk into a bar and find just one person under 21 drinking beer, then that rule has been violated.

The rules of formal logic are fairly complex, and psychologists have found that students sometimes have a hard time learning them (Nisbett, Fong, Lehman, & Cheng, 1987). The problems in formal logic take the form *if* p *then* q. Activity 13.7 gives such a problem. In this problem, all four of the cards have a letter on one side and a number on the other. The rule that describes these cards is: If there is a vowel on one side, then there must be an odd number on the other. The question is: What card(s) must you turn over to determine whether the rule is being violated?

STRATEGY SUGGESTION

Solving if–then problems involves checking two conditions: (a) the p *condition and (b) the not–*q *condition.*

If the *p* condition (a vowel) does not have a *q* on the back (an odd number), then you know the rule is being violated. Second, the not–*q* (opposite of q) must have the not–*p* condition on the front. What does that mean for the example in Activity 13.7? Because the rule is: If there is a vowel on one side (*p*) then there must be an odd number on the other (*q*), you must check the A (*p*) and the 4 (not–*q*).

ACTIVITY 13.7 *Illustration of If–Then Problem Solving*

The cards below should adhere to the following rule: If there is a vowel on one side, then there must be an odd number on the other. Which cards would you need to turn over to determine if the rule is being violated?

| A | D | 4 | 7 |

If *p* then *q* components:

A: *p*
D: not–*p*
4: not–*q*
7: *q*

Turn over the A?   YES   NO
Turn over the D?   YES   NO
Turn over the 4?   YES   NO
Turn over the 7?   YES   NO

Why are A and 4 the two cards that must be checked? First, if you turn over the A and find a non-odd (even) number, then the rule has been violated (because a card with a vowel did not have an odd number on the other side like it was supposed to). Second, if the card with a 4 has a vowel on the other side, then again you know the rule has been violated (again, a card with a vowel on one side needs to have an odd number on the other).

What about the cards we didn't need to select? First, consider the D (the not–p card). That is a consonant. Is there anything in the rule that gives any restrictions or qualifications about consonants? No. The rule places no restrictions on what a consonant can have on the other side. If you assumed a consonant must have an even number on the back, you would be making a mistake called **denying the antecedent.** What's most important to know is that it doesn't matter what is on the not–p card.

Second, consider the 7 (q). This part is confusing for many people. Most people think the 7 needs to be selected because it is the q. In fact, people confuse the actual rule—if p then q—with a different rule, if q then p. These two rules are not the same. The rule places restrictions on only cards with vowels, specifically that a vowel card must have an odd number on the other side. This confusion is the most common error in solving this type of problem. It is called **affirming the consequent.** It's important to remember that "if p then q" is not the same as "if q then p."

Such abstract problems that do not take advantage of our prior knowledge are often very hard to solve. Let's take an example with which college students may be more familiar. The drinking law can be described using formal logic: If you are under 21 years of age, then you must drink soda. Activity 13.8 gives a pictorial representation of this rule.

Beer Drinkers

The following if-p-then-q question is relatively easy to understand. Although you can probably answer the question easily, make sure you understand the logical rationale behind the answers.

Suppose you are a police officer in a bar. The squares below represent people; for two of them you know their age and for two of them you know what they are drinking. To determine if the legal drinking age (21) is being obeyed, from which of these people would you need to gather more information?

BEER	COKE	20	21

Check the age of the beer drinker (not–q)?   YES   NO

Check the age of the Coke drinker (q)?   YES   NO

Check the drink of the 20-year-old (p)?   YES   NO

Check the drink of the 21-year-old (not–p)?   YES   NO

Intuitively we know that we need to check the underage person (*p*) and the one drinking beer (not–*q*). We don't care what the 21-year-old drinks (not–*p*) or how old the Coke drinker is (*q*). Using the rules of formal logic in such a familiar domain helps us understand how the rules of logic work. Of course, we don't really need formal logic to solve a problem for which we have such clear prior knowledge. (Recall our previous discussion of how it is easier to learn more when you already know a lot.)

Rules for "If-and-Only-If" Problem Solving

Now that we have laid the foundation for formal logic by explaining if–then thinking, it should be fairly easy for you to see the extension to what is called "if-and-only-if" thinking. Whereas an if–then rule might be: "If there is a vowel on one side, there must be an odd number on the other side," an if-and-only-if rule could be: "There will be a vowel on one side if and only if there is a consonant on the other." The first one has the form "If *p* happens, then *q* must happen"; whereas the second one has the form "If *p* happens, then *q* must happen, and if *q* happens, then *p* must happen." We think it is easier to remember how to solve if-and-only-if problems because all four conditions must be checked. That is, you must check the *p*, the *q*, the not–*p*, and the not–*q*. Here is what are you are looking for:

1. The *p* must accompany the *q*.
2. The *q* must accompany the *p*.
3. The not–*p* must have a not–*q*.
4. The not–*q* must have a not–*p*.

Let's assign *p* to be the vowel and *q* to be the odd number. Using the same cards from Activity 13.7, we can verify the rule, "There will be a vowel on one side if and only if there is an odd number on the other" by doing four things:

1. Check the A to make sure it has an odd number on the other side.
2. Check the 4 to make sure that it has a nonvowel.
3. Check the 7 to make sure it has a vowel on the other side.
4. Check the D to make sure it has a non-odd number.

Notice the first two checks are the same as for if–then problems (*p* and not–*q*). In addition, we must check *q* and not–*p*. These problems are sometimes called **biconditional problems** because the logic runs in both directions: if *p* then *q* as well as if *q* then *p*. This is why all four conditions must be checked.

Let's look at if-and-only-if problem solving with the drinking example we used earlier. The if–then rule was, "If you are under 21, then you must drink soda." The analogous if-and-only-if rule would be, "You can drink soda if and only if you are under 21." We would verify this rule by checking all four people listed in Activity 13.8. As we did in the card example, we would do the following:

1. Check the person under 21 to make sure he or she is drinking soda.
2. Check the beer drinker to make sure he or she is over 21.
3. Check the soda drinker to make sure he or she is under 21.
4. Check the person over 21 to make sure he or she is drinking beer.

Again, notice how the first two checks are the same as in if–then problems (*p* and not–*q*). The difference is that *q* and not–*p* also need to be checked. In terms of this example, that means that the rule requires all soda drinkers to be under 21 and all people over 21 to be beer drinkers. Although this makes no real-world sense, perhaps it helps you see how the rules of logical problem solving can be generalized to any situation.

We suggest you simply memorize the ways to check formal logic. They are summarized in a strategy suggestion for your convenience. To remember them, try linking the information with some law or rule you are familiar with (such as the drinking example).

STRATEGY SUGGESTION

In standard problems, the conditions that need to be checked are p *and not–*q. *In if-and-only-if problems, all four conditions must be checked.*

Although people tend to have trouble solving these logic problems, you can make them easier for yourself by drawing on rules that are familiar to you. Activity 13.9 has more if–then problems to help you practice logical reasoning.

More If–Then Reasoning Problems

ACTIVITY 13.9

Try to solve these logic problems given what you have just learned.

1. If a student is a freshman, then the student is not allowed to have a car on campus. The four people you meet are Bill, a senior; Sarah, who has a car; Amy, who doesn't have a car; and Peter, a freshman. Which people will you have to ask for more information to know whether they drive a car and their year in school?

2. In a strange country there are two kinds of people: "morphs" and "dorphs." There are two kinds of food: cake and pie. The rule in the country is that if you are a morph, then you must eat pie. The four people you meet are a morph, a dorph, a pie eater, and a cake eater. From which people do you need to obtain further information to determine whether the rule is being violated?

3. All people traveling to Country X must be given the Whooping Cough vaccine. No other rules apply. At the customs desk where you work, you meet four people: one traveling to Country X, one traveling to Country Y, one vaccinated for Whooping Crane, and one vaccinated for Whooping Cough. From which people will you need to request more information (either their destination or their vaccination history) to determine whether everyone is following the rule?

PROBLEM SOLVING USING QUANTITATIVE INFORMATION: STATISTICAL REASONING RULES

In events that adhere to the reasoning rules of formal logic, the existence of just one counterexample disproves a rule. Not all events, however, follow these rules. Some events are best explained by quantitative reasoning rules, usually referred to as *statistical reasoning*. Next we state some general principles that characterize statistical reasoning. Being sensitive to these will help you in certain problem-solving situations. As in previous sections, we also give you some example problems.

More Is Better

This more-is-better principle is what statisticians call the **law of large numbers.** To understand this law, we must define two terms. First, a **population** is the set of events (usually people) that is being studied or considered. For example, in a study determining voter preference in an upcoming presidential election, the population is eligible voters in the United States. Second, a **sample** is a subset from the population that will actually be observed. In the presidential election study, we could determine voter preference by surveying registered voters. But we can't ask every single voter (122 million voters cast ballots in the 2004 presidential election). Instead, researchers select a sample of voters from the population and ask them.

What if you and a friend wanted to conduct your own presidential polls? Your friend selects 10 registered voters and asks them their preference. You, however, select 100 people. Which poll do you think will be more accurate? According to the law of large numbers, your poll will be more accurate. The law of large numbers states that as the sample size increases, the sample will reflect the true nature of the population more accurately. Let's consider a real-life example of the law of large numbers and how people fail to use this principle.

Consider athletic coaches during preseason tryouts. Tryouts for athletic teams are sometimes very brief, and coaches make decisions based on only one or two days of practice. Applying quantitative problem-solving skills tells us that this is probably not a good idea. Recall that the larger the sample, the more accurately it will reflect the population. If a coach makes a decision based on a very small sample, it is likely that the quality of play he views will deviate from the "true" performance of these players—the performance observed over the long haul. In this case, the sample is the observations during tryouts, and the population is the player's "true" ability. The population—the player's true ability—can never be completely known. Thus, we have to estimate it by taking a sample. Larger samples give more reliable estimates.

Extreme Scores Will Not Be Extreme the Next Time

The extreme-scores principle, called **regression to the mean,** is related to the law of large numbers. If a score (such as a test score, a theater audition, or an athletic tryout) is way above or way below the average (mean) one time, the score will go back ("regress") toward the population's average on subsequent observations (the next test score, the next theater or athletic tryout). In other words, if you do much worse than you normally do on a chemistry exam, it may be because of random fluctuations in scores. Regression to the mean indicates that on your next exam, you are likely to do better based simply on this principle. Many people think they do better because they try harder the next time. This may also be true, but the principle of regression to the mean says that scores will improve simply due to a statistical "correction" that steers scores back toward their true (population) mean.

Taking sports as an example, when a team plays poorly in one game, it might play much better the next time. Some people might attribute this to increased effort or a coach's conducting a rigorous practice following the poor performance.

Conversely, following an excellent performance, an athletic team might not play as well. The team could be accused of slacking off or resting on its laurels. In both of these cases, the real answer may simply lie in statistical regression: Observations way above or way below the mean will regress back toward that mean in the future.

People sometimes have a hard time believing this phenomenon when we talk about it in terms of human behavior. So let's consider a completely random process. As a way to illustrate this, we ask that you find six dice and roll them. Take the three largest values and the three smallest values and calculate the mean for each group of three. Suppose the values were 1, 2, 2, 3, 4, 6. The mean of the low group is 1.67, and the mean for the high group is 4.33. Now take the three low dice and roll them again, and the three high dice and roll them again. Is the mean for the low group higher and the mean for the high group lower on the subsequent rolls? It's quite likely. This is regression to the mean. It's based only on a statistical principle; the dice weren't trying harder or being lazy! Activity 13.10 gives examples of problems that use the law of large numbers. Try these problems to see if you understand the principles of the law of large numbers and regression to the mean.

Statistical Reasoning

ACTIVITY 13.10

Explain your answer for each of the questions below.

1. Should a casting director make auditions 2 days long (to reduce stress) or should she make them 1 week long?_____

2. Which event is more likely to result in an underdog (the team that is not favored to win) being victorious: the Super Bowl or the World Series?_____

3. Which professional tennis system will result, in the long run, in more higher-seeded (favored) players being defeated: three sets in women's matches or five sets in men's matches?_____

4. A small rural hospital delivers 10 babies per week. A large city hospital delivers 100 babies per week. Presuming that the probability of having a boy is .50, which hospital is more likely to show a week in which 60% or more of the babies born in that hospital are boys?

   a. Rural Hospital

   b. City Hospital

   c. Both are equally likely

   Why do you think so?

   _____

   _____

5. a. How surprised would you be if you flipped a coin 10 times and 7 of the flips came up heads?

   | NOT SURPRISED AT ALL | 1 | 2 | 3 | 4 | 5 | 6 | 7 | 8 | 9 | 10 | ABSOLUTELY SHOCKED |

   b. How surprised would you be if you flipped a coin 1,000 times and 700 of the flips came up heads?

   | NOT SURPRISED AT ALL | 1 | 2 | 3 | 4 | 5 | 6 | 7 | 8 | 9 | 10 | ABSOLUTELY SHOCKED |

(continued)

 *continued*

How do your answers compare? (circle one)

5a is greater than 5b   5b is greater than 5a   Both scores were the same

Explain your scores in terms of the law of large numbers:

_____

_____

_____

Don't Be Swayed by Vivid Anecdotes

The principle of regression to the mean serves as a warning to us against being influenced by vivid anecdotes. One of the weaknesses of human thinking is that we tend to place too much weight on isolated cases. We hear of single parents who are lazy, have lots of children, and receive all kinds of government handouts. We may draw the conclusion that "all single mothers are on welfare" because we hear one vivid case of a person who displays these characteristics. In fact, the data suggest just the opposite. Divorced women are more likely to be working outside the home than are married women (80% vs. 68%), single-parent households have fewer children than do married households, and only a minority of single-parent households receive some kind of government assistance (Berger & Thompson, 1995). Because we remember spectacular cases quite easily and data less easily, our impression of the truth is likely to be inaccurate.

Good problem solvers are not swayed by vivid anecdotes but instead rely on large samples of data to draw conclusions. Politicians, salespeople, and others will try to persuade you with anecdotes. Beware.

Look for Representative Samples

You now know not to be fooled by anecdotal information but that you should instead rely on large samples. We offer one more caution: The sample you use to draw your inference must be *representative*. A sample is representative if it accurately reflects the group about which you are making a judgment. Determining whether a sample is representative can be difficult, however. Consider, for example, political surveys. During election season you can find political surveys on the news every day. Suppose we found an election poll done in October 2004 of 1,000 registered voters that indicated George W. Bush was leading John Kerry by a margin of 59% to 34%, with 7% undecided. Would you be likely to believe the poll? Suppose we told you that the poll surveyed registered voters in Sioux County, Iowa, one of the most conservative (and Republican) areas of the country. If the poll sampled voters only from this geographical area, the sample would not be representative, and thus, it's likely that this poll was biased in favor of Bush. The main point is this: *For a sample to be representative, the members of that sample must be selected randomly*. In this example, the sample will be random if it is chosen randomly from all registered voters, not just those who live in Sioux County, Iowa.

Another way to ensure that a sample is random is to make sure that it is not self-selected. For example, suppose you see a commercial on TV that claims a certain product will help improve your school achievement—the Acme Academic Achievement Accelerator (AAAA). "I went from getting all Ds to getting all As," testifies one of the faithful purchasers. The commercial goes on, "The AAAA improved GPAs of those who used it by 40 percent." Will the product work? As in many problems of this sort, there's no way to know for sure. However, you should be suspicious about who is using the product. Were the people randomly selected, or did they choose to use the product themselves? If they chose the product themselves (as opposed to being randomly assigned to use the product vs. not use the product), they were self-selected. A group of people who choose to buy and use the product might be different from those who choose not to buy the AAAA. Those who are willing to invest the time and money in this product are probably going to have different attitudes toward school learning; that is, if they care enough to try AAAA, they probably are more likely to care about improving their grades. Thus, you don't really know if they improved because of the product or because of their motivation. Maybe this superior motivation would have caused their improvement anyway, without the aid of the AAAA. You may have noticed another aspect of quantitative reasoning in this example—the use of a testimonial, which is a type of anecdote. Remember, don't be swayed by one person telling you how effective something is. Avoid anecdotes. Ask for the data.

A second feature that affects whether a sample is representative is if the people who are in the sample stay in the sample. Consider the AAAA example again. Suppose it was discovered that those who stayed with the AAAA program got better grades, but that only 40% of those who originally enrolled stayed with the program. Can you conclude that the program is effective? Not really, unless you know how the ones who dropped out of the program would have done had they stayed in it. This problem is similar to the problem of self-selection. Specifically, if people who stay in the program are different (maybe in their level of motivation) from people who drop out of the program, there's no way of telling whether it's the AAAA program that caused the improvement or simply something about the people who stuck with the program that causes them to do better in school. So be careful of study programs offering you all As, of miracle diets, of tummy trimmers, and of other self-help quick fixes. The data can be deceptive because the sample may not be random.

Correlation Is Not Causation

When thinking about quantitative relations between two events—A and B—be aware that there are three possibilities:

1. There is no relation
2. There is a positive relation (as the amount of A goes up, so does the amount of B)
3. There is a negative relation (as the amount of A goes up, the amount of B goes down)

An example of a positive relation is between height and shoe size. Ask 10 people for their height and their shoe size, and plot them on a two-dimensional graph. You will likely find the line that best fits through the points will have a positive slope (go from the lower left to the upper right of the graph). An example of a negative

FIGURE 13.6 Correlation and causation.

Even if we know two events are related, we cannot assume they are causally connected. This figure demonstrates the possible causal links between two related events, A and B.

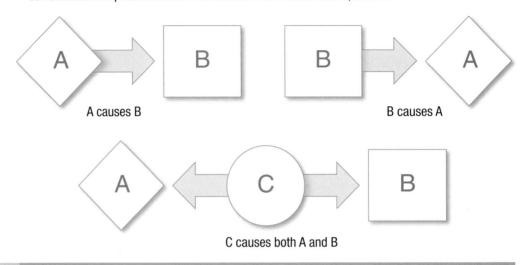

relation is between number of absences from class and course performance. Quite likely, the less often you skip class, the higher your grade.

Sophisticated thinkers will do more than recognize positive and negative relations between events. They will also notice when a relation does not exist. A common error is to assume that because two events are correlated, one event caused the other. Two events, say A and B, can be causally related in three ways: First, A could cause B. Second, B could cause A. Or third, another event, call it C, could be causing both A and B (see Figure 13.6). For example, consider the height and shoe size example. Does it make sense that height causes shoe size? No. Does it make sense that shoe size causes height? No. In this case, there is a third variable, genetics (C), that is causing both height and shoe size. Since body size is largely determined by genetics, it makes sense to posit this third variable as a cause. So, when you hear two events are correlated, be careful not to assume that you know the direction of the causal relation, or that there is a causal relation between them at all. Activity 13.11 has some correlation–causation problems for you to try.

ACTIVITY 13.11 *Correlation Does Not Equal Causation*

Can you come up with alternative explanations in the following problems?

1. People who ate Frosted Flakes as children had half the cancer rate of those who never ate it. Conversely, those who often ate oatmeal as children were four times more likely to develop cancer than those who did not. Does this mean that Frosted Flakes prevents cancer and oatmeal causes it?

2. Scientists have linked obesity with television watching, according to the *Journal of the American Academy of Pediatrics.* What are some possible explanations for this correlation? What causes what?

3. Divorce is not good for your health, claims a best-selling book. Divorced males under 70 are much more likely to die from heart disease, lung cancer, and stomach cancer. Their suicide rate is five times as high as

that of nondivorced males. And their fatal car accident rate is four times as high. Is divorce the cause of these maladies?

4. There is a positive correlation between milk consumption and incidence of cancer. Does drinking milk cause cancer?

5. In the New Hebrides Islands, the amount of body lice was *positively* correlated with good health. That is, the more body lice you had, the healthier you were. Does this mean you should hope to get infested with body lice as soon as possible? What explanation could there be for this correlation?

Note: These problems were compiled by Martin Bolt (2007).

CREATIVITY: INVENTING NOVEL SOLUTIONS TO PROBLEMS

The types of problems we have discussed so far have been ones for which one correct answer can usually be found. Sometimes we are faced with problems to solve for which more than one answer exists. The type of thinking that is required for these problems is usually referred to as **creativity.** Often, being creative implies generating a solution that is nontraditional or one that few people have thought of before.

If you are asked to think of creative solutions to problems, how might you go about doing so? Edward de Bono (1985) offered several suggestions designed to break you out of a normal way of thinking so that you can generate more unusual, creative solutions.

When being creative, allow your mind to wander to places it usually doesn't go.

If you look only at solutions that sound plausible or practical, chances are they won't be very creative either. Don't worry about judging your ideas (or the ideas of others) at first. The evaluation can come later. What is important is to generate all sorts of ideas. What may sound like a dumb or impractical idea initially may later be developed into both a creative and a practical solution to a problem. Consider three of de Bono's (1985) strategies.

Stepping-Stone Method

Sometimes we are trapped in thinking about a problem in the same way we always have thought about it. The **stepping-stone method** can help you get out of an old mode of problem solving and into a new one. Just as a stepping-stone in a river allows you to jump from one patch of ground to another without getting wet, a stepping-stone in problem solving allows you to switch from one avenue of solutions to another.

De Bono says that the stepping-stone does not need to be a feasible solution in and of itself. It only needs to redirect your problem-solving efforts. The goal of the stepping-stone method is to come up with a creative solution that otherwise would not have been generated, by going down a path you would not ordinarily take. An obviously wrong answer could serve as a stepping-stone to another, more promising solution.

Escape Method

The **escape method** is similar to the stepping-stone method, but its goal is to identify things that we take for granted in our problem solving, and to try to escape that normal way of thinking. The fact that we take something for granted suggests that we may have trouble escaping from it, because we don't tend to think about things we take for granted. The key to "escaping" is explicitly paying attention to things we assume to be true. De Bono (1985) gave the example of trying to solve the problem of long lines at phone booths in certain places (given the prevalence of cell phones, this example seems quaint and outdated but its solution is still creative). What are some things we assume about phone booths? We assume that they all cost the same amount. Questioning this assumption leads to the possibility that a few of the pay phones could cost a lot more. This would discourage people from making trivial calls on those phones, leaving them free for those with emergencies who would be willing to pay more.

Consider another of de Bono's examples: At the time de Bono wrote this book, the city of London had far fewer taxicabs than most large cities. This was at least partly because to be licensed as a cabby in London, you had to pass a detailed geography and landmarks test. It took months to learn the entire city, and the would-be cabby did not get paid for this. This requirement may have discouraged people from becoming a cab driver. The assumption behind it was that cabbies should always know exactly where they were going and how to get there. What if we challenged this assumption? Is a cabby who doesn't know where she's going of any value? Not to visitors of London, but local residents who know where they're going don't need a knowledgeable driver because the residents can instruct the driver where to go. This suggests the following solution to the cab-shortage problem: Have two classes of drivers, one group that knows the city and one group that is learning it. The former group will be used by visitors and the latter group will be used by local residents (and, de Bono says, will have a big question mark painted on their cab, indicating they don't know the city!). As they transport residents around town, they will learn the city, get paid for their efforts, and eventually get to the point they can pass the test and become a fully licensed driver who can transport visitors (and thus get the big question mark removed from the cab!).

Notice how de Bono generated this solution by first asking, "What parts of the problem do we take for granted?" By identifying the assumptions in the problem, de Bono arrived at a creative and useful solution to the problem that might not otherwise have been found.

Random Simulation Method

Advertising agencies could use the **random simulation method** to get creative juices flowing. The method is simple: Pick some random object or word and use it to open up new avenues of thinking. You can find a random object by looking out your window or by looking randomly in the dictionary. The unrelated word you start with will help you develop new connections to the problem you are trying to solve. When you are stuck in the same old mode of thinking, this technique gives you a fresh start and may help you uncover creative solutions you would not have otherwise developed. Activity 13.12 will help you practice this technique.

The Random Simulation Method

See if you can use the random simulation method to help solve a current problem with which you are dealing.

1. Identify a problem you are having in your life right now. This can be a problem with your relationships, your schoolwork, or any other area. If you can't think of a major problem, glance through a newspaper and identify a problem or controversy that is currently in the news.

2. Next, get your dictionary and turn to page 113, go to the first column, and select the ninth word in that column. (If the ninth word is not a noun, go down the column until you find a noun.)

3. Use this random word as a starting point to generate creative solutions to your current problem. What does your random word bring to mind? Does the word have any relevance to the problem you are trying to solve? You may want to write down words that come to mind, draw pictures, or make tables. Do you see any connections, any creative ideas?

Getting Stuck: Functional Fixedness and Mental Set

Another aspect of creativity is the ability to recognize when you are stuck and get "unstuck." Sometimes getting stuck means being unable to think of a solution. For example, look at Figure 13.7. The materials shown there are from one of the most famous studies of problem solving, the candle problem (Duncker, 1945). The problem is to find a way to attach the candle to the wall, using the materials shown in the diagram. This problem is difficult because people think of the tacks as the device that will secure the candle to the wall. This won't work for several reasons: First, the tack is not likely to be long enough; second, the candle wax

The candle problem.

Can you think of a way to attach the candle to the wall, using only the items shown here?

may split when pierced by the tack; and third, even if it did work, the candle would fall as it burned down near the end.

This illustrates the problem of **functional fixedness,** which is an inability to represent familiar items in new ways. We tend to think of matchboxes as holding only matches, but they can also be used to hold other things, like a candle. You could melt a little wax in the bottom of the matchbox, secure the candle to the bottom of the box, and use the tacks to attach the matchbox to the wall.

If you allow your mind to think more broadly than it normally does, you can be much more creative. The creative person is the one who sees practicality where others do not.

Another obstacle in problem solving is getting stuck in ruts—doing things the same way all the time. Maybe when you drive home from college to visit your parents, you always take a certain way. Then a friend shows you a path through rural roads that avoids heavy weekend traffic on the interstate. Even though you agree that it's faster, you always forget to take the new way until it is too late. This is an example of **mental set:** continuing to use an old method to solve a problem even when a better method has become available. The problems in Activity 13.13 illustrate mental set. Try them to see if you avoid mental set.

ACTIVITY 13.13 *Mental Set*

The table below gives five problems. In each one, the task is to measure a specified amount of water (goal) using three jars that have specific capacities (A, B, C). The capacities of the jars are shown in each problem.

Problem	Jar A	Jar B	Jar C	Goal
1	38	150	6	100
2	20	80	7	46
3	2	11	1	7
4	30	99	5	59
5	18	48	4	22

You may have discovered that the key to solving these problems is to use the formula $B - A - 2C$. This formula will work for all five problems. However, the fifth problem can be solved more easily: $A + C$. If you missed that solution, and instead used $B - A - 2C$ (which still works), you were a victim of mental set.

THE RELATIONSHIP OF PROBLEM SOLVING TO SELF-REGULATED LEARNING

Remember that the goal of this book is to make you a self-regulated learner. Earlier chapters in this book directly addressed self-regulation. For example, being a self-regulated learner means having goals and making plans (Chapters 2 and 3), having good attention and memory strategies (Chapter 6), and using effective cognitive strategies (Chapter 7). Self-regulation is also crucial to effective reading (Chapter 9) and writing (Chapter 10), because the skills of planning, reflection, and modification of reading and writing strategies are essential to success in these areas.

Self-regulation is an important aspect of problem solving as well. Being self-regulated as you approach problem-solving tasks can benefit you in three ways:

1. *Planning and setting subgoals.* A good problem solver devises an approach to problem solving. He avoids diving right into the problem without getting an overview of the problem (much as an effective reader prereads and gets an overview of a difficult text prior to reading). Once he gets an overview of the problem, he breaks the problems into subgoals. This parallels the recommendation for difficult homework assignments we made in Chapter 7 (see Activity 7.6). Understanding the components of the problem (using a task analysis like in Chapter 7) will help you break the problem into subgoals.

2. *Prior knowledge.* You have learned that memories (Chapters 6 and 7) are easier to recall if you have prior knowledge of the material you are trying to remember. Similarly, problem solving is easier if you can put the problem in terms that are familiar. Thus, a self-regulated learner tries to understand novel problems in familiar terms.

3. *Checking progress, changing strategies.* A self-regulated learner not only makes plans (Question 1 above), but also checks to see whether he is following these plans. If the goal (remember, in problem solving, the goal is to move from original state to goal state) is not being achieved, the self-regulated learner will change his problem-solving strategies.

The point is this: The skills of self-regulated learning—planning, breaking tasks into parts, using prior knowledge, checking progress, and adapting strategies to fit the task demands—are characteristic of people who are both effective problem solvers and self-regulated learners.

CHAPTER SUMMARY

In this section, we have considered a variety of ways in which people fail to solve problems successfully, and proposed solutions to help you avoid such pitfalls. We believe that effective problem solving starts with the proper mental representation (the proper picture in your head). Sometimes problems are best represented by pictures, other times by symbols, and still other times by tables or matrices. We also have suggested specific problem-solving strategies such as working backward and creating analogies. We introduced specific domains of problem solving—logical reasoning and quantitative reasoning—that follow certain prescribed rules. Knowing these rules is essential for solving problems in these domains. Finally, creativity is the ability to stretch beyond conventional mental boundaries and to see solutions where others do not. The most important lesson to learn from this chapter is this: You become a better problem solver by solving problems. We encourage you to seek out opportunities to solve problems. You will find that both your problem-solving skills and your problem-solving motivation will increase with practice.

ANSWERS TO SELECTED PROBLEMS

Activity 13.2   The Monk Problem

If you represent time on the x-axis and height on the y-axis, the problem becomes much easier to solve. You can see that no matter how fast the monk travels (in either direction), the two lines will always cross. This crossing represents what the monk refers to as the "one spot along this path that I passed at exactly the same time of day on my way up the mountain as on my way down."

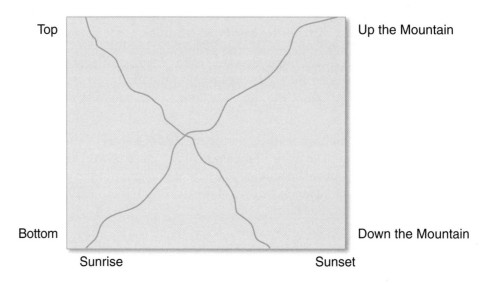

Activity 13.3   Hobbits and Orcs

A pictorial representation is helpful in this problem. (You could even draw a little boat with two seats in it to keep track of who is going across.) Update the positions of the creatures each time you move them to one side of the river or the other. A correct solution is given below.

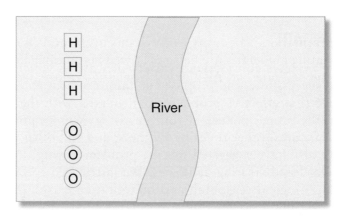

a. move 2 O's

b. return 1 O

c. move 2 O's

d. return 1 O

e. move 2 H's

f. return 1 H, 1 O

g. move 2 H's

h. return 1 O

i. move 2 O's

j. return 1 O

k. move 2 O's

Activity 13.3   Nine-Number Game

Most people represent this problem with nine slips of paper with numbers on them, and people take turns picking the slips of paper. However, an alternative representation makes this problem much easier:

8	1	6
3	5	7
4	9	2

This game should look familiar. It is identical to tic-tac-toe. All three of the rows and columns and both diagonals sum to 15. Instead of representing by choosing slips of paper with numbers on them, you can represent it this way and place Xs on your numbers and Os on your opponent's numbers.

Activity 13.3   How Old Are You?

A symbolic representation is helpful in this problem. Turn the first statement—"Mary is 10 years younger than twice Susan's age"—into symbols in this way:

$$M = 2S - 10$$

The second statement—"Five years from now, Mary will be 8 years older than Susan's age at that time"—looks like this:

$$M + 5 = S + 5 + 8$$

(Notice the 5 gets added to both sides to represent the "5 years from now.")

This gives us the standard "two equations and two unknowns" from elementary algebra. Working it through, you should find that Susan is 18 years old and Mary is 26.

Activity 13.3   International Relations

A pictorial representation is one way to solve this problem. It is easier to check that all of the seating guidelines are being followed if you can actually "see" the table at which the delegates sit. An allowable seating arrangement is:

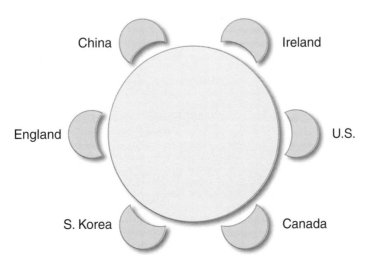

Activity 13.3   Parking Privileges

This problem can be represented by a matrix. An "X" in a cell indicates parking in that spot by that person is prohibited.

	1	2	3	4	5	6
DeVos					X	X
VanAndel	X	X	X			X
Gates	X	X		X	X	
Prince	X		X	X	X	
DuPree		X		X	X	X
Trump	X		X			

Activity 13.3   Coin Flipping

A tree diagram will be helpful for this problem. Map the possibilities for the five flips. Then count all of the tree branches that contain four heads or four tails. If you divide this number by the total number of tree branches, you have the probability that was asked for in the problem.

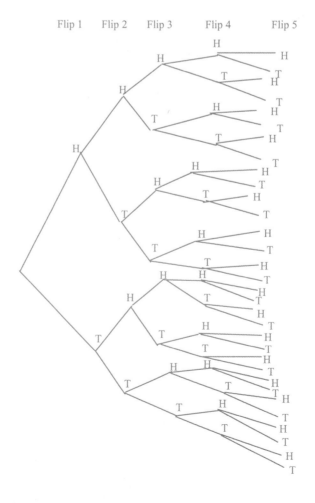

Flip 1   Flip 2   Flip 3   Flip 4   Flip 5

Activity 13.4   Water Lilies

The best way to solve this is to start at the end. At 60 days you know the pond is 100% covered. If the lilies double every day, then on the 59th day, the lilies must have covered 100% ÷ 2 of the pond. So the answer is that the pond will be 50% covered on the 59th day. (Kind of a trick question, but working backward makes it easy. In fact, there's no way to solve it working forward.)

Activity 13.4   Gambling

This problem can be solved only by working backward. It is also helpful to break it into subgoals:

1. Identify the loser of Game 3 (an arbitrary assignment).
2. Determine the dollar amounts at the end of Game 2.
3. Identify the loser of Game 2.
4. Determine the dollar amounts at the end of Game 1.
5. Identify the loser of Game 1.
6. Determine the dollar amounts before games began.

The solutions to these subgoals are:

1. Player 3 loses Game 3. (The assignment is arbitrary; it doesn't matter who won which game, but we need a place to start.)
2. Player 3 must have had more before he lost Game 3 (i.e., at the end of Game 2). Since he pays each person double what they had, and they each ended up with $8, then Players 1 and 2 must have had half of that at the end of Game 2. Thus, they each had $4. Since Player 3 shelled out $8 for losing Game 3, he must have had $8 more at the end of Game 2, so he had $16 ($8 he had afterward, plus the $8 he paid out).
3. Player 2 loses Game 2. (Again, it doesn't matter which one you pick, as long as it's not the one you picked before.)
4. Player 1 had $4 and Player 3 had $16. They won Game 2, so that means that at the end of Game 1, they had $2 and $8, respectively. This means that Player 2 had $10 more at the end of Game 1 than at the end of Game 2—$14 ($4 he had afterward, plus the $10 he paid out).
5. Player 1 loses Game 1.
6. Player 2 had $14 and Player 3 had $8. They won Game 1, so they must have started with $7 and $4, respectively. That means that Player 1 paid $11 for losing Game 1, so he had $13 ($2 he had afterward, plus the $11 he paid out).

The summary of the games looks like this:

	Player 1	Player 2	Player 3
End of Game 3	8	8	8
End of Game 2	4	4	16
End of Game 1	2	14	8
Start	13	7	4

Conclusion

ASSESSING YOUR PROGRESS, PLANNING YOUR FUTURE

Chapter Goals

This chapter will help you:

- Retake the Learning Inventory and revisit your scores on the Learning Inventory from the beginning of this book

- Identify the areas of the Learning Inventory on which you showed improvement

- Identify areas of the Learning Inventory that need further growth

- View this book, and the skills you have learned from it, as the foundation of a lifelong journey of learning

CHAPTER 14

PROGRESS ASSESSMENT

We have used the Learning Inventory as an assessment instrument whenever it has been appropriate throughout this book. You answered the Learning Inventory questions at the beginning of the book to identify strengths and weaknesses in your cognitive and motivational repertoire. We think a fitting conclusion to this book is to ask you to retake the Learning Inventory, to identify your characteristics as a learner that have changed from the time you started this book. Activity 14.1 provides a fresh copy of the Learning Inventory, and Activity 14.2 helps you compare your scores from the beginning of the book to your scores now.

ACTIVITY 14.1 *The Learning Inventory*

Mark the responses that best describe your approach to college.

GOAL SETTING

	Never or almost never	Rarely	Frequently	Always or almost always
1. When choosing between a hard class and an easy class, I consider my potential grade more than the interest or challenge the class would bring.	④	③	②	①
2. When thinking about the future, I think about the potential positive impact of doing well in college, and the potential negative impact doing poorly might have on my future.	①	②	③	④
3. When I am given a large assignment, I try to do it all in one night.	④	③	②	①
4. When faced with a large task, I make lists of things I need to do to reach the final goal.	①	②	③	④
5. I take mistakes personally and see them as a sign of failure.	④	③	②	①

Mark the responses that best describe your motivation for college.

MOTIVATION

	Never or almost never	Rarely	Frequently	Always or almost always
6. I feel trapped into taking the classes that I take. I don't feel I can take classes that interest me.	④	③	②	①
7. When faced with a difficult homework problem, I am likely to wander down the hall and ask someone in my dorm rather than work on my own.	④	③	②	①
8. I doubt whether I can succeed in college.	④	③	②	①
9. I get discouraged when courses are difficult or boring.	④	③	②	①

	None of the time	Some of the time	Most of the time	All of the time
10. Being successful in college is more a function of ability and luck than effort and persistence.	④	③	②	①
11. Even when a class is boring, I try to find something interesting to get out of it.	①	②	③	④

Indicate the extent to which you engage in these behaviors.

RESOURCE MANAGEMENT: EXTERNAL

	None of the time	Some of the time	Most of the time	All of the time
12. I set up a weekly schedule each term.	①	②	③	④
13. I make a to-do list and set priorities from that list.	①	②	③	④
14. I set aside weekly times for studying.	①	②	③	④
15. I maintain a study place free from distractions.	①	②	③	④
16. I form peer study groups in my classes.	①	②	③	④
17. I take initiative in getting help from faculty.	①	②	③	④
18. I listen to music or watch TV when studying.	④	③	②	①
19. I fall asleep when studying.	④	③	②	①

Mark the responses that best describe your approach to college.

RESOURCE MANAGEMENT: INTERNAL

	None of the time	Some of the time	Most of the time	All of the time
20. I sleep 8 hours or more each day.	①	②	③	④
21. I eat nutritionally sound meals each day.	①	②	③	④
22. I exercise three or more times per week.	①	②	③	④
23. I feel stressed about school on a regular basis.	④	③	②	①
24. I get along with people most of the time.	①	②	③	④

Mark the responses that best describe your approach to college.

ATTENTION AND MEMORY

	Never or almost never	Rarely	Frequently	Always or almost always
25. Rote memorization is my most preferred way of learning material.	④	③	②	①
26. When I have trouble remembering something, I think of things that are related to what I'm asked to remember.	①	②	③	④

27. I listen to lyrical music when I study.	④	③	②	①
28. I am easily distracted.	④	③	②	①
29. I usually study in a noisy place.	④	③	②	①

Mark the responses that best describe your approach to learning.

METACOGNITION

	Never or almost never	Rarely	Frequently	Always or almost always
30. I generate questions to help me understand class material.	①	②	③	④
31. I notice or look for examples of what I'm learning in one class in other classes or in my life outside of school.	①	②	③	④
32. I try to make comparisons and similarities between what I read in textbooks and what I hear in lectures.	①	②	③	④
33. I monitor my progress to assess whether I am learning what I set out to learn.	①	②	③	④
34. I vary my approach to learning depending on the class and type of assignment.	①	②	③	④

Mark the responses that best describe your note-taking habits.

NOTE TAKING

35. I miss class
    - ④ never
    - ③ once or twice a semester
    - ② once or twice a month (4–8 times a semester)
    - ① once or twice a week (over 15 times a semester)

36. I find it hard to concentrate
    - ① at least once per class period
    - ② at least once per week
    - ③ only one or two times a month
    - ④ I almost never have trouble concentrating in class (my mind wanders only once or twice a semester during class)

37. I ask questions or provide a comment in class
    - ④ once a week or more
    - ③ once a month or more
    - ② only one or two times a semester
    - ① I do not participate in class unless called on by the professor

38. Positive features of my note taking (mark all that apply):
    - +1 I look over my notes after class.
    - +1 I go back and expand and/or clarify my notes after class.

⊕ I review my notes with the professor or with a classmate.

⊕ People who have borrowed my notes have commented on how organized they are and easy to understand.

39. Negative features of my note taking (mark all that apply):

⊖ I try to write down verbatim what the professor says.

⊖ I lose track of what the professor is saying because I am trying to write down as much as possible.

⊖ The only time I look at my notes is a day or two before the test to review.

⊖ I have a hard time understanding my notes when I go back to them because I can't read the writing or understand the abbreviations, or there are parts missing.

Indicate the extent to which you do the activities listed while reading.

READING	None of the time	Some of the time	Most of the time	All of the time
40. I set a goal before I begin a segment.	1	2	3	4
41 I ask myself questions about the text.	1	2	3	4
42. I change my strategy based on the difficulty of the text.	1	2	3	4
43. I take notes during the reading.	1	2	3	4
44. I reread when I don't understand.	1	2	3	4
45. I listen to music.	4	3	2	1
46. I fall asleep.	4	3	2	1

Indicate the extent to which you engage in the following behaviors when you are writing.

WRITING	None of the time	Some of the time	Most of the time	All of the time
47. I make an outline.	1	2	3	4
48. I feel rushed.	4	3	2	1
49. I proofread.	1	2	3	4
50. I allow a friend to read my writing.	1	2	3	4
51. I turn in the first version I print out.	4	3	2	1
52. I have multiple pieces of information available when sitting at the computer, such as a textbook, Web sites, and note cards.	1	2	3	4

Mark the responses that best describe your approach to taking tests.

TEST TAKING

	Never or almost never	Rarely	Frequently	Always or almost always
53. After I get a multiple-choice test back, I look at the ones I got wrong and realize I made a "stupid mistake."	4	3	2	1
54. I study the same way for essay and multiple-choice tests.	4	3	2	1
55. I try to make comparisons and note similarities between what I read in textbooks and what I hear in lectures.	1	2	3	4
56. My nervousness distracts me from clear thinking during tests.	4	3	2	1
57. I jot down an outline for an essay answer before I begin writing.	1	2	3	4

Mark how true each of the following statements is of you.

CRITICAL THINKING

	None of the time	Some of the time	Most of the time	All of the time
58. I often find myself questioning things I hear or read in this course to decide if I find them convincing.	1	2	3	4
59. When a theory, interpretation, or conclusion is presented in class or in readings, I try to decide if there is good supporting evidence.	1	2	3	4
60. I treat the course material as a starting point and try to develop my own ideas about it.	1	2	3	4
61. I try to play around with ideas of my own related to what I am learning in this course.	1	2	3	4
62. Whenever I read or hear an assertion or conclusion in this class, I think about possible alternatives.	1	2	3	4

Note. The above five items are from *A Manual for the Use of the Motivated Strategies for Learning Questionnaire* (MSLQ), by P. R. Pintrich, D. Smith, T. Garcia, and W. J. McKeachie, 1993, Ann Arbor, MI: NCRIPTAL, School of Education, The University of Michigan. Reprinted with permission from W. J. McKeachie.

Mark the responses that best describe your approach to problem solving.

PROBLEM SOLVING

	Never or almost never	Rarely	Frequently	Always or almost always
63. I enjoy puzzles, problems, and brainteasers.	1	2	3	4
64. When faced with difficult problems, I have a hard time deciding how to begin.	4	3	2	1

65. When I hear someone state a position or argument,
    I skeptically try to think of alternative explanations. ① ② ③ ④

66. I am good at thinking "outside the box." ① ② ③ ④

67. I find personal testimonials on TV commercials
    convincing. ④ ③ ② ①

Scoring the Learning Inventory

Scale	Number of Items	Total Score	Scale Score (Total Score Divided by Number of Items)
Goal Setting	5		
Motivation	6		
Resource Management: External	8		
Resource Management: Internal	5		
Attention and Memory	5		
Metacognition	5		
Note Taking	5		
Test Taking	5		
Reading	7		
Writing	6		
Critical Thinking	5		
Problem Solving	5		

Strength Areas

Activity 14.3 asks you to list the areas in which your mean score is higher now than when you took the test at the beginning of this book. (For purposes of this exercise, we have defined an improvement as greater than one half of a point [0.5], but that is not a strict criterion.)

Comparing your two sets of scores, identify the areas where you have improved, according to the Learning Inventory. Next to those components, note the ways in which you have noticed the improvement in your learning (if you've noticed anything) and why you think you have improved—in other words, identify the things you are doing differently now than previously. For example, maybe you scored higher on the Critical Thinking scale when you completed the Learning Inventory in this chapter. What behaviors have you noticed in your own learning that might explain this change? Are you thinking about complex situations differently? Are you more often looking at a problem from multiple perspectives? Use Activity 14.3 to identify any changes.

ACTIVITY 14.3 *Areas of Improvement*

Component of Learning Inventory Showing a Score Increase of 0.5 or More	Reason Why You Think Increase Occurred	Courses in Which You Have Noticed a Change

Areas Needing Improvement

Activity 14.4 asks you to list the areas in which your mean score is lower on this version of the Learning Inventory than on the version you took in Chapter 1. (For purposes of this exercise, we have defined a decrease as greater than one half of a point [0.5].) Comparing your two sets of scores, identify the areas where you have shown a decrease. Next to those components, note the ways in which you have noticed that your behavior on the Learning Inventory scale is not as effective (if you've noticed anything). In other words, what things are you doing differently now than previously that may have caused your score to go down?

For example, maybe your score on the Test Taking scale is lower now than at the beginning of the semester. Can you identify reasons for this? Are your tests harder than you expected when you started the semester? Is the end of semester particularly stressful, given all you have to do before break? Most important, can you think of strategies you have learned in this course that could lower your test anxiety?

ACTIVITY 14.4 *Areas of Decline*

Component of Learning Inventory Showing a Score Decrease of 0.5 or More	Reason Why You Think Decrease Occurred	Courses in Which You Have Noticed a Change

MAKING YOU S.M.A.R.T.E.R.

The title of this book is *Learning to Learn*, which may have been a phrase you had not heard before reading this book. By now we hope you know what it means. Learning to learn is best described as a process of developing the skills, strategies, and motivation necessary to become a *self-regulated learner*. Learning to learn means teaching yourself how to learn. With the help of this book, we hope that you have achieved this.

You may have done well in high school by simply following teachers' instructions and doing what you were told. It is conceivable that you could survive in college and never learn how to learn. If you do learn how to learn, however, your performance in college will improve (your *skill*), whether you are currently doing well or not. Also, your enjoyment of and motivation for college will increase (your *will*).

You may have heard of Stephen Covey's (1989) very popular book *The Seven Habits of Highly Effective People*. We believe you can benefit from what we call the Seven Habits of a Self-Regulated Learner. The first letters of each of the characteristics form the word *SMARTER*. By following the recommendations in this book and understanding the principles underlying them, you will become a self-regulated learner, and you will make yourself smarter. A self-regulated learner is:

© Heather Jones – FOTOLIA

1. *Strategic.* A self-regulated learner employs the proper learning strategies at the appropriate time. This book has offered suggestions for learning strategies that may be used in many different settings. Chapter 6 offered ways to improve your attention and memory. Chapter 7 gave strategies to use while studying. Chapter 9 offered ways to improve your reading comprehension, and Chapter 10 discussed ways to improve your writing. Effective strategies (in all settings) are the foundation of self-regulated learning.

2. *Monitoring.* A self-regulated learner not only uses effective learning strategies, but also checks the effectiveness of the strategies. It is possible to read this book and use the strategies without checking how well they are working. A self-regulated learner, however, will set goals for learning and then monitor progress toward those goals. After reading this book, we hope that you now not only use effective strategies but also monitor to be sure the strategies are working.

3. *Adaptable.* In response to monitoring (Habit 2), self-regulated learners also adapt and adjust their learning strategies to fit the situation. We hope you now realize that the study strategies you used in high school—for example, studying the night before a test or studying only by memorization—will not work in college. To be successful in college, you will have to study consistently through the term (not just before tests), read the texts carefully, and do more than just memorize. By having many study strategies in your repertoire, you can adapt to the needs of new learning situations and change strategies to achieve the new goals.

4. *Responsive.* Not only do self-regulated learners adapt to the demands of the current task, but they are also responsive to the social influence of others around them. This characteristic is based on the idea that learning is ultimately a social endeavor—it is never done alone. At the very least, it involves your interacting with (i.e., having a "conversation" with) your textbook. Chapter 9, on reading, explored ways you can make that interaction most profitable. But even more than that, learning takes place in social situations like lectures and discussions. In

Chapter 8, we discussed ways to maximize your learning in these situations. Learning also takes place in interaction with friends and classmates. In Chapter 4, we suggested ways in which peer/group learning can work for you and that help seeking is not a crutch but a resource that, if used appropriately, can be an important feature in your learning. Finally, Chapter 5 addressed some issues of interpersonal relationships and how they impact learning. We hope we have conveyed the fact that learning does not occur in isolation. Rather, it is an interactive and social activity, and you must be responsive to social demands and take advantage of social opportunities.

5. *Thematically Organized.* We hope this book has taught you to be thematically organized in two ways. First, we hope your life is more organized now than it was before you read this book. We stressed in Chapters 2, 3, and 5 the importance of keeping the components of your life in order. Among other things, this means healthy and well-paced living, having *short-term* and *long-term* goals, keeping separate notebooks for each course, keeping papers in files, and planning and monitoring your daily life. A second type of thematic organization is the organization of your knowledge structures (*schemas*). Chapters 6 and 7 stressed the importance of keeping material organized in your mind. If you have an organized mental structure of knowledge in a course, you are far more likely to remember the material at test time. You are also far more likely to be able to use your course knowledge in flexible and meaningful ways such as writing a report or linking what you learned in class to what you experience in a service-learning project. The second feature of thematic organization stems from the first: People who lead organized lives have organized minds (a theme we stressed in Chapter 5).

6. *Effortful.* There are lots of smart people in the world, but their smartness is useless without proper effort—motivation. This is the *will* component of the book. Effective learning strategies are worth nothing if you don't try hard and put forth effort. Chapter 3 described many ways that you might be motivated for school, including intrinsic or extrinsic reasons. Maybe you are motivated by grades, maybe by the love of learning new things, or maybe by both. Throughout this book (but particularly in Chapter 3) we stressed the importance of being motivated—putting forth effort.

7. *Relevant.* Finally, we hope you have learned that the best learning is learning that means something—learning that makes a claim on your life. If what you are learning in college is relevant to your life, you will almost always do better than if you are learning inert or irrelevant facts. You can make knowledge relevant in two ways. First, you can ask yourself "So what?" in regard to what you are learning. In other words, we challenge you to find meaning and relevance in what you learn in your classes. Psychologists call this *task value*—the extent to which you see your college learning as relevant and useful. Seeing your college courses as relevant improves learning because it brings a degree of concern and interest that would not otherwise be there.

Chapters 2 and 3 discussed different ways to determine what you value and how those values affect your learning and motivation. We encourage you to find a way to care about what you are doing. This care will breed success. It is not always easy, if the class is boring or detached from your major area of study. In such courses, the challenge for you is to find some value or purpose that will enhance your motivation and learning.

The seven habits of a self-regulated learner.

FIGURE 4.1

The behaviors listed below are what make someone a self-regulated learner. Taken together, they make you SMARTER.

1. **S**trategic. A self-regulated learner employs the proper cognitive learning strategies at the appropriate time.
2. **M**onitoring. A self-regulated learner not only uses effective learning strategies, but also checks the effectiveness of the strategies.
3. **A**daptable. In response to their monitoring, self-regulated learners adapt and adjust their learning to fit the situation.
4. **R**esponsive. Self-regulated learners are responsive to the social influence of others around them.
5. **T**hematically Organized. A self-regulated learner is organized in school life, work life, and social life, and has an organized mind.
6. **E**ffortful. A self-regulated learner puts forth the appropriate amount of effort based on the difficulty and importance of the task.
7. **R**elevant. Self-regulated learners look for meaning, value, and relevance in all that they do.

The second way a self-regulated learner uses the principle of relevance is in how he or she uses his or her knowledge. Self-regulated learners learn when (and when not) to apply their knowledge. That is, they know how to use their knowledge and, thus, make it relevant. For example, they would recognize the relevance of their chemistry class to things like the weather, the environment, or even opening soda cans. For someone who is not a self-regulated learner, knowledge is inert (even in classes besides chemistry); it has no value outside of taking the test and no relevance to life outside of class.

Figure 14.1 summarizes the seven habits of a self-regulated learner. These habits are the cornerstone of college success. If you have developed them, you have learned how to learn and this book has been a success for you.

JUST THE BEGINNING: THE PATH OF LIFELONG LEARNING

You are probably reading this book near the beginning of your college journey. You may be reading it as part of a first-year experience or academic enrichment course. We hope that this book has provided useful strategies to improve your learning. We also hope that you will use these activities as they are appropriate for your learning throughout your college years.

We wrote this book to stand by itself—to be useful for almost any college student in almost any area of study. Now that you are finished, we realize that you may not refer back to it very often. However, even though you may not be using this book as a reference, we certainly hope the learning and motivational strategies you have read about will be useful to you in the future. Beyond this book and even beyond college, the book's two-pronged model of skill and will can help you approach many of life's tasks. This model is indicative of what adult learning is usually like—specifically, to succeed in life you need two things: skill and will, effective strategies and strong motivation. Whether it's being a good engineer, an informed citizen voter, or a high-quality parent, all of life takes both skill and will. One without the other is useless, and as this book stresses, you can make yourself better on each dimension.

One of the authors tells the students in his classes that the true test of a university's success is if students can say at the end of 4 years, "I don't need this place anymore." In other words, college, when it is at its best, gives you the tools to speak clearly, write convincingly, and think critically so that when new problems or concerns come along, you can handle them on your own—without the help of a professor. You are unlikely to find a college course, professor, or textbook to tell you what you should think about environmental racism, how to speak with your child's teacher when discussing what he calls a "learning disability," or whom to vote for in the city's mayoral election. Such is the learning and thinking of adult life, and college professors can only hope that by the time you graduate, the tools are in place for you to make informed decisions.

Such is the case for us. Long after you have closed this book, and maybe even long after you have forgotten this course, we hope that the tools of learning and self-regulation will remain with you. Just as a college student is to say "I don't need this place anymore," we hope that readers of this book will say "I don't need this book anymore." If you feel you don't need this book anymore, it has served its purpose. You have learned how to learn.

CHAPTER SUMMARY

It takes two things to be successful in college: skill and will. This chapter reviews the skill and will components of the Learning Inventory. By comparing your Learning Inventory scores from this chapter to your scores from Chapter 1, you can assess changes in your use of the learning and motivational strategies covered in this book. This book will not give everyone optimal performance on all aspects of college learning. We strongly believe, however, that you will see improvement in your learning and motivation relative to where you started. In the long run, using these improved strategies will help you earn better grades and make learning more fun. Long after this book is a part of your past, long after college and formal education are a part of your past, we hope that your understanding of the importance of skill and will—and how to improve them—can increase your enjoyment and success in many of life's challenges.

APPENDIX

Choosing a Major and Choosing a Career

We conclude this book with a medium-range concern—choosing a major—and a long-range concern—choosing a career. We include it as an appendix because, depending on the nature of the course you are taking, these topics may not fit well. If it is a part of your course discussions, your professor could put it any number of places in the semester, so we put these topics in an appendix for course flexibility. We have spent close to 300 pages telling you about how to succeed in college. Being a successful college student is a noble goal and should be applauded on its own merits. If that was all you cared about, we hope you have found worth in our words. But many of you believe, rightly so, that college should do something for you. It costs a great deal of money and you want that investment to pay off—perhaps with a better lifestyle, with more money, or with a job that brings you meaning and purpose. To accomplish those goals, you must ponder two important questions: What will I study? and What will I do when I graduate?

CHOOSING A MAJOR

Most students worry about choosing a major at one time or another in their college career. A significant number of students are unsure of their major when they arrive on campus and still others change their major in college.

There are many Web sites and some textbooks (e.g., Nadler, 2006) available that walk students through the process of selecting a major. Books of this nature provide students with self-assessments (similar to the learning self-assessments in this book) to determine what major is best for you. For example, the book by Nadler (2006) has 10 self-assessments that help students identify their interests, skills, and motivation. Instead of providing you with yet more self-assessments, we instead encourage you to ask yourself the following questions as you decide your major:

1. *What Do You Like?* If you are going to commit 4 (or more) years of your life to studying a particular field, it is essential that you like what you're doing. Many students come to our field of psychology with preconceptions about it that are based on television, movies, and their high school psychology course. Usually

their affection for psychology comes from interest in the subfield of clinical psychology—the diagnosis and treatment of psychological disorders. Many students arrive as first-years thinking that they would like to be clinical psychologists. As they go through their undergraduate study of psychology, they learn that there is more to psychology than simply clinical psychology. They are presented with other subfields of psychology. Some students are more attracted to these subfields, and some students leave psychology for another field that helps them enter the helping professions without having to study all of these other subfields, such as social work or nursing.

The moral of the story is that when it comes to selecting a major, don't let the tail wag the dog. In other words, don't study something simply because you think you might like it. As you progress through your study of a possible major, you could learn that the field is not what you had imagined. At that point, it is important to consider other options. In summary, it is critical to find enjoyment when you study your major. If you find it boring, tedious, or otherwise miserable, leave it and move on.

2. *What Are You Good At?* Many majors lead to careers that are very attractive in terms of prestige, salary, or entertainment. But many of these careers are also very competitive to enter. Thus, the majors that train people for those fields tend to be quite competitive. This makes sense. If high-paying or prestigious careers were easy to enter, then even more people would want those careers. In economic terms, that would lower the prestige and salary of the fields. So in certain very competitive fields, you need to have good grades. For example, at many schools admission to the undergraduate business college is more competitive than admission to the general education (i.e., science and literature) college. We've known students who are not accepted into the business college who study economics at the science and literature college and do jobs similar to those of the business-school graduates when they are finished. The main point is this: You need to make an honest assessment of your skill level and determine whether you have the qualifications to be successful in that major.

Whether or not your intended major is competitive, it is important to point out something about human ability and human success: If you look at people who are successful, they're not good at *everything*. Everyone has different skills and abilities, and when selecting a major, it is crucial to find out what your strengths are. The people who are successful find what they like and what they are good at and they strive for excellence in that area. Music majors don't need to be good at chemistry and vice versa, so the sooner you can find out where your gifts lie, the sooner you can start on your road to success.

But how should people identify those gifts? We believe the best way to do this is through taking courses. You will develop the best sense of whether you have competency in a subject area by taking a couple of classes. Specifically, if you still enjoy the area of study after taking the introductory class, we encourage you to take the methodology course in an area. (In psychology, this is research methods/statistics; in history, it is historiography.) The methodology is the "how to" class of a field that teaches you how to be a professional in that field. Beware—it is often not as exciting as other content courses in a major, and students often report that the methodology course is quite difficult. The reason we recommend taking the methods course is that if you can do well in a difficult and not terribly interesting course, then we believe you will do well in that major. On the other hand, if you struggle with this course and you lose interest in the field, you may want to reconsider your field of study.

CHOOSING A CAREER

For most people, the selection of a major is a pathway to a career. For this reason, the same two questions about major—What do I like? and What am I good at?—are relevant here, and we encourage you to ask yourself those questions as they relate to life after college. So you might really enjoy studying the course content involved in a certain major, but if you lack certain skills essential to doing the job of that major when you graduate, then you cannot be successful in that field. For example, you might be a straight-A nursing student in all the content courses, but if you are squeamish about blood or if you are unable to insert an IV into a patient's vein and cannot overcome these anxieties, then, put simply, you cannot be a nurse. We are not saying these things to scare you or to make you feel badly about things on which you need to improve. But we want you to maximize your college career, and one way to do that is by pursuing career paths that will be most profitable and enjoyable to you.

Textbooks and Web sites that assist people with career decisions use self-assessments, just like resources that help students select majors. These assessments come in at least one of two (somewhat overlapping) types. First, there are personality tests. Personality, you recall from Chapter 5, is defined as our enduring traits that stay stable over time and circumstance. When it comes to selecting a career, *personality tests* are designed to assess your enduring traits (e.g., risk taking, introversion) and how they match up with different career choices. Second, *vocational tests* measure your interest in different career choices. For example, a vocational test available at www.jobhuntersbible.com asks a series of "would you rather" career questions. One of the authors took this test and the feedback indicated that I " . . . like job responsibilities and occupations that involve creative, humanistic, thoughtful, and quiet types of activities . . . interests include abstracting, theorizing, designing, writing, reflecting, and originating, which often lead to work in editing, teaching, composing, inventing, mediating, clergy, and writing."

All in all, it's a pretty good description. But we offer a couple of critical-thinking cautions. First, the profiles tend to read a bit like horoscopes—we read into them what we want to read into them. Second, making a "would you rather" decision based on no context is difficult to interpret. That is, asking someone if they would rather be an electrician or an accountant means little to someone (like the author) who doesn't know much about being either an accountant or an electrician. So such a question does not help everyone. Third, such tests do not take into account the role of the situation when asking people to select their choices. For example, a question such as "I prefer to argue my case" versus "I prefer to avoid confrontation" depends a lot on the situation. We probably can all think of situations when we prefer to argue and some situations when we prefer to avoid confrontation. So it can be difficult to answer such questions as decisively as they are phrased by the test. Such tests can make us look less flexible than we really are. Because of these concerns, it is important to be cautious not to overinterpret such tests.

Besides the questions about interest and ability, we also encourage you to consider the following.

1. *What Matters to You?* Most college majors are 4 years, 5 years maximum. Although many people go through several job changes in their lifetimes, people tend to stay in a career for quite a while (even if they do change when they get

older). So whatever career path you choose, above anything else, it must be something that gives your life meaning. People's perception of what is meaningful is obviously varied. People can derive meaning from accomplishing tasks, earning money, winning arguments, competing, traveling, developing a philosophy of life, serving others, or some combination of these. Whatever your incentive, make sure you are true to yourself and select something that is consistent with your motives and values. Nothing is worse than feeling trapped in a career that does not give you a sense of purpose.

2. *It's a Marathon, Not a Sprint.* Life is ferociously competitive, and many people will be pushing you to make decisions and take courses as quickly as possible. Is going fast always better than going slowly? It depends. Make no mistake about it: All other things being equal, it's better to start early than to start late. Because we live in such a competitive world, many college students come to college *very* prepared, even to the point of practically having a full year of college under their belts before they even arrive on campus. For the most part, this is a good thing. But there is an irony to this also: Sometimes being ahead of everyone else means only that you finish first, but not that you end up ahead. Consider Dana, a very talented high school senior who was 2 years ahead of her peers in mathematics classes. She took calculus as a sophomore, an impressive feat indeed. However, her acceleration in mathematics meant only that she finished all her math classes before anyone else. But her junior and senior years in high school she took no math because there was no math left to take at her school. She is now poised to gain acceptance to a prestigious university, and in some ways her acceleration may prove to be a hindrance because it will have been over 2 years since she took math, and she will be asked to take math again in college. We see this also in athletics. Although it might be nice to be the best 6th-grade tennis player in your school, it would be more important to be the best 12th-grade player on your team. Athletes who start earlier in life are better than their peers at a younger age, but as others become involved in the sport and as bodies develop, those early starters might not be the best at the end of high school. The point is this: It's always a good idea to challenge yourself, but it is important to remember that completion and success are usually the main criteria—not speed.

Just as in Dana's example described above, having a "long view" about your career is equally important. Specifically, we encourage you not to think *only* about what you'll be doing when you're 25, but also when you're 45, and even (for your generation, who will be working past this point) when you're 65. What is exciting when you're younger might not be exciting when you are older. For example, many of our students want to be high school sports coaches. They grew up with sports, and they want to continue to make sports a part of their lives. They therefore seek to obtain a secondary-teaching endorsement and coach for the school that employs them. Coaching teenagers is an honorable and rewarding activity. Coaching high school sports, though, appears to be largely the purview of younger teachers. Although certainly not always the case, high school coaches tend to be early-career and middle-career teachers. As you grow older, your priorities change—you may get married and have children of your own, and you may prefer to spend time watching them play sports rather than coaching at your local high school. Also, as we age our energy level tends to drop, and we may find that it is harder to have both a teaching job and a coaching job. Also, when people are younger, they probably need the money more, so the incentive to earn extra money as a coach is not there as people age.

Take another example from our field of psychology: Many psychology majors begin working as youth counselors with troubled teens. This job is exciting because it has a lot of responsibility and brings with it a real sense that you are making a positive difference in the lives of these adolescents. As time goes on, though, the low pay becomes frustrating, the sense that the teens are not getting better becomes discouraging, and your own aging makes it harder to connect with your young clients. For this reason, we often advise our students to think about ways to move to a different kind of position as they get older—one with more supervisory responsibilities, one with more management responsibilities, or one that involves a different kind of therapeutic contact with the clients. All of these things will probably require advanced training such as an MBA or maybe a master's degree in clinical psychology or social work. These two examples simply serve to illustrate the following: What you think is a great career when you are 25 years old may not seem as great when you are 45 years old. Thus, be sure to be flexible, be willing to grow, and be willing to look over the horizon to envision a future that will be meaningful and rewarding from beginning to end.

REFERENCES

Alexander, J., & Tate, M. (1999). *Web wisdom: How to evaluate and create information quality on the Web*. Mahwah, NJ: Lawrence Erlbaum Associates.

American Psychological Association. (2001). *Publication manual of the American Psychological Association* (5th ed.). Washington, DC: Author.

Asher, S. R., & Paquette, J. A. (2003). Loneliness and peer relations in childhood. *Current Directions in Psychological Science, 12,* 75–78.

Aspinwall, L. G., & Taylor, S. E. (1992). Modeling cognitive adaptation: A longitudinal investigation of the impact of individual differences and coping on college adjustment and performance. *Journal of Personality and Social Psychology, 63,* 989–1003.

Bahrick, H. P., Bahrick, P. O., & Wittlinger, R. P. (1975). Fifty years of memory for names and faces: A cross-sectional approach. *Journal of Experimental Psychology: General, 104,* 54–75.

Batson, C. D., Fultz, J., Schoenrade, P. A., & Paduano, A. (1987). Critical self-reflection and self-perceived altruism: When self-reward fails. *Journal of Personality and Social Psychology, 63,* 594–602.

Baumeister, R. F. (2005). Self and volition. In W. R. Miller & H. D. Delaney (Eds.), *Judeo-Christian perspectives on psychology* (pp. 57–72). Washington, DC: APA Press.

Baumeister, R. F., Bratslavsky, E., Muraven, M., & Tice, D. M. (1998). Ego depletion: Is the active self a limited resource? In R. F. Baumeister (Ed.), *The self in social psychology* (pp. 317–338). New York: Psychology Press.

Baumeister, R. F., Campbell, J. D., Kruefer, J. I., & Vohs, K. D. (2003). Does self-esteem cause better performance, interpersonal success, happiness, or healthier lifestyles? *Psychological Science in the Public Interest, 4,* 1–44.

Benson, H., Greenwood, M. M., & Klemchuk, H. (1975). The relaxation response: Psychophysiologic aspects and clinical applications. *International Journal of Psychiatry in Medicine, 6,* 87–98.

Bereiter, C., & Scardamalia, M. (1987). *The psychology of written composition*. Hillsdale, NJ: Lawrence Erlbaum Associates.

Berger, K. S., & Thompson, R. (1995). *The developing person through childhood and adolescence*. New York: Worth.

Bolt, M. (2004). *Pursuing human strengths*. New York: Worth.

Bolt, M. (2007). *Instructor's resources to accompany* Myers Psychology (8th ed.). New York: Worth.

Bower, G. H., & Winzenz, D. (1970). Comparison of associative learning strategies. *Psychonomic Science, 20,* 119–120.

Bransford, J. D., & Johnson, M. K. (1972). Contextual prerequisites for understanding: Some investigations of comprehension and recall. *Journal of Verbal Learning and Verbal Behavior, 11,* 717–726.

Brown, A., & Day, J. (1983). Macrorules for summarizing texts: The development of expertise. *Journal of Verbal Learning and Verbal Behavior, 22,* 1–14.

Bruning, R., Schraw, G., & Ronning, R. (1995). *Cognitive psychology and instruction.* Englewood Cliffs, NJ: Merrill/Prentice Hall.

Bungum, T. J. (1997). Factors affecting exercise adherence at a worksite wellness program. *American Journal of Health Behavior, 21,* 60–66.

Butler, D. L., & Winne, P. H. (1995). Feedback and self-regulated learning: A theoretical synthesis. *Review of Educational Research, 65,* 245–281.

Centers for Disease Control and Prevention. (CDC). (2004). *Behavioral risk factor surveillance system survey data.* Atlanta, GA: U.S. Department of Health and Human Services, Centers for Disease Control and Prevention.

Covey, S. R. (1989). *The seven habits of highly effective people: Restoring the character ethic.* New York: Simon and Schuster.

Covington, M. V. (1998). *The will to learn: A guide for motivating young people.* New York: Cambridge University Press.

de Bono, E. (1971). *Practical thinking.* Middlesex, England: Penguin.

de Bono, E. (1985). *de Bono's thinking course.* New York: Facts on File.

Duckworth, A., & Seligman, M. E. P. (2005). Self-discipline outdoes IQ in predicting academic performance of adolescents. *Psychological Science, 16,* 939–944.

Duncker, K. (1945/1935). On problem solving. *Psychological Monographs, 58* (Whole No. 270), 1–113. [originally published in German in 1935]

Emmons, R. A., & Kaiser, H. (1996). Goal orientation and emotional well being: Linking goals and affect through the self. In A. Tesser & L. Martin (Eds.), *Striving and feeling: Interactions among goals, affect, and self-regulation* (pp. 79–98). New York: Plenum.

Eysenck, M. W. (1990). *The Blackwell dictionary of cognitive psychology.* Oxford: Blackwell Reference.

Flower, L., & Hayes, J. (1984). The representation of meaning in writing. *Written Communication, 1,* 120–160.

Geiger, M. A. (1991). Changing multiple-choice answers: Do students accurately perceive their performance? *Journal of Experimental Education, 59,* 250–257.

Gick, M. L., & Holyoak, K. J. (1983). Schema induction and analogical transfer. *Cognitive Psychology, 15,* 1–38.

Goleman, D. (1995). *Emotional intelligence: Why it can matter more than IQ.* New York: Bantam.

Hayes, J., & Flower, L. (1986). Writing research and the writer. *American Psychologist, 41,* 1106–1113.

Higbee, K. (2001). *Your memory: How it works and how to improve it* (2nd ed.). New York: Avalon.

Hofer, B. H., & Pintrich, P. R. (1997). The development of epistemological theories: Beliefs about knowledge and knowing and their relation to learning. *Review of Educational Research, 67,* 88–140.

Hofer, B. H., & Pintrich, P. R., (2001). *Personal epistemology: The psychology of beliefs about knowledge and knowing.* Mahwah, NJ: Lawrence Erlbaum Associates.

Howell, A. J., Jahrig, J. C., & Powell, R. A. (2004). Sleep quality, sleep propensity, and academic performance. *Perceptual and Motor Skills, 99,* 525–535.

Inman, M. (2005). *Attributional complexity and perceptions of racism.* Unpublished manuscript.

Jones, D. (1998). *Exploring the Internet using critical thinking skills.* New York: Neal-Schuman.

Karabenick, S., & Knapp, J. (1988). Help-seeking and the need for academic assistance. *Journal of Educational Psychology, 80,* 406–408.

Kelly, W. E. (2001). The relationship between sleep length and grade point average among college students. *College Student Journal, 35,* 84–86.

Kiewra, K. A. (1985). Learning from a lecture: An investigation of notetaking, review and attendance at a lecture. *Human Learning: Journal of Practical Research & Applications, 4,* 73–77.

Kiewra, K. A., DuBois, N. F., Christian, D., McShane, A., Meyerhoffer, M., & Roskelley, D. (1991). Note-taking functions and techniques. *Journal of Educational Psychology, 83,* 240–245.

King, A. (1992). Comparison of self-questioning, summarizing, and notetaking-review as strategies for learning from lectures. *American Educational Research Journal, 83,* 240–245.

King, P. M., & Kitchener, K. S. (1994). *Developing reflective judgment.* San Francisco: Jossey-Bass.

Light, R. (2001). *Making the most of college: Students speak their minds.* Cambridge, MA: Harvard University Press.

Macaulay, D. (1988). *The way things work.* Boston: Houghton Mifflin.

Marschark, M. (1985). Imagery and organization in the recall of prose. *Journal of Memory and Language, 24,* 734–745.

Marsh, H. W. & Kleitman, S. (2003). School athletic participation: Mostly gain with little pain. *Journal of Sport and Exercise Psychology, 25,* 205–228.

Matlin, M. W. (2002). *Cognition* (5th ed.). New York: Wiley.

McCrae, R. R., & Costa, P. T. (2003). *Personality in adulthood: A five-factor theory perspective* (2nd ed.). New York: Guilford.

McKeachie, W. J. (2005). *Teaching tips* (12th ed.). New York: Houghton Mifflin.

Miller, G. (1956). The magical number seven, plus or minus two: Some limits on our capacity for processing information. *Psychological Review, 63,* 81–97.

Nadler, B. J. (2006). *The everything college major test book.* Avon, MA: Adams Media.

Nisbett, R. E., Fong, G. T., Lehman, D. R., & Cheng, P. W. (1987). Teaching reasoning. *Science, 238,* 625–631.

Nolen-Hoeksema, S. (1998). The other end of the continuum: The cost of rumination. *Psychological Inquiry, 9,* 216–219.

Novick, L. R. (1988). Analogical transfer, problem similarity, and expertise. *Journal of Experimental Psychology: Learning, Memory, & Cognition, 14,* 510–520.

Nowak, J. (1998). *Learning, creating, and using knowledge: Concept maps as facilitative tools in schools and corporations.* Mahwah, NJ: Lawrence Erlbaum Associates

Nowak, J., & Gowin, D. B. (1984). *Learning how to learn.* New York: Cambridge University Press.

Parkhurst, J. T., & Hopmeyer, A. (1999). Development and change in the source of loneliness in childhood and adolescence: Constructing a theoretical model. In K. J. Rotenberg & S. Hymel (Eds.), *Loneliness in childhood and adolescence* (pp. 55–79). New York: Cambridge University Press.

Paul, R., & Elder, L. (1995). *Critical thinking: Tools for taking charge of your learning and your life.* Rohnert Park, CA: Foundation for Critical Thinking.

Pinto, B. M., Cherico, N. P., Szymanski, L., & Marcus, B. H. (1998). Longitudinal changes in college students' exercise participation. *Journal of American College Health, 47,* 23–27.

Pintrich, P. R. (2000). The role of goal orientation in self-regulated learning. In M. Boekaerts, P. R. Pintrich, & M. Zeidner (Eds.), *Handbook of self-regulation* (pp. 451–502). San Diego, CA: Academic Press.

Pintrich, P. R., & Schunk, D. (2002). *Motivation in education: Theory, research and applications* (2nd ed.). Upper Saddle River, NJ: Merrill/Prentice Hall.

Pintrich, P. R., Smith, D., Garcia, T., & McKeachie, W. J. (1991). *A manual for the use of the Motivated Strategies for Learning Questionnaire (MSLQ).* Ann Arbor, MI: NCRIPTAL, School of Education, the University of Michigan.

Pintrich, P. R., Smith, D. A. F., Garcia, T., & McKeachie, W. J. (1993). Reliability and predictive validity of the Motivated Strategies for Learning Questionnaire (MSLQ). *Educational and Psychological Measurement, 53,* 801–813.

Pressley, M., & Woloshyn, V. (1995). *Cognitive strategy that really improves children's academic performance.* Cambridge, MA: Brookline Books.

Ross, B. H., Ryan, W. T., & Tenpenny, P. L. (1989). The access of relevant information for solving problems. *Memory and Cognition, 17,* 639–651.

Sansone, C., Weir, C., Harpster, L., & Morgan, C. (1992). Once a boring task, always a boring task? The role of interest as a self-regulatory mechanism. *Journal of Personality and Social Psychology, 63,* 379–390.

Scheier, M. F., Carver, C. S., & Bridges, M. W. (1994). Distinguishing optimism from neuroticism (and trait anxiety, self-mastery, and self-esteem): A re-evaluation of the Life Orientation Test. *Journal of Personality and Social Psychology, 67,* 1063–1078.

Shrager, L., & Mayer, R. E. (1989). Note-taking fosters generative learning strategies in novices. *Journal of Educational Psychology, 81,* 263–264.

Sigman, M. (1995). Nutrition and child development: More food for thought. *Current Directions in Psychological Science, 4,* 52–55.

Spelke, E., Hirst, W., & Neisser, U. (1976). Skills of divided attention. *Cognition, 4,* 215–230.

Sternberg, R. (1985). *Beyond IQ: A triarchic theory of intelligence.* New York: Cambridge University Press.

Sternberg, R. J. (1997). *Thinking styles.* New York: Cambridge University Press.

Tversky, A., & Kahneman, D. (1983). Extensional versus intuitive reasoning: The conjunction fallacy in probability judgment. *Psychological Review, 90,* 293–315.

VanderStoep, S. W., Pintrich, P. R., & Fagerlin, A. (1996). Disciplinary differences in self-regulated learning in college students. *Contemporary Educational Psychology, 21,* 345–362.

Watson, D., & Tharp, R. (1997). *Self-directed behavior: Self-modification for personal adjustment.* Pacific Grove, CA: Brooks/Cole.

Whitehead, A. N. (1929). *The aims of education and other essays.* New York: Macmillan.

Wilson, T. (2005, December 29). Don't think twice, it's alright. *The New York Times*.

Wolters, C. (1998). Self-regulated learning and college students' regulation of motivation. *Journal of Educational Psychology, 90,* 224–235.

Wood, E., Woloshyn, V., & Willoughby, T. (1995). *Cognitive strategy instruction for middle and high schools.* Cambridge, MA: Brookline Books.

Yerkes, R. M., & Dodson, J. D. (1908). The relation of strength of stimulus to rapidity in habit formation. *Journal of Comparative Neurology and Psychology, 18,* 459–482.

Zimmerman, B. J. (1998). Academic studying and the development of personal skill: A self-regulatory perspective. *Educational Psychologist, 33,* 73–86.

Zimmerman, B. J. (2000). Attaining self-regulation: A social cognitive perspective. In M. Boekaerts, P. R. Pintrich, & M. Zeidner (Eds.), *Handbook of self-regulation: Theory, research, and applications* (pp. 13–39). San Diego, CA: Academic Press.

GLOSSARY

Adaptive help seeking. Seeking assistance in such a way that you strive to learn rather than simply trying to get the answers (Chapter 4).

Advanced organizer. A framework for understanding and interpreting knowledge (Chapter 1).

Affirming the consequent. A common mistake in formal logic problems; when "if p then q" is the rule, affirming the consequent means concluding that "if q then p" is also specified (Chapter 13).

Anchoring error. Quantitative estimates are based on initial numerical data, which may or may not be relevant to the estimate (Chapter 12).

Association learning. Linking what you are trying to learn with what you already know (Chapter 7).

Attributional complexity. A preference for complex reasoning, problem solving, and analyzing multiple causes of events or behaviors (Chapter 5).

Attributions. Reasons students give to explain their performance or behavior (Chapter 3).

Audience. The people for whom a particular piece of writing is intended (Chapter 10).

Automatized. Behavior that we are so familiar with that we do it without thinking (Chapter 6).

Availability error. Judgments about the frequency of events are based on how easily they are recalled from memory (Chapter 12).

Bibliography. List of materials such as books and journal articles that the authors used in preparing a book (Chapter 9).

Biconditional problems. Logic problems in which the logic and/or rules run in both directions: "if p then q" as well as "if q then p" (Chapter 13).

Big Five. Popular personality theory describing people's five major personality factors—introversion, openness, neuroticism, agreeableness, and conscientiousness (Chapter 5).

Binge drinking. Consuming four or more alcoholic beverages at one time for men and three or more for women (Chapter 5).

Choice behavior. The idea that motivation is related to individuals' decisions and choices (Chapter 3).

Cognitive interference. A disruption in your ability to process information, often caused by anxiety (Chapter 11).

Commitment. Long-term determination for achieving success (Chapter 5).

Conditional knowledge. Understanding when to activate relevant parts of long-term memory (knowing when; Chapter 6).

Contextualized relativism. The third stage in a model of critical-thinking development in which students recognize that life's issues are complex and ambiguous. Critical thinking at this stage involves evaluating the evidence and making commitments, recognizing that others might not agree, and continually evaluating one's beliefs (Chapters 5 and 12).

Creativity. In problems for which more than one answer exists, generating a solution that is nontraditional or unique (Chapter 13).

Criterion referenced. A test score that is simply a measure of your performance, independent of other people's results (Chapter 11).

Critical thinking. The ability to use acquired knowledge in flexible and meaningful ways, through understanding the problem or issue, evaluating evidence, considering multiple perspectives, and taking a position (Chapters 1, 12).

Declarative knowledge. Memory of facts, names, and other general knowledge in long-term memory (knowing what; Chapter 6).

Decode. In reading, translating letters and sounds to words (Chapter 9).

Deep processing. Encoding information while paying attention and making connections; a variety of high-level cognitive strategies that lead to more sophisticated understanding of learned material (Chapter 6).

Deep rehearsal. A memory strategy that goes beyond rote recall to develop a richer understanding (Chapter 7).

Delay of gratification. The ability to delay an immediate reward for a later reward (Chapter 5).

Denying the antecedent. A common mistake in formal logic problems; when "if p then q" is the rule, believing also that "if not–p then not–q" (Chapter 13).

Dependent help seeking. Seeking assistance in such a way that you want others to do the work rather than as a way to try to learn (Chapter 4).

Distributed practice. Spreading learning out over an extended period of time (Chapter 7).

Dualism. The first stage in a model of critical-thinking development in which students tend to see answers as either right or wrong and believe authority figures (e.g., professors) possess all the answers (Chapters 5 and 12).

Elaboration. The process of building connections and associating information with material that is meaningful to you to achieve sophisticated understanding (Chapters 7 and 8).

Emotionality. The physiological component of anxiety, which sometimes occurs during test taking (Chapter 11).

Encoding. The process by which information gets transferred from working memory to long-term memory (Chapter 6).

Escape method. A device to get out of an old mode of problem solving by identifying things that we take for granted (Chapter 13).

Expectancy. Components of motivation that involve your judgments of your capabilities as well as beliefs you have about control of yourself and the task (Chapter 3).

Expository text. Written material that conveys factual information (Chapter 9).

Extrinsic rewards. Short-term external rewards that help control and regulate effort and persistence on tasks (Chapter 3).

Faculty support. Assistance from faculty when the material is geared to a higher level than you are able to handle (Chapter 4).

Front matter. The portion of the book that comes before the main text, which includes information about the authors and the purpose of the book (Chapter 9).

Functional fixedness. Inability to represent familiar items in new ways (Chapter 13).

Fundamental attribution error. The tendency to attribute other people's behavior to internal causes (personality) and our own behavior to external forces (Chapter 5).

Generative note taking. Note taking that helps to store or encode course information (Chapter 8).

Glossary. A list of key terms cited in a book with their accompanying definitions (Chapter 9).

Goal state. A desired end to problem-solving strategies (Chapter 13).

Goals. Plans or desired achievements that both energize and guide behavior (Chapter 2).

Ill-defined problems. Problems for which not everyone will agree on the correct answer (Chapter 1).

Index. A list of terms and authors' names and the page numbers where they are discussed compiled at the end of the book (Chapter 9).

Knowledge generation. Technique employed by expert writers; actually creating new meaning while writing text instead of just reporting information (Chapter 10).

Knowledge telling. An approach used by novice writers that simply tells what is known about a topic (Chapter 10).

Law of large numbers. As a sample size increases, it more accurately reflects the entire population from which the sample was drawn (Chapter 13).

Learning strategy. An approach to completing cognitive tasks (Chapter 1).

Learning style. A preferred method of completing cognitive tasks (Chapter 1).

Loneliness. A sad or aching sense of isolation (Chapter 5).

Long-term goals. Goals concerning life in general that will not be reached in a short period of time (Chapter 2).

Long-term memory. Mental storage structure, infinite in capacity, that is said to hold all of our memories of events, actions, and people (Chapter 6).

Massed practice. Learning a large amount of material all at once, such as cramming for a test (Chapter 7).

Mastery goal. Goal that defines success in terms of improvement, mastery, progress, and learning (Chapter 2).

Mental set. Continuing to use an old method to solve a problem even when a better method has become available (Chapter 13).

Metacognition. The awareness and control you have over your own cognition; involves planning and monitoring your cognitive activity (Chapters 1, 5, and 7).

Mnemonics. Memory shortcuts and "tricks," often used for remembering lists (Chapter 6).

Motivation. How one directs and energizes his or her behavior (Chapter 1).

Multilogical thinking. The critical-thinking skill that involves examining an issue from more than one perspective (Chapter 12).

Multiple choice. The most common form of objective question; involves selecting the correct answer from a group of alternatives (Chapter 11).

Narrative text. Written material that tells a story (Chapter 9).

Norm referenced. A test score that is determined, at least in part, by the performance of others on the same task or measure, for example, grading on a curve (Chapter 11).

Optimism. The general belief in future positive outcomes (Chapter 5).

Organization. The process of identifying important information, seeing relations, and constructing connections between information (Chapter 7).

Original state. The beginning of a problem-solving situation, in which the solution is not known (Chapter 13).

Outcome goals. Goals that concern the final product of the activity (Chapter 2).

Peer-reviewed journals. Professional journals in which the articles have been evaluated by other researchers in the field (Chapter 10).

Peer support. Supportive relationships with other students that foster learning (Chapter 4).

Performance goal. Goal that defines success in competitive or comparative terms (Chapter 2).

Personality. Enduring traits of a person that stay stable over time and circumstance (Chapter 5).

Planning. Setting goals for your cognitive activity (Chapters 1 and 10).

PMI. Method for evaluating evidence that involves considering the *plus, minus,* and *interesting* aspects of a position (Chapter 12).

Population. The set of events (usually people) that are being studied or considered—the entire group from which a sample is drawn (Chapter 13).

Preface. Part of the front matter of a book in which the author states the goals for and rationale of writing the book (Chapter 9).

Primary task. Task to which you devote most of your attention (Chapter 6).

Prior knowledge. Information you already know that helps organize new information you are learning (Chapter 6).

Problem solving. The act of moving from a state of not knowing how to complete a task to being able to complete the task (Chapter 1).

Procedural knowledge. Memory of motor skills, behaviors, and other procedural tasks (Chapter 6).

Process goals. Intermediate goals that you might engage in on your way to the final outcome goal (Chapter 2).

Professor support. Assistance from faculty and teaching assistants when the course is more difficult than you expected (Chapter 4).

Quasi-reflective/relativism. The second stage in a model of critical-thinking development in which students believe all thinking is simply a matter of opinion, and that all opinions are equally valid (Chapter 12).

Random simulation method. A device to get out of an old mode of problem solving by selecting a random object or word and using it as a way to open up new avenues of thinking (Chapter 13).

Recall memory. Generating a portion of your memory on your own, without a list of alternatives (Chapter 6).

Recognition memory. Identifying the concept you are trying to remember from a set of possibilities (Chapter 6).

Reflective judgment. Critical thinking that involves moving from an understanding of knowing simply right or wrong to an understanding that the answers to life's questions are often complex and ambiguous (Chapter 12).

Regression to the mean. Extreme scores on events will not be extreme the next time, due to a random statistical "correction" that steers scores back toward their true (i.e., population) mean (Chapter 13).

Rehearsal. Low-level learning strategy that involves repeating information until it has been memorized (Chapter 7).

Reinforcers. Positive rewards used to help you achieve your goal (Chapter 3).

Representativeness error. Judgments that are based on how likely ("normal") the description is of people in general (Chapter 12).

Resource management. Effective uses of available tools and resources (Chapter 1).

Revising. Reading over your written text and fixing it to communicate better with the audience (Chapter 10).

Sample. A subset from the population that will be observed (Chapter 13).

Schema. An organized set of facts residing in long-term memory (Chapter 6).

Secondary tasks. Tasks other than the primary task to which you also devote attention (Chapter 6).

Selective attention. Ability to block out unwanted information to focus only on desired information (Chapter 6).

Self-efficacy. Self-appraisal of one's ability to master a task (Chapters 1 and 3).

Self-regulated learner. Both skillful and willful in learning; one who actively plans, monitors, and controls his or her own learning and behavior (Chapter 1).

Sensory memory. Information that is held for a very brief period of time after it has been experienced (Chapter 6).

Shallow processing. A type of learning that involves expending minimal attention or effort (Chapter 6).

Shallow rehearsal. A memory strategy that focuses mainly on learning the definition of a concept (Chapter 7).

Short-term goals. Specific goals that enable individuals to monitor their progress and regulate their behavior in pursuit of long-term goals (Chapter 2).

Skill. Knowledge and cognitive strategies that individuals learn and acquire (Chapter 1).

Stepping-stone method. A device to get out of an old mode of problem solving, with the end goal of discovering a creative solution that otherwise would not have been generated (Chapter 13).

Structural analogy. Comparison or connection that looks past irrelevant, superficial features and recognizes the abstract, structural similarities that are needed to solve a problem (Chapter 13).

Surface analogy. Comparison or connection based on superficial features that are not relevant to solving the problem (Chapter 13).

Surveillance. Being consciously aware of your surroundings (Chapter 6).

Task analysis. Figuring out the steps required and the strategies or skills you will need to use to complete a task (Chapter 7).

Test anxiety. Nervous or anxious feelings during an exam or test; related to poor performance (Chapter 1).

Translating. The actual writing of text; translates ideas from an outline into actual words, sentences, and paragraphs (Chapter 10).

Value. Components of motivation that involve your reasons for doing the task (Chapter 3).

Will. Various ways individuals attempt to motivate and regulate themselves (Chapter 1).

Working memory. Also called short-term memory; stores a limited amount of information for a limited period of time (Chapter 6).

INDEX